E/2011/50/Rev. 1
ST/ESA/333

Department of Economic and Social Affairs

World Economic and Social Survey 2011

The Great Green Technological Transformation

United Nations
New York, 2011

DESA

The Department of Economic and Social Affairs of the United Nations Secretariat is a vital interface between global policies in the economic, social and environmental spheres and national action. The Department works in three main interlinked areas: (i) it compiles, generates and analyses a wide range of economic, social and environmental data and information on which States Members of the United Nations draw to review common problems and to take stock of policy options; (ii) it facilitates the negotiations of Member States in many intergovernmental bodies on joint courses of action to address ongoing or emerging global challenges; and (iii) it advises interested Governments on the ways and means of translating policy frameworks developed in United Nations conferences and summits into programmes at the country level and, through technical assistance, helps build national capacities.

Note

Symbols of United Nations documents are composed of capital letters combined with figures.

E/2011/50/Rev. 1
ST/ESA/333
ISBN 978-92-1-109163-2
eISBN 978-92-1-054758-1

United Nations publication
Sales No. E.11.II.C.1

Printed at the United Nations, New York

Preface

The world faces important decisions on how we generate energy and manage our natural assets—choices with implications that will reverberate for generations to come. Against a backdrop of a rising global population and unceasing pressure on the natural environment, this 2011 edition of the ***World Economic and Social Survey*** can guide our collective efforts to achieve a much-needed technological transformation to a greener, cleaner global economy.

The past two decades have seen considerable economic growth, particularly in the emerging economies. Hundreds of millions of people have risen from poverty—in Asia, Latin America and, increasingly, in Africa.

But with global population expected to reach 9 billion by 2050, we need to accelerate the pace of productive economic expansion. At the same time, this growth must be balanced with respect for the human and natural capital that is its foundation, lest we risk profound and potentially irreversible changes in the planet's ability to sustain progress.

Rather than viewing growth and sustainability as competing goals on a collision course, we must see them as complementary and mutually supportive imperatives. This becomes possible when we embrace a low-carbon, resource-efficient, pro-poor economic model.

A comprehensive global energy transition is critical to this process. With data, analysis and careful projections, this ***Survey*** illustrates the feasibility of such a transformation. It also highlights the hurdles, and outlines what will be required of governments and the international community as a whole to make the most of available green technologies—and to generate new applications and inventions that meet the needs of countries at different levels of development.

The ***Survey*** also addresses the challenge of feeding a global population that will be nearly 35 per cent larger in 2050 than it is today—looking back at the first green revolution in agriculture, and ahead to future models that can be far more effective in improving the global food supply while protecting its sources.

Green economic thinking can unleash the government policies and business opportunities that will power sustainable growth, reduce poverty and protect our natural resources. By providing a wealth of information, insights and practical recommendations, this ***Survey*** can help advance the global debate on the critical role that a transformation in technology can play in ushering in a greener future. Its publication is especially timely as the world prepares for next year's Rio+20 United Nations Conference on Sustainable Development, and I commend it to policy-makers, non-governmental partners, business executives and concerned individuals everywhere who can help realize this shared goal.

BAN KI-MOON
Secretary-General

Acknowledgements

The *World Economic and Social Survey* is the annual flagship publication on major development issues prepared by the Department of Economic and Social Affairs of the United Nations Secretariat (UN/DESA).

The *Survey* was prepared under the general supervision and leadership of Rob Vos, Director of the Development Policy and Analysis Division (DPAD) of UN/DESA. Manuel F. Montes led the team that prepared the report. The core team at DPAD included Diana Alarcón, Christina Bodouroglou, Nicole Hunt, S. Nazrul Islam, Alex Julca, Mariangela Parra-Lancourt, Vladimir Popov and Shari Spiegel. Administrative support was provided by Laura Dix and Lydia Gatan. Michael Brodsky of the Department of General Assembly Affairs and Conference Management copy-edited the original manuscript. June Chesney, who also undertook critical editing, led the copy preparation and proofreading team in DPAD, which included Leah C. Kennedy, and Valerian Monteiro (content design). David O'Connor, Richard A. Roehrl and Friedrich Soltau, colleagues from the Division for Sustainable Development (DSD) of UN/DESA, were part of the core team and also provided the principal inputs to chapter II of the report. Substantive contributions were also made by Sylvie I. Cohen and Andres Figueroa Davila of the United Nations Entity for Gender Equality and the Empowerment of Women (UN-Women) and Barbara Tavora-Jainchill of the Secretariat of the United Nations Forum on Forests (UNFF).

We gratefully acknowledge the overall intellectual support for the project provided by Tariq Banuri, Director of DSD, and the background research contributions of Sally Brooks, Xiaolan Fu, Kelly Sims Gallagher, Arnulf Grübler, Tim Jackson, Bashir Jama, Michael Loevinsohn, Keywan Riahi, Jonathan R. Siegel, Aaron L. Strong and Charlie Wilson. Inputs and comments are gratefully acknowledged from across the wider United Nations system, including the Economic and Social Commission for Asia and the Pacific (Rae Kwon Chung and Masakazu Ichimura), the United Nations Conference on Trade and Development (Dimo Calovski, Angel Gonzalez-Sanz, Mongi Hamdi, Richard Kozul-Wright, Michael Lim, Anne Miroux and Padmashree Gehl Sampath), the United Nations Development Programme (Francisco Rodriguez and other staff of the Human Development Report Office) and the United Nations Industrial Development Organization (Augusto Luis Alacorta). The report also benefited from discussions with researchers at the International Food Policy Research Institute (Claudia Ringler, Mark Rosegrant and Máximo Torero) and the Centre for Policy Dialogue in Bangladesh (Fahmida Khatun and Rehman Sobhan), and from data provided by Nick Johnstone of the Organization for Economic Cooperation and Development. In addition to these contributions, we also owe thanks for the insights provided by other participants, at two workshops organized within the framework of the preparation of this report, including Elias G. Carayannis, Chantal Line Carpentier, Ronald E. Findlay and Richard Nelson.

Critical overall guidance was provided by Jomo Kwame Sundaram, Assistant Secretary-General for Economic Development at UN/DESA.

Overview

The green technological transformation

"Business as usual" is not an option

While humankind has made enormous progress in improving material welfare over the past two centuries, this progress has come at the lasting cost of degradation of our natural environment. About half of the forests that covered the earth are gone, groundwater resources are being depleted and contaminated, enormous reductions in biodiversity have already taken place and, through increased burning of fossil fuels, the stability of the planet's climate is being threatened by global warming. In order for populations in developing countries to achieve a decent living standard, especially the billions who currently still live in conditions of abject poverty, and the additional 2 billion people who will have been added to the world's population by mid-century—much greater economic progress will be needed.

Continuation along previously trodden economic growth pathways will further exacerbate the pressures exerted on the world's resources and natural environment, which would approach limits where livelihoods were no longer sustainable. Business as usual is thus not an option. Yet, even if we stop global engines of growth now, the depletion and pollution of our natural environment would still continue because of existing consumption patterns and production methods. Hence, there is an urgent need to find new development pathways which would ensure environmental sustainability and reverse ecological destruction, while managing to provide, now and in the future, a decent livelihood for all of humankind.

The green economy as the new paradigm?

To achieve this goal, a radically new economic strategy will be needed. Economic decision-making, by Governments and private agents alike, will need to focus on ways to strengthen, rather than endanger, environmental sustainability. The "green economy" has been promoted as the key concept in this regard—the concept that embodies the promise of a new development paradigm, whose application has the potential to ensure the preservation of the earth's ecosystem along new economic growth pathways while contributing at the same time to poverty reduction.

There is no unique definition of the green economy, but, however imprecisely defined, there is broad agreement on the basic idea underpinning it, namely, that enhancing economic growth, social progress and environmental stewardship can be complementary strategic objectives and that the need for possible trade-offs among them en route to their realization can be overcome. In this sense, the focus of the concept is fully consistent with that of the sustainable development concept eleborated by the United Nations, which perceives the economic, social and environmental dimensions as the three pillars of development and which stresses the importance of intergenerational equity in development, that is, ensuring that meeting the needs of the present generation does not compromise the ability of future generations to meet their own needs.

Further, the green economy concept is based on the conviction that the benefits of investing in environmental sustainability outweigh the cost of not doing so, as much as it outweighs the cost of having to protect ecosystems from the damages caused by a "non-green" (brown) economy.

A technological revolution is needed ...

Growth of the world population, per capita income, energy and resource use, waste and the production of pollutants (including greenhouse gas emissions) have all increased exponentially since the first industrial revolution. A depiction of these increases assumes the shape of a hockey stick (see figure O.1 (a) to (d)). The related increase in the level of human activity is threatening to surpass the limits of the Earth's capacity as a source and sink.

The objective of the green economy is to ensure that those limits are not crossed. One option for achieving this would be to limit income growth, as it would also, given existing production methods, limit the growth of resource use, waste and pollutants. However, doing so would complicate efforts to meet the development objective and would thus not be in the interest of developing countries, which are home to the vast majority of the world's population. Reducing population growth could be another option; but this could be achieved more effectively by improving living standards. Reducing non-renewable energy and resource use, reducing waste and pollutants, and reversing land degradation and biodiversity losses would then seem key to greening the economy.

A fundamental technological overhaul will be required. Technologies will need to undergo drastic changes so as to become more efficient in the use of energy and other resources and minimize the generation of harmful pollutants. At present, 90 per

Figure O.1 (a)
Exponential growth of world population, 1750-2050

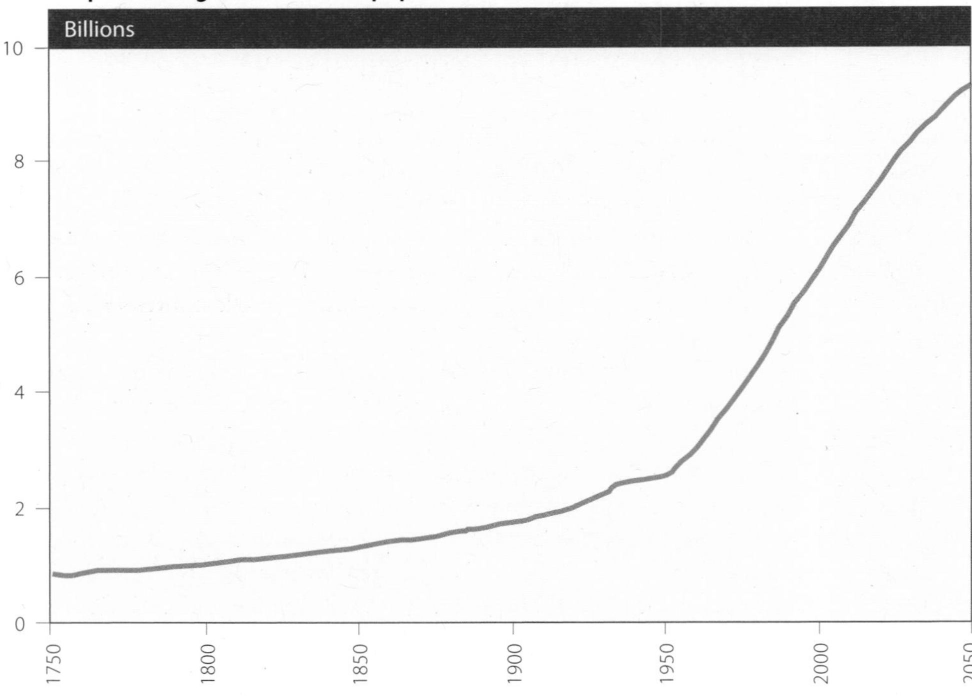

Sources: For 1750-1949, United Nations, "The world at six billion" (1999), p. 5, table 1, entitled "World population, year 0 to near stabilization"; for 1950-2050, United Nations, Department of Economic and Social Affairs, Population Division, "World Population Prospects: The 2010 Revision" (medium variant) (New York, 2011).

Note: Projections begin after 2010, and are based on the medium variant.

Figure O.1(b)
Growth of world per capita income, 1820-2008

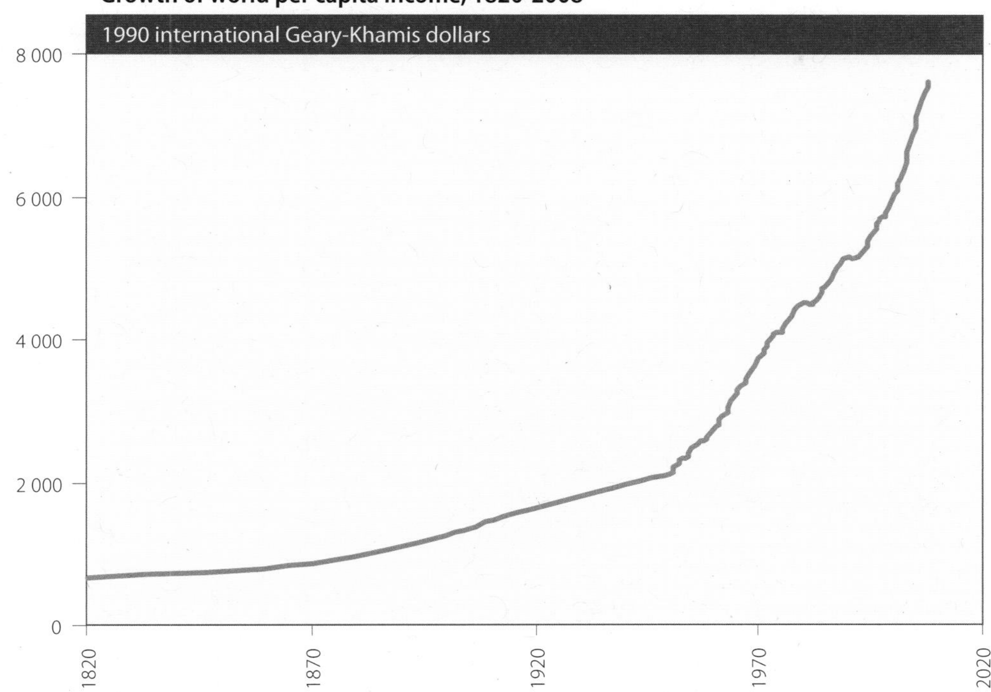

Source: Angus Maddison, "Maddison data on population and GDP". Available from http://sites.google.com/site/econgeodata/maddison-data-on-population-gdp.

cent of energy is generated through brown technologies that utilize fossil fuels, with this

Figure O.1(c)
Rise in energy consumption since the first industrial revolution, 1850-2000

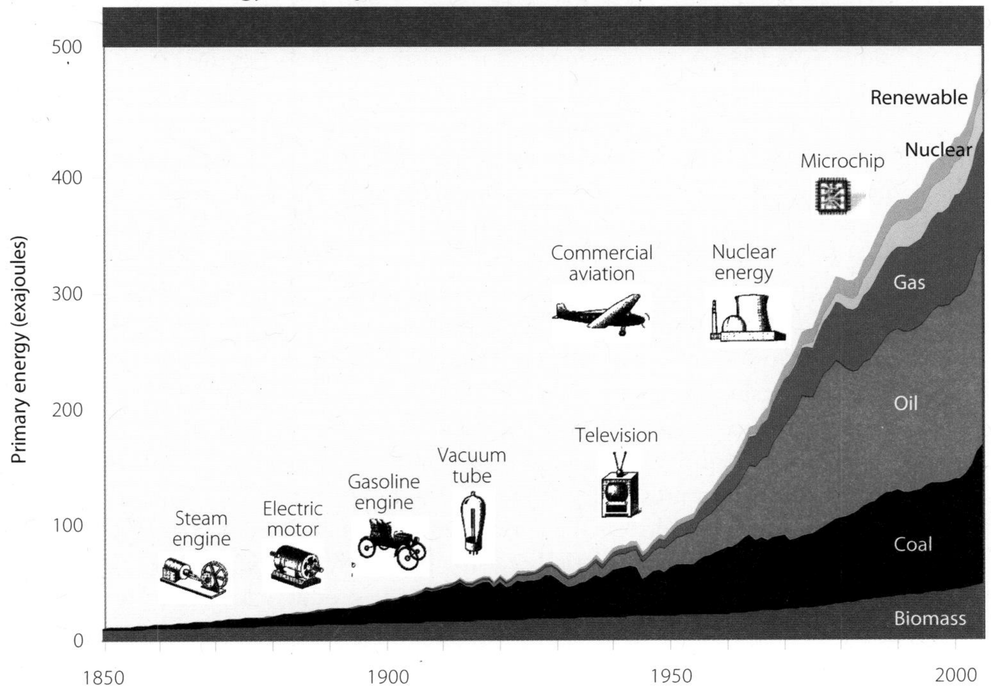

Source: United Nations (2009), figure II.4.

Figure O.1(d)
Exponential increase in greenhouse gas emissions, 1816-2008

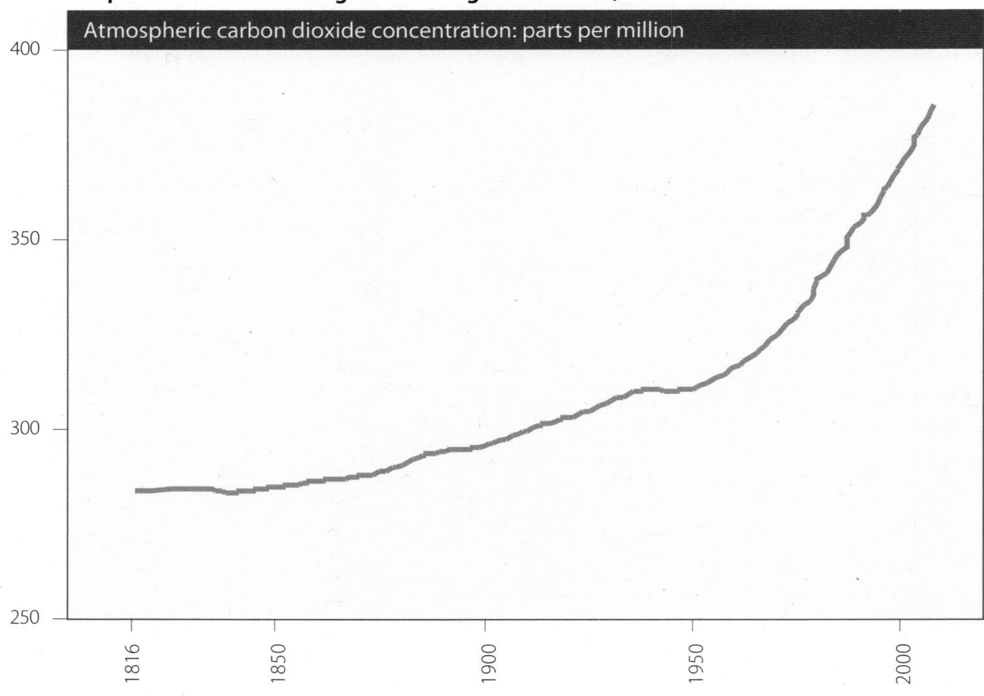

Source: United States Department of Energy, Carbon Dioxide Information Analysis Center (CDIAC) (see http://cdiac.esd.ornl.gov).

type of production being responsible for about 60 per cent of carbon dioxide (CO_2) emissions. According to the more cautious scenario, for CO_2 equivalent concentrations to be stabilized at 450 parts per million (consistent with the target of stabilizing global warming at a 2° C temperature increase from pre-industrial levels), the use of fossil fuels would need to drop by 80 per cent by mid-century. Reducing the energy use and greenhouse gas emissions associated with growing and increasingly urban populations will require drastic changes in consumption patterns, transportation systems, residential and building infrastructure, and water and sanitation systems.

Modern agriculture, which underpins global food security, currently contributes about 14 per cent of greenhouse gas emissions, and the land-use and water management related thereto are not sustainable in many parts of the world. Deforestation is contributing an estimated 17 per cent of global emissions, while causing the loss of habitat, species and biodiversity in general. As with regard to energy, technologies do exist that are known to ensure more sustainable farming and forestry management, prevention of land erosion and strict limits on water pollution by agriculture, but a great deal more innovation and knowledge sharing is needed to allow for their adaptation to local conditions. At the same time, however, inasmuch as nearly 1 billion people are undernourished and are facing serious food insecurity, global food production would need to increase by between 70 and 100 per cent from present levels by 2050 in order to feed a growing population. Thus, there is an urgent need to make agricultural production environmentally sustainable, while at the same time substantially raising productivity. It is hard to imagine how this can be attained without a major overhaul of existing production systems, technologies and supporting infrastructure.

The incidence of natural disasters has increased fivefold since the 1970s. This increase can, with a fair degree of certainty, be attributed in part to climate change induced by human activity. Deforestation, degradation of natural coastal protection and poor infrastructure have increased the likelihood that weather shocks will turn into human disasters, especially in the least developed countries. Reducing disaster risk will then entail significant technological and social change, including rebuilding of infrastructure and better land-use and water management in vulnerable areas with vulnerable social groups fully taking part in decision-making processes related to the implementation of systems of community resilience to climate change and disasters.

... which will be like no other

Many of the technologies needed for a green economy are already available, as evidenced, for example, by the range of options for generating renewable energy (wind, solar power and biofuels, among others), technologies for carbon capture and more efficient energy use, techniques to replace non-biodegradable resources, and sustainable farming and forestry techniques, as well as technologies to render coastlines and infrastructure less prone to natural disasters. These options offer readily usable starting points. The main challenges to jump-starting the shift to a green economy lie in how to further improve these techniques, adapt them to specific local and sectoral needs, scale up the applications so as to bring down significantly their costs, and provide incentives and mechanisms that will facilitate their diffusion and knowledge-sharing. Meeting these challenges successfully is easier said than done.

As so many of the components of existing economic systems are "locked into" the use of non-green and non-sustainable technologies, much is at stake in terms of the high cost of moving out of those technologies. Developing countries, especially low-income ones, with relatively low rates of electricity usage, may be able to "leapfrog" into electricity generation based on renewable forms of primary energy, for instance. The question is how to enable those countries to access, utilize and, above all, afford green technologies.

Further innovation and scaling up are also needed to drive down unit costs. Technologies will need to be "transferred"' and made accessible, since most innovation takes place in the developed countries and private corporations in those countries are the main owners of the intellectual property rights covering most green technologies. The new technologies will also need to be locked into new production processes. This would imply improving much existing infrastructure and actively promoting green technologies and industries. Consequently, the technological revolution for a green economy will be fundamentally different from previous revolutions—in three ways.

First, it will have to take place within a specific and limited time period. Given existing pressures on our ecosystem, the goal would need to be achieved within the next three to four decades—a huge challenge, given that diffusion of technologies is a slow process. Previous technological revolutions typically required a substantially longer period of time than that available now to accomplish the required green technology revolution.

Second, Governments will have to assume a much more central role, the limited time frame being one key reason for this. Under current circumstances, there needs to be an acceleration of technological innovation and diffusion, which is unlikely to occur if they are left to market forces. Equally important is the fact that the natural environment is a public good and not "priced" by the market. Markets for green technologies do exist, but they are just developing, created through government policy. Governments will also have to play a key role in promoting further research on and development of green technologies and their diffusion, inasmuch as the benefits will accrue to whole societies. In addition, since at present existing brown technologies are locked into the entire economic system, a radical shift to green technologies will mean improving, adjusting and replacing much existing infrastructure and other invested capital. Such transformations will be costly and necessitate large-scale long-term financing, which is unlikely to be mobilized in full through private initiative and will require government support and incentives. Thus, not only will strong technology policies be needed, but they must go hand in hand with active industrial and educational policies aimed at inducing the necessary changes in infrastructure and production processes.

Third, since the environmental challenges are global, the green technological revolution will need to be facilitated by intense international cooperation. The global dimension is most obvious in the case of climate change, but problems of food insecurity and deforestation have significant cross-border effects as well, stemming, for example, from food price instability and greenhouse gas emissions. Through international trade and investment, incomes and consumption in one country are linked to the ecological footprints left in the country of production. Multilateral environmental agreements, trade and investment rules, financing facilities and intellectual property rights regimes would all need to be aligned so as to facilitate the green technological transformation. Since many, although not all, existing new technologies are owned by the advanced countries and the cost of inducing green technological change will be much higher for developing countries relative to their incomes, there will be important distributional challenges connected with greening the global economy, which will also need to be addressed through the abovementioned financing facilities and other new mechanisms of international cooperation.

This year's *World Economic and Social Survey* examines the means by which the technological revolution can meet the requirements and sustain the objectives of green economy.

The complexity of technological change

The outcomes are uncertain

Technological change is a cumulative process, fraught with uncertainties as to direction and outcome. History also suggests that there is no simple technological sleight of hand for transforming production and consumption. Changes in the world's dominant technologies will lead to significant changes in social structure, market institutions, living arrangements and lifestyles.

Inevitably, radical technological change will have strong distributive effects across and within countries. Some countries and groups will be negatively affected by reduced demand for their products and resources. On the other hand, countries that keep up with research and development efforts and manage to generate new linkages with the rest of their economies will be better able to keep in step with the emerging technological trends and experience gains in wealth and welfare.

Technological change is closely linked to industrial upgrading and structural change

The biggest advances in technological capabilities and applications will have to occur in the developing world where technological upgrading involves structural changes in production. The capacity of an economy to generate new dynamic activities is key to sustainable development. Because production processes must change in order to sustain long-term growth and facilitate development, Governments must choose enabling policies. This may involve what the Austrian economist Joseph Schumpeter called "creative destruction": creating new economic activities to replace older, less productive ones. Selective investment, industry and technology policies will thus become essential for all countries pursuing sustainable development.

A Green National Innovation System (G-NIS) is needed

All countries have what has come to be called a national innovation system (NIS), which encompasses the educational system, scientific and technical research institutions, private firms' product development departments and other mechanisms through which products and production processes are redesigned. All countries have a national innovation system, whether or not policymakers are conscious of its presence. A key responsibility of an effective NIS is building domestic capacity to choose, absorb and promote the technologies that are most conducive to enhancing dynamic sustainable development. This *Survey* proposes mainstreaming sustainable development objectives into existing national innovation systems and situating those objectives at their very core so as to create what it calls Green National Innovation Systems (G-NIS). The G-NIS would also serve both to coordinate the reorientation of sector-specific innovation systems for agriculture, energy, construction, manufacturing and transport, among other sectors, towards a focus on green technologies and to ensure consistency among green technology, industrial and demand-side policies.

Accelerating the green energy transition

A radical energy transformation is needed

It is rapidly expanding energy use, mainly driven by fossil fuels, that explains why humanity is on the verge of breaching planetary sustainability boundaries through global warming, biodiversity loss, and disturbance of the nitrogen-cycle balance and other measures of the sustainability of the Earth's ecosystem. A comprehensive global energy transition is urgently needed in order to avert a major planetary catastrophe.

While climate change scenarios indicate that the transition would need to be achieved within the next four decades, history and present developments suggest that this would be virtually impossible: Previous major energy transitions took from 70 to 100 years (figure O.2). Since 1975, energy systems have stabilized around the use of fossil fuels with no visible shift in the direction of a new transition towards renewable and cleaner primary energy sources, despite national and international efforts to accelerate technological change in energy generation in response to the oil crises of the 1970s and

Figure O.2
Two grand-scale transitions undergone by global energy systems, 1850-2008

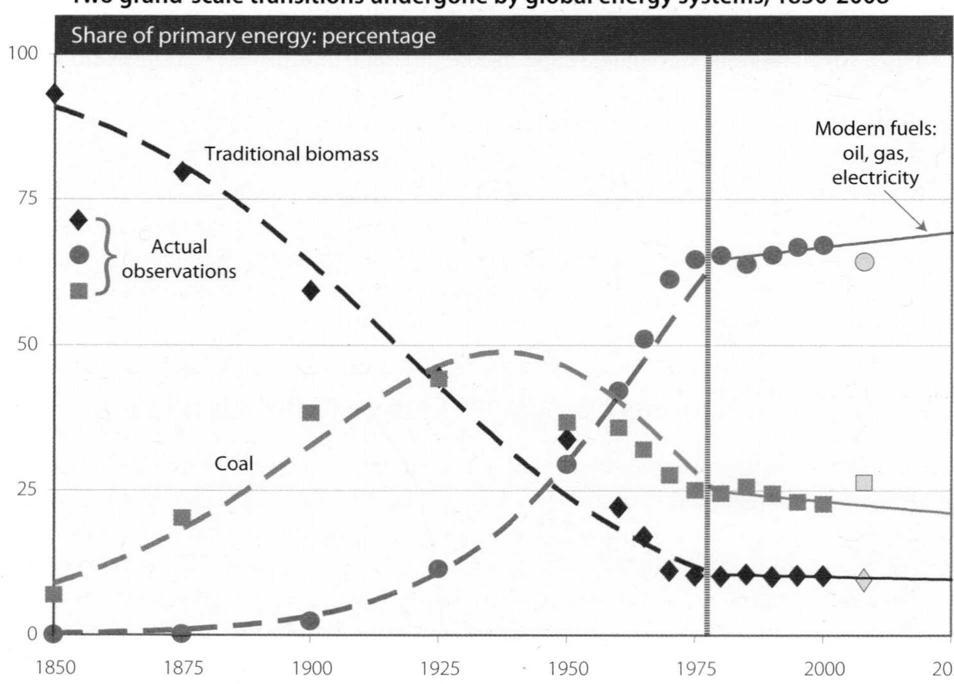

Sources: British Petroleum (2010); Grübler (2008); and International Energy Agency (2010a).

increasing concerns about global warming. Progress has been made in achieving greater energy efficiency (as determined by use of energy per unit of output) and increased use of certain types of technologies with lower carbon content, but these achievements have been greatly outweighed by rising energy demand leading to continued increases in global greenhouse gas emissions. The high levels of economic growth that developing countries will need to achieve in the coming decades in order to meet their development targets will lead to further drastic increases in energy demand. Far more drastic improvements in energy efficiency and an accelerated shift to sustainable energy will thus be required if catastrophic damage through climate change is to be averted.

Will such a transformation be feasible?

The long lifetimes of power plants, refineries, buildings and energy infrastructure make any energy transition necessarily a long-term affair. Global replacement costs of existing fossil fuel and nuclear power infrastructure are estimated at, at least, $15 trillion–$20 trillion (between one quarter and one third of global income). Some developing countries may be able to leapfrog directly to renewable energy sources, although the bulk of the energy infrastructure of most emerging and developing countries is already locked into the utilization of fossil fuels.

Many countries are already making efforts to foster a greener energy supply system, including through investments in energy innovation, feed-in tariffs and other price measures, and regulatory measures and efficiency standards designed to promote energy efficiency and diffusion of renewable and clean sources of energy. The *Survey* indicates, however, that the pace of progress of technological change is nowhere near that needed to reach the goal of full decarbonization of the global energy system by 2050. Clearly, existing efforts are just not generating a global solution; and increased efforts to accelerate change will therefore be needed in both developed and developing countries.

The task will be daunting, partly because of the massive investments locked into brown energy technology and its interdependencies with the broader economic system; and partly because, as present knowledge suggests, there may be technical limits to the massive scaling up of renewable energy technologies (such as wind and solar power), given present conversion efficiency as well as the limits to deployment of those technologies and improvements in their energy-use efficiency.

Accelerating a green energy transformation is possible—but it will be difficult

There are examples of rapid national energy transitions. Portugal, for example, increased the share of renewables (including hydroelectric power) in total energy supply from 17 to 45 per cent in just five years, between 2005 and 2010. Such accelerated transitions will likely be easier in small and resource-rich or affluent economies than in large and resource-poor or low-income countries. The 1987 Montreal Protocol on Substances that Deplete the Ozone Layer[1] is an example of a global instrument that has produced successfully a framework for inducing a worldwide radical and swift shift away from polluting technologies, with special support to developing countries for adopting new technologies.

The *Survey* concludes that accelerating the green transition will require ensuring coherence across a broad range of policies among all countries. These policies will, by and large, have to be adapted to local conditions and opportunities, and implemented at the national level. However, these national policies will need to "add up", which is now not the case, so as to meet global targets, especially those for reducing greenhouse gas emissions, given the global nature of climate change.

Global targets need to recognize differences in levels of development

A global energy transformation should simultaneously meet emission targets and facilitate an upward convergence of energy usages of developing and developed countries (the per capita income and energy availabilities of the former are on average one tenth those of the latter). The Kyoto Protocol[2] to the United Nations Framework Convention on Climate Change[3] requires signatories to reduce their yearly emissions to about 13 tons of CO_2 emissions per person by 2012, which seems achievable. This target would be coupled with declining rates of emissions increase in developing countries. To stay within the absolute CO_2 concentration limit of 450 parts per million accepted by the Copenhagen Climate Change Summit, accelerated progress towards a renewable or green energy transformation will be needed, as this limit would entail cutting annual emissions gradually to 3 tons per person by 2050, or less for any more stringent limit set to stabilize the climate.

However, given that current knowledge suggests that there may be limits to the degree to which renewable technologies can be scaled up and the extent to which energy efficiency can be increased to meet growing energy demand, caps on energy consumption

1 United Nations, *Treaty Series*, vol. 1552, No. 26369.

2 Ibid., vol. 2303, No. 30822.

3 Ibid., vol. 1771, No. 30822.

(with significant implications for production and consumption processes) to complement emission reduction targets may need to be considered. The *Survey* estimates that the emissions cap would be equivalent to primary energy consumption of 70 gigajoules per capita per year, which means that the average European would have to cut his or her present energy consumption by about half and the average resident of the United States of America by about three quarters. Most developing-country citizens would still be able to significantly increase their average energy usage for some period of time. Even so, developing countries will not be able to avoid making the green energy transformation as well to ensure that global emission reduction targets can be met.

Green energy policies need to be coherent along production and consumption chains

In accelerating technological transformation to meet emissions and energy-use targets, the *Survey* recommends that policies and actions be guided by four key goals.

Improving energy efficiency in end use without expanding consumption where energy-use levels are already high

Reducing energy use through technological change—entailing production of factory equipment, home appliances and automobiles that are more energy-efficient—is potentially as important as installing clean energy supply facilities. This will, however, require a quantum increase in support for research and deployment in a relatively neglected area. In order for macrolevel gains to be reaped from end-use efficiencies, it is important that improved energy efficiency not be allowed to become the basis for an increase in activity and consumption in developed countries and that such increases be permitted only in countries that are still overcoming energy and income deficits.

Supporting a broad energy technology development portfolio globally while adapting more mature technologies in specific locations

A wide range of technologies exist for producing clean energy and reducing energy intensity of production and consumption. Most experts concur that Governments, in particular advanced economies, should promote the development of a broad portfolio of technologies (including renewables such as solar, wind, geothermal and hydropower) along the full chain of technology development (research, development and demonstration, market formation, diffusion and commercial adaptation). Most developing countries may opt for a more focused portfolio, given that their entry into energy technological transformation would take place at mature stages of the process.

Supporting more extensive experimentation and discovery periods

Support for technological development must also allow for experimentation sufficient to ensure that the more efficient technologies are scaled up, with the end goal being, in all cases, commercial viability. Government support programmes should ensure that consistent improvement of technologies is focused towards widespread usability beyond the demonstration stage and should avoid a premature locking in of suboptimal technologies that are not viable in non-specialized situations.

Using "smart" governance and accountability strategies in energy-related technological development

It is important, at the global and national levels, to expand oversight by independent and broadly representative technical bodies of the allocation of public funds for technological development. Support programmes should have sufficient flexibility to provide and withdraw resources based on potential and opportunity cost considerations. Governments can subsidize and reward efforts by private companies to achieve progressively higher energy efficiencies in end-use products such as factory equipment, cars and home appliances. An excellent example of such an approach is Japan's Top Runner programme, which turns the most efficient product into a standard to be met by other manufacturers within a given time period. Upgrading towards technologies that are low on emissions and highly energy-efficient should be a key objective of industrial policy.

Technological change for sustainable food security

The first green revolution in agriculture was in fact not all that "green"

The recent food crises laid bare deeper structural problems within the global food system and the need to increase investment and foster innovation in agriculture so as to accelerate growth of food production in order to overcome hunger and feed a growing world population. Achieving this goal with existing agricultural technologies and production systems would entail further increases in greenhouse gas emissions, water pollution, deforestation and land degradation, which in turn would impose further environmental limits on food production growth itself.

In large parts of the world, food systems were shaped to a considerable extent by the so-called green revolution of the 1960s and 1970s, which pushed agricultural yields as much through intensive use of irrigation water and environmentally harmful chemical fertilizers and pesticides, as the introduction of new seed varieties (figure O.3).

A truly green agricultural revolution is now needed ...

Food security must now be attained through green technology so as to reduce the use of chemical inputs (fertilizers and pesticides) and to make more efficient use of energy, water and natural resources, as well as through significant improvement of storage facilities, and marketing to reduce waste. An extensive menu of already available green technologies and sustainable practices in agriculture (which have been successfully adopted with large productivity gains in developing-country contexts) can be deployed to lead the radical transformation towards sustainable food security, including technologies and practices such as low-tillage farming, crop rotation and interplanting, water harvesting and recycling, water-efficient cropping, agroforestry and integrated pest management. Further, biotechnology, genetic engineering, food irradiation, hydroponics and anaerobic digestion hold out the promise of improving the resistance of food crops to pests and extreme weather, increasing their nutritional value and reducing food contamination and greenhouse gas emissions. Development of new high-yielding varieties of crops, a central focus of the first green revolution in agriculture, should continue, provided such development is

Figure O.3
Diverging productivity growth of cereal food crops, by region, 1961-2009

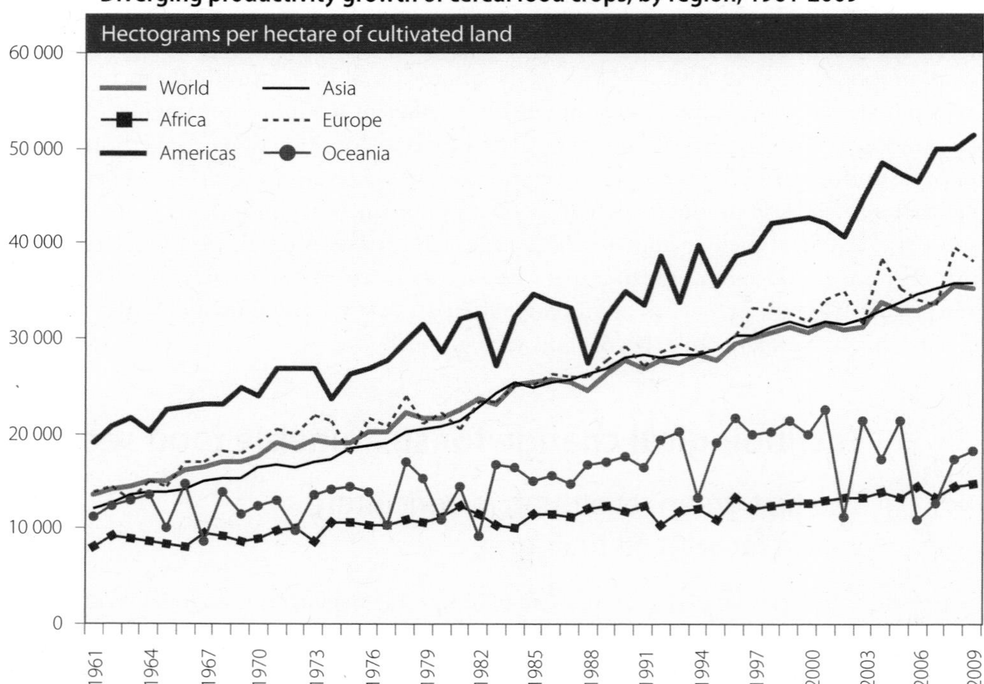

Source: Agricultural Science and Technology Indicators (ASTI), facilitated by the International Food Policy Research Institute (IFPRI). Available from http://www.asti.cgiar.org/data/.

combined with improved water management and better use of agrochemical and organic inputs so as to substantially reduce their adverse ecological impacts, as in the System of Rice Intensification (SRI) which raises crop yield while reducing water, chemical fertilizer and pesticide usage through simple changes in the times when and the means by which rice seeds are transplanted and irrigated.

… a revolution with a key focus on small-scale farming

While these technologies need to be improved further, the main challenge is to change incentive structures so as to encourage their widespread use. The *Survey* reaffirms the view taken by the international community at the 1996 World Food Summit and when defining responses to the food crisis of 2007-2008, namely, that the main policy focus on the supply side should be promotion and development of sustainable agriculture, with an emphasis on small farm holders in developing countries, since it is in this area that most gains in terms of both productivity increases and rural poverty reduction can be achieved. In developing countries, most food is still locally produced and consumed, placing small-scale farming at the heart of food production systems.

The green revolution of the 1960s and 1970s bypassed many small farm holders because of its focus on a single technological package—one that did not address the context-specific conditions of millions of farmers, mainly in Africa. Without providing adequate technologies and a larger range of supportive services (rural infrastructure, like rural roads and sustainable irrigation systems, education and training and access to land, credits, affordable inputs and market information), small farm holders are, typically, not able to take advantage of available technological improvements.

A comprehensive approach to food security is essential …

The policy challenge is thus twofold. First, effective ways must be found to adapt sustainable agricultural technologies to local conditions and the needs of small farm holders. Second, dynamic innovative processes must be introduced at the local level, including by putting in place the necessary support infrastructure and services, as well as strengthened forms of association and joint production among farmers (such as cooperatives and land consolidation), especially for crops whose cultivation benefits from economies of scale. Taking advantage of scale economies could also be appropriate in serving large markets and accessing inputs and credit. Increased agricultural productivity raises rural incomes and frees labour for the industrial sector.

The *Survey* argues that a comprehensive policy approach is needed to take on these challenges, which would involve both a comprehensive national framework for sustainable use of resources, and new technology and innovation with the capacity to increase the productivity, profitability, stability, resilience and climate change mitigation potential of rural production systems. Water conservation, soil protection and biodiversity enhancement need to form part of an integrated approach aimed at sustainable management of land and other natural resources and also need to build on synergies between the forest and agriculture sectors. In the context of competitive land uses, many solutions, involving difficult choices, will be reachable only through open and inclusive negotiation and discussion. Nevertheless, the aforementioned synergies between sectors (resulting, inter alia, in reduced deforestation and increased land productivity, and sustainable water supply) present important "win-win" options through better resource management facilitated by an enabling institutional environment.

… and will need to be supported by an enabling institutional environment

Countries should consider placing a Sustainable Agricultural Innovation System (SAIS) at the centre of a comprehensive policy approach to achieving food security and environmental sustainability. The SAIS, as the agricultural and natural resource management pillar of a Green National Innovation System, would link the multiplicity of actors that participate in national innovation systems in agriculture: universities, research institutions, firms, farmers, civil society organizations and private foundations.

Sustainable transformation of agriculture requires greater national capacities to adapt to continuous environmental and market change. A dynamic SAIS would provide the framework for the policy coherence needed to accelerate the desired transformation of agriculture, including by laying out the strategies for easing the adaptation of green technologies and sustainable crop practices, and for improving the capacity of farmers to innovate through learning and experimentation and to secure better access to input and product markets through partnerships with other actors (research institutions, private corporations, non-governmental organizations and local governments).

Research capacities will need to be rebuilt

The creation of a Sustainable Agricultural Innovation System able to assume a leadership role in the new green revolution will require a new effort to rebuild global and national research capacities in agriculture and natural resource management, including through increased financial support for agricultural research and development. Experience from the previous green revolution has shown that the adoption of new technology for food security requires long-term financial support for research and development. A significant component of that support had been channelled through the Consultative Group on International Agricultural Research (CGIAR) network, which lost much of its capacity to exercise leadership in further technological innovation when the flow of resources became unstable and decreased. The international and national public sectors have an important role to play in facilitating farmers' free access to information and technology by providing adequate incentives to the private and not-for-profit sectors to collaborate in producing public goods, and by reinvigorating and helping to reorient the focus of networks like CGIAR as part of an SAIS and international cooperation.

The previous green revolution took less than a decade to increase food production at impressive rates. The new revolution in agriculture needed to improve food security and halt the depletion of natural resources can, with adequate financial resources and political support, be produced through the incorporation of available technology in farming.

International support will be critical

The international community has much to contribute to the transformation in agriculture by removing obstacles to the transfer of technology (including privately held patents); delivering on its commitment to mobilize $20 billion in additional official development assistance (ODA) for sustainable agriculture, as pledged at the 2009 G8 Summit held in L'Aquila, Italy; providing small-scale farmers with expanded access to mechanisms for the payment of environmental services; and, in the case of Organization for Economic Cooperation and Development (OECD) member countries, eliminating agricultural subsidies.

Harm inflicted by natural events

The frequency of climate-related disasters is increasing

The frequency of natural disasters has quintupled over the past 40 years. By far, most of this increase can be accounted for by the greater incidence of hydro-meteorological disasters (floods, storms, droughts and extreme temperatures) associated with climate change. Major disruptions in the ecosystem, often referred to as "extreme events", have become more likely. Such events could already be occurring in the area of biodiversity (resulting in rapid extinction of species) and may be close to occurring in the fisheries domain and in some water systems.

Developing countries tend to suffer more from the adverse consequences of natural hazards through multiple vulnerabilities associated with lower levels of development and inadequate resources, which constrain their efforts to build more adequate and resilient infrastructure and implement adequate disaster risk management strategies.

Disaster risk management should be an integral part of national development strategies

Despite the urgent threat involved, disaster risk management and adaptation to climate change in developed and developing countries alike have not been mainstreamed into broader decision-making processes. In practice, responses are most often largely event-driven. The *Survey* emphasizes, in contrast, that investment and technology decisions related to disaster risk reduction and adaptation to climate change should be embedded in national development strategies. This approach is in line with that set out in the Hyogo Framework for Action 2005-2015: Building the Resilience of Nations and Communities to Disasters[4] for disaster risk management and in the Cancun Adaptation Framework.[5]

Existing technologies can be deployed

Reducing disaster risk in a sustainable manner will involve changes in the design of settlements and infrastructure, including roads, rail systems and power plants. Existing modern technologies, including sea walls, tidal and saltwater intrusion barriers, and improved water and crop storage, appear by and large to be adequate to the task of providing protection against most (non-extreme) hazards. Further technological innovation, which draws on indigenous knowledge, is needed to adapt disaster-resilient infrastructure, housing and natural coastal protection to local conditions and to make the technologies more affordable for developing countries.

National efforts need to be supported through regional and global cooperation

Natural hazards know no national borders and often affect larger regions. National-level disaster risk management will thus need to be linked to regional mechanisms of cooperation, including for maintaining joint monitoring, forecasting, and early warning systems, and defining risk reduction strategies.

International cooperation will also require facilitating technology transfer to developing countries in order to reduce the local harm caused by global warming. Technology transfer should ensure that recipients have the capacity to install, operate, maintain and repair imported technologies. It will be important for local adapters to be able to produce lower-cost versions of imported technologies and adapt imported technologies to domestic markets and circumstances. In the Hyogo Framework for Action and the United Nations Framework Convention on Climate Change, the international community identified the need for external financial support for local adaptation and disaster resilience efforts, including through the mobilization of resources for dedicated multilateral funding.

Technology transfer and international cooperation

Multilateral trading rules and international finance need to be "greened"

A sustained scaling up and reform in international cooperation and finance are required to achieve the global technological revolution. Scaling up and reforms require action in three areas. First, an international regime for green technology-sharing will have to be established to facilitate technology transfers to and development in developing countries. This will include using a broader set of tools in intellectual property and multilateral trade policies.

4 A/CONF.206/6 and Corr.1, chap. I, resolution 2.

5 United Nations Framework Convention on Climate Change, 2011, decision 1, CP.16, sect. II.

Second, securing adequate development finance and policy space to energize developing-country efforts to upgrade production technologies towards environmental sustainability is indispensable. Third, international governance and cooperation have to be upgraded.

An effective global technology development and diffusion regime needs to be established

Expanding action in nurturing and upgrading green production and consumption technologies in developing countries must be a key goal of international cooperation. However, publicly guided international mechanisms of technological diffusion have limited precedents, since, historically, the bulk of technological knowledge has been embodied and transferred as private property through the operations of private companies. The successful experience of CGIAR is an example of how rapid worldwide diffusion of new agricultural technologies can be effected through a publicly supported global and regional network of research institutions. In the climate change area, building international public policymaking capability can draw upon the experiences already existing in international scientific networks and the example of multi-stakeholder cooperation provided by the work of the Intergovernmental Panel on Climate Change. The international community took the first step towards meeting this challenge in reaching an agreement at the Conference of the Parties to the United Nations Framework Convention on Climate Change at its sixteenth session, held in Cancun, Mexico, from 29 November to 10 December 2010, to set up a Technology Executive Committee (TEC) as a policymaking body[6] to implement the framework for meaningful and effective actions to enhance the implementation commitments on technology transfer.[7] At the same session, agreement was reached on establishing an operational body to facilitate a networking among national, regional, sectoral and international technology bodies, to be called the Climate Technology Centre and Network (CTCN).[8]

The intellectual property rights regime needs to be changed

Managing global intellectual property rights is also crucial, as patenting is highly aggressive in various areas of green technology. For example, a small group of private companies is actively patenting plant genes with a view to owning the rights to the genes' possible "climate readiness" in the future. Granting intellectual property rights constitutes, and should always remain, a public policy action, one whose intention is to consistently stimulate—not restrict—private initiative in technological development. At the present time, the granting of a patent is the most widespread and lucrative technological development incentive.

Obtaining agreement among countries on the public policies needed to accelerate invention and diffusion is critical. Currently, protecting private intellectual property rights by enforcing exclusive use and deployment by its owner is the main approach. Internationally, spurring green technological development will require a wider mix of public sector strategies, which guarantee a commercial incentive substantial enough to enable private parties to use subsidies and public purchases of technology at reasonable cost

6 Ibid., para. 117(a).

7 Ibid., para. 119.

8 Ibid., paras. 117(b) and 123.

in their research undertakings, while constraining monopolistic practices which restrict diffusion and further development.

Public policy tools could include global funding for research, to be placed in the public domain for widespread dissemination under the same modality utilized in the green revolution in food agriculture in the 1960s and 1970s. With technology funds, it should be possible to establish international innovation networks within different areas of technology. The overall strategy could also include global awards for the formulation of technical solutions to well-defined problems, and public purchase at appropriate prices of private technology for deployment in the public domain. The private sector must continue to play a vital role in technological development, particularly in developing and adapting basic inventions for actual application.

The new international regime should allow special and differential access to new technology based on level of development. For example, developing-country Governments and firms could be allowed to adapt technology but begin paying royalties only when its use has begun to yield commercial returns. Where exclusive private-sector rights of use to vital technology are a hindrance to the development of other needed technology or to widespread use, the technology regime must have a mechanism (such as exists in certain areas of public health) for granting a "compulsory licence" that places said technology in the public domain.

Multilateral trading rules should grant greater flexibility to developing countries in their conduct of industrial policies

Present project-oriented loan conditionality and the proliferation of international financing mechanisms thwart developing countries' efforts to design and implement coherent strategies for sustainable development. Investment measure-related restrictions (from the multilateral trade regime and bilateral treaties) shackle attempts to implement industrial policy at a time when developed-country industrial interventions for building green technologies are proliferating. Thus, it is important to guarantee developing countries sufficient policy space for industrial development.

The multilateral trading system should allow developing countries higher levels of bound tariffs and a greater range in those levels than were proposed under the Doha process. It is also important to consider recognizing industrial policies encompassing, for example, domestic content and technology transfer requirements so as to enable developing countries to undertake sector-specific programmes aimed at building dynamic local industries.

Environmental standards have served as effective industrial policy instruments for accelerating technological transformations. At present, technical standards are often determined by Governments (unilaterally or through agreements among a reduced number of countries) or set by private companies. Wider participation of all parties in the setting of these standards, especially developing countries, should guarantee that the introduction of environmental standards (including through green labels and ecological footprint certificates) will not become a means of practising unfair trade protectionism. The Montreal Protocol process through which the substances to be banned and the pace of their elimination were identified may serve as an example in this regard.

Financing of green technology transfers will require domestic and international financial reforms

To facilitate the introduction of the new green technologies, investment rates in developing countries will have to be stepped up considerably. Inadequate financing has been consistently identified by developing countries as the greatest obstacle to their rapid adoption of clean technologies (figure O.4).

Using scenarios that are consistent across sectors, the ***Survey*** estimates that incremental green investment of about 3 per cent of world gross product (WGP) (about $1.9 trillion in 2010) would be required to overcome poverty, increase food production to eradicate hunger without degrading land and water resources, and avert the climate change catastrophe. Given the limited time frame for achieving the required technological transformation, the required global level of green investments would need to be reached within the next few years.

At least one half of the required investments would have to be realized in developing countries. Enhanced domestic resource mobilization (private savings and public revenues) should be key to financing the additional investment effort over the medium run. Many developing countries have poorly developed markets for long-term financing and a weak fiscal basis, which limit the scope for substantial increases in domestic funding for long-term investment in the near term. Other constraints on investing domestic resources in developing countries originate from deficiencies in the global financial and payments system. A number of developing countries hold a significant portion of domestic savings as international reserves, which in large measure have been invested in financial assets in developed countries. The volatility of global capital and commodity markets are an important determinant underlying this form of self-insurance and substantial net

Figure O.4
Economic and market barriers to technology transfers reported in technology needs assessments

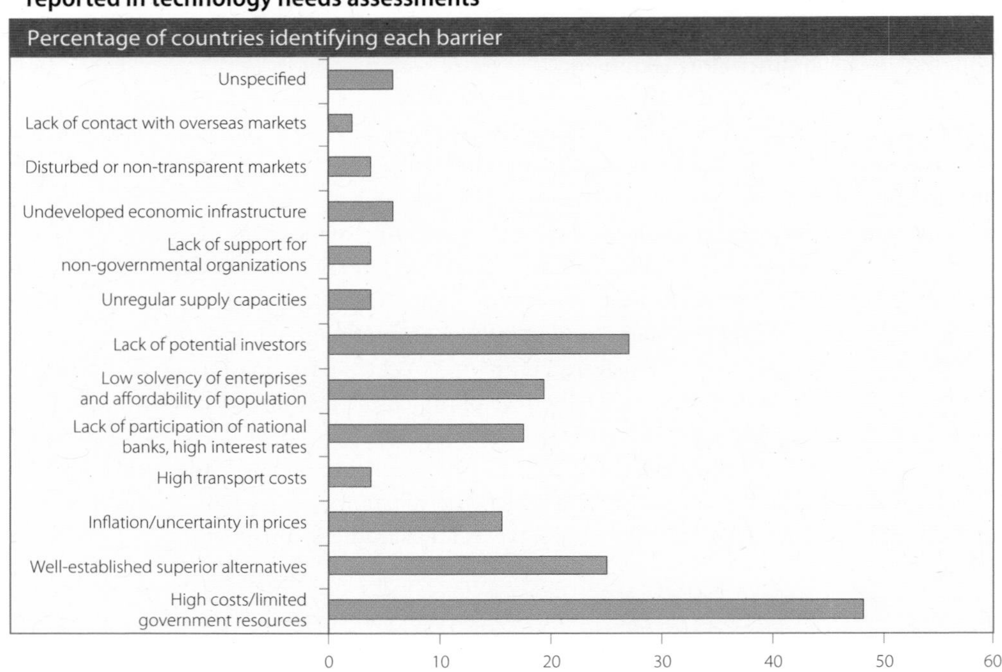

Source: United Nations Framework Convention on Climate Change, Subsidiary Body for Scientific and Technological Advice (2009), figure 6.

transfer of financial resources to advanced market economies. Reforms of the international payments and reserve system that would stem global market volatility and reduce the need for reserve accumulation by individual developing countries could liberate substantial resources (including from sovereign wealth funds through the use of special drawing rights) for long-term financing in green investments. Moreover, this would facilitate effective net resource transfers to developing countries.

The external financing currently available for green technology investments in developing countries is far from sufficient to meet the challenge. The Global Environment Facility and climate change trust funds under the management of the World Bank managed to disburse no more than $20 billion per year in the last two years. Consequently, at present most of the financing for technology transfer is dependent on foreign direct investment (FDI) flows, technical cooperation provisions in external assistance grants and loans and export credit agency funding. However, all of these mechanisms lack incentives and policy contexts conducive to investment in green technologies.

The commitment set out in the Copenhagen Accord to mobilize $30 billion for the period 2010-2012 and $100 billion per year by 2020 in transfers to developing countries is more of a step in the right direction, but that commitment has yet to be realized. The ***Survey*** estimates that developing countries will require a little over $1 trillion a year in incremental green investment. While a large proportion of the incremental investment would ultimately be financed from developing countries' public and private resources, international financing will be indispensable, particularly in the early years, in jump-starting green investment and financing the adoption of external technologies. The Copenhagen pledges do not appear to match the required scaling up of the global effort. The scaling up likely also comes too late, given the limited time available.

Global governance capabilities need to be strengthened

The proposed reshaping of national development efforts and strengthened international commitment in the areas of technological development and cooperation, external assistance, investment finance and trade rules will require stronger mechanisms of global governance and coordination. Within the next three to four decades, all of these efforts must "add up" to achieving what today seems to be a set of almost unattainable targets, including a reduction in per capita carbon emissions by almost three fourths and the eradication of poverty, which will require an almost 10 times greater availability of modern energy sources by those now counted as poor.

The *Survey* recognizes that the bulk of the efforts to carry out a technological transformation must occur at the country level and build upon local conditions and resources. The need for an effective global technology policymaking body has already been indicated. If the overall global objectives are to be achieved, two critical conditions need to be fulfilled. First, more effective monitoring and verification of performance on international commitments are needed. As regards establishing the corresponding mechanisms of common accountability, lessons can be drawn from existing modalities in other areas, such as the trade policy review process of the World Trade Organization.

Second, much greater coherence will be required among the now noticeably disjointed multilateral architectures for environment, technology transfer, trade, aid and finance so as to facilitate coordination among what will likely be a diverse set of country strategies for green growth and ensure that they add up to global targets for environmental sustainability.

At the United Nations Conference on Environment and Development, held in Rio de Janeiro from 3 to 14 June 1992, the community of nations reached agreement on a "precautionary principle" to serve as a guide to public policy. According to that principle, in the absence of scientific consensus that a particular action or policy is harmful to the public or to the environment, the burden of proof that the suspect action or policy is *not* harmful rests with the party or parties implementing it. The precautionary principle determines that there exists a social responsibility to protect the public from exposure to harm in cases where scientific investigation has found a plausible risk of harm, which implies that all possible means should be applied towards achieving sustainable development.

Sha Zukang
Under-Secretary-General
for Economic and Social Affairs
May 2011

Contents

Boxes

Figures

Tables

Explanatory Notes

The following symbols have been used in the tables throughout the report:

..	**Two dots** indicate that data are not available or are not separately reported.
–	**A dash** indicates that the amount is nil or negligible.
-	**A hyphen** indicates that the item is not applicable.
−	**A minus sign** indicates deficit or decrease, except as indicated.
.	**A full stop** is used to indicate decimals.
/	**A slash** between years indicates a crop year or financial year, for example, 2010/11.
-	**Use of a hyphen** between years, for example, 2010-2011, signifies the full period involved, including the beginning and end years.
	Reference to "dollars" ($) indicates United States dollars, unless otherwise stated.
	Reference to "billions" indicates one thousand million.
	Reference to "tons" indicates metric tons, unless otherwise stated.
	Annual rates of growth or change, unless otherwise stated, refer to annual compound rates.
	Details and percentages in tables do not necessarily add to totals, because of rounding.

The following abbreviations have been used:

CAFE	Corporate Average Fuel Economy (standards) (United States of America)
CCS	carbon capture and storage
CDM	Clean Development Mechanism (Kyoto Protocol)
CERs	certified emissions reductions
CGIAR	Consultative Group on International Agricultural Research
CH_4	Methane
CO_2	carbon dioxide
CSP	concentrating solar power
DAC	Development Assistance Committee (OECD)
DOE	Department of Energy (United States of America)
EGTT	Expert Group on Technology Transfer (UNFCCC)
EJ	exajoules
ESTs	environmentally sound technologies
EU	European Union
FAO	Food and Agriculture Organization of the United Nations
FDI	foreign direct investment
FFS	Farmer Field Schools
FIT	feed-in tariff
F-gases	fluorinated gases
GATT	General Agreement on Tariffs and Trade
GDP	gross domestic product
GE	genetically engineered
GEA	Global Energy Assessment
GHG	greenhouse gas
GJ	gigajoules
G-NIS	Green National Innovation System
Gt	gigatons
GtC	gigatons of carbon
GW	gigawatts
ICT	information and communications technology
IEA	International Energy Agency
IFPRI	International Food Policy Research Institute
IGCC	integrated gasification combined cycle
IMF	International Monetary Fund
IPCC	Intergovernmental Panel on Climate Change
IPM	integrated pest management
kg	kilogram
kWh	kilowatt-hour
LECZ	low-elevation coastal zone
MCDA	multi-criteria decision analysis
mpg	miles per gallon
$MtCO_2e$	metric tones of CO_2 equivalent
Mtoe	millions of tons of oil equivalent
MW	megawatt
NDVI	normalized difference vegetation index
N_2O	nitrous oxide
NPP	net primary productivity
NIMBY	not in my backyard
NIS	National Innovation System
ODA	official development assistance
OECD	Organization for Economic Cooperation and Development
PES	payments for environmental services
POP	persistent organic pollutant
ppm	parts per million
ppmv	parts per million by volume
PPP	purchasing power parity
PV	photovoltaic
R&D	research and development
RD&D	research, development and demonstration
SAIS	sustainable agricultural innovation system
SBSTA	Subsidiary Body for Scientific and Technological Advice (UNFCCC)
SCC	social cost of carbon
SDRs	special drawing rights
SHS	solar home systems
SRI	System of Rice Intensification
SUV	sport utility vehicle
TRIPS	Agreement on Trade-related Aspects of Intellectual Property Rights
TW	terawatts
UNCTAD	United Nations Conference on Trade and Development
UN/DESA	Department of Economic and Social Affairs of the United Nations Secretariat
UNDP	United Nations Development Programme
UNEP	United Nations Environment Programme
UNESCO	United Nations Educational, Scientific and Cultural Organization
UNFCCC	United Nations Framework Convention on Climate Change
UNICEF	United Nations Children's Fund
UNWTO	United Nations World Tourism Organization
WEFM	World Economic Forecasting Model (of the United Nations)
WGP	world gross product
WHO	World Health Organization
WTO	World Trade Organization
VC	venture capital
ZJ	zettajoules

The designations employed and the presentation of the material in this publication do not imply the expression of any opinion whatsoever on the part of the United Nations Secretariat concerning the legal status of any country, territory, city or area or of its authorities, or concerning the delimitation of its frontiers or boundaries.

The term "country" as used in the text of this report also refers, as appropriate, to territories or areas.

For analytical purposes, unless otherwise specified, the following country groupings and subgroupings have been used:

Developed economies (developed market economies):

Australia, Canada, European Union, Iceland, Japan, New Zealand, Norway, Switzerland, United States of America.

Group of Eight (G-8):

Canada, France, Germany, Italy, Japan, Russian Federation, United Kingdom of Great Britain and Northern Ireland, United States of America.

Group of Twenty (G-20):

Argentina, Australia, Brazil, Canada, China, France, Germany, India, Indonesia, Italy, Japan, Mexico, Republic of Korea, Russian Federation, Saudi Arabia, South Africa, Turkey, United Kingdom of Great Britain and Northern Ireland, United States of America, European Union.

European Union (EU):

Austria, Belgium, Bulgaria, Cyprus, Czech Republic, Denmark, Estonia, Finland, France, Germany, Greece, Hungary, Ireland, Italy, Latvia, Lithuania, Luxembourg, Malta, Netherlands, Poland, Portugal, Romania, Slovakia, Slovenia, Spain, Sweden, United Kingdom of Great Britain and Northern Ireland.

EU-15:

Austria, Belgium, Denmark, Finland, France, Germany, Greece, Ireland, Italy, Luxembourg, Netherlands, Portugal, Spain, Sweden, United Kingdom of Great Britain and Northern Ireland.

New EU member States:

Bulgaria, Cyprus, Czech Republic, Estonia, Hungary, Latvia, Lithuania, Malta, Poland, Romania, Slovakia, Slovenia.

Economies in transition:

South-eastern Europe:

Albania, Bosnia and Herzegovina, Croatia, Montenegro, Serbia, the former Yugoslav Republic of Macedonia.

Commonwealth of Independent States (CIS):

Armenia, Azerbaijan, Belarus, Georgia,[a] Kazakhstan, Kyrgyzstan, Republic of Moldova, Russian Federation, Tajikistan, Turkmenistan, Ukraine, Uzbekistan.

Developing economies:

Africa, Asia and the Pacific (excluding Australia, Japan, New Zealand and the member States of CIS in Asia), Latin America and the Caribbean.

Subgroupings of Africa:

Northern Africa:

Algeria, Egypt, Libyan Arab Jamahiriya, Morocco, Tunisia.

Sub-Saharan Africa:

All other African countries, except Nigeria and South Africa, where indicated.

Subgroupings of Asia and the Pacific:

Western Asia:

Bahrain, Iraq, Israel, Jordan, Kuwait, Lebanon, Occupied Palestinian Territory, Oman, Qatar, Saudi Arabia, Syrian Arab Republic, Turkey, United Arab Emirates, Yemen.

South Asia:

Bangladesh, Bhutan, India, Iran (Islamic Republic of), Maldives, Nepal, Pakistan, Sri Lanka.

East Asia:

All other developing economies in Asia and the Pacific.

Subgroupings of Latin America and the Caribbean:

South America:

Argentina, Bolivia (Plurinational State of), Brazil, Chile, Colombia, Ecuador, Paraguay, Peru, Uruguay, Venezuela (Bolivarian Republic of).

Mexico and Central America:

Costa Rica, El Salvador, Guatemala, Honduras, Mexico, Nicaragua, Panama.

Caribbean:

Barbados, Cuba, Dominican Republic, Guyana, Haiti, Jamaica, Trinidad and Tobago.

---

a As of 19 August 2009, Georgia officially left the Commonwealth of Independent States. However, its performance is discussed in the context of this group of countries for reasons of geographical proximity and similarities in economic structure.

Least developed countries:

Afghanistan, Angola, Bangladesh, Benin, Bhutan, Burkina Faso, Burundi, Cambodia, Central African Republic, Chad, Comoros, Democratic Republic of the Congo, Djibouti, Equatorial Guinea, Eritrea, Ethiopia, Gambia, Guinea, Guinea-Bissau, Haiti, Kiribati, Lao People's Democratic Republic, Lesotho, Liberia, Madagascar, Malawi, Maldives, Mali, Mauritania, Mozambique, Myanmar, Nepal, Niger, Rwanda, Samoa, Sao Tome and Principe, Senegal, Sierra Leone, Solomon Islands, Somalia, Sudan, Timor-Leste, Togo, Tuvalu, Uganda, United Republic of Tanzania, Vanuatu, Yemen, Zambia.

Small island developing States and areas:

American Samoa, Anguilla, Antigua and Barbuda, Aruba, Bahamas, Barbados, Belize, British Virgin Islands, Cape Verde, Commonwealth of the Northern Mariana Islands, Comoros, Cook Islands, Cuba, Dominica, Dominican Republic, Fiji, French Polynesia, Grenada, Guam, Guinea-Bissau, Guyana, Haiti, Jamaica, Kiribati, Maldives, Marshall Islands, Mauritius, Micronesia (Federated States of), Montserrat, Nauru, Netherlands Antilles, New Caledonia, Niue, Palau, Papua New Guinea, Puerto Rico, Saint Kitts and Nevis, Saint Lucia, Saint Vincent and the Grenadines, Samoa, Sao Tome and Principe, Seychelles, Singapore, Solomon Islands, Suriname, Timor-Leste, Tonga, Trinidad and Tobago, Tuvalu, United States Virgin Islands, Vanuatu.

Parties to the United Nations Framework Convention on Climate Change:

Annex I Parties:

Australia, Austria, Belarus, Belgium, Bulgaria, Canada, Croatia, Czech Republic, Denmark, Estonia, European Community, Finland, France, Germany, Greece, Hungary, Iceland, Ireland, Italy, Japan, Latvia, Liechtenstein, Lithuania, Luxembourg, Monaco, Netherlands, New Zealand, Norway, Poland, Portugal, Romania, Russian Federation, Slovakia, Slovenia, Spain, Sweden, Switzerland, Turkey, Ukraine, United Kingdom of Great Britain and Northern Ireland, United States of America.

Annex II Parties:

Annex II parties are the parties included in Annex I that are members of the Organization for Economic Cooperation and Development but not the parties included in Annex I that are economies in transition.

Chapter I
Introduction: why a green technological transformation is needed

Summary

- The cumulative effects of the degradation of the Earth's natural environment has increased the scale of the sustainable development challenge enormously. Provisioning for human life using the current technology is expected to be increasingly infeasible as population continues to increase and the harmful impacts of human production and consumption multiply.
- Business as usual is not an option. An attempt to overcome world poverty through income growth generated by existing "brown technologies" would exceed the limits of environmental sustainability.
- A global green technological transformation, greater in scale and achievable within a much shorter time-frame than the first industrial revolution, is required. The necessary set of new technologies must enable today's poor to attain decent living standards, while reducing emissions and waste and ending the unrestrained drawdown of the earth's non-renewable resources.
- Staging a new technological revolution at a faster pace and on a global scale will call for proactive government intervention and greater international cooperation. Sweeping technological change will require sweeping societal transformation, with changed settlement and consumption patterns and better social values.

The development challenge and the emerging environmental crisis

The current pattern of economic growth has led to the environmental crisis

Since the first industrial revolution, major transformations in energy technology (from muscle power to water, then steam, and later hydrocarbons) and other innovations have generated substantial increases in production and human activity. However, the same technologies that enabled the quantum increases in material welfare have also come at a lasting cost with respect to the degradation of the world's natural environment. To continue to tread the pathways of past economic development would further enhance pressure on natural resources and would destabilize the Earth's ecosystem. Even if we were to now stop global growth engines, the depletion and degradation of the world's natural environment would continue because of existing consumption habits and production methods. Much greater economic progress is needed in order to lift the poor out of poverty and provide for a decent living for all, including the additional 2 billion people who will inhabit the planet by mid-century. Hence, there is an urgent need to seek out new development pathways that will ensure environmental sustainability and reverse ecological destruction, and at the same time serve as the source of decent livelihoods for all of today's population and for future generations.

Unremitting increases in population and income

The increases in population and production have exhibited a "hockey stick" pattern

Both population and incomes have grown exponentially over the past two centuries. While world population size had remained relatively stable for much of human history, it started to increase at an accelerated pace with the first industrial revolution (figure I.1).[1] The world population increased from about 1 billion in 1800 to about 6.5 billion by 2010 and is likely to increase, according to United Nations projections, to about 9 billion by the end of this century.

Figure I.1
Exponential population growth in the modern era

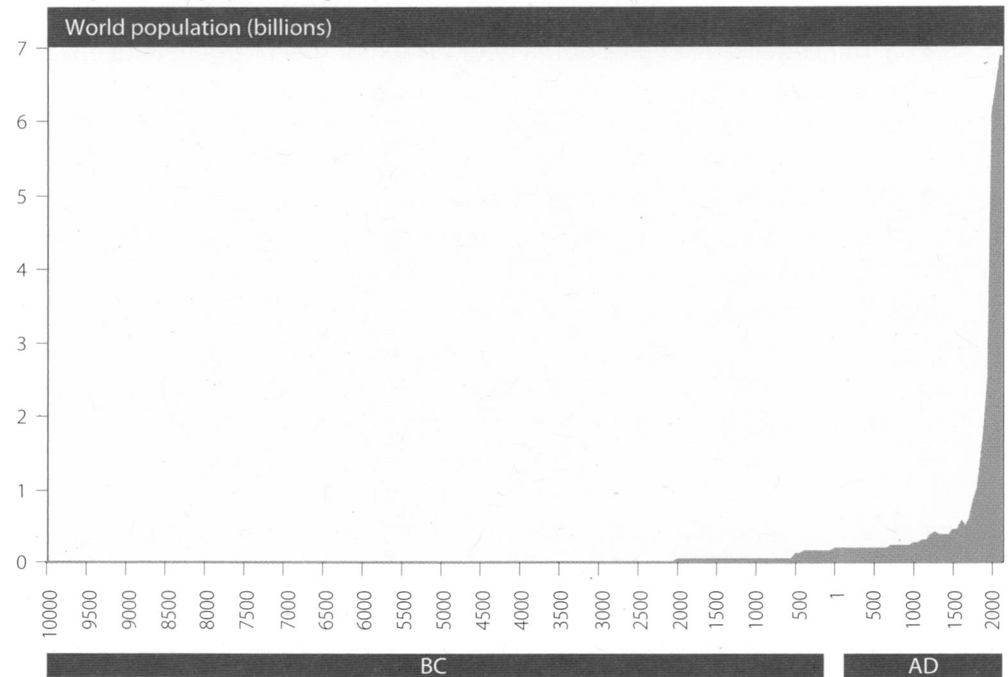

Sources: For 10,000 BC-1749, United States Census Bureau online (www.census.gov/ipc/www/worldhis.html); for 1750-1949, United Nations, "The world at six billion" (ESA/P/WP.154) (12 October 1999), table 1; for 1950-2010: United Nations, Department of Economic and Social Affairs, Population Division, World Population Prospects: The 2010 Revision (medium variant) (New York, 2011).

Similarly, human per capita welfare is believed to have increased at a very slow pace for most of human history, having taken off only with the industrial revolution.[2] Since 1820, income growth, like population size, has exhibited a "hockey stick pattern" (see figure I.2), with per capita income increasing 24 times faster than during the period 1000-1820.[3]

1 It is estimated that even in 10,000 BC, at the onset of the Neolithic revolution, the world population was only about 1 million. Population increased with the successes of Neolithic agriculture and the Bronze- and Iron-Age civilizations. However, even at the onset of the first industrial revolution (1750 AD), world population was limited to only 750 million. Since 1820, population has increased at the rate of 1 per cent per year, a rate that is 6 times higher than that prevailing during the period 1000-1820 (Maddison, 2007, p. 69).

2 According to Maddison (2007), average world income increased by only about 50 per cent between 1000 and 1820 AD. His research suggests that annual per capita income of most ancient societies was about 400 international PPP dollars (IPPP$). DeLong (1998) places this figure much lower, at IPPP$ 90. In any case, until 1820, economic growth, by and large, was extensive, serving mainly to accommodate the fourfold increase in population.

3 Since 1820, per capita income has increased by 1.2 per cent per year (Maddison, 2007).

Figure I.2
Accelerated growth of world per capita income in the modern era

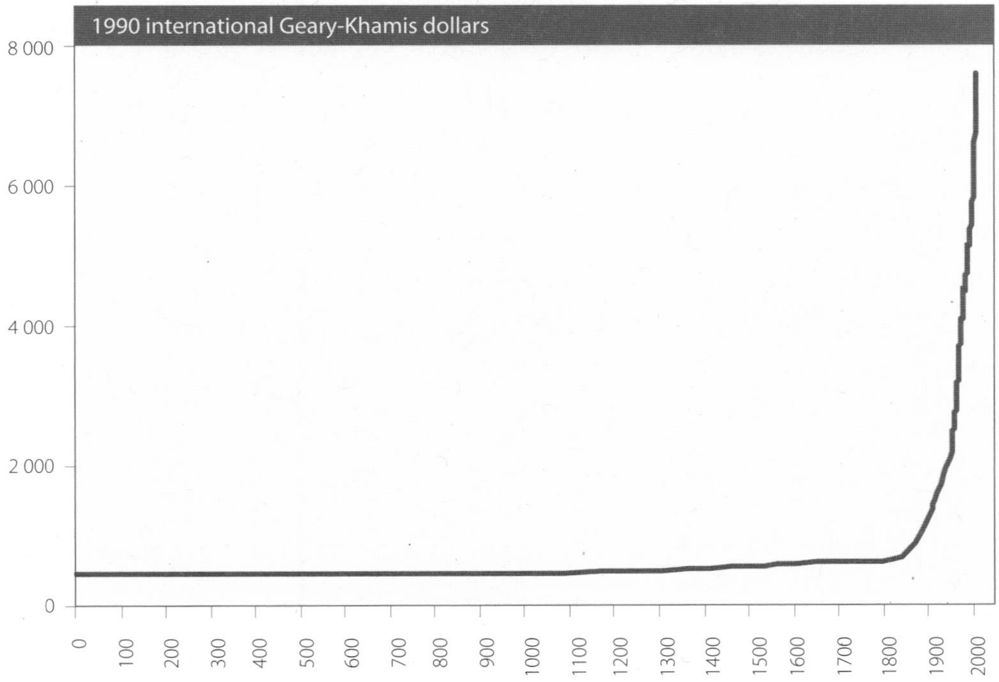

Source: Maddison data on population and GDP. Available from http://sites.google.com/site/econgeodata/maddison-data-on-population-gdp.

Lopsided distribution of population and income growth

The distribution of income and population growth has been very uneven

Most of the observed per capita income growth has been concentrated in the currently developed part of the world (figure I.3). Much smaller gains have been observed in much of Asia, Africa and Latin America. Income growth in developed countries was accompanied by drastic declines in birth and mortality rates and increases in longevity, accelerating a demographic transition. By contrast, developing countries still face much higher birth rates relative to mortality rates, coupled with the slower income growth and, as a result, see much faster population growth (figure I.4).[4] This lopsided distribution of income and population has aggravated the environmental crisis in many ways.

Environmental impact of increased population and income

The limits of the Earth's capacity as "source" and "sink" are being reached …

The Earth has a double function in ensuring human survival—serving as both "source" of the natural resources necessary for, and "sink" for the waste (including pollution) generated by, production and consumption. The impact on that double function of dramatic increases in population and average income, in combination with other conducing factors, has sown the seeds of an environmental crisis.

The hockey-stick patterns of population and income growth are mirrored by the exponential increase in energy consumption (figure I.5).[5] Increased energy consumption has led to a commensurate increase in emissions of carbon dioxide (CO_2) into the

4 Between 1750 and 2008, the combined populations of Europe, North America and Oceania increased almost sevenfold, from 167 million to 1,103 million, while the combined populations of Asia, Africa and Latin America (including the Caribbean) increased ninefold, from 624 million to 5.6 billion.

5 Primary energy consumption had increased from a little over 10 exajoules (EJ) in 1850 to about 500 EJ by 2000.

Figure I.3
Diverging growth of per capita income, by region, 1820-2008

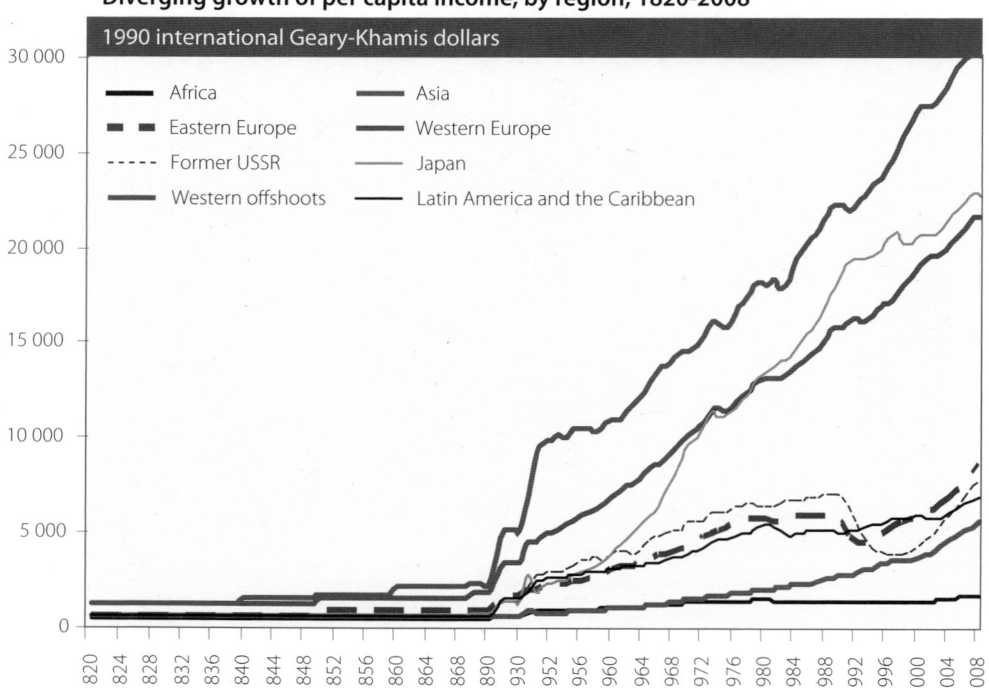

Source: Maddison data on population and GDP. Available from http://sites.google.com/site/econgeodata/maddison-data-on-population-gdp.

Figure I.4
Regional divergences in population growth, 1750-2150

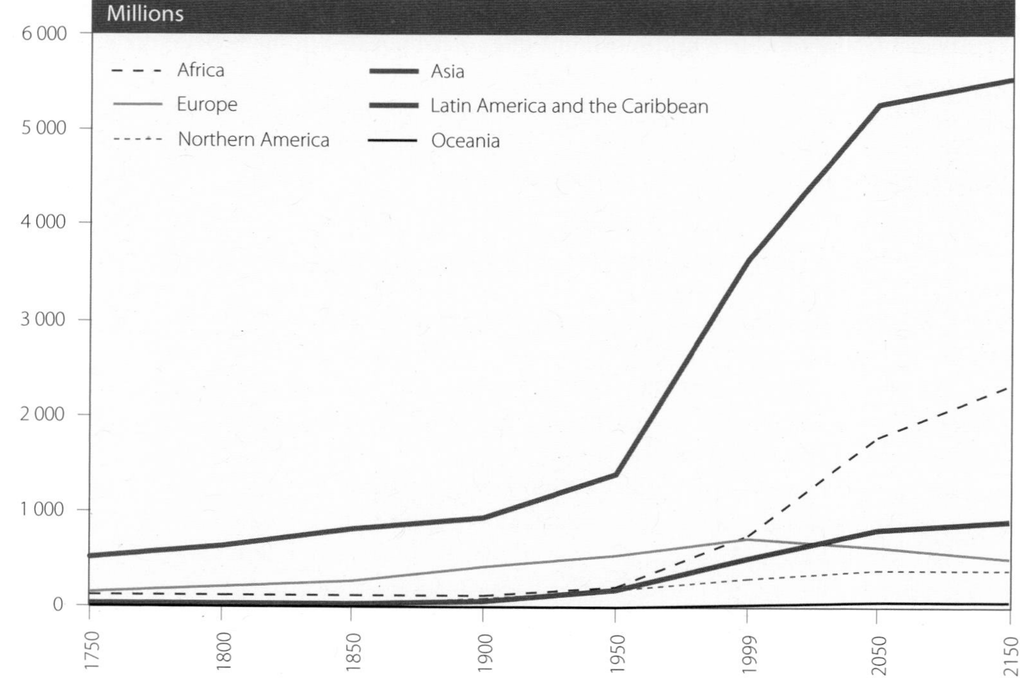

Source: United Nations, "The world at six billion" (ESA/P/WP.154) (12 October 1999), table 2.

Note: Population estimates beyond 2008 are based on the medium-variant projection of the Population Division, UN/DESA.

Figure I.5
Rise in energy consumption since the first industrial revolution

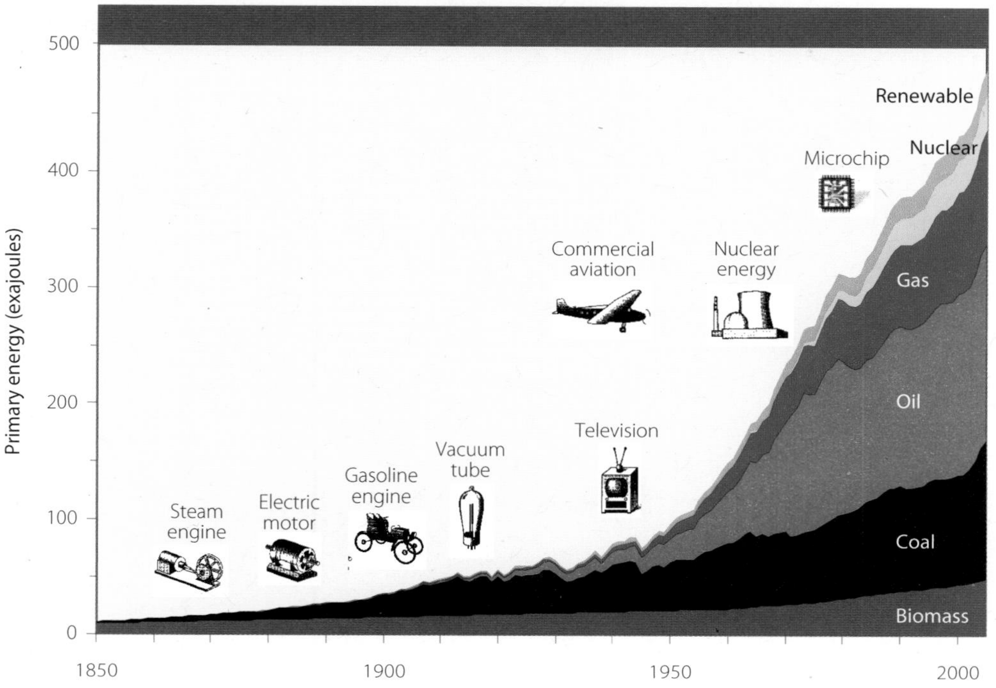

Source: United Nations (2009), figure II.4.

atmosphere, from a pre-industrial level of about 260 parts per million (ppm) to close to 400 ppm in 2010 (figure I.6).[6] Rising concentrations of CO_2 and other greenhouse gases have caused a similarly steep increase in average global temperatures, which are now about 1° C above those observed around 1850 and in the centuries before (figure I.7). With trends in greenhouse gas emissions continuing, global temperatures are set to increase further, and will likely average between 2° C and 5° C above pre-industrial levels by the end of the century (figure I.8), surpassing the limits for a stable climate and becoming high enough to cause cataclysmic changes (United Nations, 2009). The extreme weather events whose incidence has increased in recent years prove how devastating these changes can be (see chap. IV).

There also has been a secular rise in the volume of waste accompanied by alarming changes in its composition. Waste is becoming increasingly non-biodegradable, toxic and radioactive. For example, non-biodegradable plastic now far outweighs such natural materials as timber, paper, iron, copper, lead, aluminium, phosphorus and potash in GDP (figure I.9).

... causing severe damage to the planet's environment and ecosystem

This brief survey demonstrates that, since the first industrial revolution, there has been a switch from an almost horizontal to an almost vertical pattern of rise in population, income, resource use and waste dumped into the Earth's ecosystem. This switch has caused irreparable damage to the Earth's ecosystems and is knocking it off balance. According to the Millennium Ecosystem Assessment (2005):

- Sixty per cent of a group of 24 ecosystems are now degraded or exploited beyond ecological limits

6 From a pre-industrial level of less than 5 gigatons (Gt), which is roughly the atmosphere's absorptive capacity, the amount of CO_2 emitted has increased to about 40 Gt.

Figure I.6
Rise in atmospheric carbon dioxide concentration, 1000-2008

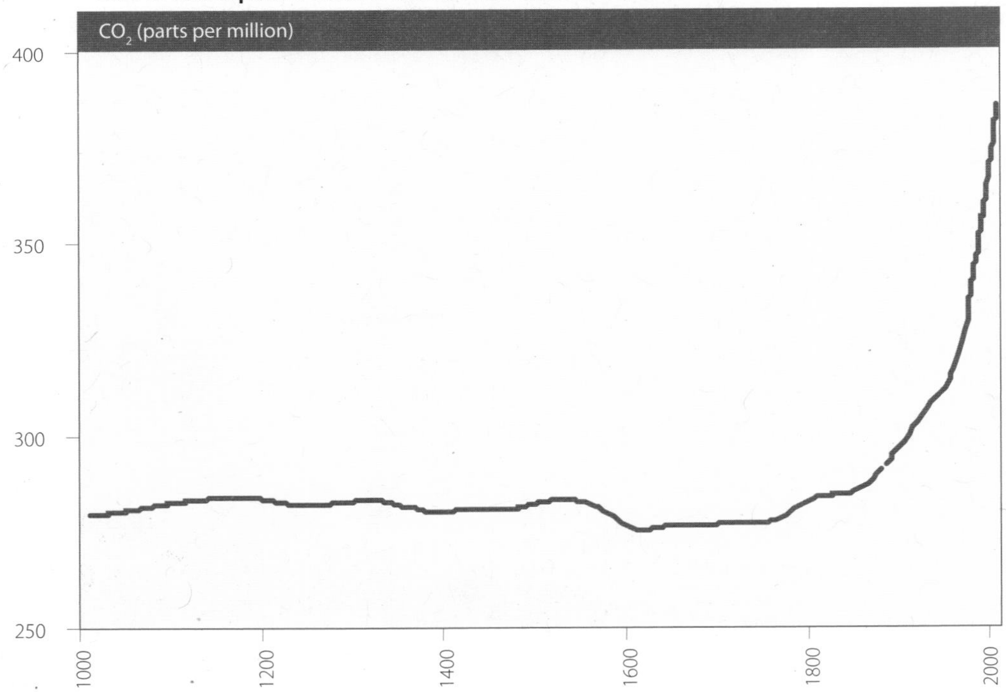

Source: United States Department of Energy, Carbon Dioxide Information Analysis Center (CDIAC). Data available from http://cdiac.esd.ornl.gov.

Figure I.7
Rise in global temperature, 1880-2010

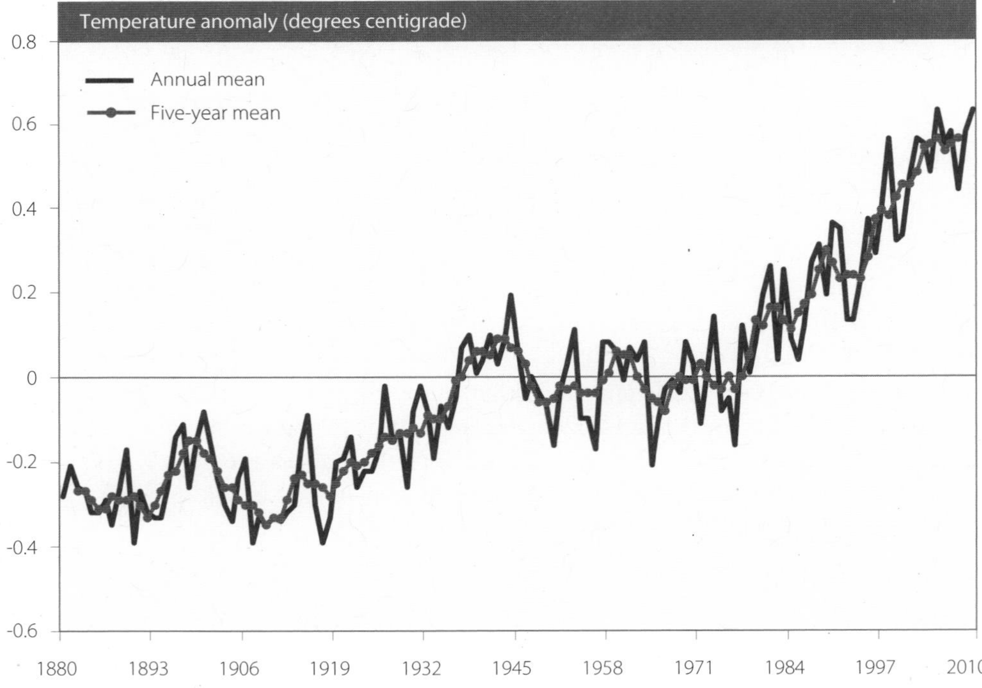

Source: National Aeronautics and Space Administration, Goddard Institute for Space Studies (GISS). Data available from http://www.data.giss.nasa.gov/gistemp/graphs.

Figure I.8
Observed and projected rises in global temperature, alternative scenarios, 1850-2100

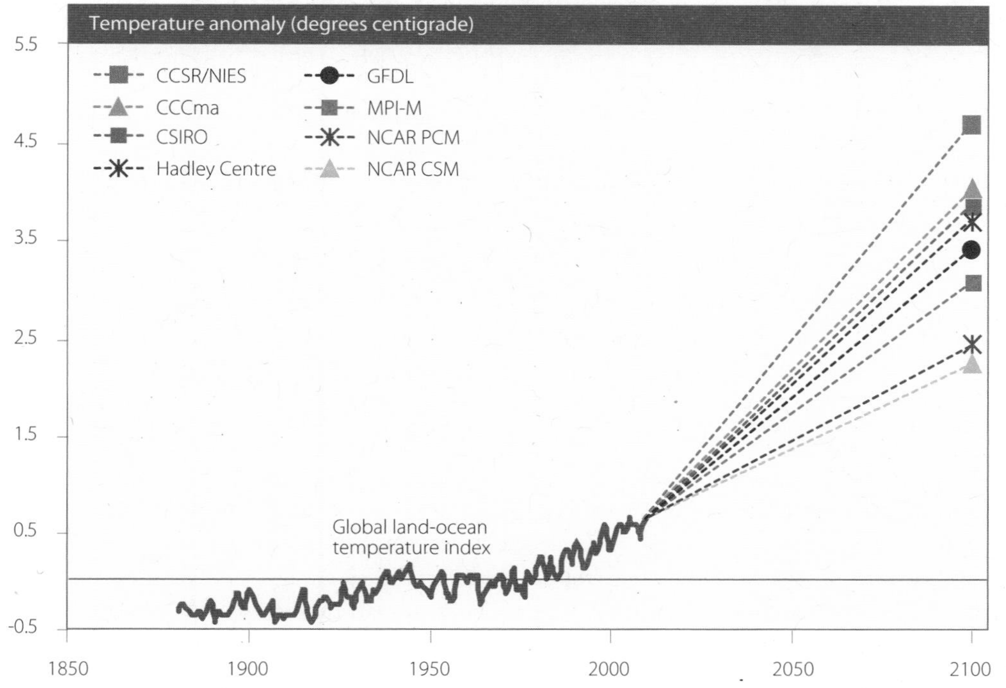

Sources: For 1850-2010: Goddard Institute for Space Studies (GISS): data available from http://www.data.giss.nasa.gov/gistemp/graphs; for 2100: data available from http://en.wikipedia.org/wiki/File:Global_Warming_Predictions.png.

Note: All the predictions shown in this figure are based on the A2 scenario of the Intergovernmental Panel on Climate Change (IPCC) (see IPCC, 2007b, for details). This scenario is based on specific assumptions about, inter alia, the future growth of output and population, and integration of the global economy. Variations among the predictions come from different assumptions regarding emissions and their impact on temperature rise.

Figure I.9
Increased use of non-biodegradables, 1900-2000

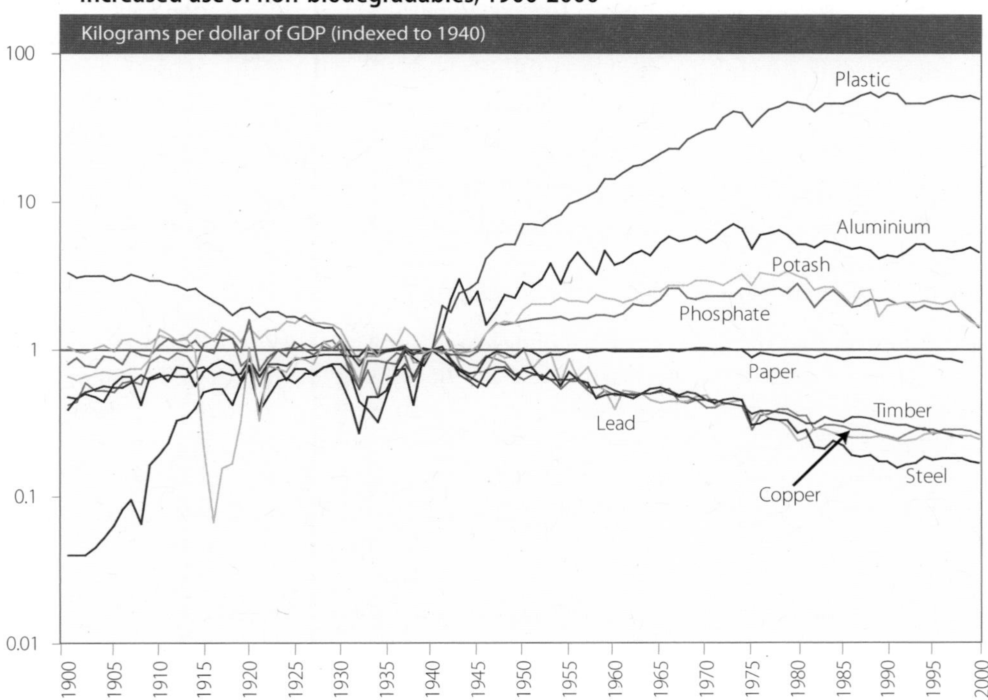

Source: Wernick and others (1997).

- The world has lost 50 per cent of its wetlands since 1900
- More land was converted to cropland in the 30 years after 1950 than in the period 1700-1850
- Forest area has shrunk by about 40 per cent over the past 300 years
- Twenty-five countries have completely lost their forests and 29 countries have less than 10 per cent forest cover
- The current species extinction rate is about 1,000 times higher than the rates that prevailed over the planet's history
- The world has lost 50 per cent of its mangrove forests since 1980
- Agriculture accounts for 70 per cent of worldwide water use
- Dams contain four times more water today than in 1960
- There is now from three to six times more water in reservoirs than in natural rivers

The pandemic spread of diseases and the extinction of species are imminent threats

The ecological degradation and destruction, as detailed above, are having alarming effects on the Earth's function as a source of natural resources, including through the adverse impacts on the quality of land, land-use patterns and food production, which are aggravating food insecurity (as discussed in chap. III). The risk of non-linear changes which could provoke sudden catastrophes and destabilize ecosystems has increased substantially. The collapse of fisheries, the pandemic spread of diseases and the extinction of species are imminent threats. Ecological degradation and destruction are aggravating human vulnerability, particularly for those people who are forced to settle in areas susceptible to risk. For example, the degradation of mangrove forests was one of the reasons for the high toll exacted by the Indian Ocean tsunami of December 2004 (see chap. IV for a discussion of rising trends in the frequency and intensity of natural disasters and their impact).

Clearly, the current hockey-stick pattern of development with its concomitant steep rises in resource use and waste is not sustainable. The question is what can be done to ensure that development does not exceed the limits of the Earth's carrying capacity while assuring that all of its inhabitants have fulfilling lives, based, inter alia, on the convergence of the living standards of currently developed and developing parts of the world.

Sustainable development and the green economy paradigms

The concept of sustainable development

Sustainable development entails combining economic and social development and environmental protection

The argument that the current pattern of development is not sustainable had already been made several decades ago, but has yet to lead to a change of direction. To amalgamate existing forces and direct them towards implementation of new policy approaches, the World Commission on Environment and Development (the Brundtland Commission), in its 1987 report entitled *Our Common Future* (World Commission on Environment and Development, 1987), proposed the now widely agreed definition of the concept of sustainable development as the process that "meets the needs of the present without compromising the ability of future generations to meet their own needs" (p. 8). However, this definition, while being widely accepted, gave rise (owing to its somewhat general focus) to many different interpretations and explications.[7] Nevertheless, within the framework of the international agreement reached at the 1992 United Nations Conference on Environment and Development, as reflected in its adoption of the Rio Declaration on Environment and Development (United Nations, 1993) and Agenda 21 (ibid.), the concept of sustainable development is perceived as encompassing the pursuit of three goals: economic development, social development and environmental protection.

Sustainable development is also a goal of developed countries

The Brundtland Commission report paid particular attention to the interrelationships among these three goals, noting two-way connections between any given pair.[8] In particular, noting that social development was necessary for sustaining both economic development and environmental protection, the Commission observed that "(a) world in which poverty is endemic will always be prone to ecological and other catastrophes"[9] and that "the distribution of power and influence within society lies at the heart of most environment and development challenges".[10] It also emphasized that sustainable development is not a goal applicable only to developing countries but must be a goal of developed countries as well.

Finding ways to force action on the commitments set out in Agenda 21 required agreement by Member States on the concrete steps to be taken

The work of the World Commission on Environment and Development led to the decision of the Governing Council of the United Nations Environment Programme (UNEP), at is fifteenth session, to recommend to the General Assembly that it convene a United Nations Conference on Environment and Development (United Nations, General Assembly, 1989). The Conference, popularly known as the Rio Earth Summit, was held in June 1992. The aforementioned Rio Declaration on Environment and Development proclaimed, inter alia, the right to development (principle 3) and that, in view of the different contributions to global environmental degradation, States had common but differentiated responsibilities (principle 7). Agenda 21 laid out before the international community a very broad set of objectives to be achieved in the twenty-first century. Finding ways to compel action on the commitments contained in Agenda 21 required agreement among Member States on concrete steps towards development cooperation, or at least on concrete indicators. The formulation of the Millennium Development Goals in 2000 can be seen as a further step forward towards agreement on concrete indicators of achievement of social development targets.[10]

At the start of the twenty-first century, then, the world community had both a broad-ranging agenda for sustainable development encompassing economic development, social development and environmental protection; and a set of indicators for the achievement of specific social development goals whose pursuit has already spurred notable action and policy initiatives.

7 For instance, for some, the concept of sustainable development implies that the current generation must leave for the next generation the same amount of "natural capital" as it had inherited from the previous generation. In other words, conservation of the stock of natural capital constituted a condition for development to be considered sustainable. See Pearce, Markandya and Barbier (1989) for a compilation and discussion of various definitions of sustainable development.

8 The distinction between "economic development" and "social development" as used here follows common usage in the mainstream literature, according to which reduction of poverty and inequality, increase in access by and empowerment of the poor and disadvantaged groups of the society, among other objectives, are to be considered a social (rather than an economic) goal. In contrast, other theoretical perspectives would regard poverty reduction, decrease in inequality of income and assets and improvement in access to productive resources as equally important *economic* goals and conditions for enhancing economic efficiency and growth.

9 See document A/42/427 of 4 August 1987, annex, overview, para. 27.

10 Ibid., chap. 1, para. 43.

The concept of a "green economy"

The concept of a green economy constitutes a response to the further aggravation of the environmental crisis

While the 'green economy' had been before,[11] its current application is sometimes associated with the 2008 crisis and the environmental sustainability context of the stimulus packages that were considered in an effort to overcome it. Influenced, in part, by the climate change-related negotiations on the eve of the fifteenth session of the Conference of the Parties to the United Nations Framework Convention on Climate Change,[12] held in Copenhagen from 7 to 19 December 2009, many argued for making these stimulus packages "green". Some countries actually did make a conscious effort to include in their stimulus packages projects that would be directed towards protection of the environment and mitigation of climate change. Over time, other expressions besides green economy—such as green growth, green stimulus, green technologies, green sectors, green business and green jobs—have entered common parlance.

However, despite its increasing utilization, the concept of a green economy is not well defined. Noting the many different ways in which the concept is used, the Secretary-General, in a report to the General Assembly, concluded that "'green economy' is an omnibus term" (United Nations, General Assembly, 2010a, para. 57) and therefore asked for "greater conceptual clarity with regard to the links between a green economy and sustainable development" (ibid., para. 57(a)).

Insisting on the green economy concept can be risky for a variety of reasons

In general, the concept of a green economy is invoked in an attempt to stress environmental sustainability and protection while pursuing sustainable development. Possibly because of the lack of a clear definition, the current interest in greening economies has revived concerns and debates harking back to the days when the Brundtland Commission was struggling to effect a consensus on the concept of sustainable development. In the current debate, many developing-country representatives have expressed the view that the insistence on a green economy is risky for a variety of reasons (Khor, 2011a). They are concerned: (a) that it could lead to a one-dimensional focus on environment and a corresponding marginalization of social development goals, and that if adopted at the global level, a focus on the green economy might thereby undercut the importance and urgency of developing countries' right to development; (b) that such a focus could lead to a "one size fits all" approach through which developed and developing countries would be judged by the same yardstick, thereby diluting the aforementioned principle of "common but differentiated responsibilities" adopted at the Earth Summit; (c) that the efforts to green the world's economy could induce developed countries to impose new trade restrictions on developing countries; and (d) that a green economy framework could lead to the attachment of new policy conditionality to international development assistance (ODA) and lending to developing countries.

Green economy-related efforts should fit within the sustainable development framework

Such concerns can be addressed by ensuring that the green economy concept does not undermine a balanced approach to sustainable development. Enhancing economic growth, social progress and environmental stewardship can be seen as complementary strategic objectives. As already indicated, because of the exponential increase in the level of human activity, the limits of the Earth's capacity as both a source and a sink are being or already have been reached. Emphasizing the need for green economies can help focus attention on these constraints and limits. In this sense, the concept of a green economy stresses the importance of intergenerational equity in economic and social development, that is to say, ensuring that meeting the needs of the present generation does

11 See, for example, Pearce, Markandya and Barbier (1989).

12 United Nations, *Treaty Series*, vol. 1771, No. 30822.

not compromise the ability of future ones to meet their own needs; further, it is based on the presumption that the benefits of investing in environmental sustainability outweigh the cost of not doing so, because the cost of having to protect ecosystems from the damages associated with a "non-green" (brown) economy are larger that the projected costs of investing in sustainability.

The need for a fundamental technological and structural transformation

Remaining within the limits of the Earth's capacity requires ...

To ensure that no limits are crossed that would destabilize the Earth's ecosystem, a fundamental technological overhaul and structural transformation of production and consumption processes towards a green economy will be needed, entailing achievement of at least the following five objectives:

(a) Reduction of resource requirements in general and of energy requirements in particular, in both absolute terms and relatively, per unit of output;

(b) Substitution of renewable for non-renewable resources, given the total resource use;

(c) Substitution of biodegradables for non-biodegradables, at any given level of output or waste;

(d) Reduction of waste (including pollution), at any given level of resource use;

(e) Protection of biodiversity and ecosystems.

... substitution of renewable resources for non-renewable ones

These green economy objectives are interrelated. For example, replacement of non-renewable by renewable resources helps to overcome resource constraints (first objective) and reduce waste (fourth objective). Similarly, reduction of resource extraction and waste generation is the most effective means of protecting biodiversity and ecosystems (fifth objective). To determine what is required to achieve these objectives, they must be examined in some detail.

Reducing resource requirements

There have been some increases in resource-use efficiency ...

Reduction of resource requirements, in both absolute terms and per unit of output, should be a key objective of greening the economy. Many observers have pointed out that there is much scope for drastically reducing resource intensity of production and consumption processes; and there is considerable evidence of greater resource efficiency, reflecting trends towards a "decoupling" of the growth of resource use from output growth. For example, physical resource use per unit of output decreased by about half in Organization for Economic Cooperation and Development (OECD) member countries during the period 1975-2000 (figure I.10). Moreover, the energy intensity of output has decreased substantially since the 1970s, with global energy intensity now about 30 per cent lower than in 1970. Energy intensity in both the United States of America and the United Kingdom of Great Britain and Northern Ireland is about 40 per cent lower now than in 1980 (Jackson, 2009a, p. 48).[13]

... but no reduction in total resource requirements

However, despite this progress in reducing input intensity, the absolute worldwide volume of material and energy utilized in production and the amounts of waste

13 It should be noted, however, that much of the reduction in material and energy intensity of output in developed countries has been achieved by relocating material- and energy-intensive manufacturing operations within developing countries.

Figure I.10
Material intensity of output in OECD countries, 1975-2000

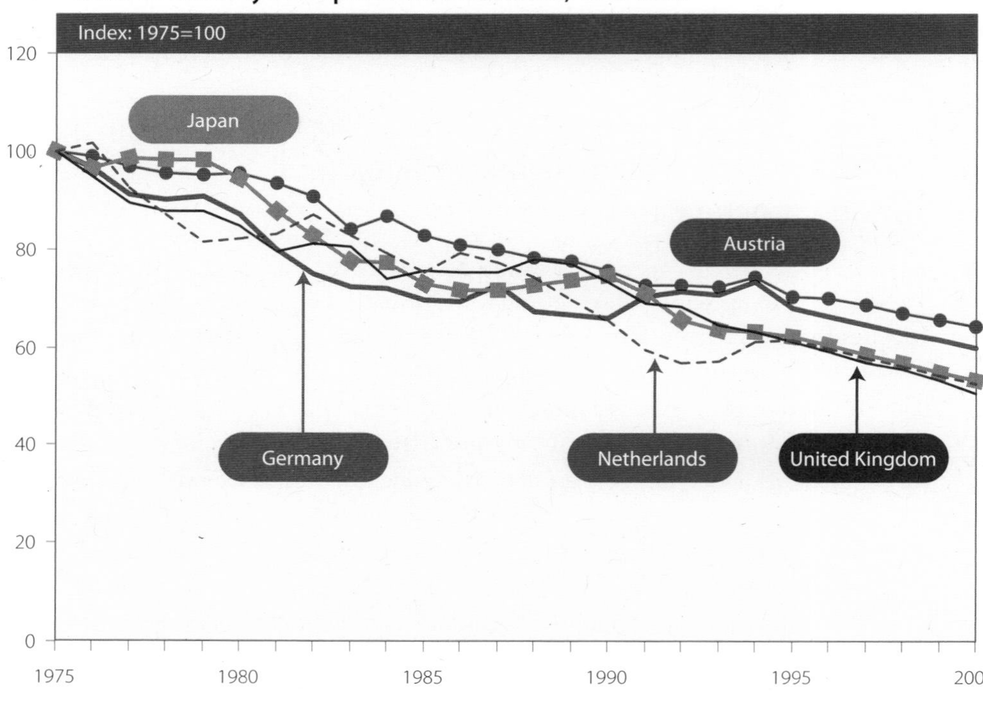

Source: Jackson (2009b), p. 70.

generated continue to increase, as evidenced, for example, by the continued upward trends in world consumption of metals such as iron, nickel, bauxite, copper and zinc (figure I.11). While fast growth in some major developing countries is responsible in part for this continued trend, the fact remains that in developed countries, too, resource use has continued to increase despite low population growth and improvements in resource efficiency in production (figure I.12). The evidence therefore makes it clear that despite some progress in relative decoupling, achieving the objective of absolute decoupling remains elusive.

Substitution of renewable for non-renewable resources

The substitution of renewable for non-renewable resources can often lead to win-win solutions

The Earth's limits as a source of natural resources should be overcome further through the substitution of renewable resources for non-renewable ones. Since many renewable resources (for example, solar energy and wind power) are also less waste-generating, their substitution for non-renewable resources would result in a win-win solution, as it would allow constraints on the Earth's functions as both a source and a sink to be overcome.

Thus far, progress in replacing non-renewable with renewable resources has been too slow to significantly reverse ongoing trends. Since the first industrial revolution, there has been an unremitting increase in the total use of non-renewable energy sources, especially of fossil fuels like coal, gas and oil; and the rate of increase in their use has accelerated since 1950. As a result, non-renewable carbon-intensive energy sources accounted for about 85 per cent of total energy use in 2000 (figure I.13). Weaning human societies away from non-renewable resources and guiding them towards renewable ones have therefore become urgent tasks.

Figure I.11
Global trends in primary metal extraction, 1990-2007

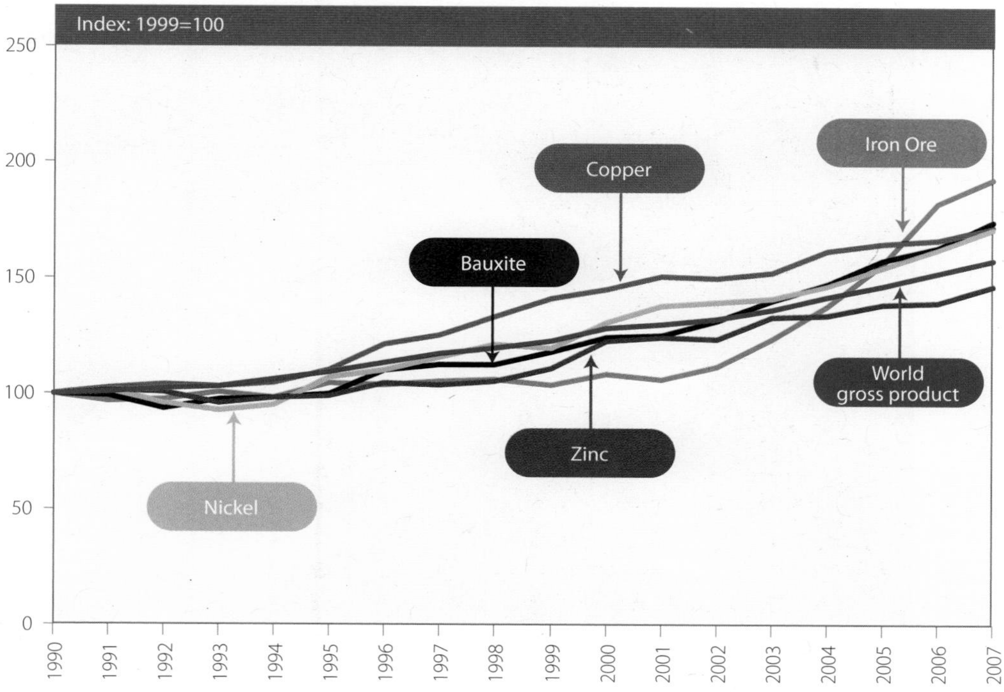

Index: 1999=100

Iron Ore
Copper
Bauxite
World gross product
Zinc
Nickel

Source: Jackson (2009b), p. 74.

Figure I.12
Direct material consumption in OECD countries, 1975-2000

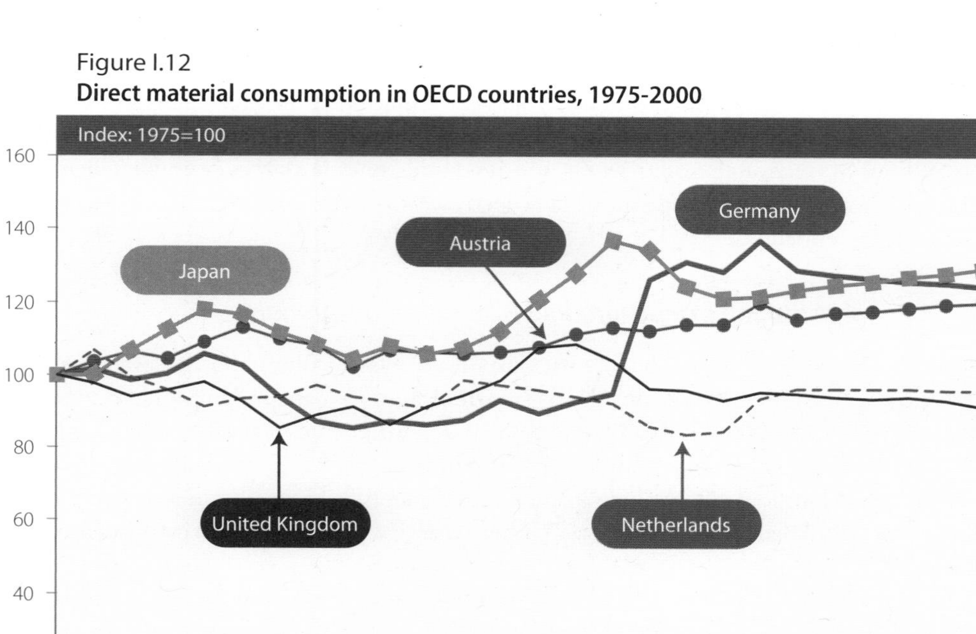

Source: Jackson (2009b), p. 72.

Figure I.13
History and possible future of the global energy system under the B1 stabilization scenario for relative shares of the most important energy sources

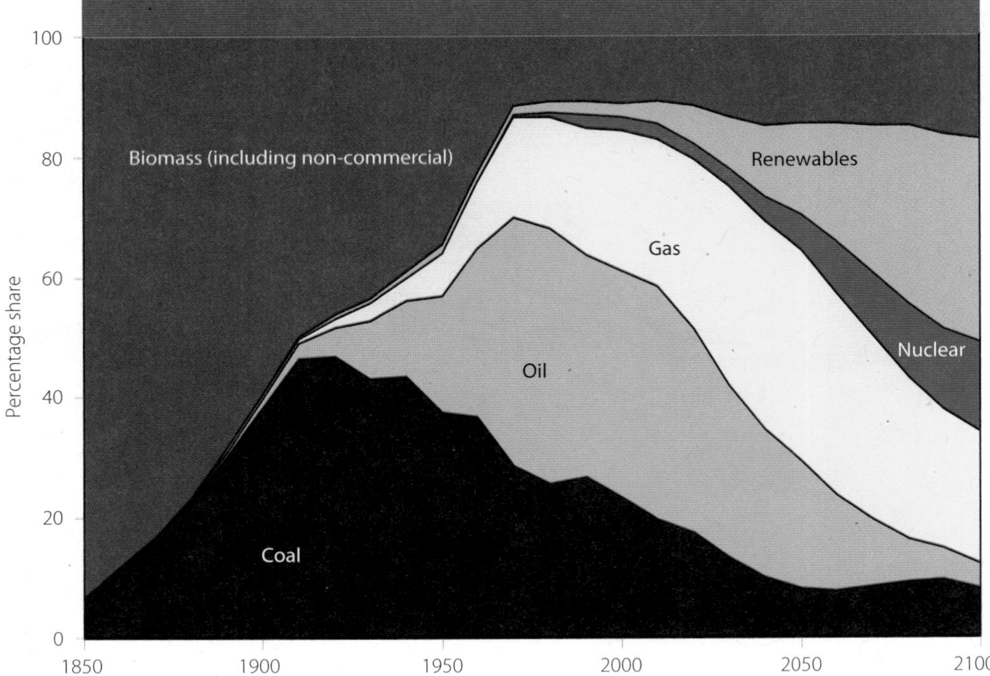

Source: United Nations (2009), figure II.6.

Note: B1 is one of the stabilization scenarios considered by the Intergovernmental Panel on Climate Change (IPCC). It is one of the ideal scenarios among the possible ones and stipulates fast economic growth, rapid changes towards a service and information economy, population rising to 9 billion by 2050 and then declining, a reduction in material intensity and the introduction of clean and resource-efficient technologies, and a more integrated world. Further details on B1 and other scenarios are provided in IPCC (2007a, p. 44).

The production of renewable energy can, in some cases, be more resource-intensive

However, in some cases, production of renewable energy (for example, certain biofuels) can be more resource-intensive, so that replacement of non-renewable with renewable resources will not necessarily reduce overall resource requirements. Nevertheless, substitution of renewable resources for non-renewable ones is always desirable when such substitution does not increase and in fact decreases the overall volume of resources used and waste generated.

Substitution of biodegradables for non-biodegradables

Substitution of biodegradables for non-biodegradables is an urgent task

Preponderance of non-biodegradables in output and waste volume has become a serious threat to the Earth's environment. As was shown in figure I.9, the weight of plastic in gross domestic product (GDP) has steadily increased over time and now far surpasses that of such natural inputs as timber, paper and metals. Unfortunately, most of the plastics currently used are non-biodegradable. Although some defenders of plastic maintain that widely used plastic bags will break down in 500 years, there is actually no reliable basis for such claims (Lapidos, 2007).

Fortunately, there is now increasing awareness of the harmful effects of plastic; as a result, many communities, cities and countries are taking measures to restrict its use. In the United States of America, for example, the State of California, in 2007, imposed restrictions on the use of plastic bags. Several cities in Europe have taken similar measures. Among developing countries, Bangladesh, for example, reimposed a ban on the use of plastic bags in 2002.

Technologies already exist to produce biodegradable plastics. Currently available degradable plastic materials are of two main types: polyester polymers (biodegradable) and synergistic and hybrid polymers (bio-based) (Alire, 2011; Kaeb, 2011).

Technologies for producing biodegradable plastics already exist

However, efforts to substitute biodegradable plastics for non-biodegradable ones face a number of hurdles, including the difficulty of finding appropriate substitutes for certain types of non-biodegradable materials currently used in a range of applications; and the fact that, although the production of biodegradable and bio-based substitutes is technically feasible, the cost of producing them is generally higher.

Reduction of waste

Although the limits to the Earth's capacity as a source of resources has received more attention historically, limits to its capacity as a sink for waste are now proving to be a more constant focus. That the limits of Earth's capacity as a sink are fixed is most evident in the context of the global warming threat, which is a direct result of excessive emissions of greenhouse gases, especially CO_2 into the atmosphere. The threat of exceeding the Earth's limits as a sink was made evident even earlier by the ozone hole resulting from excessive chlorofluorocarbon emissions. Thus, the reduction of waste (especially pollution) should be an overriding objective of the green economy.

The limits of the Earth's capacity as a sink for waste and pollution are fixed

The task of reducing CO_2 emissions is particularly daunting. To limit any further increases in the Earth's temperature to less than 2° C above the pre-industrial average, as agreed internationally, the concentration of CO_2 in the atmosphere should not exceed 450 ppm. With a projected world population of 9 billion by 2050 and assuming 2 per cent income growth per year on average between 2007 and 2050, the average CO_2 emission intensity per unit of output will have to decrease from 768 grams in 2007 to 6 grams by 2050 if destabilizing the climate is to be averted (figure I.14).

The reduction in material and energy intensity of output has helped reduce, to a certain extent, the world average CO_2 intensity of GDP somewhat (figure I.15).[14] However, as was the case with resource use, the reduction in the carbon intensity of GDP growth has not resulted in a reduction in the global volume of CO_2 emissions (figure I.16). In fact, despite climate change-related efforts, the growth of CO_2 emissions seems to have accelerated since 2001. Ironically, much of this increase has been due to increased emissions by Annex 1 countries, which under the Kyoto Protocol to the United Nations Framework Convention on Climate Change[15] were obliged to reduce their emission volumes.

The reduction in material and energy intensity of output has helped to reduce the average carbon intensity of GDP

Moreover, the composition of waste has further worsened, with the rising share of non-biodegradables having already been noted. The increasing share of electronic waste ("e-waste"), often containing radioactive elements, is another growing concern. In general, waste is becoming more hazardous, toxic and radioactive (Baker and others, 2004).

Protection of biodiversity and ecosystems

Agricultural production by its very nature depends heavily on the quality of the environment. Unfortunately, the modernization of agriculture, which has led to significant increases in food productivity, has not been conducive to conservation of natural capital, as

Unfortunately, the modernization of agriculture has not been conducive to the preservation of the natural capital

14 The global carbon intensity declined by about one quarter from just over 1 kg of CO_2 per United States dollar in 1980 to 770 grams in 2006. However, much of this decline seems to have been the result of a sharp decline in CO_2 intensity of GDP in China up to 2000, after which the country's downward trend suffered some reversals.

15 United Nations, *Treaty Series*, vol. 2303, No. 30822.

Figure I.14
Carbon intensities, current, and those required to stay within the 450 ppm limit of CO_2e concentrations under alternative scenarios

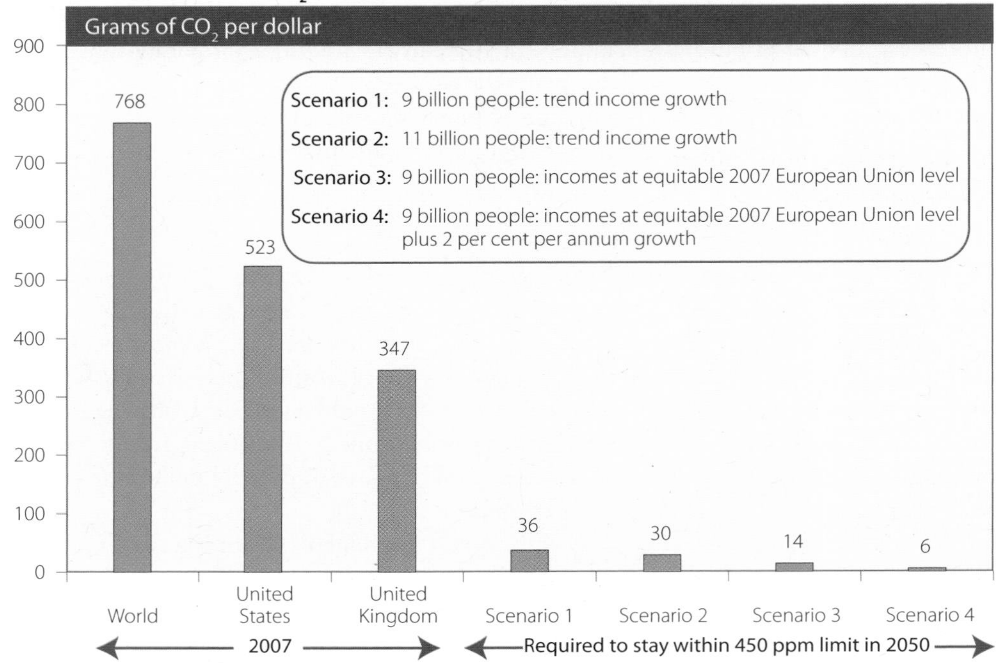

Source: Jackson (2009b), p. 81.

Figure I.15
Intensity of CO_2 emissions per unit of output, world and selected countries and regions, 1980-2006

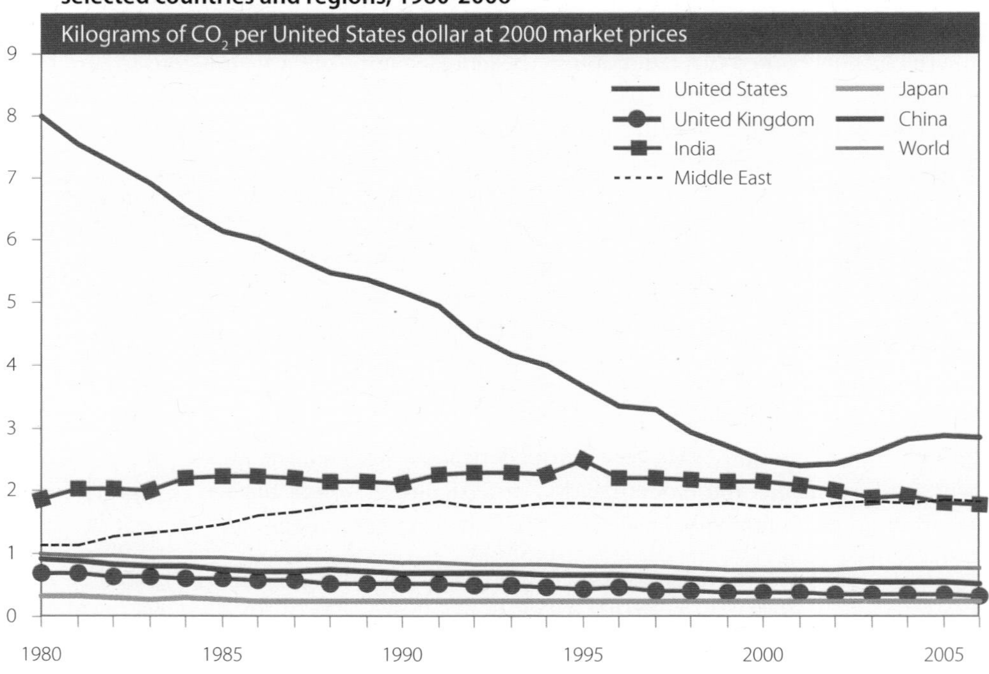

Source: Jackson (2009b), p. 70.

discussed in chapter III. In many areas, modern technologies and production systems have accelerated land degradation, clearing and degradation of forests, depletion of groundwater sources and degradation of surface-water bodies, including rivers. Worldwide, the agriculture sector currently contributes about 14 per cent of greenhouse gas emissions, and related land-use and water management are not sustainable in many parts of the world. Deforestation and degradation of forests are contributing an estimated 17 per cent of global emissions, while causing the loss of habitat, species and biodiversity in general. At the same time, nearly 1 billion people are undernourished and face serious food insecurity. Global food production needs to increase by between 70 and 100 per cent from present levels by 2050 in order to feed a growing population. Thus, there is an urgent need to make agricultural production environmentally sustainable, while at the same time substantially raising productivity. It is hard to imagine how this can be achieved without a major overhaul of existing production systems, technologies and supporting infrastructure.

The incidence of natural disasters has increased fivefold since the 1970s, as analysed in chapter IV of this *Survey*. With a fair degree of certainty, this increase can be attributed in part to climate change induced by human activity. Deforestation, degradation of natural coastal protection and poor infrastructure have increased the likelihood that weather shocks will turn into human disasters, especially in the least developed countries.

Further, in any society, loss of natural capital affects the poor and vulnerable more than the well off. Because of their greater reliance on, inter alia, smallholder agriculture, open-capture fishing, harvesting of forest products, inter alia, the poor depend more on natural capital-related services.

Equitable growth within environmental boundaries

The world needs both "convergence upward" and "convergence downward"

Principle 7 of the Rio Declaration on Environment and Development, on the right to development, has often been interpreted in terms of economic "convergence", whereby developing countries would be helped in catching up with developed countries as regards income levels and living standards. "Convergence upward" would require income levels and living standards in developing countries to grow faster to enable the gap with those of developed countries to be closed. According to the parallel notion of "convergence downward", the per capita ecological footprints in developed countries should decrease so as to approach the low levels currently observed in developing countries.

Despite development efforts for more than half a century, progress with respect to development and poverty reduction remains uneven and patchy. Using the international poverty line of $1.25 per person per day (in 2005 purchasing power parity (PPP) value), as defined by the World Bank, 1.4 billion people, representing about 26 per cent of the developing world's population, lived in poverty in 2005. The incidence of poverty was 50.4 per cent in sub-Saharan Africa and 40.3 per cent in South Asia.

Economic growth is a precondition for poverty alleviation

Shared growth is necessary for poverty reduction

Economic growth is a precondition for poverty reduction and improvement in other economic and social indicators. In the recent period, this has been illustrated by the experience of East Asia, in particular of China. As a result of its faster economic growth for more than three decades, China has been able to lift about 600 million people out of poverty. The number of poor in China, as defined by the $1.25 cut-off, decreased from 835.1 million in 1981 to 207.7 million in 2005, which meant a drop in poverty incidence from 84.0 to 15.9 per cent. Similarly, in Viet Nam, the poverty rate declined from 90.4 to 17.1 per cent between 1981 and 2005. By contrast, sub-Saharan Africa, a region that failed to achieve fast economic growth, also failed to achieve poverty reduction. As a result, the number of poor in this region increased from 212 million to 388 million during 1981-2005.

There is hardly any evidence of the achievement of sustained poverty reduction without fast economic growth over several decades. The impact of economic growth on poverty reduction depends very much on how it is shared. As Besley and Cord, eds., (2007, p. 1) note: "Growth is less efficient in lowering poverty levels in countries with high initial inequality or in which the distributional pattern of growth favours the non-poor."

Growth in turn requires structural transformation and sector-specific policies

The capacity of an economy to generate new dynamic activities is key to its sustaining economic growth (Ocampo, 2011a). The emergence of new dynamic activities involves the movement of workers and resources from low-productivity to higher-productivity sectors, resulting in increased economic output and higher incomes. In a globalized economy, this process, in turn, requires identification of sectors in which a country has comparative advantage or in which the country can build up its comparative advantage for the future. Successful development and transformation therefore require the adoption of industrial (or production sector) policies and the necessary space within which to conduct such policies.

Growth and environmental protection

Growth must be achieved while at the same time respecting the limits of the Earth's capacity

Rapid economic growth, based on existing technology, generally requires more input and generates more waste. Because of this factor, it is often suggested that there will be a trade-off between economic growth and environmental protection. However, this need not be the case. The precise objective of investing in greater resource efficiency and sustainable development is to overcome the need for such a trade-off. Moreover, as such investments will generate new economic activities, continued economic growth (especially for developing countries) may well be feasible without surpassing the limits of environmental sustainability.

A recent report of the United Nations Environment Programme (2011) estimates that 2 per cent of current world gross product (WGP) would need to be invested annually between now and 2050 in order to shift development onto a path of green growth and thereby address the current broad range of environmental concerns. Utilizing model-based projections, the report determines that the green economy scenario would permit the sustaining of higher—not lower—GDP growth than under the business-as-usual (BAU) scenario. These required investment estimates may be at the lower end, however. The *World Economic and Social Survey 2009* (United Nations, 2009) and chapter II of the present *Survey*, report that about 2.5 per cent of WGP (or about $1.6 trillion) per annum would need to be invested to effect the energy transformation necessary to meet climate change mitigation targets alone. This analysis further suggests that public investments would need to be frontloaded in order to unleash private sector financing. Moreover, simulations using the United Nations Global Policy Model showed that such a green investment scenario would accelerate economic growth in developing countries (ibid.).

While the outcomes of such scenario analyses rest on the assumptions embedded in the modelling frameworks, they do suggest that it may well be feasible to combine fast growth with environmental protection in developing countries.

Limits to growth in developed countries?

The assumptions underlying the aforementioned global sustainable growth scenarios include the supposition that green technologies can be effectively scaled up quickly and that their costs will not prove to be prohibitive. However, as discussed in chapter II, there are reasons to temper such technology-related optimism, as enormous technical hurdles need to be surmounted to accelerate innovation and ensure widespread application of resource-efficient and waste-reducing technologies, especially those related to energy. Hence, if, for instance, emission reduction targets cannot be met through accelerated technological progress in energy efficiency and renewable energy generation, it may be necessary to impose caps on energy consumption itself in order to meet climate change mitigation targets in a timely manner.

Quality of life does not necessarily increase beyond a certain level of material consumption …

Proposals to put limits on economic growth can be viewed in this context. Advocates of such an approach emphasize, in particular, a voluntary acceptance of certain limits to output and consumption growth by developed countries, so as to cap the production of waste and utilization of non-renewable resources. They base their proposals on a number of arguments: first, acceptance of limits by developed countries would make it easier for the world as a whole to stay within the Earth's carrying capacity; second, acceptance of such limits by developed countries would result in a freeing up of more space for the growth of developing countries, thereby facilitating convergence upward; third, acceptance of limits by developed countries would also facilitate convergence downward, through a more rapid reduction of the ecological footprint in developed countries; and fourth, voluntary limits to growth would be beneficial for developed countries themselves, because a further expansion of the current pattern of consumption would damage the quality of life rather than improve it. On these bases, voluntary limits to growth in developed countries could be beneficial for both developed and developing countries.

… suggesting that developed countries could focus on quality-of-life issues rather than on material growth

The argument that there are limits to growth is not a new one. In the 1970s, studies commissioned by the Club of Rome had drawn attention to the limits of resource availability. The follow-up studies reiterated the necessity for accepting limits to growth, while putting more emphasis on the limits of the Earth as a sink. The need to consider placing certain limits on the total volume of world output and consumption was also recognized by the Brundtland Commission in its report, which noted that the concept of sustainable development did imply limits, although they might need to be imposed gradually. The report recommended that "those who are more affluent adopt lifestyles within the planet's ecological means"[16] and, within the context of the responsibility of political leaders who felt that their countries had reached a "plateau", took note of the fact that "many of the development paths of the industrialized nations are clearly unsustainable".[17]

Does the quality of life stop improving beyond a certain level of per capita income?

Recently, a number of studies have put increasing emphasis on the fourth argument above for limiting growth in developed countries. To make their case, many of them presented evidence from cross-country data showing that the quality of life does not improve much beyond a certain level of per capita income. For example, taking life expectancy as an objective measure of the quality of life, it can be seen that life expectancy does not increase much beyond a per capita income level of about $10,000. Similarly, as indicated in chapter III of this *Survey*, cross-country evidence suggests that there are no significant additional gains in human development (as measured by the human

16 See A/42/427, annex, chap. 1, para. 29.

17 Ibid., Chairman's foreword.

development index) beyond the energy-use level of about 110 gigajoules (GJ) (or 2 tons of oil equivalent (toe) per capita).

While capping the use of energy and other resources by setting limits to growth in developed countries might have worldwide benefits, to many the prospect of "prosperity without growth" may not be very appealing. One reason for the difficulty involved entails what Jackson (2010) refers to as the "dilemma of growth"—the fact that while the current pattern of growth is unsustainable, the current structure of the economy and of society is such that an economy without growth is unstable. Acceptance and implementation of prosperity without growth will therefore require major structural transformations of economies and societies.

The great green technological transformation

With or without the acceptance of limits to growth in developed countries, putting global development on a sustainable path will require greening economic growth. The attainment of technological progress will be essential and in many respects will entail a major overhaul of existing production methods and consumption habits.

What kind of technological revolution?

Industrial development so far has meant material growth at the cost of environmental protection

As explained above, the technological overhaul is required to undo the undesired effects of the past technological revolutions, while preserving their positive achievements and propelling the relationship between humankind and nature to a new stage. Up until the first industrial revolution, humans had mostly been at the mercy of nature. The main source of energy was the muscle power of animals and of humans themselves. This dependence on muscle power limited the extent to which humans could extract natural resources and convert them into consumption goods. As a result, the material standard of living remained low for thousands of years. However, the fact that growth during the pre-industrial era was mostly horizontal, involving expansion into new territories and an increase in the density of population, does not mean that impressive technological achievements were not produced in this period.[18]

The first industrial revolution ushered in an era of dependence on fossil fuels

The technological revolution that was at the heart of the first industrial revolution succeeded in abolishing the sovereignty of nature, so to speak, and in establishing the supremacy of humans over it. Many have deemed this revolution a Faustian bargain, by which mankind opted for continuously increasing material consumption at the expense of nature. Subsequent technological revolutions have only expanded the capacity of humankind to impose its will on nature—a victory attested by a sharp rise in population and rising levels of income and consumption. However, a point has now been reached where humans need to restore the sovereignty of nature, not because they lack the capacity to go on conquering it but because overtaxing nature's capacity is detrimental to humans themselves.

What are the concrete dimensions of this new technological revolution? Understanding the character of past technological revolutions can help answer this question. The first industrial revolution had been preceded, accompanied and followed by many changes, including radical transformations in social organization and ideology, as aptly described by the nineteenth century classical economists and later by Karl Polyani (1944).

18 On the basis of the pre-industrial experience, the work of most classical economists was conceptualized in terms of a "stationary state" rather than of continuous growth.

From the technological perspective, however, the main change consisted in the replacement of muscle power by the steam engine as the main motive force. Yet, this came at a price, since steam engines require coal, which ushered in the era of humans' increasing dependence on fossil fuels. The subsequent invention of electricity permitted energy to be applied among a vast range of machines in terms of scale and application; but as generation of electricity also relies primarily on fossil fuels, their use has grown exponentially (figure I.15).

Figure I.16
Trends in fossil fuel consumption and CO_2 generation, 1980-2007

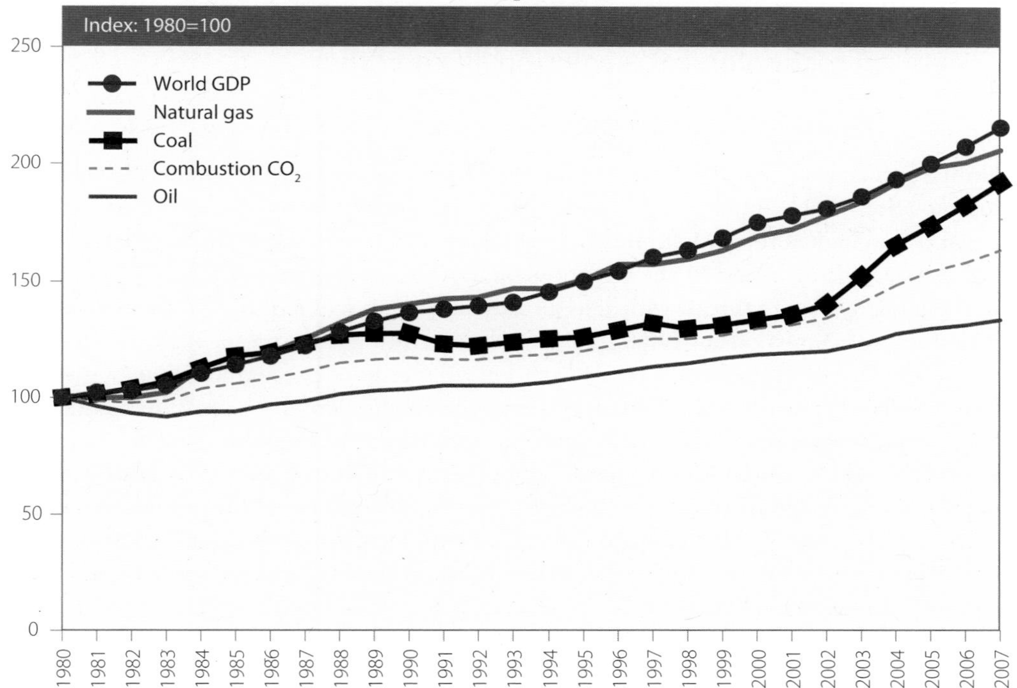

Source: Jackson (2009a), p. 50.

The second industrial revolution introduced harmful non-biodegradables

While the first industrial revolution changed the nature of the energy source, enabled production using machines (instead of muscle) and increased the importance of metal (which was necessary to produce those machines), the second industrial revolution's major achievement was the development of the chemicals industry, which resulted not only in the processing and refining of substances already available in nature but in the manufacture of new ones. Unfortunately, many of these new products, such as plastics, turned out to be non-biodegradable.

The introduction of new energy sources and new materials has gone hand in hand with the development of an ever increasing range of products, at least in developed countries. At the same time, progress has also led to the production of spurious articles of consumption and the shortening of product life, both of which have led to the waste of physical and human resources.

The new technological revolution has to overcome dependence on fossil fuels and non-biodegradables

The new technological revolution will have to reverse the undesirable impacts of the past technological revolutions, while preserving and enhancing their positive achievements, which means: reversing the dependence on fossil fuels; reversing the trend towards increasing use of non-biodegradables; conserving resources by reducing the resource requirement per unit of output and the production of luxury consumption goods, and by increasing the durability of goods produced; reducing waste by a switch to renewable inputs, and by making reuse and recycling of non-renewable inputs almost universal; reversing the process of land degradation and making it possible to feed the additional 3 billion people who will inhabit the Earth by 2050, without exceeding its capacity; and making it easier for societies, particularly in more vulnerable parts of the world, to protect themselves against natural hazards which are becoming more frequent.

To be successful in achieving the goals set out above, the technological revolution for a green economy will possess certain features that are critically different from those of previous revolutions.

A technological revolution like no other

A compressed time frame

Only three or four decades are left!

Unlike previous technological revolutions, which were by and large spontaneously unfolding processes which could take as much time as they needed to attain their objectives, the green technological revolution must be carried out within a much more compressed time frame given the acuteness of the environmental crisis. Its gravity is reflected most clearly in the climate change threat, which, as already indicated, will require drastic cutbacks in greenhouse gas emissions by 2050 in order to avert risking catastrophic impacts. In other words, the related technological transformation will need to be accomplished over the next four decades. Many other dimensions of the environmental crisis—such as loss of species, land degradation and desertification, deforestation and loss of freshwater and groundwater reserves—call for a similar urgency and compressed time-frame. However, achieving the necessary technological transformation under such constraints will be a huge challenge, since it is well known that diffusion of technology is a slow process and that previous technological revolutions typically took much longer (about 70 years or more) (Wilson and Grübler, 2010; and chap. II).

Greater social guidance and a greater public role

Governments played important roles in past technological revolutions ...

Contrary to conventional wisdom, Governments played an important role in previous technological revolutions. For example, machine-based cotton textile production during England's first industrial revolution would not have flourished without the support of the British Government's colonial and trade policies, which ensured that colonies served as sources of raw materials and as captive markets. Steam engines would not have developed as they had without the Government's decision to fit out all Royal Navy vessels with steam engines. The rise of the chemicals industry in the second industrial revolution derived great benefits from the protectionist policies of the Governments of the second-generation industrializing countries. More recently, the development of nuclear power plants has owed much to the war-related focus on the development of the atom bomb. Finally, the development of the Internet owes much to the communications-related projects of the United States Department of Defense. At the same time, a large part of technological diffusion has depended on market-based processes.

... and will have important roles in the technological revolution needed now

Governments will have to play a much more central role in inducing the technological transformation needed to achieve the objectives of the green economy for a number of reasons. First, there is the aforementioned matter of the faster pace required: The needed acceleration of technological innovation and diffusion is unlikely to occur if left to spontaneous market forces. Equally important is the fact that the natural environment is a public good and consequently not "priced" by the market. Although there are markets for green technologies, they are just developing through the implementation of government policy. Governments will then have a key role to play in promoting more extensive research and development and diffusion of green technologies, inasmuch as the benefits accrue to societies as whole. In addition, since existing brown technologies are presently locked into the entire economic system, a radical shift to green technologies will mean adjusting, improving or replacing much of the existing infrastructure and other investments. Such transformations will be costly and will require large-scale long-term financing, which it is unlikely will be mobilized in full through private initiatives. Hence, government support and incentives will be required. Thus, not only will strong technology policies be required, but they will need to go hand in hand with active industrial and educational policies designed to generate the necessary changes in infrastructure and production processes.

Industrial policies are necessary for inducing the new technological revolution

Industrial policies will be needed to actively promote production activities and processes that reduce resource requirements, substitute renewable inputs for non-renewable ones and replace non-biodegradables with biodegradables. Such active government intervention will be essential inasmuch as prices, as determined in unregulated markets, would not be reliable indicators of environmental impacts and long-term resource constraints and hence would be incapable of guiding decisions on incentives to investments and resource allocation for sustainable production. The core of this strategy should be a strong technology policy with a focus on adaptation and dissemination of green technologies and the treatment of green economic activities as "infant industries" which require appropriate support (subsidies, preferably time-bound, access to credit and perhaps some level of trade protection). A green industrial policy would give preference to new public and private investment that contributes to sustainable development, has good prospects as regards generating backward and forward linkages in the economy, and is aligned with broader development priorities. Such actions should be supported by public sector investments directed towards developing the necessary infrastructure and providing the poor with access to basic energy and water and sanitation. This would also include implementing appropriate regulation, pricing policies, taxes and subsidies designed to limit pollution and emissions, to control overexploitation of natural resources and to ensure that prices better reflect environmental values, as well as mainstreaming environmental criteria into government procurement policies. Under no circumstances, however, should the poor be penalized, especially when the products or services concerned are essential ones. Thus, if water is generally underpriced, then when its price is being revalued, a system of differential pricing should be put in place so as to ensure access for the poor.

Greater international cooperation

New technologies will involve "public goods" and, often, "global public goods"...

The green technological revolution will also necessitate greater international cooperation than was required in carrying out previous ones, as the result of several factors. First, the foci of many of the green technologies are regarded as public goods. The protection of these components of global commons, encompassing, inter alia, the atmosphere, oceans, open-capture fish stock, biodiversity and ecosystems, is not possible through efforts of individual nations only. Instead, cooperation of all nations is necessary for the development and deployment of technologies that can protect these commons.

... and hence the technological revolution will require global cooperation

Second, through international trade and investment, incomes and consumption in one country are linked to the ecological footprints left by the countries of production. Multilateral environmental agreements, trade and investment rules, financing facilities and intellectual property right regimes would all need to be aligned so as to facilitate the green technological transformation. Since the majority, though not all, of existing new technologies are owned by the advanced countries and the cost of stimulating green technological change will be much higher for developing countries relative to their incomes, there will be important distributional considerations associated with greening the global economy, which will also need to be addressed through financing facilities and other new mechanisms of international cooperation.

Developing countries will have an important, role to play as "partners" in the new technological revolution

The required greater international cooperation emphasized above must encompass greater cooperation between developed and developing countries. During previous technological revolutions, beginning with the first industrial revolution, the role of developing countries was a limited one. Mainly, they were relegated to the status of colonies supplying material resources and providing captive markets. Based on their historical role, these countries continue, generally, to be viewed primarily as receivers of the technologies produced in developed countries. However, if the technology revolution for a green economy is to be successful, developing countries will need to be true partners in developing, utilizing and generally sharing the new technologies.

In actual fact, developing countries themselves now constitute quite a diverse group, embracing a wide range of technological capabilities. Countries such as China, India and Brazil are already playing a leading role in developing, manufacturing, deploying and exporting (including to developed countries) various green technologies (such as solar panels, wind turbines and biofuel technologies). Moreover, global value chains, which extend across developed and developing countries and represent a new global division of labour, cannot be subsumed under the traditional technology transfer paradigm based on the "provider-receiver" relationship. Instead, many developing countries are already partners in the innovation, production and deployment of green technologies. This role will likely become increasingly important and its impact more widespread in the future. Further, even developing countries that do not participate in the current global division of labour associated with engagement in the development and production of green technologies can play a significant role as potential markets for these greener technologies. Expansion of scale is the most important means by which the current high cost of many green technologies can be brought down. The large populations of developing countries can provide that scale if they, too, develop and can afford these new technologies and products. Thus, adaptation of green technologies by agents in developing economies will be essential in accelerating the processes whose aim is to make the green technologies commercially viable.

The development-related aspirations of developing countries offer both a challenge and an opportunity in the context of the green technological transformation

Thus, the development-related aspirations of developing countries pose both a challenge and an opportunity for the green technological transformation. Those aspirations pose a challenge to the extent that the green economy-related objectives will have to accommodate developing countries' pressing need to achieve higher levels of material welfare. At the same time, their aspirations present an opportunity, because many developing countries are still at the early stage of urbanization, entailing the transition from traditional to modern fuels and other hurdles. Hence, switching (or leapfrogging) to green technologies may prove easier in some developing countries than in developed countries, which face the task of converting already built brown technologies and infrastructures into green ones. Developing countries can therefore provide experiences of greening which may be instructive for developed countries.

Societal transformations

Greening the economy will require major societal transformations for reasons related to supply and demand. On the supply side, policies and institutions required to foster the necessary technological transformation may not be implementable without a societal transformation. On the demand side, consumption habits and living patterns must adapt to changes in the nature and packaging of products and modern conveniences. Moreover, as noted above, the desired technological transformation might not evolve at the necessary pace and scale, so that supply-side changes may not prove sufficient: demand-side changes would then be required, such as those discussed above under "limits to growth". These demand-side changes, however, could not be expected without a radical societal transformation. The examples below illustrate these interconnections.

Societal changes are necessary as both a precondition for and a complement of technological transformation

Transforming settlement, transportation and consumption patterns

Much of the material and energy consumption of a society is determined by the settlement patterns, as illustrated by Japan's compact form of urbanization, which partly explains why the energy intensity of its economy is significantly less than that of the United States of America (Duro and Padilla, 2011). It is true that Japan's compact urbanization has been, to a large extent, dictated by the country's mostly mountainous physical terrain, where whatever limited space for settlement and urban development exists is found around the mouths of rivers. Nevertheless, Japan's experience does demonstrate that opting for compact urbanization is one way to keep material and energy requirements down.

Societal changes can conduce to the achievement of necessary changes in consumption patterns

Settlement and transportation patterns also influence consumption patterns. Spending on housing and household goods and services now constitutes the most important share of personal consumption. By contrast, the share of food in total consumption in developed countries is now very limited. Meanwhile, spending on housing and household goods depends critically on the size of houses, which depends in turn on the settlement pattern. Compact urbanization generally leads to apartment living, whereas urban sprawl leads to residence in large-sized houses, which require more energy, more furniture—more, in fact, of almost everything.

The world is poised to experience further urban growth in the near future, especially in developing countries. Along with urban income growth, this will give rise to shifting consumption patterns. Protein-rich food consumption will rise, with commensurate increases in the pressure on land stemming from the demand for its use in livestock production. The demand for non-food consumption should also be expected to rise along with resource use and waste production, if the demand is to be satisfied through prevailing technologies. Such trends will enhance the need for the green technological transformation, but they would also suggest that policies designed to influence consumer behaviour will be just as critical in facilitating the transition towards a sustainable development path.

Urban income growth will generate shifting consumption patterns

Changes in the social value system

The required technological and societal transformations necessary for greening the economy and ensuring sustainable development and poverty reduction without exceeding the limits of the Earth's capacity will not be possible without changes in the social value system. Communities have to begin placing greater value on the Earth's natural environment as constituting a resource to be shared among current and future populations. Social and political discourse and public priorities must increasingly reflect such a change in

Societal changes will require changes in social value systems

values; and societies must ensure that the tools they use for measuring social and economic trends, such as the concept of economic output,[19] also reflect those values, so that feedback can be provided on the progress being made in respect of their integration in people's lives. Changing individual and social values is likely to be an even greater challenge than that of transforming technology, production processes and consumption patterns.

The agenda

The dimensions of societal transformation that have been presented in this chapter extend beyond the scope of the present *Survey*. Still, by keeping these issues in the foreground, this *Survey* will be better able to focus on the technological transformation challenge within a few key areas. Chapter II explores the issues of transformation as related to the energy sector, where progress is critical to overcoming poverty, mitigating global warming and protecting the Earth's natural environment. Chapter III, which calls for a truly green agricultural revolution, examines the challenges of protecting ecosystems and ensuring sustainable management of land and forests. Chapter IV focuses on how human societies can protect themselves against the increasing incidence and intensity of natural hazards, many of which arise through profligate resource extraction and waste generation. Chapter V examines in detail national institutional arrangements that are conducive to the necessary technological transformation. The final chapter considers the issues of global coordination and institution-building, which are vital to the achievement of the green technological transformation.

19 See United Nations and United Nations Environment Programme (2000) for an example of efforts directed towards integrating the environmental dimension with national income accounting; and also chap. 29 of the 2008 SNA (European Commission, International Monetary Fund, Organisation for Economic Cooperation and Development, United Nations and World Bank, 2009) (http://unstats.un.org/unsd/nationalaccount/docs/SNA2008.pdf) where the concept of environmental accounting is fully embedded in the system of national accounts.

Chapter II
The clean energy technological transformation

Summary

- A global sustainable energy transition needs to be achieved within four decades, a significantly faster rate than in the past.
- Global sustainable energy policy must take into special consideration the 3 billion poor people who aspire to gaining access to electricity and modern energy services.
- The scope of current national and global policies and programmes does not "add up" to the scale of actions needed to meet global emission reduction targets. Paradoxically, they are also overly ambitious in terms of their expected outcomes and are inconsiderate of certain biophysical, techno-economic and socio-political limits to scaling up known technologies. A reality check of current plans is needed so that realistic and well-targeted initiatives can be devised at a far greater scale.
- There is a need for comprehensive, strategic and systemic approaches that emphasize performance goals, niche markets and technology portfolios, especially those related to end-use. In order to take pressure off the technological innovation imperative, individual limits of 70 gigajoules (GJ) primary energy use per capita and 3 tons of carbon dioxide (CO_2) emissions per capita by 2050 may need to be considered. Such energy-use and emissions caps would not affect the development-related aspirations of developing countries.
- The sustainable energy transition offers significant economic opportunities for both developed and emerging market economies, but poses additional development challenges for poorer and more vulnerable countries, which would therefore require enhanced support from the international community.

Introduction

Energy technologies[1] have been greatly shaping society and the environment for the past two centuries. In fact, modern civilizations are largely dependent on fossil fuel energy technologies, which make high-density urban settlements possible. While technological progress has eliminated many problems, it has also added new and often unexpected ones (Grübler, 1998; Diamond, 2005). Emissions of greenhouse gases (GHGs) arising from the combustion of fossil fuels have been the main cause of anthropogenic global warming. All energy technologies, whether they are fossil-based or not, consume resources, use land and

1 For the purpose of the present chapter, energy technology shall comprise not only material inputs and equipment, but also software (that is, explicit and tacit knowledge and human skills) and "orgware" (that is, institutions, regulations and cultural norms) (Dobrov, 1979).

pollute air, water and the atmosphere. Energy use has reached a scale at which planetary boundaries are being breached for a range of essential Earth-system processes, including in terms of global warming and biodiversity loss, which is likely to lead to catastrophic environmental change (Rockström and others, 2009).

The declared goal of establishing a renewable and low-carbon energy system on a global scale remains elusive

Despite two decades of climate change policies; thousands of programmes, initiatives, regulations, market-based instruments and international agreements; and the disbursement of hundreds of billions of dollars in subsidies, funds, research and development (R&D) efforts and development aid, the declared goal of establishing a renewable low-carbon energy system on a global scale remains elusive. In 2005, fossil fuels accounted for 85 per cent of the global primary energy mix, while low-carbon nuclear power accounted for 6 per cent, hydroelectricity for 3 per cent and biomass for 4 per cent. Modern renewables jointly accounted for less than 1 per cent.

New fossil fuel-based plants will remain operational for decades

Global CO_2 emissions have increased at an annual rate of more than 3 per cent, considerably faster than in previous decades (van Vuuren and Riahi, 2008). The past decade was the first in two centuries with increasing CO_2 emissions intensities, owing to a "coal revival", in contrast with the rapid conversion to natural gas in the 1990s. In 2010, the global share of coal reached an estimated 29 per cent, which in relative terms was higher than, and in absolute terms about twice as large as, at the time of the first oil crisis, in 1973. In the 2000s, China alone added more coal power capacity *each year* than the total installed capacity in the United Kingdom of Great Britain and Northern Ireland (International Energy Agency, 2010b, p. 202). These trends, which are diametrically opposed to declared greenhouse gas mitigation goals and targets, are by no means limited to emerging economies. Even in Germany, a country with one of the most ambitious Government goals for greenhouse gas mitigation, 10 coal power plants were under construction and another 12 coal power plants were in the pipeline (Bundesnetzagentur, 2009). These fossil-fuel-based capacities will remain operational for decades and make greenhouse gas reduction efforts increasingly difficult.

In contrast with the actual trend of ever more rapid increases in greenhouse gas emissions, *global* emissions would need to be *reduced* by 50-80 per cent by 2050 and turn *negative* in the second half of this century, in order to stabilize CO_2 concentrations at about 450 parts per million by volume (ppmv), a target recommended by the Intergovernmental Panel on Climate Change (IPCC) and agreed upon at the sixteenth session of the Conference of the Parties to the United Nations Framework Convention on Climate Change,[2] held in Cancun, Mexico, from 29 November to 10 December 2010. Essentially, this would require making the power and transport sector carbon-free *worldwide* by mid-century, in view of the limitations associated with replacing industrial processes based on fossil fuels. Today's CO_2 emitting devices and infrastructures alone imply cumulative emissions of about 496 gigatons (Gt) of CO_2 from 2010 and 2060, leading to atmospheric concentrations of about 430 ppmv (Davis, Caldeira and Matthews, 2010). In other words, even an immediate *global stop* to building new fossil-fired capacities would lead close to the envisaged global target of 450 ppmv by mid-century. This puts into perspective the enormous ambition of the global target, given the long-lived capital stock and rapidly rising energy demand.

Forty per cent of humanity, or 2.7 billion people, continues to rely on traditional biomass, such as wood, dung and charcoal

At the same time, about 40 per cent of humanity, or 2.7 billion people, continues to rely on traditional biomass, such as wood, dung and charcoal. Air pollution from inefficient stoves leads to an estimated 1.5 million premature deaths per year, more than from malaria, tuberculosis or HIV. About one fifth of humanity or 1.4 billion people,

2 United Nations, *Treaty Series*, vol. 1771, No. 30822.

continues to live without access to electricity, mainly in South Asia and sub-Saharan Africa (International Energy Agency, United Nations Development Programme and United Nations Industrial Development Organization, 2010). Many more, especially in urban areas, have access but cannot afford to make full use of it. The United Nations Secretary-General's Advisory Group on Energy and Climate Change proposed the goal of universal access to modern energy services by 2030 (United Nations, 2010a). It is important to note that bringing universal access to modern energy services to almost 3 billion people would require only about 3 per cent higher electricity generation, less than 1 per cent more demand for oil and less than 1 per cent more CO_2 by 2030 (International Energy Agency, United Nations Development Programme and United Nations Industrial Development Organization, 2010). Thus, the development aspirations of the world's poor are not in conflict with efforts to solve the climate problem. The 500 million richest people, who constitute only 7 per cent of the world population, are responsible for half of all greenhouse emissions. They live in every country of the world and earn more than the average citizen of the United States of America. In contrast, the poorest 3.1 billion people are responsible for only 5-10 per cent of the total (Pacala, 2007; Chakravarty and others, 2009).

The global energy challenge is immense, as evidenced by the multiple global objectives explored by the Global Energy Assessment (GEA) (Riahi and others, forthcoming): (a) to ensure universal access to electricity and modern cooking fuels by 2030; (b) to reduce premature deaths due to air pollution by 50 per cent by 2030; (c) to limit global average temperature change to 2° C above pre-industrial levels by 2100 (with a probability of greater than 50 per cent); and (d) to establish energy security, for example, to limit energy trading and increase diversity and resilience of energy supply by 2050. Meeting GEA objectives requires a complete transformation of the global energy technology system in the course of one generation, which is a considerably shorter time-frame than was the case for historical energy transitions. Governments have called for concerted actions to accelerate technology change towards cleaner energy technology. Many technology optimists believe such acceleration is essential and have in this regard coined the term "energy technology innovation imperative" (Holdren, 2006). Innovation in this context encompasses the full spectrum ranging from incremental improvements to radical breakthroughs and from technologies and infrastructure to social institutions and individual behaviours (Wilson and Grübler, 2010).

Several Asian Governments are pursuing energy technology-focused industrial policies, with mostly positive developmental benefits

Simplistic solutions dominate present national and global debates on how to meet the energy technology innovation imperative. Technology optimists suggest "big push" policies to scale up available technologies. Others focus on market incentives and hope that the necessary technological transformation will come about by "getting prices right" through internalizing environmental externalities. Several Governments in Asia are pursuing energy technology-focused industrial policies, with mostly positive developmental benefits. However, evidence suggests that none of these approaches has the potential to sufficiently accelerate energy technology change on the required global scales. Indeed, most Government energy technology programmes and private sector projects have not met their overambitious goals in recent decades. Reality checks are needed to enable Governments to devise better policies and programmes at scales commensurate with the challenge. Better-focused and greater efforts to move to cleaner and renewable energy will be needed to ensure climate stabilization while allowing developing countries to satisfy their rapidly increasing demand for commercial energy which is linked to their development aspirations. Historically, such huge challenges were addressed consecutively rather than concurrently.

Global energy technology transitions

Past energy technology transitions provide lessons for current efforts and can inform future visions of energy technology change in the twenty-first century.[3]

The global energy system

Specific energy technologies should not be analysed in isolation

The global energy system is a planetary-scale complex network of energy converters and energy flows. Figure II.1 illustrates the associated global flows of "exergy", that is, the energy available to be used, at the most aggregate level, from extraction at the primary level through the secondary, final and useful energy levels. It illustrates the dominance of fossil fuels and the low overall efficiency of the global system. It should also be noted that most greenhouse gas mitigation efforts focus on electricity supply, even though most losses are incurred from the final to the useful level. Useful energy is divided into motion (transport and machines), heat (mainly buildings) and non-energy (dominated by six materials). The underlying global reference energy system of interlinked energy technologies is even more complex. As the overall system is more than the sum of its components, for most purposes neither specific energy technologies (such as a wind power plant) nor specific parts of the system (such as renewable energy) should be analysed in isolation.

Figure II.1
Global exergy system flows, 2005

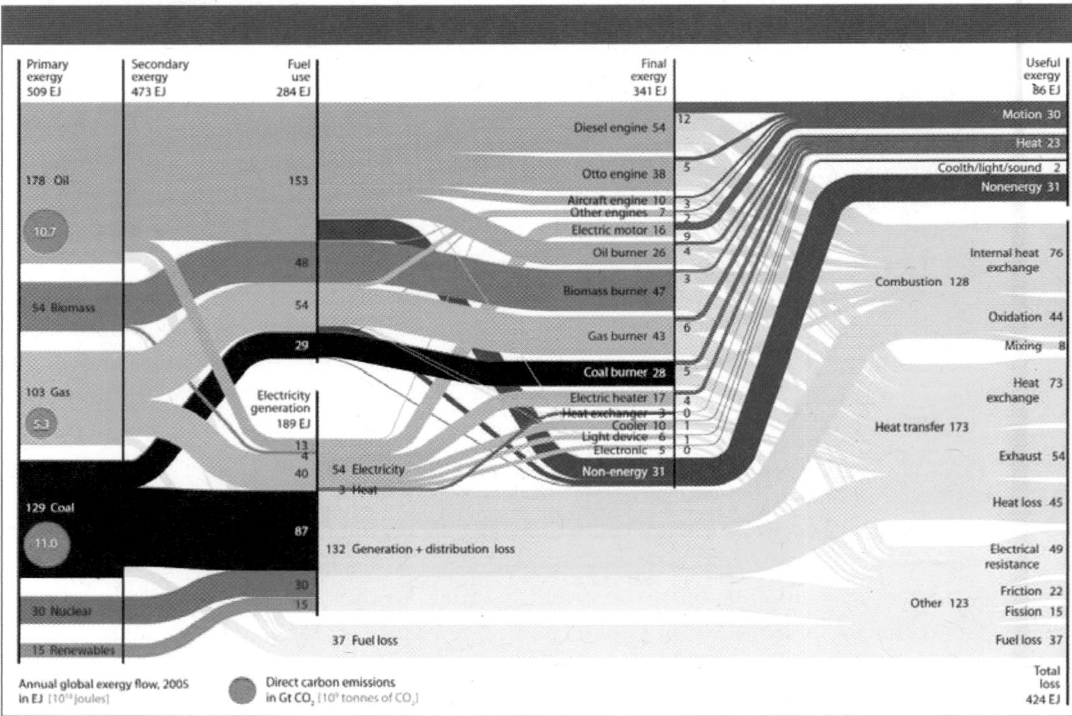

Source: Cullen and Allwood (2009).

---

3 The present subsection draws upon Wilson and Grübler (2010) and Grübler and others (forthcoming).

History of global energy transitions

Over the past 200 years, global energy use has grown by a factor of 25-530 exajoules (EJ) in 2009, compared with a sevenfold increase in population, driven by demand for higher-quality energy services made possible by underlying energy technology change. Throughout the twentieth century, total energy use in developed countries had been much higher than in developing countries. In recent decades, however, energy demand in China, India and other emerging economies has grown rapidly, so that by 2009, more than half of primary energy was used in developing countries. This share is expected to continue to increase to at least two thirds over the coming decades. At present, 2.7 billion people continue to rely on traditional, non-commercial fuels typical for pre-industrial societies. They use only between 15 and 50 GJ of primary energy per capita, delivering about 2-5 GJ of per capita in useful energy services. Growth of per capita energy use in developing countries has accelerated since 1975, whereas use in developed countries has stagnated (figure II.2).

There are persisting differences between the development trajectories of countries, spanning the extremes of highly energy-intensive and highly energy-efficient. Initial differences in resource endowments or social configurations can be perpetuated over time by differences in economic activity, technology adoption rates, consumption patterns and infrastructure, which shape the direction of path-dependent energy technology change (Wilson and Grübler, 2010). At 1990 levels of energy conversion efficiency, a minimum level of 40-50 GJ primary energy per capita would be associated with a decent quality of life (Smil, 2004). Cross-country evidence suggests that, typically, no additional human development gains are obtained through primary energy use above 110 GJ per capita at prevailing conversion efficiencies. Improving overall global energy conversion efficiency from the present 11 per cent to 17 per cent would result in provision of the same level of energy services using 70 GJ of primary energy per capita.

Typically, no additional human development gains are obtained with primary energy use above 110 GJ per capita

Figure II.2
Trends in per capita energy use and population in developed and developing countries, 1800-2009

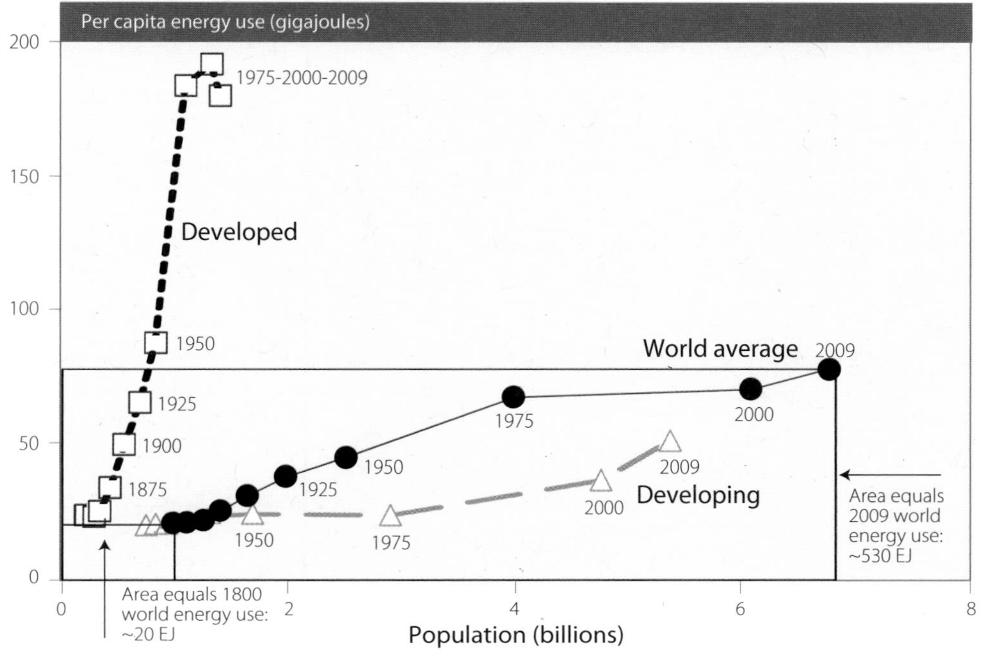

Source: Wilson and Grübler (2010).

Note: Non-commercial energy sources are included. Countries are classified using the United Nations Framework Convention on Climate Change categories as Annex I (developed or industrialized) or non-Annex I (developing) countries. Data are from Grübler (2008) and updated from British Petroleum (2010) and International Energy Agency (2010a). Data prior to 1950 are estimates.

History of global energy technology transitions

Two major energy technology transitions have shaped the structure of the global energy system and the qualitative dimension of energy use since the onset of the industrial revolution (Nakicenovic, Grübler and McDonald, 1998). The first, associated with the emergence of steam power relying on coal (Landes, 1969), took more than a century to unfold (figure II.3). The second, characterized by the displacement of the coal-based steam technology cluster by electricity and petroleum-based technologies, is only about half-complete, with 2.7 billion people still lacking access to modern energy services (Global Energy Assessment, forthcoming).

There is no evidence of any differences in the speed of energy technology change across a wide range of technologies

These transitions towards higher-quality energy fuels took place through successive substitutions going from traditional fuels to oil, gas and nuclear. At the global level, these substitutions had occurred at intervals of 70-100 years for the 250 years until 1975 (Marchetti and Nakicenovic, 1979). Since 1975, however, this process has slowed to a global transition time of about 250 years, primarily as a result of government interventions and politically induced high and volatile oil prices. In addition, at the level of plants and units, there is no evidence of any differences in the speed of energy technology change across a wide range of technologies since the nineteenth century (Wilson, forthcoming). The historical energy technology transitions have been characterized by a number of stylized patterns (Wilson and Grübler, 2010):

- End-use applications drive supply-side transformations
- Quality/performance dominates cost in the initial market niches
- Energy technologies do not change individually but in clusters, with "spillovers"

Figure II.3
Two grand-scale transitions undergone by global energy systems, 1850-2008

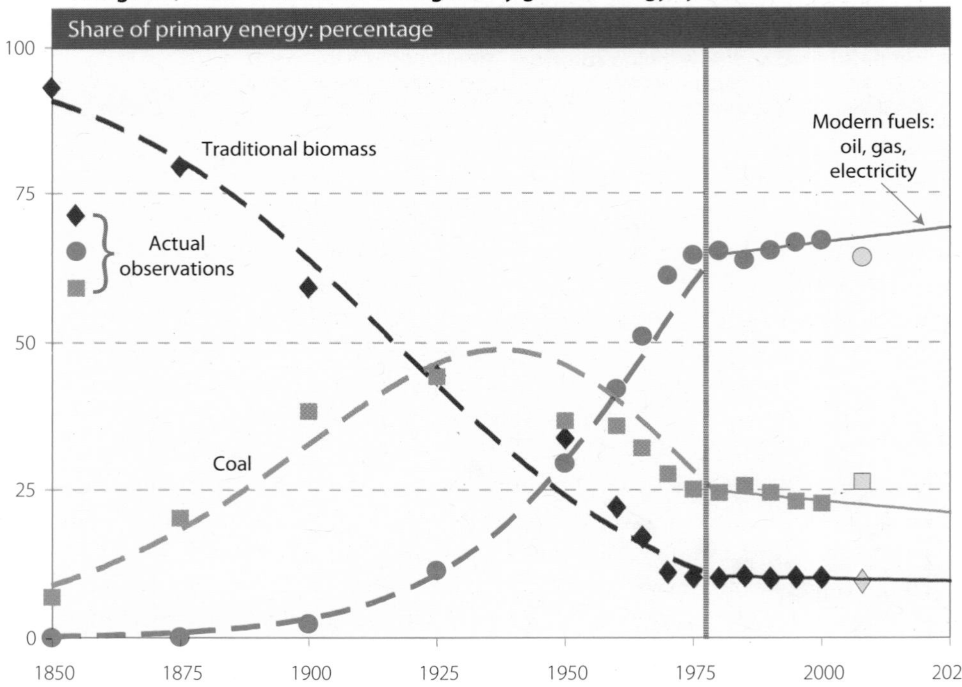

Sources: British Petroleum (2010); Grübler (2008); and International Energy Agency (2010a)

Note: The diamonds, dots and squares are actual data points, including estimated values for 2008. The broken lines are coupled logistic equations fitted on the data over the period 1850-1975.

- Time periods for energy technology change are decades, not years
- Experimentation and learning precede "upscaling" and widespread diffusion
- The size and the rate of expansion of energy conversion capacity are inversely related
- Diffusion in late "adopter" regions is faster than in initial "innovator" regions, but maximum market penetration levels are lower
- Both sufficient time and resources are needed for energy technology learning

Future scenarios

From 1950 to 1990, energy-related global greenhouse gas emissions increased by about 3 per cent per year, mainly owing to increases in population (+1.8 per cent) and incomes (+1.9 per cent), the effect of which was moderated by lower energy intensity consumption patterns (-0.3 per cent) and better, lower-carbon technologies (-0.4 per cent) (Waggoner and Ausubel, 2002). Policy has typically focused on technology as the main lever for reducing emissions and it is indeed a powerful driver. Future energy technology change will be as important for determining future greenhouse gas emissions levels as long-term demographic and economic developments over the course of the twenty-first century (Roehrl and Riahi, 2000). Alternative technology strategies result in a divergence of emissions levels only gradually, after several decades or more, owing to the long lifetimes of power plants, refineries, buildings and energy infrastructure (Grübler, 2004); but near-term technology and policy decisions will have sown the seeds of subsequent divergences, translating into different environmental outcomes as new technologies gradually replace older ones.

Claims that "the technology exists to solve the climate problem" underestimate the scale of efforts required

Scenario analysis has helped to identify robust energy technology portfolios across a wide range of assumptions with respect to energy demand, resource constraints and availability and cost of technologies, and the extent of greenhouse gas constraints (Roehrl and Riahi, 2000; Riahi, Grübler and Nakicenovic, 2007; Grübler and Riahi, 2010). Figure II.4 illustrates the contributions of energy technologies to greenhouse gas emissions reductions, under a high-emissions baseline scenario, required for stabilization at a concentration of 550 ppmv CO_2e by 2100. The top two "mitigation wedges" show the contributions (in annual gigatons of carbon (GtC)) of (supply-side) carbon intensity improvements and (demand-side) energy intensity improvements in the baseline relative to a "frozen" state of technological development in 2000. This difference illustrates the innovation challenge of incremental energy efficiency improvements. Popular claims that "the technology exists to solve the climate problem" reflect the idea that no necessarily disruptive revolutionary changes (for instance, to nuclear fusion) would be needed, but such beliefs underestimate the challenge of achieving continued incremental improvements in line with historical trends.

The ranking of these mitigation wedges is quite robust across scenarios, with energy conservation and efficiency accounting for more than half the emissions reductions. Indeed, across the wide range of scenarios, energy efficiency contributed about 59 per cent of the cumulative greenhouse gas emissions reductions from 2000 to 2100, compared with the much lower contributions of renewables (18 per cent), nuclear (9 per cent), fossil fuels (6 per cent) and other means (8 per cent) (Riahi, Grübler and Nakicenovic, 2007).

Several global scenarios have explored feasible levels of lower per capita energy use and low greenhouse gas emissions that do not compromise economic development. For

Figure II.4
"Robust" climate change mitigation wedges, 2000-2100

Share of primary energy: percentage

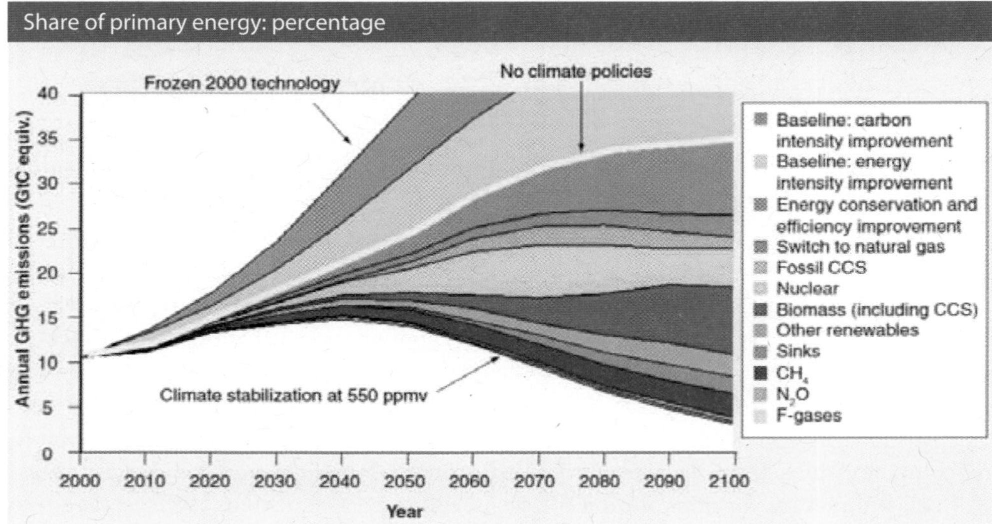

Source: Riahi, Grübler and Nakicenovic (2007)
Abbreviations: CCS, carbon capture and storage; CH_4, methane; N_2O, nitrous oxide; F-gases, fluorinated gases.

example, the GEA efficiency scenario shows that the world's average primary energy use per capita can decrease from 71 to 63 GJ from 2010 to 2050, with average per capita gross domestic product (GDP) still tripling (in constant dollar terms). This implies an improvement in eco-efficiency by a factor of 3.2, which is almost as ambitious as the "factor 4" goal of doubling wealth and halving resource use, originally suggested by von Weizsäcker, Lovins and Lovins (1998). Thus, even world average levels of energy use of less than 70 GJ per capita would be achievable by mid-century, in line with the target suggested by the present *Survey* (see below).

Efforts to accelerate energy technology change

The pace of the global energy transition has slowed significantly since the 1970s

The pace of the global energy transition has slowed significantly since the 1970s, despite national and international efforts to accelerate energy technology change in response to the oil crises of the 1970s, current concerns about global warming, and the goal of ensuring universal access to modern energy services.

The international energy technology agenda

A complex system of organizations and institutions has emerged at the international level to promote energy technology cooperation and provide both financial resources for clean energy investments and price signals to favour low-carbon energy technologies; and a global system for the transfer of hundreds of billions of United States dollars is in the making.

The International Energy Agency (IEA) maintains 40 multilateral technology initiatives, also known as implementing agreements, covering the full range of energy technologies, including programmes with voluntary participation designed to accelerate the deployment of clean energy technologies and cost-effective technologies for carbon capture and storage (CCS). Thus far, however, these international efforts have had a relatively small effect on the global energy transition.

CDM investments have been concentrated in a handful of large emerging economies, such as China, Brazil and India

The Clean Development Mechanism (CDM) under the Kyoto Protocol to the United Nations Framework Convention on Climate Change,[4] for instance, was expected to greatly stimulate clean energy technology transfer to developing countries and significantly reduce costs for developed countries. The market value of Clean Development Mechanism transactions had reached $6.5 billion in 2008, but dropped thereafter by about 60 per cent as a result of the financial crisis and uncertainty about the future climate policy regime. Looking ahead to 2012, renewable energy projects are estimated to make up 61 per cent of the total number of CDM projects, accounting for 35 per cent of certified emissions reductions (CERs), with industrial gas and methane projects accounting for just under half of the remainder of CERs. If fully implemented, CDM projects contracted during the period 2002-2008 would require $106 billion worth of low-carbon investment, primarily in "clean" energy (Kossoy and Ambrosi, 2010). CDM investments have been concentrated, however, in a handful of large emerging economies, such as China, Brazil and India.

From 1991 to 2009, the Global Environment Facility (GEF), which serves as a financial mechanism for the United Nations Framework Convention on Climate Change, allocated more than $2.7 billion to climate mitigation activities while leveraging an additional $17 billion in financing. In 2008, the World Bank also established the Climate Investment Funds which represent a collaborative effort among the multilateral development banks to address climate finance gaps. By 2010, contributors had pledged $6.4 billion in new funds. One component, the Clean Technology Fund finances the scaling up of demonstration, deployment and transfer of clean technologies and focuses on countries with significant mitigation potential. The first round of investment plans encompasses 13 countries, energy efficiency projects, bus rapid transit, concentrating solar power, and wind power.

The need to transfer environmentally sound technologies is recognized under the United Nations Framework Convention on Climate Change

The transfer of environmentally sound technologies is recognized under the United Nations Framework Convention on Climate Change, but action on the ground has progressed relatively slowly. The Conference of the Parties at its sixteenth session, agreed to establish a Climate Technology Centre and Network, which aim to support technology transfer and local technology innovation capacity.

National plans for clean energy technology

Efforts of emerging and other developing economies to support clean energy technology have typically focused on the creation of domestic manufacturing and export capacities

Recent efforts in developed economies to support clean energy technology have typically focused on economic instruments for creating niche markets and promoting the commercial diffusion of new technologies. Efforts of emerging and other developing economies to support clean energy technology have typically focused on domestic research, development, manufacturing and export capacities. China's Twelfth Five-Year Plan, endorsed in March 2011, encompasses a green growth strategy geared towards building technology leadership, through special efforts to develop and deploy wind, solar, hydro, nuclear, energy efficiency, electric cars, "smart grids", infrastructure and high-speed rail. It includes a plan to install 10 million charging stations for electric cars and to increase installed renewable energy capacity by 47 per cent by 2020. It plans to invest €57 billion in new ultra high voltage (UHV) transmission lines by 2015, and €460 billion to develop smart grids, and to increase nuclear power capacity from 10 to 50 GW, although most investments will continue to be for "clean" coal. South Africa aims to slow its greenhouse gas emissions growth and reduce those emissions after 2030, through increased energy efficiency,

4 United Nations, *Treaty Series*, vol. 2303, No. 30822.

feed-in tariffs for renewables, development of carbon capture and storage for coal-fired power plants and coal-to-liquid plants, a levy on coal-fired power and the introduction of a carbon tax. The Republic of Korea is implementing a green growth strategy and five-year action plan which aim for a 46 per cent reduction in energy intensity by 2030 and for an 11 per cent share of renewable energy. The national energy plan for 2008-2030 foresees investments in low-carbon transport, hybrid vehicles, renewable energy technologies and the construction of 10 nuclear power plants. Mexico has set an indicative reduction target for its greenhouse gas emissions by 50 per cent from 2000 to 2050, and its Special Climate Change Programme makes provisions for wind power, cogeneration, efficient household appliances and lighting, promoting rail freight, and 600,000 efficient cooking stoves.

Energy plans of the poorest and most vulnerable economies have aimed to find a balance between Governments' immediate priorities and the priorities of aid donors, in order to leverage development assistance. For example, energy plans and policies of a number of small island development States aim to address their special vulnerabilities and promote renewable energy. For example, Maldives announced its goal of achieving a carbon-neutral energy sector by 2020; Tuvalu aims to achieve 100 per cent renewable energy utilization by 2020; there have been positive experiences with thermal solar water heating in Barbados, Mauritius and Palau; hybrid solar-diesel power generation is being piloted in Maldives and Tuvalu; and geothermal energy is in the early phases of exploration in Saint Kitts and Nevis and Saint Lucia. Despite such commitments, however, fossil-fuel use has continued to increase faster than renewable-energy use in most small island development States (United Nations, 2010a).

National plans for universal access to modern fuels and electricity

Globally, less than 65 per cent of the rural population had access to electricity in 2008

Globally, less than 65 per cent of the rural population had access to electricity in 2008 (International Energy Agency, 2009). Two thirds of the people without electricity access were in sub-Saharan Africa and South Asia. Only 11 per cent of the rural population in sub-Saharan Africa have access to electricity. From 1970 to 1990, more than 1 billion people had gained electricity access, half of whom were in China alone. From 1990 to 2008, almost 2 billion additional people secured electricity access (Global Energy Assessment, forthcoming). However, there is no evidence for acceleration or deceleration of electrification over the past 100 years. Historically, the process of electrification has taken several decades in all countries. The United Kingdom and the United States needed about 50 years to achieve universal access around 1950. Among the emerging economies, Mexico, China, Brazil, Thailand and Mauritius achieved universal access in the 1990s. India and South Africa, however, still have some way to go, as do all least developed countries. The time needed to achieve universal access to electricity has ranged from about 20 years in Thailand and 40 years in China to 90 years in Mexico. Countries with low population densities or those consisting of dispersed islands face special challenges. Electrification in remote islands remains limited owing to high capital costs, despite special efforts made by small island developing States. For example, Fiji completed about 900 rural electrification community projects between 2005 and 2009, in order to be able to reach universal electricity access by 2016 (United Nations, General Assembly, 2010b).

The benefits of electrification are clear. For poor households in developing countries, having household lighting has been estimated to add between $5 and $16 per month in income gains. The added benefits of access to electricity in general would be in the order of $20-$30 per household per month through enhanced entertainment, time savings, education and home productivity (World Bank, Independent Evaluation Group, 2008). These benefits outweigh by far the $2-$5 per month that poor households typically pay for the cost of electricity.

For poor households in developing countries, household lighting adds between $5 and $16 per month in income gains

Energy efficiencies of kerosene, candles and batteries for lighting are very low. As a result, lighting services with kerosene cost as much as $3 per kilowatt-hour (kWh), which is higher than the cost of lighting with solar electricity, at about $2.2 per kWh in poor countries. In poor countries, diesel generators and micro-utilities typically provide lighting at a cost of $0.5-$1.5 per kWh, compared with centralized traditional utilities which often provide lighting at an effective cost of less than $0.3 per kWh. However, for traditional utilities, providing services to poor households becomes economically interesting only at demand levels of higher than 25 kWh per month, whereas poor households already derive great benefits per unit of cost in the range of 1 to 4 kWh per month.

For the poorest people in developing countries, cooking (and space heating in cold climates) can account for 90 per cent or more of the total volume of energy consumed (World Energy Council and Food and Agriculture Organization of the United Nations, 1999). Relatively simple and inexpensive improved stoves can reduce by as much as 30 per cent the amount of fuel needed for cooking (Global Energy Assessment, forthcoming). Some of these cooking stove programmes, including their costs, are described below.

Relatively simple and inexpensive improved stoves can reduce by as much as 30 per cent the amount of fuel needed for cooking by the poorest people in developing countries

National energy technology innovation strategies

An increasing number of Governments—notably, those of China, Japan and the Republic of Korea—and the European Union (EU) have adopted or followed some kind of national energy technology innovation strategy. Such strategies are typically part of national innovation systems, as discussed in chapter V, and provide a framework for coherent packages of policies and programmes that encompass all stages of the technology life cycle. The EU Lisbon Strategy provides a broad framework for a set of research, development and demonstration (RD&D) framework programmes. The fact that Japan has long focused on the promotion of performance targets for specific technologies has made the country the world leader in energy efficiency. China and the Republic of Korea have implemented industrial policies that focus on rapid adoption, local research, and manufacturing and deployment capacity, supported by flexible financial and regulatory support to accelerate qualitative improvements.

In China, energy technology R&D has expanded rapidly and is dominated largely by Government-owned enterprises which provide 85 per cent of all energy-related R&D. Similar to those of Organization for Economic Cooperation and Development (OECD) member countries, the energy R&D portfolio is dominated by supply-side options, of which more than half entailed fossil fuel-related technologies and 30 per cent, electric power, transport and distribution. Most recently, the Government has strengthened its patent system, with the number of filings having boomed since 2002, which will soon make China's patent office the world's largest. The wind power sector offers a good example of China's rapid creation of local capacities. The market share (of *cumulative* installed wind power capacity) of foreign manufacturers in China declined from 75 per cent in 2004 to 38 per cent in 2008, while the share of domestic manufacturers increased from

China's patent office will soon be the world's largest

23 to 59 per cent.[5] Such rapid replacement of firms' market position has been unheard of in other countries' energy markets (see chap. V).

Investments in research, development and demonstration (RD&D), market formation, and diffusion

Table II.1 provides global estimates of public and private investments in energy innovation, market formation, and diffusion (Wilson and Grübler, 2010; Grübler and others, forthcoming). In 2010, investments in commercial diffusion amounted to between $1 trillion and $5 trillion, substantially more than the $150 billion-$180 billion invested in market formation and the $50 billion for RD&D. RD&D and Government-driven market formation investments focused on power and fuel supply, whereas the majority of private sector diffusion investments were for end-use and efficiency.

Table II.1
Global estimates of public and private investments in energy innovation, market formation, and diffusion, 2010

Billions of 2005 United States dollars

	Innovation RD&D	*Market formation*	*Diffusion*
End-use and efficiency	>>8	5	300-5,000
Fossil fuel supply	>12	>>2	200-550
Nuclear	>10	0	3-8
Renewables	>12	~20-60[a]	>20
Electricity generation, transmission and distribution	>>1	~100	450-520
Other[b] and unspecified	>>4	<15	..
Total	**>50**	**<150-180**	**1,000-5,000**

Sources: Grübler and others (forthcoming); and International Energy Agency (2010b).
a The high estimate is from International Energy Agency (2010b).
b Hydrogen, fuel cells, other power and storage technologies, and basic energy research.

Investment in research, development and demonstration (RD&D)

Today's level of public spending for energy-related research and development in developed countries is still well below that of the 1970s and early 1980s

Only one fifth of the $50 billion in public and private RD&D investments was for end-use technologies and energy efficiency in 2010. The R&D intensity of the energy supply industry was comparable with that of the textile industry, but much lower than that of manufacturing. Public investment in energy-related RD&D continues to be low in developed countries, amounting to 5 per cent of total public RD&D. It had increased rapidly in response to the oil crises of the 1970s, but collapsed in the mid-1980s in line with falling oil prices and privatization, only to recover from 2000 in response to concerns about global warming. Today's level of public spending for energy-related RD&D in developed countries is still well below that of the 1970s and early 1980s, even though overall (not just energy) RD&D budgets have doubled since the 1980s (Nemet and Kammen, 2007). Public spending on RD&D of nuclear, fusion, fossil fuels and renewable energy technologies is lower in each case than in 1980.

5 Data from Tan and others (2010).

Over the past 20 years, emerging economies have become leaders in terms of public RD&D expenditures. They are also emerging as leaders in terms of renewable energy patents. Energy RD&D in Brazil, the Russian Federation, India, Mexico, China and South Africa was about $19 billion (in PPP terms), which is more than the total public energy RD&D budget of all IEA countries combined (estimated at $12.7 billion in PPP terms). This challenges the conventional wisdom that new energy technologies are developed in OECD countries and transferred to developing countries. Energy RD&D investments in emerging economies were focused on fossil fuel and nuclear energy, with renewables and energy efficiency underrepresented (table II.2).

Table II.2
Public and private spending on energy-related RD&D in selected emerging economies and the United States of America, 2004-2008[a]

Millions of 2008 United States dollars at PPP

	Fossil (including CCS)	*Nuclear (including fusion)*	*Electricity, transmission, distribution and storage*	*Renewable energy sources*	*Energy efficiency*	*Energy technologies (unspecified)*	***Total***
China	7 044	19	..	..	161	5 885	**14 772**
Brazil	1 246	8[b]	122[b]	46[b]	46[b]	196	**1 664**
Russian Federation	430	..	22[b]	14[b]	25[b]	553	**1 045**
India	800	965[b]	35[b]	57[b]	..	..	**1 857**
Mexico	140	32[b]	79[b]	..	263[c]	19[c]	**534**
South Africa	164	164	26[c]	7[c]	..	9[b]	**370**
Subtotal	**9 624**	**>1 187**	**>285**	**>124**	**>497**	**>6 662**	**>18 580**
United States	1 821	804	319[b]	699[b]	525[b]	2 510	**6 678**

Source: Gallagher and others (forthcoming).
a Most recent year available.
b Government only.
c Private sector only.

Investment in market formation

Market-formation interventions include public and private investments in the early stages of technological diffusion and public procurement

Market-formation investments, which include public and private investments in the early stages of technological diffusion, are sometimes also referred to as "niche market" investments. These include public procurement and government subsidies for certain technologies, as well as private investments involving renewable performance standards, carbon taxes and feed-in tariffs (chap. V). About $100 billion out of the total of $150 billion-$180 billion in global investments for market formation was for electricity generation, transmission and distribution, $20 billion-$60 billion for renewables and about $5 billion for end-use and efficiency. The niche market investments for renewables are expected to increase rapidly in the coming years, in view of current Government plans in developed and developing countries alike. International Energy Agency (2010b) has estimated that government support for renewables will rise from $57 billion in 2009 to $205 billion in 2035 (figure II.5).[6] By comparison, fossil-fuel consumption subsidies amounted to $312 billion in 2009 (ibid.). These numbers do nonetheless indicate that Governments favour renewables, since, excluding grid investments, Government subsidies for modern renewables amounted to $9.7/GJ compared with $0.8/GJ for fossil fuels.

6 This assumes that world average support per unit will drop from 5.5 cents/kWh in 2009 to 2.3 cents/kWh in 2035, but does not take into account the additional costs of integrating intermittent renewable sources into the network.

Figure II.5
Annual global support for renewables in the IEA New Policies Scenario, 2007-2035

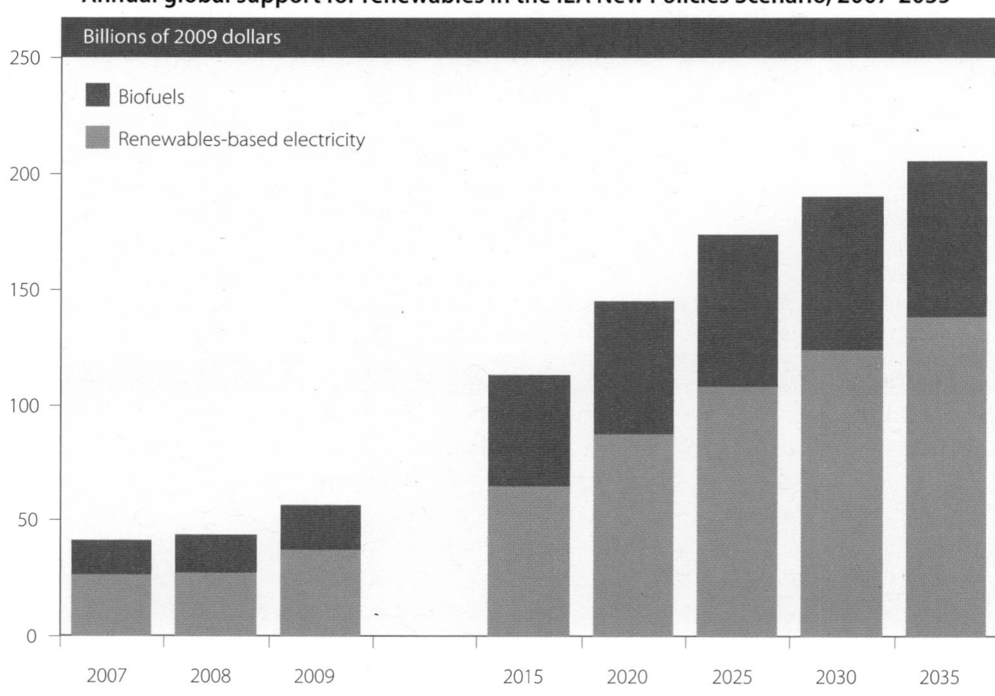

Source: International Energy Agency (2010b).

Note: The IEA New Policies Scenario assumes cautious implementation of recently announced commitments and plans, even if not yet officially adopted.

Investment in diffusion

Global investments in energy and end-use technologies were more than double supply-side investments

Global supply-side energy investment was about $740 billion in 2010, with $70 billion for renewables. These investments were dominated by electricity generation, transmission and distribution (51 per cent) as well as upstream investments in fossil fuel supply (46 per cent), including the oil exploration and production component and the gas exploration and production component which accounted for 19 and 13 per cent, respectively. The most important renewables investments were in large-scale hydropower (annual capacity additions of 25-30 gigawatts (GW)) and biofuels ($20 billion, of which $8 billion was for Brazil's ethanol). Global investment in energy end-use technologies was more than double the supply-side investments, and reached an estimated $1.7 trillion in 2005, of which almost $1.2 trillion was for road vehicles (Grübler and others, forthcoming).

Public-private partnerships in energy investments have become increasingly popular, accounting for almost $40 billion in the first semester of 2009 despite the global financial crisis. Other private sector investments in energy technology include investment by angel investors, companies' internal investments, debt instruments, project finance, mergers and acquisitions, and investments in publicly listed energy technology firms. Energy-related venture capital investments boomed in EU and North America in recent years, reaching $15.5 billion, or 10 per cent of all private investments in energy technology diffusion in 2008 (International Energy Agency, 2009). Most of these investments were for solar, biofuels, biomass, battery technologies, smart metering, software, and high-efficiency engines.

Government energy technology programmes

The following selected examples of government energy technology programmes offer important lessons for future programmes.[7] Most of the programmes have focused on power supply or alternative fuels.

Ethanol in Brazil, the United States and Mauritius

In response to the oil crisis and the erosion of trade preferences for sugar exports, Brazil's military Government launched the world's first large-scale ethanol programme in 1975, with producer subsidies and user incentives aimed at a rapid shift towards dedicated engines running on ethanol. In response to low gasoline prices in the mid-1980s, a national research programme was started which achieved a reduction in production costs from $35/GJ (in 2004 United States dollars) to less than $10/GJ in 2009, mainly through higher yields. In Brazil, ethanol derived from sugar cane has a high energy return of 8.3 times the energy input (ranging from 3.7 to 10) and high yields of about 5,500 litres per hectare. In addition, the introduction of flexible fuel engines (developed with foreign automobile companies) allowed users to choose the desired mix of ethanol and gasoline, thus creating fuel competition and a hedge against lower future oil prices from 2003. The cumulative subsidy aimed at making up for the difference between the higher ethanol production cost and world oil prices between 1975 and 2004 amounted to an estimated $50 billion. Rising oil prices in recent years meant that ethanol production costs became cheaper than world oil prices after 2004. Flexible fuel engines have been highly successful, reaching 81 per cent of the light-vehicle registrations by 2008 (Brazil, Associação Nacional dos Fabricantes de Veículos Automotores, 2008). In this context, it should be noted that, in January 2009, gasoline prices were again lower than ethanol production costs owing to the global recession, but this had again been reversed by January 2011.

In the United States, commercial production of fuel ethanol from corn had started in 1980, reaching 5 billion litres in 1995 and 35 billion litres in 2008. In 2007, the United States Congress passed a bill that mandated the production of 140 billion litres of corn ethanol by 2022, which would be equal to about 13 per cent of United States gasoline demand. If this goal were to be achieved domestically, it would require using the entire United States corn harvest.

In recent years, many developing countries in tropical zones have tried to learn from Brazil's experience with ethanol, and experimented with various local crops. An interesting case is that of Mauritius, which created a local sugar cane and biofuel research institute. While lower sugar cane yields and a smaller scale of operation led to ethanol prices that were about twice as high as those of Brazil, Mauritius has successfully deployed economical bagasse-based cogeneration. It should be noted, however, that, even if all tropical countries attained sugar cane yields as high as Brazil's and all of the world's sugar cane production (19 million hectares in 2005) were shifted to ethanol production, the resulting yield would meet only about 6 per cent of the world's gasoline demand.

Even if all of the world's sugar cane production were shifted to ethanol production, the resulting yield would meet only about 6 per cent of the world's gasoline demand

7 The present subsection draws upon the module on energy technology innovation of the Global Energy Assessment (Grübler and others, forthcoming), which also provides a series of detailed case studies.

Coal-based synthetic fuels in the United States

In response to the second oil crisis, the United States embarked on a large-scale programme to produce synthetic fuels from coal. In 1980, it had established the Synthetic Fuels Corporation which was to improve technologies and produce 2 million barrels of liquid fuel per day by 1992, at a cost of $60 per barrel, in order to replace about 25 per cent of United States oil imports. Against the backdrop of the collapse of oil prices, the programme was cancelled after five years, with production having reached only 10,000 barrels per day and incurred costs having amounted to $5 billion (at 1980 prices) (Gaskins and Stram, 1991). Despite its failure to reach its envisaged goals, the programme did develop coal-gasification technologies that paved the way for highly efficient integrated gasification combined cycle (IGCC) coal power plants which were deployed around the world from the 1990s.

Hydrogen production in the United States

In contrast with the large diffusion investments in ethanol and synthetic fuels, support for hydrogen production and handling (that is, materials science) has been small-scale and limited to R&D. However, hydrogen has found a performance niche in certain industrial processes. Annual production in the United States from 1971 to 2003 increased more than 10-fold and production costs were reduced by a factor of 5, without any subsidies and despite the material challenges associated with handling hydrogen (Ausubel, 2007). A hydrogen pipeline is being operated between Louisiana and Texas; and some are considering the old idea of mixing hydrogen into the national natural gas pipeline system.

Nuclear power in the United States

The fact that, initially, safety was not a key performance criterion for nuclear power has had far-reaching consequences

Experience with nuclear power offers a prime example of an ambitious "big push" experiment which Governments have carried out in order to accelerate development, deployment and diffusion of a new energy technology. As noted earlier, more than half of all cumulative energy-related public RD&D support in IEA countries since 1974 has been for nuclear power technologies. Exuberant expectations by early promoters of nuclear power from the 1950s are reflected in the statement by Lewis Strauss in 1954 that nuclear power would become "too cheap to meter". In the beginning of the 1970s, the International Atomic Energy Agency (IAEA) had expected global installed nuclear power to reach at least 2.5 terawatts (TW) by 2000, as compared with what was in fact the actual total of 351 gigawatts (GW). The first nuclear power plant started operating in the United Kingdom in 1956. In the United States, as many as 65 plants were ordered between 1965 and 1969, and by the end of 1970, the country had 107 units on line, under construction or purchased. Rapid scaling up of unit size to beyond 1 GW brought costs down to less than those of coal power plants in the early 1970s. Thereafter, increasingly large cost and construction time overruns made nuclear power increasingly uncompetitive. Between 1978 and very recently, no new plant was ordered in the United States. Reasons included low oil prices (for much of the 1980s and 1990s) and increasing costs associated with safety regulation. The "Atoms for Peace" programme launched by the United States in 1953 was a typical Government big-push technology undertaking which shortened the formative phase during which, typically, different designs are tested. In the end, the design of the pressurized water reactor used in nuclear submarines became the sole dominant operational commercial reactor design. Yet, it was compactness and little need for refuelling that had been the main performance criteria of reactors in submarines. Safety was not a key performance criterion, which has had far-reaching consequences. When accidents in commercial nuclear power plants made it increasingly clear that safety had to be increased, it was achieved with retrofitting and increased regulation. By the year 1978, an average of 1.3 new regulations were being added *every day* in the United States. The result was the introduction of additional risks related to an increasingly complex technology system and cost overruns due to retrofitting. In short, the well-intended Government push for rapid commercialization of nuclear power without a link to appropriate performance criteria led to lock-in of inferior designs. Alternative designs, such as passive safety systems and high-temperature reactors, came too late.

Wind power in Germany, Denmark, the United States, the Netherlands, China and India

Premature scaling up of inferior technology can be an obstacle to building a sustainable industry

The first wind power plants had been developed in the 1880s, but it was not until the 1970s that the currently dominant design was settled upon and deployed. Denmark, the United States, Germany, the United Kingdom, Sweden and the Netherlands were early movers in wind energy innovation but followed different approaches. In the 1970s and 1980s, Germany and Sweden had focused on public R&D support for a quick scaling up to a range of 2-4 megawatts (MW), but provided only limited support for market formation. Premature scaling up failed to build a sustainable industry (Meyer, 2007) and established utilities had little incentive to deploy high-cost, intermittent wind turbines which were difficult to maintain. Denmark, the Netherlands and the United States focused on R&D and deployment of smaller-scale and simpler wind turbines in niche markets. Denmark established a test station for wind turbines in 1978, issued type approvals from 1979 and introduced investment and production subsidies in the same year (Grübler and others, forthcoming). The result was sustained growth of the industry, the entry of new actors (farmers and municipalities), and very high reliability (98 per cent in 1985) (Heymann, 1998). While the Netherlands had also established a test field in 1981, it focused on competition rather than cooperation among manufacturers, which led to much slower progress and to lower reliability. In the United States, a number of subsidy schemes were introduced that led to a boom in wind power so that, by 1986, California had installed 1.2 GW of wind power which, at the time, constituted 90 per cent of the world total. However, "subsidy harvesting" by the private sector spurred hasty development and inadequate operational testing. By 1985, only 38 per cent of wind-power plants in the United States were operating properly; and the industry collapsed in 1986 when Government subsidies were reduced.

From the 1990s, many increasingly large wind power projects were undertaken in Denmark, Germany and Spain. The cost per kWh of wind power was halved between 1980 and 2000, and reliability, efficiency, level of turbine noise, and grid stability greatly improved. Germany introduced feed-in tariffs, and average wind farm and turbine prices declined by 30 per cent from 1991 to 1996 (a learning rate of 10 per cent), with export prices at about half the average domestic price (Junginger, Faaij and Turkenburg, 2005). Germany's feed-in tariffs effectively cross-subsidized technology transfer and the development of wind power industries in other countries, including China and India. From 1996 onward, prices began to increase in Germany, owing to rapidly expanding demand both domestically and for exports to emerging economies and later owing to higher commodity prices.

China and India have used industrial policy, including legal provisions, duties, taxes and subsidies, to support domestic wind power research and the wind power industry since the 1990s

China and India have used industrial policy, including legal provisions, duties, taxes and subsidies, to support domestic wind power research and the wind power industry since the 1990s (see chap. V). Further, China mandated domestically produced components and, along with India, instituted domestic technology certification programmes. As in the case of Europe, wind power plants were not necessarily built in the most suitably windy locations: the local policy environment was a much more important factor. For example, in India in 2004, 57 per cent of wind power capacity was installed in Tamil Nadu which only has 7 per cent of the wind resources (Global Wind Energy Council, World Institute of Sustainable Development and Indian Wind Turbine Manufacturing Association, 2011). By the end of 2010, 194 GW of wind power capacity had been installed worldwide (figure II.6), of which 84 GW were in EU, 40 GW in the United States, 42 GW in China and 13 GW in India. In 2010, 35.7 GW of new capacity were installed, which was 6 per cent less capacity than in 2009. More than half of this new capacity was installed in China (16.5 GW) and India (2.1 GW), compared with 9.8 GW in EU and 5.1 GW in the United States (Eurobserver, 2011).

Photovoltaics in Germany, the United States, Japan, China and Kenya

Solar photovoltaics (PV) was invented in the United States but was not deployed there on a large scale. For several decades, through its R&D, and its "Sunshine Programme" from 1994 to 2004, Japan refined the technology and successfully reduced the costs of a 3kW roof system from 6 million to 2 million yen. The Sunshine Programme was remarkable in that it phased out its solar PV subsidies (which peaked at about $250 million in 2001) over

Figure II.6
Global installed wind power capacity, 1993-2010

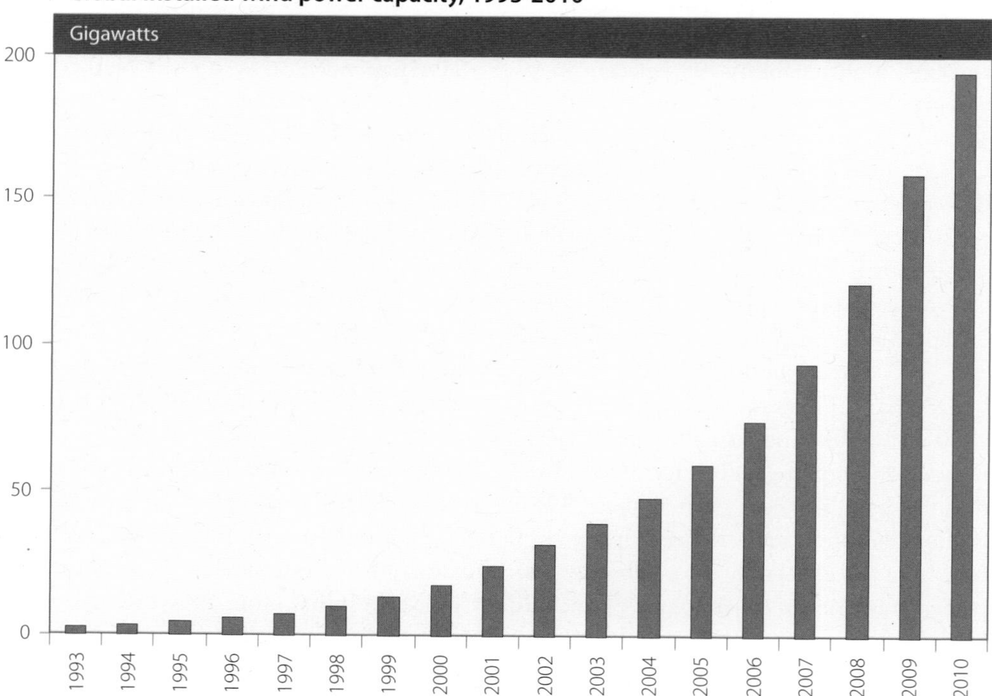

Source: Eurobserver (2011).

the duration of the Programme. Despite its low insolation levels, Germany is today by far the largest solar PV market in the world, owing to its generous feed-in tariffs. China produces and exports the majority of solar panels, most of which are sold in Germany, which remains the producer of machines needed in the manufacturing plants. Most recently, off-grid solar PV has become increasingly popular in poor areas without access to electricity, in view of the prevailing high electricity prices and low demand levels. The examples of Kenya and Bangladesh are described in chapter V.

Solar water heaters in the United States and China

Research in United States national laboratories and universities had improved solar water heater technology in the 1970s. A key breakthrough was the production of selective coatings which would absorb more sunlight. Driven by United States Federal and State subsidies and expectations of high future energy prices, the solar water heater industry boomed from the late 1970s and a $1 billion industry was created. In the 1980s, there was rampant abuse of generous subsidies (subsidy harvesting) which resulted in poorly installed systems. Within a few years, about half the systems were no longer functioning (Taylor, 2008). In 1984, tax credits for new installations expired and the solar water heater industry in the United States collapsed, with the technology being by and large abandoned for two decades. The perception of poor reliability persists and, with the industry's size currently at about $30 million, has proved difficult to overcome. More successful was a programme in Hawaii that made consumer rebates contingent on an inspection. The technology is currently cost-effective, especially in large installations with high demand for hot water. While the quality of the technology has improved since 1976, unit costs have not been reduced significantly and, instead, have been determined mainly by the price of steel and glass (Taylor and others, 2007). In contrast, solar water heaters have been rapidly adopted in China which now accounts for most of the 100 GW capacity that is installed worldwide today.

More successful than efforts of the United States to improve solar water heater technology was a programme in Hawaii that made consumer rebates contingent on an inspection

Concentrated solar power in the United States, Germany, Spain and North Africa

The United States, Germany and Spain have led long-standing research programmes in solar thermal electricity, which included experimentation with a variety of designs.[8] The first modern concentrating solar power (CSP) plant with 1 megawatt (MW) capacity had been built in Italy in 1968. The parabolic trough design of a 354 MW plant built in California in 1984 became dominant. Different types of working fluids (such as molten salt), which are a key determinant of the efficiency, have been used. Overall deployment remains much lower than that of wind power, owing to higher cost and water-use conflicts in desert areas. In the United States, costs of producing CSP are about 12-18 cents per kWh compared with 2 cents for nuclear power, although costs as low as 5 cents might be achievable in the future with heliostat mirrors and gas turbine technology.

Overall deployment of solar power remains much lower than that of wind power, owing to higher costs and conflicts over water use in desert areas

An industrial consortium, consisting mainly of German companies, has recently been formed with the goal of constructing a country-size CSP facility in North Africa and linking it to the EU power grid with high-voltage alternating current (HVAC)

8 Designs include the parabolic trough, the dish stirling, the concentrating linear Fresnel reflector and the solar power tower.

lines. The initiative is commonly known as DESERTEC. The consortium has plans for a €400 billion CSP facility together with solar PV and wind power over an area of 17,000 square kilometres (km^2) in the Sahara which might deliver as much as 15 per cent of Europe's power by 2050. Besides the costs, the main obstacle to the realization of the DESERTEC goal continues to be geopolitical in nature.

Micro-hydroelectricity and biogas in China

China has the largest hydroelectricity potential in the world. During the "Great Leap Forward" (which started in 1958), there had been plans to build 2.5 GW of micro-size hydroelectricity plants by 1967, but only about 0.5 GW were completed (Carin, 1969). In a new wave of construction from 1970 to 1979, their number increased from 26,000 to 90,000, with mean size doubling to only 70 kW. Much larger hydro plants in the MW and GW ranges have been built since the 1980s. Many technical and maintenance problems (silting, drought, leaks) with hastily built microplants meant low load factors and relatively high costs (Smil, 2010a). In 2006, China completed the world's largest hydropower plant, with a capacity of 18.2 GW. From the early 1970s, China had promoted microscale biodigesters running on animal dung, human faeces, garbage and waste water. A 10 cubic metre (m^3) biodigester was deemed sufficient to provide biogas for a family's cooking and lighting needs. Some 30,000 were completed by 1973 and 400,000 by 1975. China's official target for 1985 was 20 million units, but in reality their numbers fell to less than 4 million by 1984, as millions of the units were abandoned owing to lack of the necessary skills for maintenance (ibid.).

Efficient cook stoves in developing countries

There is a wide range of cooking-stove models tailored to local needs, fuel supply, available technical skills and affordability

The Global Energy Assessment reviewed 51 programmes, conducted since 1980 in 8 Asian, 12 African and 9 Latin American countries, whose aim has been to distribute clean cooking stoves to poor households. Included in the review were costs, efficiency and technologies used. The review highlighted the wide range of cooking-stove models tailored to local needs, fuel supply, available technical skills and affordability. Energy efficiencies ranged from 15 per cent for simple mud stoves running on straw and twigs (several thousands of which were constructed by trained artisans in Viet Nam at a cost of $1.8) to as high as 40 per cent in the case of a programme in China involving 300,000 clay stoves running on coal briquettes and constructed in local workshops since the 1980s. There was no evidence of systematically increased efficiencies or reduced costs over time. Programmes in Latin America tended to be smaller in size, but were mostly subsidized to varying degrees, including 100 per cent in some cases in Guatemala, Bolivia (Plurinational State of) and El Salvador, whereas in Asian and African countries, there was a wide range of subsidy levels, depending on the type of stove. Noteworthy are the large-scale programmes designed to distribute since the 1990s more than 5 million Chulha stoves, running on a range of fuelwood, straw, dung and agricultural waste, with efficiencies between 20 and 28 per cent, and delivered at costs of only $1.80-$4.60, depending on the subsidy levels (which ranged from zero to 78 per cent subsidy). Manufactured metal stoves in India, Zimbabwe, Rwanda, Mali, the Niger, Burkina Faso and Guatemala, were about 10 times more expensive than Chulha stoves, but typically achieved efficiencies that were somewhat higher—close to 30 per cent.

Top Runner Programme on end-use efficiency in Japan

Japan has maintained mandatory energy efficiency standards for appliances and automobiles since 1980, which were not very successful, however, as they were largely based on negotiations with industry. In 1998, Japan initiated the Top Runner Programme to improve energy efficiency of end-use products, as a cornerstone of its climate change policy. The idea is that the most energy-efficient product on the market during the standard-setting process establishes the "Top Runner standard" which all corresponding product manufacturers will aim to achieve in the next stage.[9] Energy efficiency standards are discussed and determined by the Ministry of Economy, Trade and Industry and its advisory committees comprising representatives from academia, industry, consumer groups, local governments and mass media. The scope of the Programme is reviewed every two to three years. It started with 9 products and had been expanded to 21 products by 2009 (Grübler and others, forthcoming). The targeted products account for more than 70 per cent of residential electricity use. To date, all targets set by the programme have been achieved or overachieved. For example, the energy efficiency of room air conditioners improved by 68 per cent, of refrigerators by 55 per cent, of TV receivers by 26 per cent, of computers by 99 per cent, of fluorescent lights by 78 per cent, of vending machines by 37 per cent and of gasoline passenger cars by 23 per cent (Japan, Energy Conservation Center, 2008), representing enormous technical improvements and attaining one of the highest levels of energy efficiency in the world. Yet, it is not clear whether the Programme can be replicated successfully outside Japan. Specific success factors include a limited number of domestic producers with high technological capacity, which were willing to comply with the standards even without sanctions.

Under the Top Runner Programme, the most energy-efficient product on the market during the standard-setting process establishes the standard that all corresponding product manufacturers will aim to achieve in the next stage

Car fuel efficiency standards in the United States

The typical efficiency of United States cars in the early 1970s had been the same as in the 1930s—13 miles per gallon (mpg), which meant 85 per cent of the gasoline was wasted (Smil, 2010a). The Corporate Average Fuel Economy (CAFE) standards, which were introduced in 1975, doubled the average efficiency of United States passenger cars to 27.7 mpg by 1985, but no further improvements were made until CAFE standards were revised in 2007. In fact, the popularity of sport utility vehicles (SUV), vans and pickup trucks depressed United States vehicle fleet efficiency, which reached only 22 mpg by 2006. The 2007 revision of CAFE no longer exempts light trucks classified as SUVs or passenger vans (unless they exceed a 4.5 t gross vehicle weight rating), and the aim is to increase fleet efficiency to 35 mpg by 2020. For comparison, the 1913 Model T Ford, which was the world's first mass-produced automobile, averaged 25 mpg. All new cars in New Zealand currently rate between 34 and 62 mpg. The EU corporate vehicle standard of 130 gCO_2/km, to be achieved by 2012, is equivalent to 47 mpg (or 5 litres (l)/100 km) for a gasoline-fuelled car.

The popularity of sport utility vehicles (SUVs), vans and pickup trucks depressed United States vehicle fleet efficiency

Lessons from market-based measures

Oil price spikes, high gasoline taxes, subsidies and permit trading schemes are "natural" experiments which provide insights into the impact of market measures, such as energy or carbon taxes.

9 The Top Runners set the standard, with consideration given to technological potential. Differentiated standards are set based on various parameters.

Carbon price signals and emissions trading

The volatility of emissions trading schemes holds back investment in low-carbon infrastructure

The social cost of carbon (SCC) corresponds to the externality of a unit of carbon emitted over its lifetime in the atmosphere. Under an optimal climate policy, the emission reduction target should be set so that the cost of reducing emissions (marginal abatement cost) is equal to the SCC. SCC estimates vary. For instance, estimates previously used by the Government of the United Kingdom for policy and project evaluation ranged from \$41 to \$124 per ton of CO_2, with a central case of \$83. Estimates from other models, for example, the Dynamic Integrated model of Climate and the Economy (DICE), are substantially lower. Recently, the market price of allowances in the EU Emissions Trading Scheme (ETS) has fluctuated around \$20 per ton of CO_2. With respect to individual behaviour, calculations done by MacKay (2008) suggest that only with very high carbon prices would there be a noticeable impact on activities like driving and flying. For instance, he concluded that at \$150 per ton, domestic users of gas would notice the cost of carbon in their heating bills; a price of \$250 per ton would increase the effective cost of a barrel of oil by \$100; at \$370, carbon pollution would cost enough to significantly reduce people's inclination to fly; and at \$900, driving habits might be significantly changed. The prevailing allowance prices appear too low to foster "market pull" of low-carbon technologies, and the volatility of emissions trading schemes holds back investment in low-carbon infrastructure.

Emissions trading markets require careful design and a sophisticated regulatory framework which explicitly takes into account strategic gaming behaviour of actors. For example, in the case of emissions trading in Germany, the design of the first National Allocation Plan (NAP I, 2005-2007) led to "windfall" profits for high emitters and further increased an already existing preference for investments in coal compared with natural gas (Pahle, Fan and Schill, 2011). In contrast, alternative allocation rules, such as full auctioning of permits or a single best available technology benchmark, would have substantially increased natural gas investment incentives. A total of 10 coal power plants (11.3 GW) are currently under construction in Germany, and plans for an additional 12 coal power plants exist, which together would account for about 32 per cent of German peak electricity demand in 2008 (Bundesnetzagentur, 2009). In other words, the details of institutional design are at least as important as the overall choice of policy instrument.

Gasoline taxes

In November 2010, gasoline retail prices in different countries ranged from about 2.2 cents to 256 cents per litre, the wide range being due to massive government intervention in the form of gasoline subsidies and taxes (Deutsche Gesellschaft für Internationale Zusammenarbeit, 2011). This wide range is not limited to gasoline retail prices, but is typical of most energy markets. Fifteen countries (mainly oil producers) had "very high subsidies", with retail prices ranging from 1 to 51 cents per litre, which was below the world crude oil price of \$81 per barrel at the time. Eight countries (mostly very poor) had retail prices ranging from \$0.52 to \$0.76 per litre, the latter being the prevailing level in the United States at the time. The majority of developing countries had retail prices ranging from \$0.77 to \$1.46 per litre, the latter being at the level of the lowest price level in EU (which was that of Romania). A mixed group of countries, including almost all EU members, Japan, high-income oil producers (Norway and the United Kingdom) and a few least developed countries (Senegal and Malawi) had retail prices ranging from \$1.46 to \$2.54 per litre. High gasoline prices have not halted the growth of vehicle miles in affluent countries, but they have created a preference for smaller and more fuel-efficient vehicles. Nonetheless, absent regulations, income has been the main driver of transport energy demand, regardless of the level of gasoline retail prices.

These cases illustrate the limitations of a policy approach based on price incentives. In the context of the debate about a global CO_2 tax, it is useful to note that gasoline taxes were equivalent to carbon taxes of $248 per tCO_2 in China, $451 in Japan, $575 in Germany, $753 in the Netherlands and $832 in Turkey, whereas subsidies for gasoline in the Bolivarian Republic of Venezuela were equivalent to a carbon rebate of $202 per tCO_2.[10] The implied carbon taxes are between 10 and 100 times higher than the prevailing carbon prices under the Clean Development Mechanism or in EU-ETS markets. They are also higher than carbon taxes deemed necessary for the energy sector as a whole with respect to the declared 450 ppmv stabilization, according to most mitigation scenarios (see, for example, Global Energy Assessment, forthcoming; and Intergovernmental Panel on Climate Change, 2001). Yet, only regulatory measures (such as those of the Top Runner Programme in Japan) have had significant impacts on fuel efficiency and emissions of road vehicles.

Many experiences illustrate the limitations of a policy approach based on price incentives

Feed-in tariffs

Feed-in tariffs (FITs) guarantee suppliers of renewable electricity a price that covers their costs with a profit, even though the price is higher than that paid for the fossil fuel-based alternative. The FIT consists in either fixed prices based on generation cost, independent of the market (as in Germany), or a fixed premium on top of the market price for electricity (as in Spain). FIT policies have been adopted in some 75 national and subnational (State/provincial) jurisdictions worldwide (REN21, 2010). A study of support policies for electricity from renewable sources in OECD and selected developing countries concludes that jurisdictions with FITs had the highest market growth for renewables and that payments per kWh tend to be lower under FITs than under standard renewable portfolio schemes (International Energy Agency, 2008a). However, as with any subsidy instrument, careful design and periodic re-calibration are necessary to ensure that objectives are achieved at the lowest cost to society, and this requires strong government capacity. Regulatory capture, where entrenched industry interests are able to extract subsidies even after the legislative objective has been attained, is common.

Careful design and periodic re-calibration of feed-in tariffs are necessary to ensure that the objectives are achieved at the lowest cost to society

Does every little bit help: a critical assessment of current approaches

The previous section painted a picture of massive Government intervention and private sector responses to the need to promote clean energy technology research, development and deployment in response to the oil crises and the climate change challenge. Yet, energy technology change has slowed considerably at the level of the global fuel mix since the 1970s, and there is no evidence to support the popular notion of an acceleration of energy technology change, either at the fuel or at the sector, plant or unit levels. In order to reconcile these facts, a science-based reality check is needed, in order to assess the implications of current plans and practices.

10 A gasoline tax of $0.01 per litre is equivalent to $4.14 per tCO_2.

Plans need to add up globally

At the most basic level, initiatives need to add up (in arithmetic terms) to the declared ambitions at the national and global levels. Despite impressive growth rates for the diffusion of renewable energy technologies since 2000, it is clear that the current trajectory is nowhere near attaining a realistic path towards complete decarbonization of the global energy system by 2050. Similarly, the renascence of nuclear power has barely made up for losses of older capacities that are increasingly being phased out.

Planetary-scale transformations are required to meet emissions targets

By making simple order-of-magnitude assessments, MacKay (2008) and Smil (2010a) illustrate the infeasibility of prominent existing plans and proposals. MacKay (2008) also traces that contours of low-carbon energy plans for the world, the United States, the United Kingdom and the rest of Europe: the plans add up in terms of global emissions targets, but to achieve these targets, planetary-scale transformations are required. And MacKay shows that existing energy plans do not add up to such a transformation. All actions help but, if small, they help only a little. For example, systematically switching off a phone charger saves about as much energy as is used up in three seconds of driving a car.

At the international level, global environmental problems and especially global warming are often thought of as problems of developed countries, but in fact populous emerging developing economies increasingly dominate growth in global emissions and resource use. Without participation and actions by today's developing countries, no realistic solution is possible to any one of the global environmental problems. For example, the majority of today's energy-related investments are in developing countries. During 2010-2050, the cumulative cost of the energy system (including investment and operating costs) is estimated at about $60 trillion in developed countries and about $80 trillion in developing countries (Global Energy Assessment, forthcoming).

Plans also need to add up at the system level

Plans also need to add up in terms of both the requirements of the energy system and the overall progress measures such as global eco-efficiency, because energy technologies are part of a complex interdependent system and because measures devised to achieve eco-efficiency at the local or even at national levels do not necessarily add up to a globally eco-efficient system.

The net result of a successful national climate policy could be an overall increase in emissions worldwide if production plants are simply transferred abroad

First, plans need to add up in terms of the *global* energy-economy-environment (E3) system. For example, satisfying about 20 per cent of today's demand for gasoline, diesel and kerosene with modern biofuels is possible in technical and economic terms from the perspective of the energy system alone. However, this would likely have enormous impacts on agriculture, food prices, ecosystems, water availability, the nitrogen cycle, energy demand and prices and, most importantly, the livelihoods of the poor in rural and urban areas alike (see also chap. III). Thus, a 20 per cent share might not be enough. With respect to the United Kingdom's climate policy, its implementation has led to decreasing greenhouse gas emissions and the country's early achievement of its commitments under the Kyoto Protocol; but while this achievement is commendable, what needs to be ascertained is whether lower emissions are indeed the result of fundamental changes in technologies or consumption patterns. In fact, when greenhouse gas emissions that are embodied in products that had been imported to the United Kingdom are included, the overall greenhouse gas emissions associated with energy and product demand in the United Kingdom increased by 12 per cent between 1992 and 2004 (Minx and others, 2009). In other words, greenhouse gas pollution was exported abroad. In addition, it is highly likely that such production, most of which was moved to emerging economies, is carried out with lower energy efficiency and higher emission intensities. Thus, the net result of the commendable United Kingdom climate policy was quite possibly an overall increase in greenhouse gas emissions worldwide—the opposite of the objective intended. This example highlights the importance of global coordination and the need for reality checks of measures from a systems and global perspective.

Second, plans also need to add up in terms of the *national* E3 system. One phenomenon to consider in this regard is the "rebound effect" (the Jevons paradox), that is, the increased energy use resulting from increased energy efficiency. While the rebound effect may be small at the local level, it is typically large at the level of the national or of the global economy. Thus, an increase in energy efficiency of a manufacturing plant, while highly desirable from an eco-efficiency perspective at the corporate level, may be partially or wholly offset through reduced energy prices and increased real incomes. Additional measures and regulations are needed to prevent or at least limit the rebound effect.

There is still a relatively large potential for efficiency increases in end-use appliances

At the same time, incentives to increase energy efficiencies are large, especially in end-use. For example, the typical compounded efficiency of the energy chain from crude oil at the well to useful transport services is about 2 per cent only (assuming single occupancy of a passenger car with five seats). While in this case, the efficiency of transforming primary to final energy is as high as 93 per cent (including transport, refining and distribution), the efficiency of transforming final to useful energy efficiency is only about 10 per cent (that is, the result of 20 per cent engine efficiency and 50 per cent efficiency of drivetrain and car). Full occupancy of the car would increase the compounded efficiency from 2 to 10 per cent. In contrast, no conceivable future engine technology could achieve the same overall efficiency increase for a single occupancy vehicle. Engine efficiency would need to be 100 per cent, which is a thermodynamic impossibility. It should also be noted that there is only limited potential for efficiency improvements in power supply technologies, some of which, such as gas combined cycle and integrated gasification combined cycle (IGCC) plants, operate not far from their theoretical limits. Similarly, the so-called cumulative degree of perfection is high for diesel oil and natural gas, compared with other materials, implying only modest room for improvements in this area (Szargut, 1988). In contrast, there is still a relatively large potential for efficiency increases in end-use appliances.

At present, there are no good substitutes for fossil fuels as industrial feedstocks

Third, plans need to add up at the level of the energy systems themselves. For example, at present, there are no good substitutes for fossil fuels as industrial feedstocks. Coke made from coal is needed as a reduction agent for smelting iron from ore. The historical alternative of charcoal cannot be used in modern blast furnaces, and even if it could be used in some form, about 3.5 Gt of dry wood per year would be needed for pig iron smelting alone, which requires plantations that are about two thirds the size of the forests of Brazil. Similarly, there are no plant-based substitutes for hydrocarbon feedstocks (about 100 giga cubic metres (Gm^3) of natural gas per year) used in making plastics and synthesizing ammonia for fertilizer production. As a result, any proposal to phase out fossil fuels requires targeted research into alternative industrial processes.

The installation of a wind farm does not necessarily lead to a reduction in emissions when backup capacity is provided by coal power

Fourth, plans need to add up at the level of power systems. For example, owing to its intermittency and need for backup capacity, the potential reduction in greenhouse gas emissions that can be achieved by wind power depends almost entirely upon the existing power system to which it is added. In fact, the installation of a wind farm does not necessarily lead to a reduction in emissions, in particular when backup capacity is provided by coal power. The "performance credit" of wind power in Germany was estimated to have been about 10 per cent in 2010 and is expected to fall to 3 per cent in 2030, with increasing installed wind power capacity (assuming a target of 99 per cent power grid reliability) (Deutsche Physikalischen Gesellschaft, 2010). This means that for each GW of newly installed wind power capacity, an additional 0.9 GW backup power capacity (for example, coal, gas or nuclear) is needed to ensure grid reliability, owing to wind's intermittency. Thus, expansion of wind power in Germany (and many other countries) primarily reduces fossil fuel demand, but hardly substitutes fossil-fired power plant capacities in the European grid, which explains the high systemic estimates of CO_2 mitigation costs for wind power of €40-€80 per tCO_2, compared with lower estimates based on assuming a full substitution of fossil-fuelled power capacities (Deutsche Energie-Agentur (DENA), 2005).

Ambitious plans for deployment of intermittent renewables need to be based on plans for the development of smart grids. The Global Energy Assessment (forthcoming) has estimated that the required share of zero carbon energy in 2030 would need to be about 22 per cent, in order for the target of staying below a 2° C increase from pre-industrial levels to be achieved with a probability of at least 50 per cent. Only the most ambitious technology-optimistic scenarios achieve such a high share, as illustrated by a literature review of renewable energy scenarios (Hamrin, Hummel and Canapa, 2007). The most technology-optimistic of the IEA scenarios (IEA ETP tech plus) barely reaches this level; the others include the EU World Energy Technology Outlook-2050 (WETO-H2) scenario with CO_2 constraint, and the Greenpeace "revolution" scenario. Assumptions in these scenarios are heroic indeed, requiring unprecedented technological progress, international cooperation and transfers. The same review also shows that under these and even less ambitious renewable energy scenarios, it is expected that a global share of more than 5 per cent of intermittent modern renewable power will be reached by 2020. This will require some sort of smart grid to deal with load balancing, which in turn means that these scenario plans assume the rebuilding of the existing power grids in most large economies within the next 10 years, an extraordinarily ambitious undertaking (comparable undertakings in previous energy transitions took more than 50 years).

National plans announced across the world do not add up to action sufficient to achieve the global targets for emission reductions

The International Energy Agency (2010b) has presented a "New Policies Scenario", which assumes implementation of recently announced commitments and plans, including those that are being discussed but have not yet been adopted. In this scenario, demand for all types of energy increases in non-OECD countries, while in OECD, demand for coal and oil declines. Globally, most new primary energy demand will be for fossil fuels until 2035, even in this very ambitious and optimistic scenario (figure II.7), which means that, ss a result, fossil fuels would maintain their central role in the primary energy mix, with their share declining from 81 per cent in 2008 to 74 per cent in 2035. Global emissions would continue to rise, but at a decreasing pace, reaching 35 Gt in 2035 (which is 21 per cent higher than the 2008 level). Developing countries would account for essentially all the increase, whereas developed countries' emissions would peak before 2015 and then fall. This would lead to stabilizing GHG (equivalent) concentrations at over 650 ppmv, resulting in a likely temperature rise of more than 3.5° C in the long term. In other words, national plans announced across the world plus what was agreed at the Cancun session of the Conference of the Parties in 2010 do not add up to action sufficient to achieve the global targets for emission reductions.

Figure II.7
Incremental primary energy demand in the IEA New Policies Scenario, 2008-2035

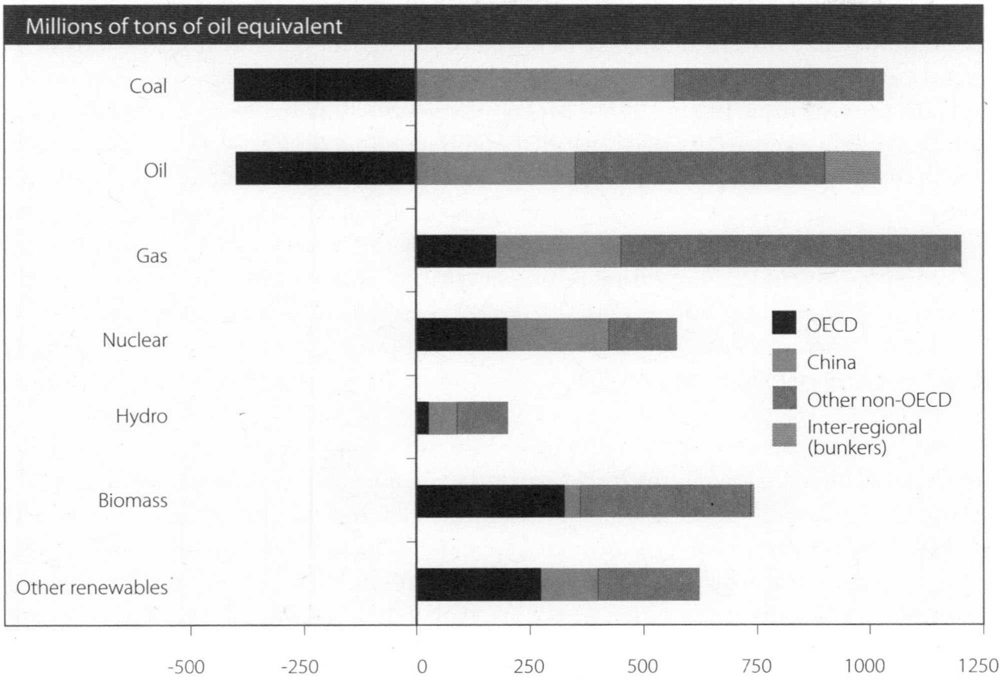

Source: International Energy Agency (2010b).

Feasible timescales for transitions

The comprehensive account given by Smil (2010b) of energy transitions suggests that the scale of the envisaged global transition to non-fossil fuels is about 20 times larger than the scale of the historical transition (fossil fuel use was about 425 EJ in 2010, compared with 20 EJ for traditional biomass in 1890). The physical magnitude of today's energy system based on fossil fuels is enormous, indeed. There are thousands of large coal mines and coal power plants, about 50,000 oilfields, a worldwide network of at least 300,000 km of oil and 500,000 km of natural gas pipelines, and 300,000 km of transmission lines. Globally, the replacement cost of the existing fossil fuel and nuclear power infrastructure is at least $15 trillion-$20 trillion. China alone added more than 300 GW of coal power capacity from 2000 to 2008, an investment of more than $300 billion, which will pay for itself only by 2030-2040 and will run maybe until 2050-2060. In fact, most energy infrastructures have recently been deployed in emerging economies and are completely new, with typical lifetimes of at least 40-60 years. Clearly, it is unlikely that the world will decide overnight to write off $15 trillion-$20 trillion in infrastructure and replace it with a renewable energy system having an even higher price tag. At the same time, it should be noted that the long-term incentive to change the existing energy system should be powerful, too, particularly in view of the fact that oil importers spent about $2 trillion to buy crude oil in 2007.

The growth of modern renewables from 1990 to 2008 was much slower than historical expansions of oil-based energy at 8 per cent per year from 1880 to 1900

Globally, modern renewables (wind, geothermal, solar photovoltaic, solar thermal and modern biofuels) accounted for 0.45 per cent of primary energy in 1990 and 0.75 per cent in 2008, which in relative terms corresponds to an average growth of 2.9 per cent per year. Over the same period, this was faster than the average annual growth of coal (1.6 per cent), crude oil (1.5 per cent) and natural gas (1.2 per cent). In absolute amounts, however, this growth amounted to the addition of 50 Mtoe of modern renewables, compared with much larger additions of coal (760 Mtoe), of oil (1,080 Mtoe) and of natural gas production (990 Mtoe). The growth of modern renewables from 1990 to 2008 was much slower than historical expansions of coal, at 5 per cent per year from 1850 to 1870; oil extraction, at 8 per cent per year from 1880 to 1900; and natural gas production, at 8 per cent per year from 1920 to 1940. Modern renewables (half of which was wind power) accounted for 3 per cent of global electricity production in 2008.

Meanwhile, internal combustion and diesel engines, which were first deployed in the late nineteenth century, still power about 1 billion cars, trucks, trains, ships and heavy machinery, with a combined capacity of about 150 terawatts (TW) (corresponding to 10 times the world's energy demand) (Smil, 2010b). Solutions that do not build on the prevailing prime movers and existing energy infrastructure will require decades to make significant dents in the primary energy mix. Unprecedented and worldwide coordinated measures are needed to transform the global energy system into an almost carbon-free one by 2050.

Small, resource-rich or affluent countries can achieve much faster transitions than large, resource-poor or low-income countries

Completion of some national energy transitions has been achieved more rapidly. For example, following the discovery of the giant Groningen natural gas field in the Netherlands, the natural gas share went from 1 per cent in 1958 to 5 per cent in 1965 and to 50 per cent in 1971. Portugal increased its share of renewables, including hydro, from 17 to 45 per cent in a matter of five years, from 2005 to 2010, and plans to become the first country to inaugurate a national network of charging stations for electric cars in 2011. However, it needs to be emphasized that small, resource-rich or affluent countries can achieve much faster transitions than large, resource-poor, or low-income countries.

One way to speed up the deployment of modern renewables is to rebuild the national grids so as to make them smart as well as to strengthen cross-border power interconnections. Current ambitions would require a rebuilding of the majority of the power grids in the world within the next 10 years, another achievement that would be completely unprecedented, which is not to say that it would be technically impossible, but only that it would come at a significant social and economic cost and would divert resources from other pressing needs, especially those of the world's poor.

Staying within limits

Energy plans must take account of certain types of limits:

- *Biophysical limits*: what is possible within planetary limits and according to the laws of nature?
- *Scientific-technical limits*: what is doable technically?
- *Economic limits*: what is affordable?
- *Socio-political limits*: what is acceptable socially and politically?

Biophysical limits have to be taken into account in making energy plans

When proponents and adversaries of energy technologies make opposing statements about their potential, the differences are often a reflection of the different types of limits that are being considered (MacKay, 2008). For example, a solar power proponent might state that the potential for solar radiation absorbed by land is 790 zettajoules (ZJ), which was about 2,000 times the figure for fossil fuel extraction in 2010. Smil (2010b, p. 110) notes that "direct solar radiation is the only form of renewable energy whose total terrestrial flux far surpasses not only today's demand for fossil fuels but also any level of global energy demand realistically imaginable in the twenty-first century". However, this is what is biophysically available—not what it is technically possible to harness. Leaving aside unsuitable locations constituting about half of the world's land area (those characterized by weak insolation or inaccessibility) about 470 ZJ are available. Yet, it would be technically possible to harness only a small fraction of this, and even less would be economically or politically acceptable. For example, the very ambitious Global Energy Assessment efficiency scenarios assume a techno-economic potential for solar PV, solar thermal and solar water heating of 2.6 ZJ.

MacKay (2008) provides per capita estimates of technical potentials for harnessing renewable energies for Europe, the United Kingdom, the United States and the world. Even leaving aside any economic and socio-political limits, he provides a low-carbon energy plan for the world and estimates the global potential for non-solar renewable energy to be about 83 GJ per capita (table II.3). In other words, without tapping at least some form of solar energy, it is technically impossible to provide for the level of energy use prevailing in Western Europe today. One billion people in Europe and North Africa could

Without tapping at least some form of solar energy, it is technically impossible to provide for the level of energy use prevailing in Western Europe today

Table II.3
Renewable energy plans for the world

	MacKay (2008)			*Riahi and others (forthcoming)*
Renewable source	*Technical potential (EJ)*	*Technical potential per capita (GJ)*	*Comments and assumptions*	*Techno-economic potential for Global Energy Assessment scenarios by 2050*
Wind	189	27.4	Onshore and offshore. Estimate of Greenpeace and the European Wind Energy Association	170
Hydro	28.8	4.11	Estimate by the International Hydropower Association and the International Energy Agency	28
Tide	1.2-2.6	0.18-0.37		..
Wave	3.9	0.57	10 per cent of raw wave power converted at 50 per cent efficiency	..
Geothermal	63.1	9.14	Extrapolation of United States geothermal potential for the world	17
Biofuels	284	41	All of the world's arable or cropland (27 million km^2) used for biofuels! Power density of 0.5 W/m^2, and losses of 33 per cent in processing and farming	117+28
Total non-solar	**571**	**83**	Sum of the above	**360**
Solar photovoltaics (PV)	..	..		1 650
Concentrating solar power (CSP)	..	..		990
Total solar: solar heaters, PV and CSP	**370 EJ**	**>54**	One billion people in Europe and North Africa could be sustained by country-size solar power facilities in deserts near the Mediterranean; and half a billion in North America could be sustained by Arizona-size facilities in the deserts of the United States and Mexico	**2 640**

Source: MacKay (2008); and Riahi and others (forthcoming).
Note: Data converted and adjusted for the world population of 6.9 billion in 2010.

be sustained by country-size solar power facilities in deserts near the Mediterranean; and half a billion in North America could be sustained by Arizona-size facilities in the deserts of the United States and Mexico.

The impacts of such a global energy plan on socio-economic and ecological systems would be enormous. For example, the harnessing of 284 EJ of biofuels would require using all of the world's arable or cropland of about 27 million km^2 for biofuels, which is clearly infeasible. For comparison, the land requirements of today's global fossil fuel infrastructure are less than 30,000 km^2, which is about the size of Belgium (Smil, 2010b). MacKay's order-of-magnitude estimates provide an illustration of the existing technical limits and what, in principle, could technically be achieved with extraordinary political and financial commitments.

Wind requires very large areas of land and power infrastructure to provide power to urban areas

Technical limits of renewables are essentially based on spatial power densities of the technologies, their conversion efficiencies and their deployment potential. Solar power reaches spatial power densities that are two orders of magnitude higher than for wind and three orders of magnitude higher than for photosynthesis. Solar power can in principle reach power densities commensurate with demand densities in houses and some smaller cities. However, industry, high-rise buildings and megacities (in which the majority of the world's population will live) require even higher power densities than solar could offer. These were made available by fossil fuels and nuclear power which exhibit power densities that are higher than the demand of even high-rise buildings (Smil, 2010a). In contrast, wind power or biomass, with power densities less than 0.5 W/m^2, require very large areas of land and power infrastructure to provide power to urban areas. In fact, the energy demand footprint for England and large parts of Central Europe is larger than what it would be possible to provide with non-solar renewables (MacKay, 2008).

Economic limits and affordability receive the most attention in the global debate on the potential for low-carbon energy technologies. While it is correct that, aside from hydro (the potential of which is low but of high quality) and wind (which provides low-quality power), modern renewables continue to be significantly more expensive, economic limits are ultimately a lesser constraint, as they can be overcome with political will and special efforts.

In poorer countries, higher energy prices typically mean higher food prices and, potentially, increased poverty, social conflict and even revolts

Socio-political limits are difficult to overcome. In fact, most energy technology debates completely disregard associated socio-political limits. In pluralistic democracies, the "not-in-my-backyard" (NIMBY) attitude is a powerful factor. There are civil movements against pipelines, coal power plants, wind and solar power plants and, especially, nuclear power installation. Italy has phased out nuclear power and Germany, Sweden and Belgium took phase-out decisions at some point in time. An extreme example involves the licensing of the Konrad radioactive waste depository in Germany which took 25 years and included public consultations with almost 289,387 people who formally raised more than 1,000 issues. Similar NIMBY movements exist against power transmission lines and pipelines. In Germany, there is already a NIMBY movement against CCS long before its commercialization (Roehrl and Toth, 2009). In poorer countries, higher energy prices typically mean higher food prices and potentially lead to increased poverty, social conflict and even revolts.

The NEEDS project of EU quantified the full (direct and indirect) costs for energy technologies used in European countries. In addition, a multi-criteria decision analysis (MCDA) process was organized with decision makers who were given the full information/data on externalities. Decision makers' preference ratings of energy technologies differed greatly from both the direct and the full costs, reflecting different socio-political preferences

(Hirschberg and others, 2009). Such differences are a robust finding across MCDA carried out among utilities and policymakers, both in Europe and in China (Hirschberg and others, 2006; 2009). Such results do not bode well for full-cost pricing solutions to clean energy, because the binding constraint will be socio-political rather than techno-economic.

The proposal by the United Nations Environment Programme (UNEP), but also voiced among the G20, to phase out fossil fuel subsidies offers another example of the importance of socio-political limits. In 2009, most of global fossil fuel consumption subsidies amounting to $312 billion were in developing countries. Of this amount, oil products received $126 billion, natural gas $85 billion, fossil-fired electricity $95 billion and coal $6 billion. Fossil fuel consumption subsidies in countries with low levels of access to modern energy[11] amounted to $71 billion, and subsidies in these countries for residential use of kerosene, electricity and liquefied petroleum gas (LPG) (sometimes labelled "fuels for the poor") were less than $50 billion (International Energy Agency, 2010b). Thus, the problem of energy access is one mainly of distribution, not of absolute amounts of available resources. IEA estimates that universal access to modern energy services could be achieved by redistributing just 12 per cent of fossil fuel consumption subsidies in developing countries so as to deal with this problem in the poorest developing countries.

The problem of energy access is one mainly of distribution, not of absolute amounts of available resources

Limits to improving energy efficiency

As discussed above, energy-efficiency improvements when combined with limits on energy consumption have great potential to help achieve global targets. However, it is clear that there are a number of barriers to deployment and adoption of more efficient energy converters, as well as techno-economic limits to be considered. Solutions to overcoming the known barriers exist, but they require long-term commitment and a stable systemic approach by decision makers.

Technical limits to energy efficiency improvements must be taken into account. In 2005, the overall efficiency of global energy conversion (from primary energy to services) was about 11 per cent (Cullen and Allwood, 2010a). In other words, global primary energy demand could be reduced to only one ninth, while the same energy services were provided, if all energy conversion devices were operated at their *theoretical* maximum efficiency. In more practical terms, but still assuming an almost perfect world, global primary energy demand could be reduced by 73 per cent (or to less than one fourth), while the current level of energy services were provided, mainly through a shift to passive systems (Cullen, Allwood and Borgstein, 2011). This is in line with the popularized overall "factor 4" and "factor 5" improvements (von Weizsäcker, Lovins and Lovins, 1998).

If all energy conversion devices operated at their theoretical maximum efficiency, global energy demand could be reduced to one ninth of current levels

In 2005, primary-to-final exergy conversion efficiency was as high as 67 per cent (fuel losses, generation and distribution losses) but final-to-useful exergy conversion efficiency was only about 25 per cent (from conversion loss). Thus, 509 EJ primary exergy provided only about 86 EJ of useful exergy (in the form of motion, heat, cool/light/sound and other non-energy forms), while 128 EJ were lost in combustion, 173 EJ in heat transfer and 123 EJ through electric resistance, friction, fission and other fuel-related phenomena. In addition, a system loss is incurred in converting useful energy into final services ("service efficiency").[12]

11 Defined as countries with electrification rates of less than 90 per cent or with access to clean cooking facilities of less than 75 per cent.

12 Global energy-related services provided included passenger transport, freight transport, structure, thermal comfort, sustenance, hygiene, communication and illumination (Cullen and Allwood, 2010b).

It is important to consider the compounding of energy efficiencies across the chain. For example, if the conversion loss of each device in the chain had been reduced by only 1 per cent (and commensurate limits applied so as to avoid invoking the Jevons paradox), about 33 EJ, or 7 per cent of world primary energy of 475 EJ, could have been saved—an amount almost equal to the energy demand of China at the time. In this example, upstream (fuel transformation and electricity generation) efficiency gains would save only 5 EJ, whereas downstream (end-use conversion devices) efficiency gains would be much larger, at savings of 28 EJ (Cullen and Allwood, 2010b).

It is through efficiency improvements in electric heaters, diesel engines, electric motors, biomass burners, gas burners and factory equipment that the highest potential savings would be achieved

Cullen and Allwood (2010b) estimated and ranked the cumulative global conversion losses of end-use devices along their energy chain, relative to their theoretical ideal (table II.4). The table shows the highest potential savings that would be achieved through efficiency improvements of electric heaters, diesel engines, electric motors, biomass burners, gas burners and Otto engines. The smallest absolute gains were possible with light devices, electronic devices and aircraft engines. In other words, current policies focusing on energy-efficiency improvements in light bulbs, standby losses and aircraft engines are expected to add up to little on the global level.

Table II.4
End-use devices ranked by their cumulative global conversion losses along their individual flow paths

End-use device	*Efficiency (percentage)*	*Loss (EJ)*
Electric heater	7	54
Diesel engine	20	47
Electric motor	17	46
Biomass burner	6	46
Gas burner	12	41
Otto engine	12	36
Cooler	2	33
Coal burner	17	26
Oil burner	14	24
Heat exchanger	2	20
Light device	4	17
Electronic	2	16
Aircraft engine	25	8
Other engine	18	8

Source: Cullen and Allwood (2010b).

Policy options and recommendations

Energy technology innovation matters. It concerns everyone and is often highly politicized. Energy technology policy needs to be comprehensive and supported by industrial policy, especially in the context of support at the market formation phase of technology life cycles (chap. V). Most importantly, global and national energy policy is also development policy and thus must demonstrate special consideration of the poor. Governments need to devise institutional designs that ensure a science-based reality check of energy technology policies. A wide range of policy instruments are available, including economic instruments, regulatory measures and cooperation (table II.5). Optimal policy packages

Table II.5
Examples of public policy measures for inducing the sustainable energy transformation

Type	*Category*	*Examples*
Economic Instruments	Subsidies	Gasoline subsidies Feed-in tariffs Fiscal incentives Direct subsidies to R&D Loan softening/guarantees Subsidies for public transport for the poor
	Taxes	Gasoline taxes R&D tax credits Carbon taxes
	Permit trading	Carbon trading market Renewable energy credit trading
	Public procurement/ investments	Green procurement Public investment in R&D infrastructure Government funding of demonstration projects Government-sponsored R&D, national laboratories National/State-funded or -run venture capitalism Public investment in education and training Government investments in science and technology parks
Command-and-control measures	Standards and regulations	Standards for biofuel blending Energy-efficiency standards Renewable energy obligations Cooking stove standards
	Goals and targets	Sectoral energy intensity targets Greenhouse gas mitigation targets Energy access targets
Cooperation	Domestic	Promotion of collaborative RD&D Public-private partnerships and knowledge exchange
	International	Official development assistance (ODA) for energy access and clean technologies Trade preferences for specific technology clusters Bilateral and plurilateral agreements on technology cooperation

Source: World Business Council for Sustainable Development (2011).

depend strongly on a country's institutions, development stage, resource endowments and socio-political preferences, and will change over time. In-depth analysis needs to be included in the process of designing policy packages, while simplified prescriptions can be counter-productive. However, insights from past experience suggest broad guiding principles and performance targets which should guide the analysis (Grübler and others, forthcoming; Wilson and Grübler, 2010).

The need for comprehensive, strategic and system approaches

Comprehensive, strategic and systems approaches are needed (see chap. V for further details). The choice of individual technology-related policy instruments needs to be tailored to technology and national and local circumstances. Ignoring the systemic characteristics of technological change often leads to a partial view and fragmented or even contradictory policies. Simplistic approaches need to be avoided, as they are commonly based on

Ignoring the systemic characteristics of technological change often leads to a partial view and fragmented or even contradictory policies

myths rather than factual evidence. The co-benefits of comprehensive approaches can be substantial. For example, the costs of halving premature deaths due to air pollution by 2030 and of ensuring energy security could be reduced to one fourth, if these goals were pursued jointly with ambitious greenhouse gas reduction measures. Bringing universal access to electricity and modern cooking fuels by 2030 would not be in conflict with the other objectives (Riahi and others, forthcoming).

Learn from but be aware of the inevitable discontinuities of the historical past

Policy-induced scaling up and deployment of new technologies without lengthy formative periods of experimentation and testing could lead to additional risks and might lock in inferior technologies (Wilson, forthcoming). Historically, performance and quality advantages of new energy technologies compared with the lower energy quality (intermittency and low power density) of modern renewable energy technologies, led to their early adoption among price-insensitive consumers. Fossil fuel resource constraints together with externality pricing might make renewables more cost-competitive, but competing land use will be a constraint on the large-scale deployment of renewables. Also, overcoming vested interests is essential, in view of the fact that, historically, it is political efforts and public infrastructure investment that have set innovator countries apart from laggards (Moe, 2010).

Manage uncertainties with portfolio diversification, scenario analysis, and a balanced mix of technology-neutral and technology-banded approaches

Picking technological winners ex ante should be avoided, while developing broad technology portfolios should be promoted. Doing this will provide a hedge against the risks of inherently uncertain outcomes of technological innovation. Failures vastly outnumber successes in both the private and public sectors. Sufficient time and resources need to be committed for experimentation before scaling up, so as to prevent any premature locking in of suboptimal technologies and clusters (van den Bergh and others, 2007).

Technology portfolios should represent the whole energy system and consider all innovation stages

Technology portfolios should represent the whole energy system and consider all innovation stages, so as to keep options open, but should avoid large-scale transfer of technology risks to the public sector. It should also be noted that less capital-intensive, smaller-scale (for example, granular) technologies tend to be associated with lower overall risk. Scenario analysis can be used for risk hedging through identification of "robust" technology portfolios. In this context, a careful balancing of technology-neutral policies (for example, carbon taxes) and technology-banded ones (for example, feed-in tariffs), as well as short- and long-term policy targets, should be considered (Sandén and Azar, 2005).

Pursue policies that promote high-performance innovations in niche markets

Policies designed to create market niches based on superior-quality technologies should be prioritized in order to shield them from full commercial competition during the initial development stages when experience is gained (Schot and Geels, 2008). At present, there are only a few evident niches in which cost-insensitive end-users might be persuaded to pay for environmental public goods.[13] Historical evidence supports the market niche approach and illustrates the practical problems associated with efforts to "buy down" the learning curve in order to reduce unit costs. New technologies may not need subsidies if they exhibit high performance despite much higher costs.

Pursue innovation policy that is stable, credible, aligned and well timed

Stable and consistent expectations about the direction and shape of the innovation system, in contrast with existing practices which are mostly characterized by stop-go policies, are necessary if innovation actors are to commit resources (Bosetti and Victor, 2011). Innovation policies need to be aligned, which requires coherent support throughout the technology life cycle, but misalignment appears to be the norm in most countries.[14] Dynamic technology standards can be effective, as evidenced by the Japanese Top Runner Programme for energy-efficient appliances. It is important to choose realistic goals for technology programmes and to manage the expectations of innovation system actors, since programmes have often been discredited in the past simply because they did not achieve their irrationally exuberant goals. Most importantly, policies should be avoided that compress the formative phase unduly and support premature scaling up, as does the current approach taken in promoting CCS, for instance.

Policies should be avoided that compress the formative phase unduly and support premature scaling up

Innovations in end-use technologies are important

Public innovation expenditures for highly energy efficient end-use technologies need to be increased. Support for such technologies in the past has proved both cost-effective and successful, thereby generating high social returns on investment (Fri, 2003). Much greater emphasis needs to be put globally on improving end-use energy efficiency, complemented by behavioural change and limits imposed on energy, land, water and materials use.

A global "Top Runner Programme"

A global programme that follows the rationale of Japan's Top Runner Programme should be considered. Such a programme would promote cooperation among countries, communities and individuals so as to achieve lower primary energy use and lower greenhouse gas emissions. Those with the best performance in groups with similar characteristics would successively set the standard for the next phase which laggards will aim to achieve. For example, Japan might be the top runner that sets the standards and targets to be achieved by other technologically advanced economies in terms of end-use energy efficiency. Other examples might include business people responsible for highly energy-intensive patterns of consumption of transport services, or high-income house-owners.

Furthermore, the programme might also strive to achieve individual primary energy use and greenhouse gas emissions targets. Given the already indicated technological limits to fast-tracking the sustainable energy transformation, per capita caps on energy use and emissions may be needed to ease the challenge. The above analysis suggested that

A reasonable primary energy use limit could provide powerful incentives to increase energy efficiency

13 Some examples are: no fuel inputs (solar PV in remote off-grid applications), quiet operation (nuclear power in submarines) and storage capacity (fuel cells for grid backup).

14 For example, support for low-carbon technologies is undermined by fossil fuel subsidies and efficiency improvements in transport are swamped by higher demand.

a limit of 70 GJ per capita would seem a reasonable long-term target to be achieved by 2050. This limit would be similar to the figure for the present per capita primary energy use in China and that for the world average (figure II.8). It should be noted, however, that the suggestion is for a limit on primary energy (not final energy), which is most relevant for the environmental impact. In fact, a reasonable primary energy use limit could provide powerful incentives to increase energy efficiency and could ensure the continued provision of more and better energy end-use services despite lower primary energy use.

In environmentally conscious Western European societies, such as that of Denmark, primary energy use is at about 150 GJ per capita, which could be brought down to the 70 GJ target with increased energy efficiency combined with measures to minimize the rebound effect. This would be much more of a challenge for the United States, which currently uses 340 GJ per capita. Such a limit would still allow ample space for energy demand growth in poor countries, such as India, with a per capita use of only 15 GJ. The target of 70 GJ per capita primary energy use would ideally be applied as averages not to countries, but to individuals, in line with the principle of individual fairness. Energy use within countries is highly uneven, with the world's richest 500 million people (7 per cent of the world population)—who live in both developed and developing countries—using more than half of all primary energy (Pacala, 2007). Burden-sharing among countries based on the principle of individual fairness would differ significantly from sharing based on countries' averages, except for the poorest countries which would have almost no commitment either way.

Figure II.8
National greenhouse gas emissions per capita versus power use per capita, selected countries and areas

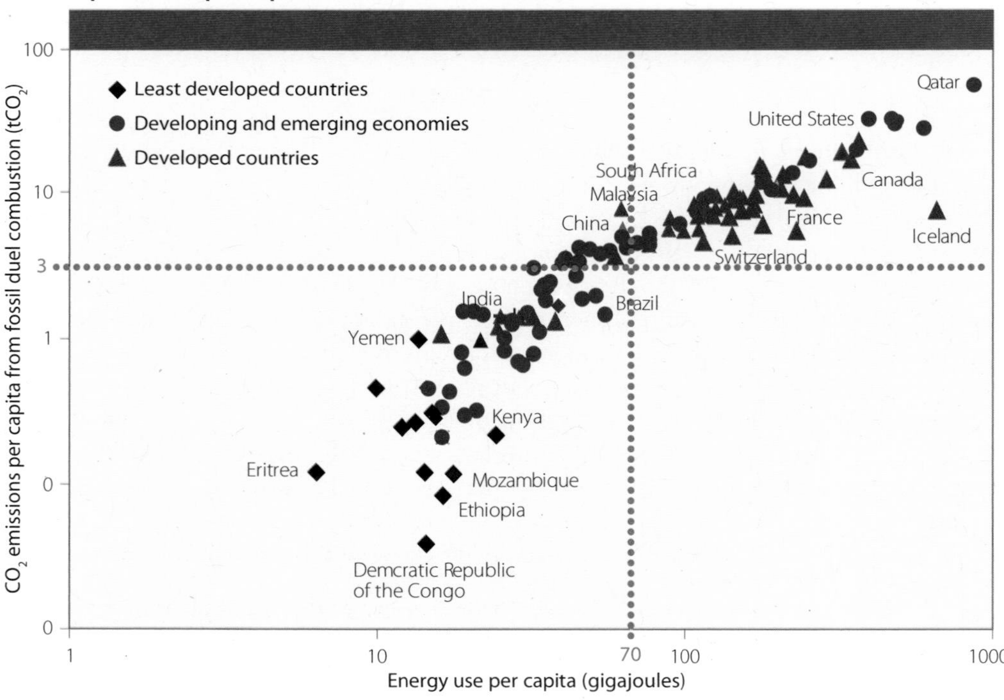

Source: World Bank, World Development Indicators, 2011. Available from http://data.worldbank.org/data-catalog/world-development-indicators.

Higher energy efficiency and lower primary energy use would take much of the pressure imposed by the imperative of rapid decarbonization off highly energy-intensive economies. Indeed, this chapter has provided ample evidence for why it might prove impossible to achieve the desired pace of global energy transition towards low-carbon and renewable energy without limits on primary energy use. A recent study on how to achieve a 100 per cent renewable energy system in Denmark by 2050 concluded that such an envisioned outcome was realistically achievable only if primary energy use was halved to 70 GJ per capita (Lund and Mathiesen, 2009).

Higher energy efficiency and lower primary energy use would take much of the pressure imposed by the imperative of rapid decarbonization off highly energy-intensive economies

Closely associated with the target of energy use per capita would be a *cap on individual CO_2 emissions of 3 tCO_2* to be achieved by 2050.[15] Such a limit would again be ideally based on individual fairness, rather than fairness across nations. From 2007 to 2030, such limits would then touch only people with annual earnings of more than $40,000 per capita (in PPP terms). For comparison, in 2007, the figure for average energy-related CO_2 emissions per capita[16] of the 60 poorest countries and areas was less than 1 tCO_2. It was 1.4 tCO_2 in Viet Nam and India; 1.9 tCO_2 in Brazil and Indonesia; 2.3 tCO_2 in Egypt; 3 tCO_2 in Mauritius and French Polynesia; 5 tCO_2 in Switzerland, Sweden and China; 6 tCO_2 in France and Venezuela (Bolivarian Republic of); 7.7 tCO_2 in Iceland and Italy; 10 tCO_2 in Germany, Japan, the Russian Federation and the Republic of Korea; 19 tCO_2 in the United States and Australia; 20 tCO_2 in Brunei Darussalam; and as much as 55 tCO_2 in Qatar (United States Department of Energy, Carbon Dioxide Information Analysis Center, 2011).

Among major global scenarios, the Global Energy Assessment mix scenario appears to be roughly in line with the focus and targets proposed here. The scenario foresees cumulative global energy-related investments of $65 trillion between 2010 and 2050, or about $1.6 trillion per year. About $23 trillion of this amount would be needed for improving efficiencies, $12 trillion for smart grids (transmission and distribution), $8 trillion for renewable electricity and a combined amount of $4 trillion for fossil-fired and nuclear power plants. An amount of $13 trillion would be needed for fossil fuel extraction and $2 trillion for biomass-related technology deployment (Riahi and others, forthcoming).

Global energy-related investments of $65 trillion between 2010 and 2050, or about $1.6 trillion per year, are required

"Reality checks" through independent centres for energy systems analysis

Conceptually, policymakers could mandate technology-neutral performance targets and avoid favouring any specific technologies. They would still become involved in all phases of the innovation cycle, in order to ensure coherence and continuity, but would focus resources on research, development and possibly demonstration. In practice, most countries are already engaging in picking winners, directly or indirectly. In late industrializing countries which can draw on existing technologies, current information about these technologies will reduce the uncertainties associated with investing in specific sectors. This makes it particularly important that technologies-related information be accessible at reasonable cost to developing countries and not unduly restrained by private intellectual

In practice, most countries are already engaging in picking winners, directly or indirectly

15 Pacala (2007) suggests that a "fair" personal CO_2 emissions limit be brought down to 3.6 tCO_2 over the next 50 years, in order to reach stabilization of concentrations at 450 ppmv. However, considering the uncertainty surrounding climate change projections and applying the precautionary principle, setting the target at 3 tCO_2 per capita by 2050 would ensure a sufficiently high probability that the stabilization target could be achieved (Jonas and others, 2010).

16 All emission estimates are production-based. Only the United Kingdom has useful numbers of greenhouse gas emissions based on consumption.

property or monopolistic practices. Even in advanced countries, the practice of picking winning technology is perceived to be unavoidable. The important questions would be who should do the picking—and how. In general, policymakers should focus, preferably, on setting broad political goals, rather than on detailed technology-specific issues. Strategic long-term planning is essential in order to coordinate actions by many different actors in different parts of the complex, interdependent energy system. Markets can help coordinate to some extent, but no market has ever been devised that could efficiently coordinate the evolution of the global energy system towards achievement of global policy objectives.

In the majority of developing countries, Governments continue directly or indirectly to "run" the energy system (apart from some regulated independent power production). Energy and economic planning units typically provide in-depth assessments of government plans and targets. While, in theory, energy plans would be based on their independent assessments, in practice, energy planning units are not always independent and assessments are either tweaked to support political decisions or sidelined.

Energy assessments undertaken by academics are not necessarily independent

In countries with liberalized energy markets, Governments have also picked winners directly (for example, through feed-in tariffs or renewable energy standards) or indirectly (for example, through institutional design). These countries typically abolished planning units a long time ago, with analysis being carried out by academic institutions and, more recently, by regulators. However, in-depth energy assessments undertaken by academics are not necessarily independent, since they are typically funded through extrabudgetary resources provided by Governments, professional associations or lobbyists. Further, regulators are (typically) responsible only for subcomponents of the energy system (for example, electricity markets) and have strategic interests of their own.

Hence, Governments, regardless of the level of market liberalization and development stage, might consider the creation of *energy system analysis centres with full independence from politics* which ensure reality checks and alignment of policies and initiatives. These centres would also promote global coherence and compatibility with green growth and sustainable development aspirations, through participation in a global network. A global hierarchy of eco-efficiency targets might be a simple means of systematizing coordination.

One size does not fit all

By their very nature, energy policy interventions will induce structural economic change. Energy policies also tend to have strong distributive effects, benefiting some industries and household groups more than others. The degree and nature of the required structural change related to a sustainable energy transformation will also vary from country to country. The distributive impacts will also differ accordingly.

Poorer and more vulnerable countries require enhanced support from the international community

The sustainable energy transition offers significant economic opportunities for both developed and emerging developing countries, but poses additional development challenges for the poorer and more vulnerable countries, which would require enhanced support from the international community.

Table II.6 provides a highly stylized presentation of the potential impacts for groups of countries, classified for present purposes by income level and status as net fuel exporters or importers. Clearly, the global and national distributive effects will depend on a range of factors such as the degree of dependence on fossil fuel imports and exports, the expected economic growth impacts of local technology capacity development,

Table II.6
Stylized potential impacts of sustainable energy transitions, by groups of countries

Driver	*Country group*					
	Low-income		*Middle-income*		*High-income*	
	Oil/commodities exporters	*Oil/commodities importers*	*Oil/commodities exporters*	*Oil/commodities importers*	*Oil/commodities exporters*	*Oil/commodities importers*
Energy import and export bills (oil price and quantities)	No significant change expected, since mainly medium-cost producers	Lower import bills	No significant change expected, since mainly medium-cost producers	Lower import bills	Export revenues reduced for high-cost producers (for example, in the North Sea area, Canada), and no significant change for low-cost producers (Middle East)	Lower import bills
Economic growth impacts of development of local technology capacities	Possibility of using recent oil/ commodity gains to diversify into green technologies. Huge challenge of competing with emerging economies	Serious challenge in any case	Potential for leadership in "green" technologies development and manufacturing, due to rapidly growing markets, relatively low costs		Challenge associated with opportunity to diversify into green technology niches linked to existing oil infrastructure; for example, in places with high isolation; and develop and deploy solar reactors for the purpose of delivering synthetic gasoline	Continued challenges of deindustrialization and offshoring independent of transition. Can leverage research to maintain technological leadership
Manufacturing, industrialization and deindustria-lization (for example, offshoring)						
Policy-related markets (for example, carbon trading)	Depends on details of market energy					
Poverty, employment and social impacts	Intercountry distribution depends on many factors (for example, climate vulnerability). Intracountry distribution depends on national socio-economic policies and measures					
Unequal distribution of pollution impacts						

Source: UN/DESA.

and opportunities for countries to attract manufacturing of new technologies in efforts to industrialize. Estimating the welfare and distributive effects of those challenges and opportunities is not the purpose of this *Survey*. Yet, such effects will need to be fully considered when designing global and national policies.

The fact that the major emerging economies have large markets for energy technologies provides an opportunity to develop local technology capacities and upgrade industrial capabilities, as is the case for China. Oil-rich countries with high insolation would also have a number of opportunities to diversify their industrial base and leverage the existing oil infrastructure (for example, through manufacturing and deployment of

The fact that major emerging economies have large markets for energy technologies provides an opportunity to develop local technology capacities and upgrade industrial capabilities

solar reactors in desert areas near existing oil facilities, with the reactors transforming CO_2 and water into gasoline).

At present, those opportunities would be considerably greater in the case of innovation of new technologies, since the market and intellectual property position in mature technologies is dominated by firms in the developed world.

The sustainable energy transition poses challenges to the poorest countries which face greater obstacles (including small market size) in developing local technology capacities. Industrialized economies would continue to face the challenges of deindustrialization and offshoring, trends which are independent of the sustainable energy transitions, and their main opportunities will be in leveraging their highly developed research capacities so as to maintain technological leadership in technology-intensive market segments.

Chapter III
Towards a truly green revolution for food security

Summary

- The recent food crises have revealed deep structural problems in the global food system and the need to increase resources and foster innovation in agriculture so as to accelerate food production. Food production will have to increase between 70 and 100 per cent by 2050 to feed a growing population. With current agricultural technology, practices and land-use patterns, this cannot be achieved without further contributing to greenhouse gas emissions, water pollution and land degradation. The consequent environmental damage will undermine food productivity growth.
- Achieving sustainable food security would provide a long-term solution to the challenge of combating hunger and malnutrition, mitigating food price volatility and protecting the environment. It will require, however, a radical change in existing policies—a change that would result in a strengthening of currently fragmented systems of innovation and an increase in resources for agricultural development and sustainable resource management.
- The main challenge is to improve incentives so that they promote and lead to the development of sustainable agriculture by small farm holders. Evidence has shown that, for most crops, the optimal farm is small in scale and it is at this level that most gains in terms of both sustainable productivity increases and rural poverty reduction can be achieved.

The global food crisis

The recent global food crises laid bare long-term threats to food security

The increase in prices underlying the 2007-2008 food crisis and the new food price spikes in 2011 have exposed the presence of serious threats to the sustainability of the global food system and its capacity to provide adequate and affordable access to food. Meeting the challenge of expanding food production to feed the world population over the coming decades requires a major transformation in agriculture. The so-called green revolution of the 1960s and 1970s helped boost agricultural productivity worldwide, but did not conduce to a sustainable management of natural resources, nor to food security for many of the world's poor. The world now needs a truly green revolution in agriculture—one conducive to the kind of technological innovation that aims to radically improve the productivity of small farm holdings through environmentally sustainable natural resource management embedded in broader developmental agricultural support measures.

Persistent food insecurity

Almost 1 billion people are undernourished worldwide...

The dramatic food price increases in 2007–2008 and the ensuing economic crisis saw the global number of undernourished people surpass 1 billion in 2009, signalling a threat to world economic, social and political stability. Although the number and proportion of hungry people, particularly in Asia, declined in 2010, amid signs of economic recovery, those figures remain above pre-crisis levels, leaving 925 million people undernourished (Food and Agriculture Organization of the United Nations, 2010a) (figure III.1).

... with two thirds living in seven countries

The World Food Summit Plan of Action (Food and Agriculture Organization of the United Nations, 1996) considered food security as existing "when all people, at all times, have physical and economic access to sufficient, safe and nutritious food to meet their dietary needs and food preferences for an active and healthy life" (para. 1). Based on this definition, undernourishment is thus a key indicator of food insecurity. The overwhelming majority (98 per cent) of the world's undernourished people live in developing countries, with two thirds of them concentrated in seven nations (Bangladesh, China, the Democratic Republic of the Congo, Ethiopia, India, Indonesia and Pakistan). Most hungry people (578 million) reside in Asia and the Pacific, although the highest share (30 per cent, or 239 million people) are found in sub-Saharan Africa (figure III.2).

While progress varies from country to country, developing countries as a group have not moved closer to the food security targets established at the World Food Summit: the number of undernourished people increased by almost 10 per cent between 1990–1992 and 2010.[1]

Figure III.1
Undernourished population worldwide, 1969-2010

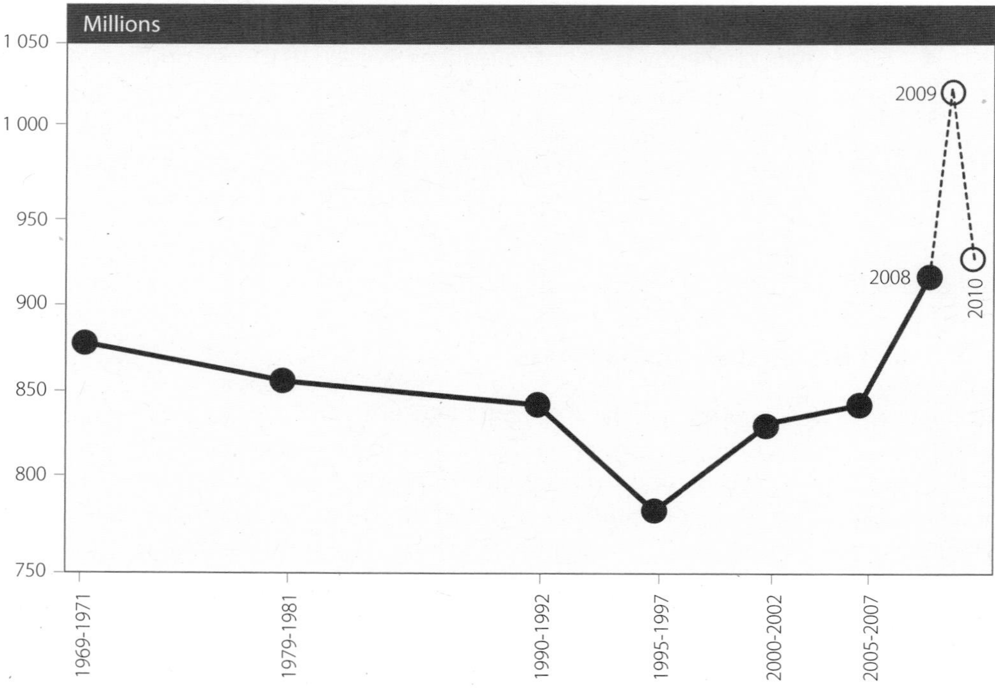

Source: Food and Agriculture Organization of the United Nations (2010a).
Note: Undernourishment exists when caloric intake is below the minimum dietary energy requirement, which is the amount of energy needed for light activity and a minimum acceptable weight for attained height. It varies by country and over time depending on the gender and age structure of the population.

1 Commitments agreed to at the 1996 World Food Summit included the call for at least halving the number of undernourished people in the world by the year 2015 (Food and Agriculture Organization of the United Nations, 1996, para. 7).

Figure III.2
Undernourished population by region, 2010

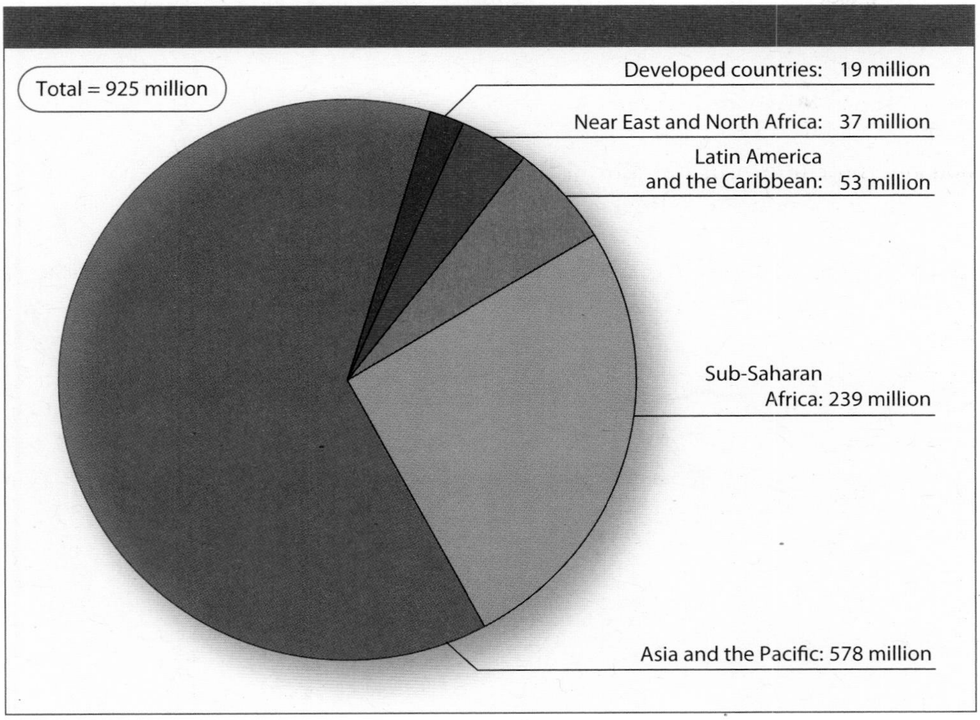

Source: Food and Agriculture Organization of the United Nations (2010a).

The 22 countries regarded as facing a "protracted food security crisis" are home to over 165 million undernourished people (about 20 per cent of the world's total). The proportion of undernourished people ranges from under 15 per cent in Côte d'Ivoire to almost 70 per cent in the Democratic Republic of the Congo (Food and Agriculture Organization of the United Nations, 2010a).

Impact of the 2007-2008 world food price spike

Following the 2007-2008 food price crisis, the number of people living in poverty increased by an estimated 100 million

World food prices increased dramatically in the period 2007–2008. Prices for corn, wheat and rice more than doubled between 2006 and 2008. While prices declined in late 2008, food prices have since rebounded, attaining new record highs in February 2011 (figure III.3). Despite conflicting evidence, it would appear that recent price rises have also been accompanied by higher volatility, which increases uncertainty, thereby hindering investment in human and physical capital, technology and innovation (Food and Agriculture Organization of the United Nations, 2009a) (figure III.4).

Global food prices have rebounded to record highs in 2011

The severe impact of the 2007-2008 food crisis on living conditions was attested by the riots that broke out in over 30 countries. Evidence shows that 41 countries lost between 3 and 10 per cent of gross domestic product (GDP) to rising energy and commodity prices in 2007-2008 (World Bank, 2008a). Increasing food prices have had a particularly negative impact on the poor who spend 50-70 per cent of their income on food (von Braun, 2009). Higher food prices are estimated to have pushed a further 100 million people into poverty in 2007-2008 and nearly 50 million in the latter half of 2010 (World Bank, 2008b; 2011).

Figure III.3
Real food price indices, annual averages, 1990-2011

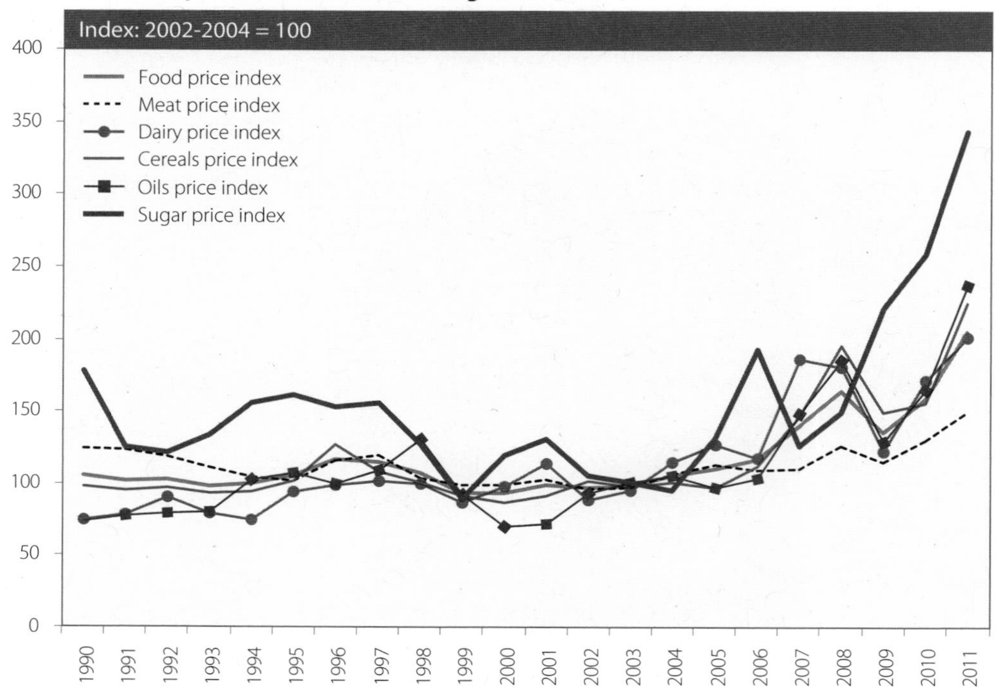

Source: Food and Agriculture Organization of the United Nations. Available from http://www.fao.org/worldfoodsituation/wfs-home/foodpricesindex/en.

Figure III.4
Annualized volatility of nominal cereal prices, 1957-2009

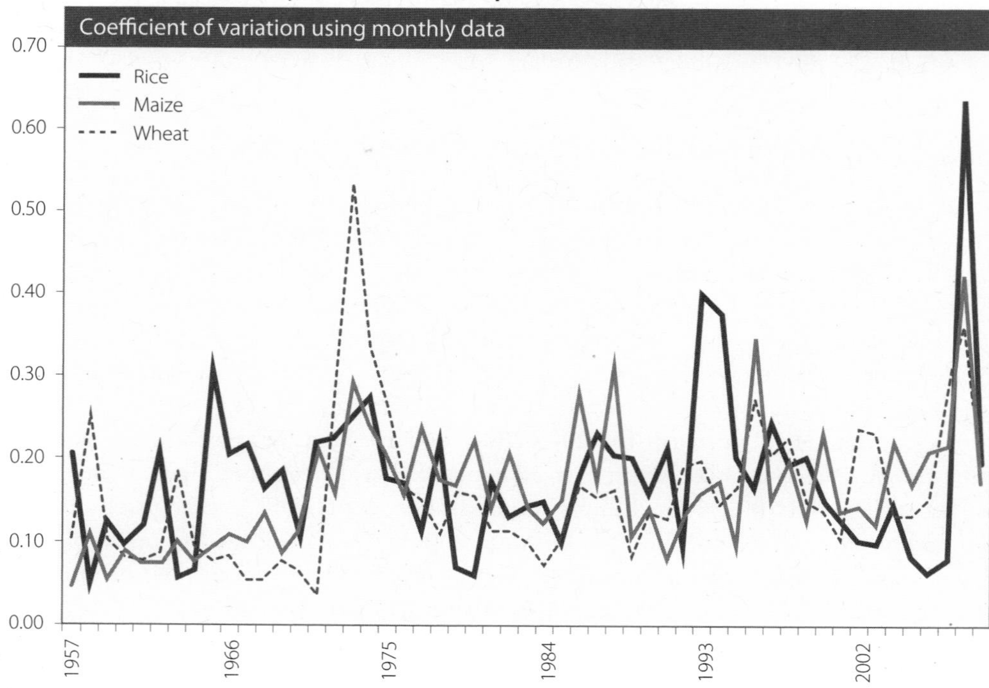

Sources: Organization for Economic Cooperation and Development and Food and Agriculture Organization of the United Nations (2010).

The nature of the impact of price rises depends on countries' economic structure, sectoral linkages, trade position, poverty levels and diet diversification (Rapsomanikis, 2009). Although higher prices provide incentives to increase production, many small farm holders are unable to respond owing to lack of access to finance, agricultural inputs, markets and technology (United Nations, 2008a). Nevertheless, in developing countries with a large share of net producing households, high food prices boost demand for rural labour and incomes (Chant, McDonald and Verschoor, 2008). While countries like India, China and Indonesia have limited the domestic impact of higher international food prices through export restrictions on rice and other crops (Timmer, 2009), evidence from the latest price spikes (2010-2011) points to greater convergence of trends in national and international food prices, which is a cause for concern, given the recent steep upward trajectory of global prices (Ortiz, Chai and Cummins, 2011).

Causes of the food price crisis

The world food crisis was the result of overlapping demand and supply crises (in 2006-2008, for example, world grain production fell short of consumption (figure III.5)).

Demand-side causes

Over the past 20 years, continued global population growth, principally in developing countries (see figure O.1(a)), and rising incomes, particularly in South-East Asia, have not only raised food consumption, but also altered dietary patterns, as reflected in a greater demand for animal protein (and hence food grains). Meat consumption in China and

Food prices have been pushed up by growing and wealthier populations, commodity speculation, trade policies and United States dollar depreciation

Figure III.5
World production and consumption of grains, 1990-2011

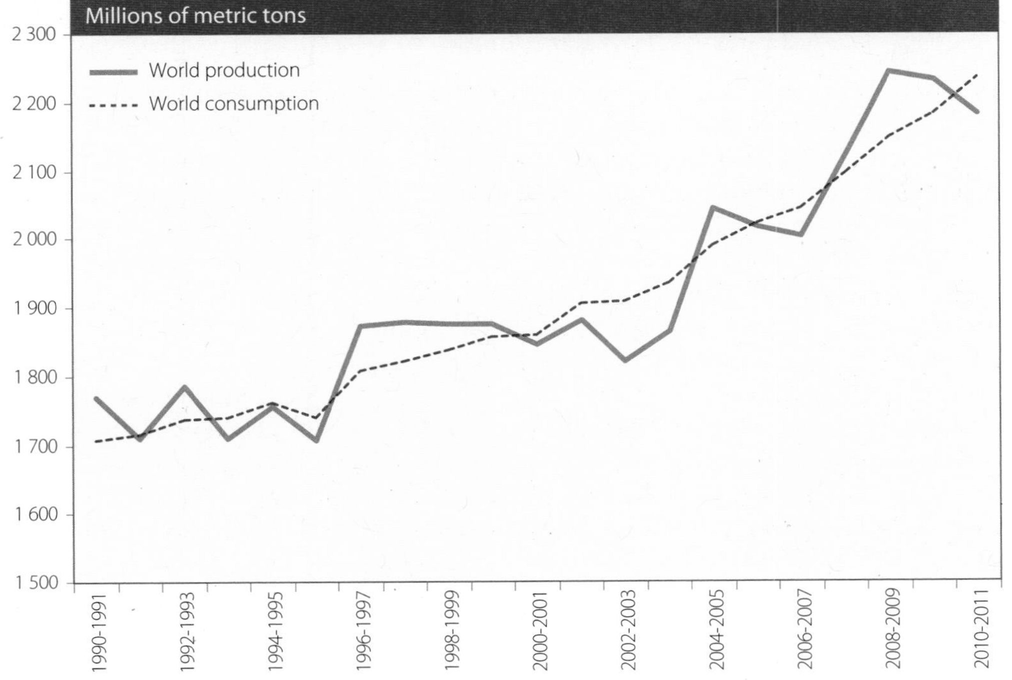

Source: United States Department of Agriculture (USDA) Production, Supply and Distribution (PSD) database.

India rose by about 25 per cent and 140 per cent, respectively, in the last decade (HM Government, 2010).

The significant depreciation of the United States dollar in 2008, in which most food commodity prices are denominated, also contributed to higher prices. The Food and Agriculture Organization of the United Nations (FAO) estimates that for each 1 per cent depreciation of the United States dollar, agricultural commodity prices increase by between 0.3 and 0.8 per cent (Sarris, 2009). In addition, attempts by Governments to insulate domestic markets from escalating international food prices and prospective shortages through trade protection measures further increased the level and volatility of global prices. The persistence of high and volatile food prices has also been attributed to a notable recent increase in financial speculation in commodity futures markets (Gilbert, 2008; United Nations, 2011).

Supply-side causes

Competition for land, climatic conditions, biofuel policies, high energy prices and structural problems in agricultural production and investment were supply-side factors

Land available for food cultivation has been shrinking owing to degradation and competition for other uses such as urban development and production of non-food crops. Deforestation is mainly driven by competition for agricultural land, be it for subsistence farming in Africa or for establishment of large-scale cattle and soy plantations in Latin America (Stern, 2007). In addition, increased purchases of farmland by foreign investors has resulted in the favouring of exports over domestic food production. An estimated 56 million hectares of land in developing countries were bought by foreigners in 2009, a 10-fold rise from the previous decade, with two thirds of these sometimes controversial "land grabs" occurring in Africa (Deininger and others, 2010).

Adverse weather conditions in 2005-2006, including drought in Australia, possibly related to climate change, resulted in poor harvests and exerted upward pressure on prices (Food and Agriculture Organization of the United Nations, 2008). Similarly, harmful climatic phenomena in the Russian Federation and Ukraine, particularly the recent heatwaves, are thought to be the main drivers behind the most recent international price spikes (World Bank, 2011).

Perhaps the most important contributing factor to the 2008-2009 food crisis, albeit still subject to debate, is the diversion of food commodities to biofuel production (Mitchell, 2008; Food and Agriculture Organization of the United Nations, 2009a). In 2007, three quarters of the annual increase in world maize use was absorbed by ethanol plants alone, accounting for 12 per cent of total maize production. In the United States, one third of the domestic use of corn supply was for ethanol production and the biodiesel sector accounted for about 60 per cent of the rapeseed oil output of the European Union (EU) (Food and Agriculture Organization of the United Nations, 2009a). United States and EU biofuel production has been supported by State subsidies and tariffs, which cost developed countries $11 billion in 2007 (United Nations, 2008a). Studies that attempt to explain the impact of biofuel demand on world food prices exhibit marked differences in their findings, which suggest that demand could explain anywhere from 15 to 70 per cent of the 2007-2008 food price hike. Direct competition between food and fuel has led to calls for support for a new generation of biofuels that do not compete with food (Vos, 2009).

In 2007-2008, oil price rises positively impacted the level and volatility of food prices by raising fertilizer, freight and other food production costs, as well as by creating incentives for biofuel expansion (United Nations, 2008a).

A number of structural impediments to the expansion of food production have been identified, including declining agricultural investment, partly owing to lower public investments and earlier low food prices (United Nations, 2008a). The share of total overseas development assistance (ODA) allocated to agriculture fell from a peak of 18 per cent in 1978 to 4 per cent in 2009, with ODA earmarked for agriculture having decreased significantly in the 1990s (United Nations, 2008a) (see figure III.6). In this context, the International Monetary Fund (IMF), the World Bank and other institutions have been criticized for providing foreign aid conditional on the implementation of policies (such as abolishing fertilizer subsidies and favouring cash crops) that have undermined food self-sufficiency and raised imports (Stiglitz, 2002). At the same time, donor nations have continued to engage in provision of distortionary agricultural subsidies to producers and consumers (amounting to $376 billion of Organization for Economic Cooperation and Development (OECD) expenditure in 2008), undermining the ability of farmers in developing countries to compete (United Nations, 2010b).

The world faces a proliferation of instances of localized chronic food insecurity

The intertwined factors examined above contributed to the global food crisis. In this context, the fact that the number of undernourished people worldwide (1 billion) is matched by the number of those who are overfed and obese, and that hunger in the world has continued to increase in recent decades despite continuous agricultural productivity growth and, generally, low food prices, calls poignantly into question the effectiveness of the global food distribution system (Godfray and others, 2010a). Yet, between 75 and 90 per cent of staple foods are produced and consumed locally, which suggests that the world faces the prospect of a proliferation of cases of localized chronic food insecurity (United Nations Conference on Trade and Development, 2010).

Figure III.6
Total volume and share of ODA allocated to agriculture, 1995-2009

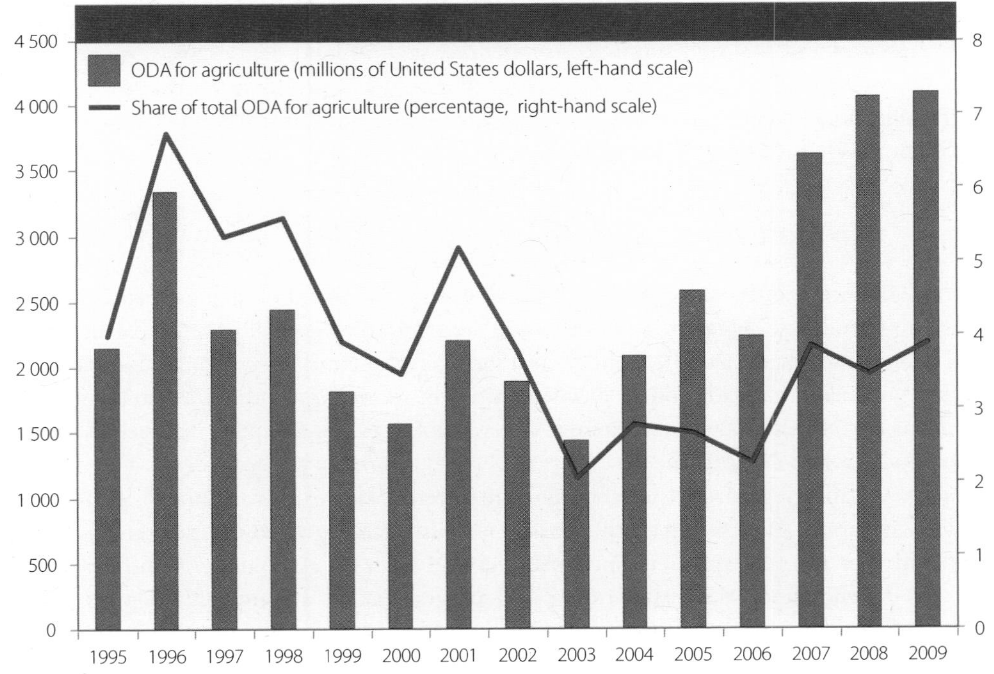

Source: OECD StatExtracts.

Policy responses to the food crisis

Escalating global food prices prompted an international commitment of $20 billion in external assistance

The food price surge induced prompt policy reactions at both national and international levels. For instance, at the G8 Summit in Hokkaido Toyako in 2008, donors pledged to provide $10 billion in ODA to fight hunger (Group of 8, 2008); and, at the G8 Summit in L'Aquila, Italy, in 2009, $20 billion over three years to address food insecurity in a sustainable manner (Group of 8, 2009).

At the national level, countries responded differently, with a wide range of mainly short-term policy measures including import tariff reductions, price controls, export restrictions, stock reductions, food programmes, new biofuel policies, and commodity futures markets regulation (Organization for Economic Cooperation and Development and Food and Agriculture Organization of the United Nations, 2010). A study evaluating such responses in 10 emerging economies revealed the importance of providing targeted safety nets for the poor as emergency responses to food shortfalls. While trade protection and building food inventories may enhance national food availability in the short run, such measures may at the same time prove to be costly in terms of expenditure and contribute to keeping food prices high by restricting food supply in international markets (Jones and Kwiecinski, 2010).

Unsustainable natural resource management as a threat to both food security and the environment

Technology in use in agriculture has led to adverse environmental outcomes ...

A range of fundamental natural resources (such as land, water, air and biodiversity) provide the indispensable base for the production of essential goods and services upon which human survival depends. During the past half-century, shrinkage in the availability of natural resources occurred more rapidly than in any comparable time in history, driven in great part by human intervention in the environment in the form of agricultural activities. Although vital to the production and supply of food, feed and fuel, these have had negative environmental and socio-economic consequences, such as land degradation, water pollution, climate change, biodiversity loss, reduced long-term productive capacity, poverty, migration and ill health (International Assessment of Agricultural Knowledge, Science and Technology for Development, 2009).

Environmental impacts

... including severe depletion of natural resources

Land degradation is among the world's greatest environmental challenges, with the potential to destabilize societies, endanger food security and increase poverty (Millennium Ecosystem Assessment, 2005). Defined as a long-term decline in ecosystem function and productivity, land degradation is driven mainly by poor land and water management, including over-cultivation, overgrazing, deforestation and inadequate irrigation (Berry, Olson and Campbell, 2003).

Almost half of the world's surface has been degraded

Land degradation is increasing, in severity and extent, in many parts of the world, with about 40 per cent of the world's land surface degraded (25 per cent has been degraded over the past quarter-century alone) and with an estimated 1.5 billion people directly dependent on agriculture (Bai and others, 2008). Figure III.7 depicts global change in land productivity (in terms of carbon dioxide (CO_2) fixation) over the period

Figure III.7
Global change in net primary productivity, 1981-2003

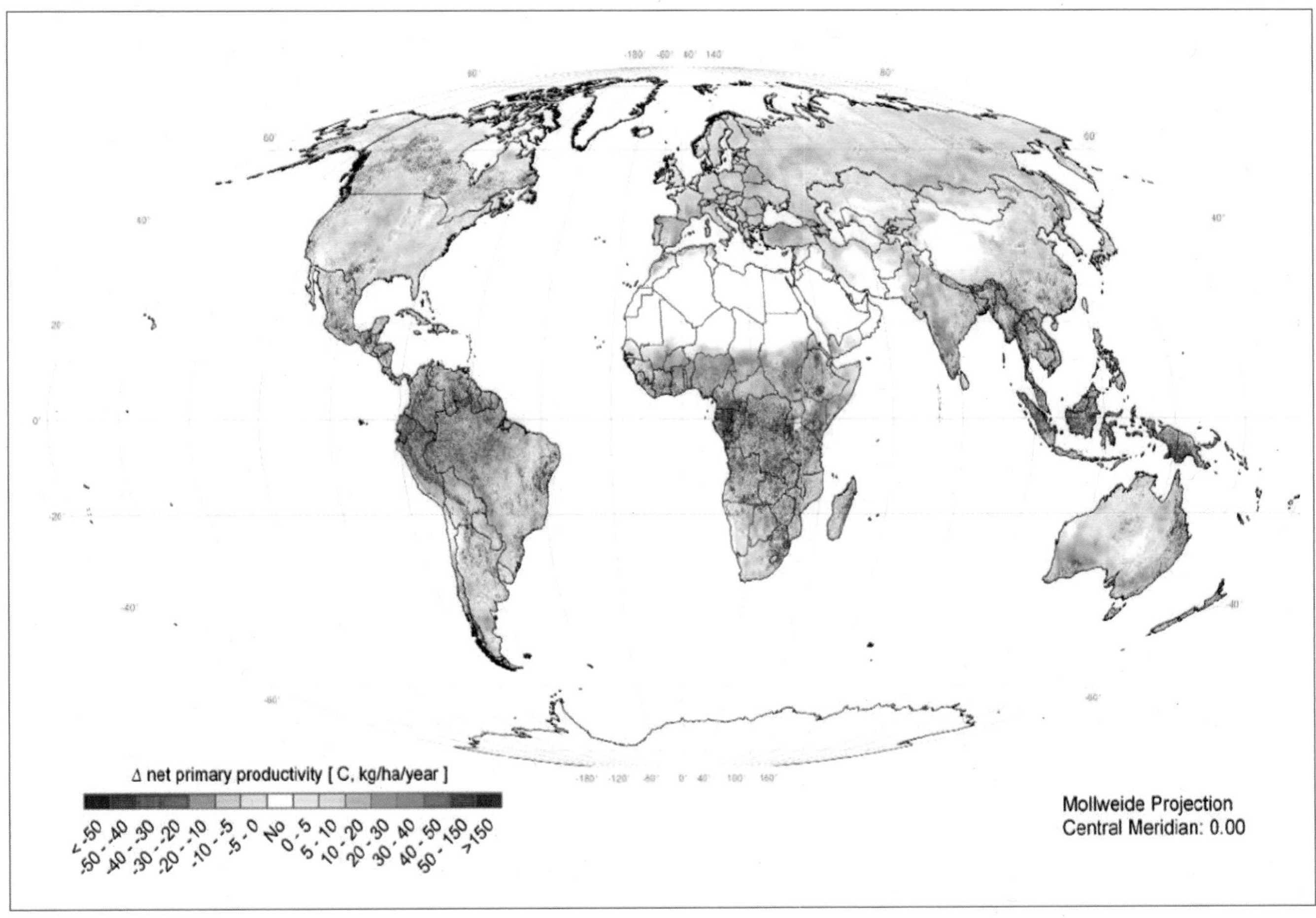

Source: Bai and others (2008), figure 2.

1981-2003.[2] Degrading areas are mainly in: the part of Africa that is south of the Equator, in South-East Asia and southern China, in north-central Australia, in the pampas and in swathes of boreal forest in Siberia and North America (ibid.).

Agriculture is a cause as well as a casualty of climate change

Land degradation has negative effects on climate, biodiversity, water ecosystems, landscape and other ecosystem services (see table III.1). While agriculture contributes significantly to the problem of climate change, it is also vulnerable to its effects. Climate change impacts agriculture in many ways, with changes in temperature, precipitation and climatic variability affecting the timing and length of growing seasons and yields and thereby exacerbating land degradation and contributing to water scarcity (Agrawala and Fankhauser, eds., 2008; and table III.2). Notably, in this regard, with temperature rises, crop productivity is forecast to increase at mid-high latitudes and decrease at lower

2 Land degradation is measured by the change in the normalized difference vegetation index (NDVI), scaled in terms of net primary productivity (NPP). NPP is the rate at which vegetation fixes CO_2 from the atmosphere less losses through respiration; deviation from the norm is used as an indicator of land degradation or improvement. As a proxy, the remotely sensed NDVI, which has been shown to be related to biophysical variables that control vegetation productivity and land/atmosphere fluxes, is also used to estimate vegetation change (Bai and others, 2008).

Table III.1
Global environmental impacts of land degradation

Environmental component or process	*Bases of impact of land degradation*
Climate change	• Land-use change, deforestation in particular, is a critical factor in the global carbon cycle • Soil management changes can result in the sequestration of atmospheric carbon • Agriculture is a major source of methane (CH_4) and nitrous oxide (N_2O) emissions • Land surface change (for example, as regards albedo and roughness) plays an important role in regional and global climate change • Human activities accelerate the occurrence of sandstorms • Biomass burning contributes to climate change
Biodiversity	• Deforestation leads to loss of habitat and species • Land-use change and management, including fragmentation and burning, lead to loss of habitat and biodiversity • Non-point pollution from crop production damages aquatic habitats and biodiversity
Water resources	• Agricultural activities are a major source of water pollution • Land-use and cover change alters the global hydrologic cycle • Atmospheric deposition of soil dust damages coral reefs
Persistent organic pollutants (POPs)	• Soil contains a major pool of POPs • Biomass burning produces POPs

Source: University of East Anglia, Overseas Development Group (2006).

latitudes (Intergovernmental Panel on Climate Change, 2007a). For instance, it is estimated that, in Southern Africa, yields could fall by up to 50 per cent between 2000 and 2020 (Intergovernmental Panel on Climate Change, 2007b); and that, by 2080, 600 million additional people could be at risk of hunger as a direct consequence of climate change (United Nations Development Programme, 2007, overview, p. 9).

There are important feedback mechanisms, however, as agriculture activity and land degradation generate greenhouse gas (GHG) emissions and thus contribute to climate change. They also impact land-surface albedo so as to engender adverse weather patterns (University of East Anglia, Overseas Development Group, 2006). Notwithstanding significant uncertainty in estimates, agricultural activities account for about 30 per cent of emissions of greenhouse gases (carbon dioxide (CO_2), methane (CH_4) and nitrous oxide (N_2O)) (Baumert, Herzog and Pershing, 2005). Agriculture is a significant emitter of CH_4 (50 per cent of global emissions) and N_2O (70 per cent) (Bhatia, Pathak and Aggarwal, 2004). Emissions from cattle and other livestock account for just over one quarter of CH_4 emissions.

There is much interest in the climate change mitigation potential of the reverse of this process, carbon sequestration, in both vegetation (forests in particular) and soil. Table III.3 summarizes the contribution of agriculture to greenhouse gas emissions.

Globally, agriculture is the main source of depletion and pollution of water resources

Access to sufficient and safe water is crucial for food production, poverty reduction and human health. However, increasing and competing demands for water have

Table III.2
Projections of climatic changes and corresponding impacts on agriculture

Projected change	*Likelihood of future trends based on projections for the twenty-first century*	*Projected impacts on agriculture*
Warmer and fewer cold days and nights; warmer and more frequent hot days and nights over most land areas	Virtually certain	Increased yields in colder environments; decreased yields in warmer environments
Warm spells/heatwaves: frequency increases over most land areas	Very likely	Reduced yields in warmer regions due to heat stress at key development stages; increased danger of wildfire
Heavy precipitation events: frequency increases over most areas	Very likely	Damage to crops; soil erosion, inability to cultivate land due to water-logging of soils
Area affected by drought increases	Likely	Land degradation; lower yields/ crop damage and failure; increased livestock deaths; increased risk of wildfire
Intense tropical cyclone activity increases	Likely	Damage to crops; windthrow of trees
Increased incidence of extreme high sea level	Likely	Salinization of irrigation and well water

Source: Intergovernmental Panel on Climate Change (2007a), table 3.2.

Table III.3
Contribution of agriculture to global greenhouse gas and other emissions

Greenhouse gas	Carbon dioxide	Methane	Nitrous oxide	Nitric oxide	Ammonia
Main effects	Climate change	Climate change	Climate change	Acidification	Acidification Eutrophication
Agricultural source	**Land-use change, especially deforestation**	Ruminants (15)	Livestock (including manure applied to farmland) (17)	**Biomass burning (13)**	Livestock (including manure applied to farmland) (44)
		Rice production (11)	Mineral fertilizers (8)	Manure and mineral fertilizers (2)	Mineral fertilizers (17)
		Biomass burning (7)	**Biomass burning (3)**		**Biomass burning (11)**
Agricultural emissions as a proportion of the total emissions from anthropogenic sources (percentage)	15	49	66	27	93

Source: Food and Agriculture Organization of the United Nations (2003).
Note: Sources of land degradation are in bold. Percentage contribution of each type of emission to total global emissions appears in parentheses.

led to serious depletion of surface-water resources (Smakhtin, Revenga and Döll, 2004). Agricultural irrigation accounts for some 70 per cent of all water withdrawals.

Moreover, it appears that water quality has been degraded partly owing to intensive agriculture, which has become the main source of water pollution in many developed and developing countries, rendering it unsustainable and a source of risks to human health (Molden and de Fraiture, 2004). Intensive livestock production is probably the largest sector-specific source of water pollution (Steinfeld and others, 2006). Excessive use of agrochemicals (pesticides and fertilizers) also contaminates waterways. The capacity of coastal and marine ecosystems to produce fish for human harvest is highly damaged by overfishing and loss of wetlands and other water habitats.

Deforestation is a major cause of biodiversity loss

Biodiversity underpins agriculture and food security through the provision of the genetic material needed for crop and livestock breeding, and raw materials for industry, and other ecosystem services (International Assessment of Agricultural Knowledge, Science and Technology for Development, 2009). The past century has seen the greatest loss of biodiversity through habitat destruction, primarily through the conversion of forests for agriculture.

While the last quarter-century has witnessed an increase in forest area in industrialized countries, developing countries have experienced an average decline of about 10 per cent (Food and Agriculture Organization of the United Nations, 2007) (figure III.8). The problem of deforestation is particularly severe in the humid tropics (Moutinho and Schwartzman, eds., 2005). Africa and South America suffered the largest net loss of forests from 1990 to 2005, with Africa accounting for over half of recent global losses, even though the continent hosts just over 15 per cent of the world's forests (University of East Anglia, Overseas Development Group, 2006). Habitat destruction and degradation

Figure III.8
Trends in forest area, 1990, 2000 and 2010

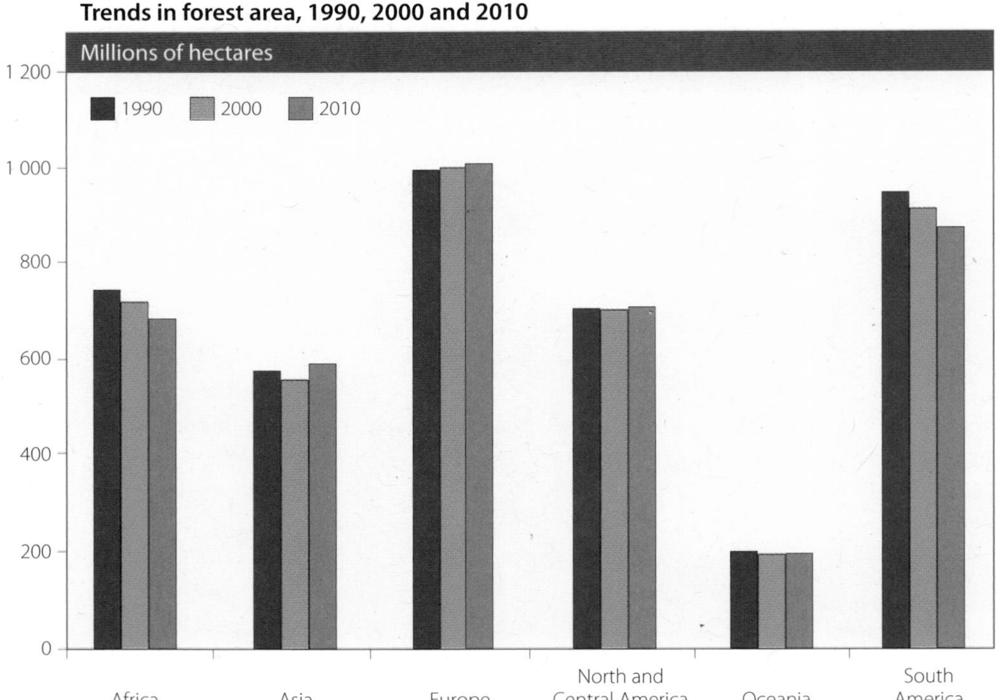

Source: Food and Agriculture Organization of the United Nations (2010b).

is the major global threat to birds and amphibians, affecting almost 90 per cent of threatened species (IUCN, Species Survival Commission, 2004). This is particularly evident in the case of tropical forests, which cover less than 10 per cent of the earth's land area, yet harbour 50-90 per cent of the planet's terrestrial species (Millennium Ecosystem Assessment, 2005).

The spread of industrial agriculture has also promoted the simplification of agro-ecosystems, with reductions in the number of and variety of species. Further, production of monocultures increases environmental risks by reducing biodiversity, ecosystem functions and ecological resilience (International Assessment of Agricultural Knowledge, Science and Technology for Development, 2009). In addition, over-exploitation of marine resources is so severe that an estimated 20 per cent of freshwater fish species have become extinct (Wood, Sebastian and Scherr, 2000), while certain commercial fish and other marine species are threatened globally (International Assessment of Agricultural Knowledge, Science and Technology for Development, 2009).

Socio-economic impacts

Unsustainable natural resource management has negative socio-economic consequences …

Unsustainable natural resource management also has adverse socio-economic consequences. In particular, land degradation can lead to substantial productivity losses, thereby posing risks to food security (Sanchez, 2002). While productivity impacts vary largely by region, the areas mostly affected are those whose populations are already suffering from poverty and hunger (Oldeman, 1998). The productivity of some lands has declined by 50 per cent owing to soil erosion and desertification (Dregne, 1990). Globally, the annual loss of 75 billion tons of soil costs about $400 billion per year, or approximately $70 per person per year (Lal, 1998). Soil compaction has caused yield reductions of between 40 and 90 per cent in West African countries (Kayombo and Lal, 1994). Nutrient (nitrogen, phosphorus, and potassium) depletion also has a severe global economic impact, especially in sub-Saharan Africa. In South Asia, annual economic loss is estimated at $500 million from waterlogging, and at $1.5 billion due to salinization (Food and Agriculture Organization of the United Nations, 1994). Deforestation can also exacerbate food insecurity, as forests provide food, inputs and services that support crop and livestock production (Food and Agriculture Organization of the United Nations, 2006). In a case-study analysis of seven developing countries, Berry, Olson and Campbell, (2003) estimated that problems of sustainable land management reduced agricultural GDP by between 3 and 7 per cent.

… including reduced long-term productive capacity, poverty, migration and ill health

There is often a strong association between the distribution of poor people reliant on agriculture and fragile environments. Poor people are likely to be farming steeper land and drier, less fertile soils and in more remote areas (World Bank, 2003). Sub-Saharan Africa and South Asia experience the highest intensity of soil degradation, population growth and food insecurity (Bai and others, 2008; Food and Agriculture Organization of the United Nations, 2010a). In Mexico, land degradation contributes to migration (Berry, Olson and Campbell, 2003). Deforestation will likely have a particularly adverse impact on many of the 1.5 billion persons who depend on forests for their livelihoods, especially as they represent 90 per cent of those living in extreme poverty (World Bank, 2004).

Natural resource degradation may also exacerbate gender inequalities by increasing the time requirement for fulfilment of female responsibilities such as food production, fuelwood collection, and soil and water conservation. For instance, in rural

Rajasthan, India, approximately 50 person-hours per month are required for households gathering fuelwood (Laxmi and others, 2003). In Malawi, women spend between 4 and 15 hours per week collecting firewood (Rehfuess, Mehta and Prüss-Üstün, 2006).

Agricultural production systems can further adversely affect human health. Water pollution from inorganic fertilizers and livestock waste undermines the safety of drinking water and aquatic food. Pesticides negatively affect the health of farm workers (World Water Assessment Programme, 2003). Transportation of agricultural products has also promoted the cross-border spread of pests and diseases (International Assessment of Agricultural Knowledge, Science and Technology for Development, 2009). In addition, desertification-induced dust storms can cause respiratory disorders, including bronchitis (Millennium Ecosystem Assessment, 2005).

Drivers of unsustainable natural resource management

Natural resources degradation is driven by poor land and water management practices

In explaining the unprecedented global degradation and depletion of land, water and biodiversity, a combination of natural and human-induced factors can be identified, including *indirect* factors such as population pressure, and *direct* factors, such as land-use patterns.

Deterioration of natural resources are most commonly caused by poor land and water management practices in a process driven by socio-economic and political factors (Bai and others, 2008). Land fragmentation and limited farm size contribute to inappropriate livestock management, resulting in land degradation. In addition, human-induced climate change aggravates resource degradation through floods, droughts, fires, soil changes and biodiversity loss. On the other hand, people can be a major asset in reversing resource degradation through reforestation and other sustainable land, water and forest management practices and technologies (Eswaran, Lal and Reich, 2001).

Underlying unsustainable management of natural resources are numerous interconnected economic and socio-political drivers, including poverty, inequality, demographic trends, national resource allocation, land distribution and rights, political stability, governance and institutions, societal perceptions of and values on land, and behavioural consumption and production patterns. For instance, poor small-scale farm holders can over-exploit natural resources, particularly when facing population pressure and scarcity of suitable land, as is the case in the *minifundias* in the Andean highlands of Latin America. On the other hand, large-scale farming can also be a cause of land degradation through the excessive use of chemicals and the engagement in unsustainable land management practices in order to increase productivity and profits.

Food security and small farm holders

Small farm holders are at the heart of the battle against poverty and hunger

To the extent that most food is locally produced and consumed, small farm holders are at the heart of the food security challenge. The majority of the extremely poor and about half of the undernourished people in the world live in a total of 500 million farms in developing countries (almost 90 per cent of farms worldwide), each comprising less than two hectares (ha) of land (International Food Policy Research Institute, 2005).

The scale of farming varies by region, with the average farm size ranging from 1.6 ha in Africa and Asia to over 120 ha in North America (table III.4). There is evidence to suggest that average farm size among small farm holdings is decreasing owing to population pressure and land scarcity. The bottom 25 per cent of rural agricultural households

Table III.4
Approximate average farm size by world region

Region	*Average farm size (hectares)*
Africa	1.6
Asia	1.6
Latin America and the Caribbean	67.0
Europe[a]	27.0
North America	121.0

Source: von Braun, 2009.
a Data for Western Europe only.

in several African countries farm, on average, less than 0.1 ha of land per capita (Jayne and others, 2003).

Women make up almost half of the rural workforce …

Small farm holders dominate agriculture in developing countries, where the presence of women is highly significant, typically in subsistence farming. In Africa and East and South-East Asia, women make up over 40 per cent of the agricultural workforce (Food and Agriculture Organization of the United Nations, 2011). Estimates of the share of female employment in that work force range from 36 per cent in Côte d'Ivoire and the Niger to 60 per cent in Lesotho. However, female farmers have less access to land, credit, markets and technology: Only 5 per cent of landholders in North Africa and West Africa are women, only 15 per cent in sub-Saharan Africa and only 25 per cent in a sample of countries in Latin America; furthermore, the average farm size is significantly smaller (ibid.).

… but they have restricted access to land, credit, markets and technology

In low-income countries, there are 3 billion people in rural areas; 2.5 billion are involved in agriculture and 1.5 billion make a living from small farms (Food and Agriculture Organization of the United Nations, International Fund for Agricultural Development and International Labour Organization, 2010; Foresight, 2011). Countries and communities based mainly on small-scale farming are not only among the poorest, but also among the most threatened by ecosystem degradation (United Nations Environment Programme, 2002). For instance, in countries such as China and India (which, despite having invested heavily in rural development, are home to most of the world's undernourished people), the areas most vulnerable to food insecurity often contend with poor natural conditions and fragile ecologies (Xiao and Nie, 2009; M S Swaminathan Research Foundation and World Food Programme, 2008).

With small-scale farms likely to dominate the agricultural landscape in the foreseeable future, addressing the particular challenges they face is vital to combating poverty and hunger (Dixon, Gibbon and Gulliver, 2001). While there is an emerging consensus among international organizations regarding the importance of strengthening the role of small farm holders in order to ensure the achievement of greater food security, effective policies need to be in place to secure the viability of small farm holders, particularly in view of intensification of international competition and strengthening of marketing chains and quality standards, and natural resource degradation (Hazell and others, 2010).

Small-scale and diversified farming has advantages in terms of productivity, food production and environmental protection …

Most of the findings presented in the literature dealing with agricultural development in low-income countries indicate that small farm units tend to show higher productivity than large-scale farms. Small farm holders not only tend to make more intensive use of land and labour but also face lower transaction costs for labour. These advantages may disappear, however, for certain crops whose cultivation benefits from significant economies of scale and input-intensive technologies, or when conditions critical for efficient farming—like marketing opportunities, quality assurance, and access to inputs, markets, credit and information—are lacking for small farm holders.

... but without proper support it may lead to unsustainable use of natural resources

Poverty among small farm holders may create incentives for more intensive non-sustainable resource extraction as a short-term survival strategy (Lutz, ed., 1998). In northern Zambia, for instance, labour-rich households have higher incomes but they also cause the most deforestation (Holden, 1991). Nevertheless, Altieri (2008) notes that small-scale and diversified farming continues to have significant advantages over large-scale monoculture systems in terms of productivity (20-60 per cent higher yields), food production and environmental protection (including climate change mitigation).

Notwithstanding recognition of the challenges faced by small farm holders, these findings reinforce the view that they should be assigned a prominent role in food security strategies. Female farmers play a particularly important role; in Africa, for example, they account for more than half of the agricultural output (Mehra and Rojas, 2008). Small farm holders in developing countries often experience undernourishment themselves, while remaining the main suppliers of food to urban areas. Hence, improving food security and even economic growth will critically depend on removing the barriers faced by small farm holders and expanding their productive capacity, while paying particular attention to the needs of female farmers.

Towards a true green technological revolution in agriculture

A radical transformation in agriculture is needed ...

The preceding analysis makes clear that combating hunger and malnutrition in a sustainable manner and guarding against high and volatile food prices will require a radically different approach addressing the structural constraints on food production within a wider framework of sustainable natural resource management. This would entail both the establishment of a comprehensive national framework for sustainable use of resources, and a harnessing of the technology and innovation needed to increase the productivity, profitability, stability, resilience and climate change mitigation potential of rural production systems and forests. Water conservation, soil protection and biodiversity enhancement need to form part of an integrated approach of sustainable land and forest management,[3] which must also integrate biophysical with sociocultural, institutional and behavioural variables, while recognizing the multifunctional nature of agriculture.

... to build synergies between increased food production and sustainable natural resource management...

A holistic, cross-sectoral approach should, for instance, consider trade-offs and build on synergies between the forests and agriculture sectors. In view of their competitive land uses, many solutions, involving difficult choices, will be reached through open and inclusive discussion and negotiation. On the other hand, the aforementioned synergies among the sectors (resulting, inter alia, in reduced land degradation and increased productivity; sustainable water supply; and green energy infrastructure and buildings) present important "win-win" options through better resource management facilitated by an enabling institutional environment.

3 Sustainable land management is defined as "the use of land resources, including soils, water, animals and plants, for the production of goods to meet changing human needs, while ensuring the long-term productive potential of these resources and the maintenance of their environmental functions" (United Nations, 1993). Although there is no universally agreed-upon definition for sustainable forest management (SFM), the United Nations Forum on Forests (UNFF) states that "sustainable forest management, as a dynamic and evolving concept, aims to maintain and enhance the economic, social and environmental value of all types of forests, for the benefit of present and future generations" (United Nations Forum on Forests, 2007).

... within a comprehensive national framework for sustainable resource use

An appropriate institutional setting is also crucial in respect of supporting small-scale farming so as to increase agricultural investment and productivity and preserve natural resources. The State has an important role to play in building rural infrastructure (including roads, storage facilities and irrigation systems); improving market access (including for credit, inputs and insurance); providing extension services and technological capacity-building; encouraging coordination among multiple stakeholders; and securing property rights (including land redistribution).

Sustainable agriculture should also be a priority in developed countries to ensure more efficient use of energy and a reduction in use of chemical fertilizers and pesticides. Large subsidies to agriculture in OECD countries, including subsidies for the production of biofuels (entailing a shift in production away from food crops), have led to severe imbalances in the economics of agricultural production and consumption worldwide.

An agricultural innovation system approach can help accelerate the new green revolution

Government policies to stimulate a new technological revolution in agriculture will have to build on the rich experiences associated with innovation in the last 30 years. The recent literature on innovation in agriculture is using the concept of agricultural innovation systems to "denote the network of economic and non-economic actors, and the linkages amongst these actors (to) enable technological, organizational and social learning of the kind needed to devise context-specific solutions" (United Nations Conference on Trade and Development, 2010, sect. 1.6). We propose to utilize the concept of a sustainable agricultural innovation system (SAIS) to focus on developing a comprehensive policy framework for innovation which can respond to the double challenge of increasing productivity in food production and environmental sustainability. The SAIS constitutes the agricultural pillar of the larger concept of greening the National Innovation System (G-NIS), as discussed in chapter V.

After a brief overview of the SAIS framework, the present section identifies existing processes linked to technological innovation in agriculture and management of natural resources, including a brief review of recent experiences of innovation in sustainable agriculture compared with the experience of the green revolution of the 1960s and 1970s. Against this background, four critical objectives are singled out whose attainment requires strategic policy support to effect the transformation to sustainable agriculture, namely: (a) improved access to the whole range of technological options; (b) better access to supportive services, including removal of the political obstacles that prevent faster productivity growth among small-scale farm holders; (c) gender sensitivity in agricultural innovation processes; and (d) strengthening cooperation and partnerships to accelerate innovation.

The sustainable agricultural innovation system framework

All actors, institutions and processes, within the whole food chain must be part of the policy innovation framework ...

The SAIS perspective facilitates the recognition of the multiplicity of actors that produce and use global knowledge (including universities, research institutions, firms, farmers, extension workers, civil society organizations and private foundations), their interests, the institutional contexts within which interactions occur in the innovation process, and the dynamics of learning and institutional change (Spielman, 2005). The SAIS perspective also serves to underline that innovation is important, in relation not only to production, but also to improving processes, products and marketing, and strengthening organizations and partnerships within different parts of the system through the engagement of different actors.

An innovation systems perspective enables the recognition of the evolutionary nature of innovation—its achievement through the cumulative effect of interactions between agents on the supply and demand sides of the system, within a framework of formal and informal institutions, supportive policies and stakeholder involvement, as illustrated by the cases presented in box III.1 (Brooks and Loevinsohn, 2011).

Box III.1

Innovation in agriculture

The development of agricultural research and experimentation has not been weak, even in the most challenged regions in Africa (United Nations Conference on Trade and Development, 2010), although they have lacked appropriate support to ensure widespread benefits. The two successful experiences discussed below illustrate the contribution of multiple stakeholders to achieving rapid improvement in the productivity of small farm holders with environmentally sustainable practices. Direct participation of small farm holders in a process of continuous learning and adaptation was a key factor of success.

The System of Rice Intensification (SRI)

Rice is the single most important staple of the poor, especially in Asia. Under current practices of the continuous flooding of fields and the heavy use of inorganic fertilizers, rice production is one of the main sources of methane gas emissions and one of the main causes of the contamination of land and water. It is estimated that 24-30 per cent of the freshwater utilized worldwide is for the production of rice.

With support from Africare, Oxfam America, the WWF-ICRISAT Project and the World Bank, an innovation known as the System of Rice Intensification (SRI) has been successfully tested in 40 countries with impressive results. With simple changes in the management of crops entailing transplantation into non-flooded fields of fewer seeds at a younger age and with wider spaces between them, in addition to broader use of organic fertilizers and integrated pest control management, crops become more resistant to climate variations, pests and diseases. Depending on local conditions, yields may increase by up to 50 per cent. Water savings have ranged between 25 and 50 per cent; input cost savings per hectare are estimated to be 23 per cent, due mainly to the use of fewer agrochemicals; and farmers' incomes have increased substantially.

According to Brooks and Loevinsohn (2011, p. 11): "In India, which appears to have the largest area under SRI, 'learning alliances' have been formed that exchange experiences and take the lead in interactions with government ... (especially at local level) ... notably in Andhra Pradesh, Tamil Nadu and Tripura." However, the involvement of formal research institutions has been more marginal, with some positive experiences in China and Indonesia. The Governments of Cambodia, China, India, Indonesia and Viet Nam have endorsed these innovations and included them as part of their national strategies for food security (Africare, Oxfam America and WWF-ICRISAT Project, 2010, p. 3).

The Farm Field School approach

Prompted by widespread environmental pollution and occupational poisoning in South-East Asia as a result of heavy use of pesticides, research institutions have developed the underpinnings of an integrated approach to improving pest control management through the conservation of beneficial insects (spiders and planthoppers, among others) and better management of the ecology of farmers' fields. Farmer Field Schools (FFS), which were developed over 10 years in the Philippines and Indonesia, have provided an opportunity for farmers to learn through observation and experimentation in the field.

With support from the Government of Indonesia, the United States Agency for International Development and the Food and Agriculture Organization of the United Nations, the FFS approach has spread to other developing countries (namely, Bangladesh, Cambodia, China, India, the Lao People's Democratic Republic, Nepal, the Philippines, Sri Lanka, Thailand and Viet Nam) and been adapted to various farming systems. The range of management skills has been extended to include the production of vegetables, cotton, potatoes, tree crops, fruits, maize, poultry and dairy cows, soil fertility management, land and water management, groundwater management, conservation agriculture, land degradation management, agroforestry, community forestry, fishing and preservation of biodiversity.

The agricultural innovation system that emerged from the experiences of integrated pest management and the Farmer Field Schools was made possible through active participation of multiple stakeholders. National and international research institutions in the Philippines and Indonesia have provided scientific knowledge to the Farmer Field Schools while non-governmental

Box III.1 (cont'd)

organizations in Indonesia have developed the pedagogic process needed to facilitate adult learning. Bilateral donors and international organizations (such as FAO) were critical in supporting the creation of Farmer Field Schools in other countries through financial contributions, provision of information and advocacy.

There are now FFS projects operating in 87 countries in Asia, sub-Saharan Africa, Latin America and the Caribbean, East and North Africa, Central and Eastern Europe, the United States of America and Western Europe. The FFS approach has contributed to the development of improved skills among farmers, a greater demand for information and a greater flexibility in the managing of their crops.

Sources: Brooks and Loevinsohn (2011); Braun and Duveskog (2008); and Africare, Oxfam America and WWF-ICRISAT Project (2010).

… so as to be able to support the design of effective mechanisms for enhancing innovation in sustainable agriculture

The policy challenge is how to move beyond the recognition of a multiplicity of innovative experiences towards the design of interventions and policies capable of stimulating and supporting the innovative capacity of the actors (farmers, civil society organizations and corporations) that are part of the food production system. The literature identifies two trajectories for fostering and supporting innovation: the "orchestrated trajectory" induced by policy and the "opportunity trajectory" triggered by market signals. Brooks and Loevinsohn (2011) extends this framework by adding an "endogenous" trajectory which emerges in local contexts.

These parallel trajectories intersect in each country at the point where knowledge and innovation are generated. Policies should aim to strengthen interactions among the various processes so as to ensure that innovation contributes simultaneously to poverty reduction, food security and environmental sustainability. Those objectives are not served if innovation is driven merely by profit motives, as is the case for most agricultural activities. Further, traditional public-private partnerships have not been very successful in directing innovation efforts towards achieving the objectives set out in a sustainable development agenda (Hall, 2010).

Policy must support local innovations

The challenge for policymakers is how to identify and support promising innovation trajectories in a context where the adoption of new technology and crop management practices has a mixed record of successes and failures and where many contentious issues are not easily resolved. Questions about what constitutes effective interventions persist, including: should the priority be building technical capacity of farmers or promoting established technological practices and products (Brooks and Loevinsohn, 2011); and should the strategy be one of strengthening farmers' organizations or improving their links with input suppliers. In order to respond to these questions, the management of rural development programmes needs to undergo a deep transformation of its own. The application of public policy and project management tools (logical frameworks and monitoring and evaluation systems) needs to become less rigid and more flexible and adaptive so as to be able to move beyond a narrow focus on *outcomes* and towards the strengthening of innovative *processes* (Berdegué, 2005). The very common practice, for example, of focusing on the replication (or scaling up) of successful innovative experiences may be too narrow to stimulate experimentation and learning, which would necessarily include the capacity to learn from failure.

A policy agenda with the capacity to stimulate innovation demands radical changes in the institutions and mechanisms that presently support agricultural development. A process of learning and innovation needs to unfold within public institutions—one that facilitates the adoption of a strategic focus on innovation and nationwide institutional changes in support of a techno-institutional agenda for food security under which local innovations can prosper (Leeuwis and Hall, 2010).

Building on existing approaches to technological innovation in agriculture and natural resource management

Local innovation in sustainable agriculture

Local communities and farmers are constantly innovating in response to shocks ...

Local farmers and communities have shown great capacity to innovate in response to weather and other shocks. There are thousands of successful experiences of localized enhanced pest and weed management, water efficiency and biodiversity, including stories of highly successful innovation in the most challenging circumstances characterized by a poor natural resource base and widespread poverty (World Bank, 2007a, 2008c; Thapa and Broomhead, 2010; Spielman and Pandya-Lorch, 2009; Africare, Oxfam America and WWF-ICRISAT Project, 2010; Pretty and others, 2006).

... and many of their innovations entail the adoption of environmentally sustainable practices ...

Pretty and others (2006) assessed 286 sustainable innovation experiences in 57 poor countries encompassing 37 million hectares.[4] In four years, and with wide variations across the 12.6 million farms evaluated, there were large and significant increases in crop yields (79 per cent on average), greater water efficiency, evidence of carbon sequestration and a reduction in pesticide use of 70.8 per cent associated with an average yield increase of 41.6 per cent.

... but they often lack the resources to expand production and apply their experiences beyond the local context

Most often, innovation experiences among local farmers and rural communities are part of their survival strategies in response to soil depletion, water scarcity, HIV/AIDS, catastrophic events and other negative factors; however, typically, the conditions needed to utilize these experiences on a larger scale are lacking. While indigenous female workers have experience in the management of biodiversity and traditional knowledge for sustainable agriculture, poor access to land, inputs and credit has often prevented the expansion of that successful experience (World Bank, 2009).

Nevertheless, there are several well-known examples of innovations with large-scale impacts. The integrated pest management (IPM) approach, proliferating Farm Field Schools and the System of Rice Intensification (SRI) are good examples of creative innovation that achieved large-scale impacts through highly effective collaboration among multiple stakeholders (see box III.1).

Other large-impact innovations encompass the networks of millers and politicians that popularized the use of NERICA (New Rice for Africa) in Africa, the handmade paper industry in Nepal, the organization of small-scale producers to export mangos in India, the diffusion of micro-irrigation in Bangladesh (Hall, Dijkman and Sulaiman, 2010) and watershed management in India (box III.2), among many others.[5]

---

4 Agricultural sustainability centres on the adoption of technology and practices designed to increase food production without negative environmental impacts. The projects evaluated encompassed 3 per cent of cultivated area in developing countries.

5 The World Bank (2007a) documented eight case studies in Asia, Africa and Latin America; and more recently, Juma (2011) published several case studies from around the world. However, there are many more case studies in the literature, including on the practice of national and international non-governmental organizations, some of which are available from http://www.fara-africa.org/; http://www.fodderinnovation.org/; http://www.cos-sis.org/; http://www.papandina.org/; http://www.oxfam.org/en/search/apachesolr_search/food%20security%20oxfam%20programs; http://www.worldvision.org/content.nsf/learn/ways-we-help-foodsecurity?Open&lpos=bot_txt_Food-Security#response; http://www.agra-alliance.org/; http://www.sristi.org/cms/; and http://www.prolinnova.net/.

Box III.2

Watershed development in India

In India, watersheds—namely, land drained by a common watercourse—have been the focus of increasing development efforts in recent decades. These areas of intense poverty and food insecurity tend to be characterized by eroded slopes and degraded pastures and forests.

Early watershed restoration projects had focused on the physical symptoms of degradation by building infrastructure designed to retain water and slow erosion, as well as by banning grazing and harvesting of forest products on the ridges. While these projects achieved striking visual results and benefited farmers in the lower reaches, they nevertheless negatively impacted women and landless and marginalized peasants who depended on fodder and forest products from the upper parts.

In the 1970s, a number of innovative village-level projects were initiated, granting landless people, including women, rights to use the additional surface water that was generated, in exchange for their collaboration in conserving soil and vegetation in the upper watershed. They were then able to sell the water to farmers or use it on rented land.

The substantial environmental and socio-economic benefits conferred by these projects inspired further efforts by both Governments and non-governmental organizations, including the expansion of employment opportunities based on natural resources and local opportunities outside agriculture. When well conceived and executed, such programmes can result in significant gains in farm output, ecological protection, employment for the landless, gender parity and female empowerment.

Overall, watershed development in India highlights the importance of the participation of diverse actors and attention to local contexts in harnessing environmental innovations that can produce multiple, equitable and sustainable benefits.

Source: Brooks and Loevinsohn (2011).

... are based on explicit support from Governments, multilateral and civil society organizations, and donors working directly with local farmers

The adoption of sustainable practices in agriculture is supporting the application of the emergent concept of "sustainable agriculture intensification", also known as the "agroecological approach", "ecologically intensive agriculture" and "low-external input technology" (International Fund for Agricultural Development, 2011). Those practices have several points in common:

- Successful experiences have been based on direct involvement of farmers in learning and innovation aimed at adapting knowledge, technology and management practices to the local context
- Active participation by various actors including Governments, non-governmental organizations, and multilateral organizations has been critical not only to scaling up innovations, but also to disseminating knowledge, building capacity among farmers, fostering trust and reducing the risks associated with new technology and agricultural practices
- Adjustments in the rules, norms and values of the institutions governing agricultural research and development (R&D), and practices, have also been important in inducing behavioural change among farmers (to encourage them to adopt new practices), redefining the role of women and establishing closer interacting networks

Successful innovative experiences with large welfare gains for small-scale farm holders, rural communities and the poor are those where technical knowledge is made relevant and accessible to farmers and is accompanied by an enabling environment within which they can overcome the constraints that they face in respect of adopting new technology and agricultural practices (Berdegué, 2005).

Agricultural research and development during the green revolution of the 1960s and 1970s

As in the original green revolution, sustainable agriculture for food security needs long-term research support, adequate investments for rural development, and institutional reform

Not too long ago, developing countries and donors had responded to widespread poverty and food insecurity with policies that induced a profound transformation of the rural economy. The so-called green revolution of the 1960s and 1970s brought new technology and innovation to farmers in Asia and Latin America as part of an effort to increase food production at a time when close to one third of the world's population (1 billion people) were vulnerable to hunger and malnutrition (Spielman and Pandya-Lorch, 2009).

Technological innovations were based on breeding new crop varieties, mainly wheat, rice and maize that were more resistant to pests and disease and more responsive to chemical nutrients and that allowed double- and even triple-cropping (International Food Policy Research Institute, 2002). In Asia, cereal production increased from 313 million to 650 million tons per year between 1970 and 1995; and countries in Asia and Latin America saw higher calorie intake per person and a substantial increase in real per capita income, with subsequent poverty reduction (Hazell, 2009).

The technological innovation and diffusion triggered by the green revolution were facilitated by a large and interconnected system of international research centres, coordinated by the Consultative Group on International Agricultural Research (CGIAR) and sustained with adequate funding from developed and developing countries and private donors. These centres sustained research operations, gene banks and nursery programmes in an environment of open and free exchange of information and plant genetic materials (Dubin and Brennan, 2009). The budgets available to CGIAR centres grew from $15 million in 1970 to $305 million in 1990 (Pardey and Beintema, 2001).

Governments expanded rural roads, irrigation and electrical power facilities, and improved storage facilities. Basic education, agricultural research and extension services to support farmers also improved, and international lending for agricultural development was prioritized.

Unfortunately, the "technical package" that accompanied the green revolution was not replicable in regions with different agroecological conditions in terms of climate, soil, weeds and pests, most notably sub-Saharan Africa, and where the consumption of staples was more diversified so as to include millet, sorghum, and cassava, of which improved varieties would come much later. Also, the technology arising from the green revolution was based on intensive use of fertilizers, chemical pesticides and water, which had negative environmental impacts.

Three lessons can be learned from the first green revolution

Three important lessons derived from the experience of the green revolution are relevant to the discussion of a new wave of transformations in agriculture, namely, that: (a) the development of new technology requires long-term financial support for R&D and effective and free flow and dissemination of information; (b) the adoption of new technology requires an enabling institutional framework and large investment in infrastructure, and capacity development among farmers, as well as access to inputs, credits and markets; and (c) innovations in agriculture require long-term commitments from national Governments and other international stakeholders. Going forward, the environmental impact of agriculture is a major concern. New technology and a radical reform in agricultural practices will be needed to reduce greenhouse gas emissions, land degradation, and over-exploitation and contamination of water tables, and to increase the carbon sequestration capacity of agriculture and forestry.

Multiple technological options need to be made available in response to multiple challenges

In contrast with the experience of the green revolution, which relied on the adoption of a "technical package" on a large scale, achieving food security in today's context will require faster productivity gains among a large number of small-scale producers in very different agroecological regions. There is no single "technical solution" to simplify the quest for more rapid productivity and environmental sustainability gains. Instead, a whole range of technical options need to be made available to farmers.

There is no one technology that fits all …

An extensive menu of technologies and a wealth of sustainable practices in agriculture are available to spearhead the radical transformation required to increase food production without a major expansion of cultivated areas and a further depletion of natural resources. A recent study found that important productivity gains, of the order of a two- to threefold increase in average yields in Africa, for example, can be achieved through better use of existing knowledge and technology (Foresight, 2011). Similarly, FAO (2011) estimates that with better access by women to land, external inputs and technology, agricultural production in developing countries could increase by as much as 2.5-4.0 per cent, and the number of undernourished people could decline by between 12 and 17 per cent (that is, 100 million-150 million people could be free of hunger).

… but a wide range of technology options need to be made available to meet farmers' specific needs …

Traditional technologies and practices have proved their relevance to increasing productivity and ensuring environmental sustainability: for example, low-tillage farming, crop rotation and interplanting, water harvesting and recycling, water-efficient cropping, green manure utilization, agroforestry and integrated pest management have been successfully adopted with large productivity gains.

… including traditional knowledge and practices

The technology that emerged from the green revolution will continue to play an important role in the development of new crop breeding and higher-yielding varieties with substantial productivity gains, although continuing innovations will be needed for reducing the use of external inputs and increasing efficiency of water so as to reduce negative environmental impacts.

While modern developments in biotechnology, genetic engineering, food irradiation,[6] hydroponics and anaerobic digestion promise to improve the resistance of food crops to pests and extreme weather, increase their nutritional value, and reduce food contamination and greenhouse gas emissions, appropriate incentives to expand research on crops and processes of relevance to the poor need to be put in place.

There is very little that can be said, in general, about the choice of technologies that respond to the specific needs of farmers in diverse agroecological regions except that making those technologies available as options to small farm holders requires a new policy framework and additional investments in rural development. In Asia and some countries in Latin America, where the technologies derived from the green revolution led to overuse of agrochemicals and the depletion of water tables, Governments may need to reconsider whether to continue subsidizing the use of fertilizers and pesticides or to facilitate access to sustainable technology in order to increase the use of organic fertilizers and efficient water management. In sub-Saharan Africa, where small-scale farm holders generally use a fraction of the recommended levels of external inputs, decreasing food insecurity may require

6 Food irradiation is a physical process that exposes foods to a highly penetrating form of energy—gamma rays or high-energy electrons—which can uniformly deactivate the DNA of unwanted microorganisms without changing the basic nature of the treated food. It is a safe and cost-effective way to eliminate food contaminants.

the devising of new incentives to increase the use of chemical inputs in combination with sustainable technology and practices.

A radical rethinking of policy objectives and tool design is required ...

From a policy perspective, the problem is how to increase awareness and stimulate the adoption of sustainable technology and crop management practices. The policy challenge becomes ever more complicated when there are trade-offs between increasing food production and halting environmental degradation, as in the case of the extensive provision of subsidies to agrochemicals so as to increase food production in spite of their negative environmental impact. In many developing countries, reconciliation of these two objectives—food security and environmental sustainability—will require a radical transformation of current policy objectives, including a wider dissemination of information and technical support to small-scale farmers through adequate extension services, the removal of political constraints and appropriate incentives for building stronger partnerships with a multiplicity of stakeholders, as discussed below.

Expanding support services and land reform and overcoming political obstacles to agrarian change

... along with increased investments in rural infrastructure and expanded access to credit and technology

In the context of food-insecure countries, striking a delicate balance between large productivity gains and environmental sustainability will require additional investments and improved capacities to implement national strategies for food security that lead to: an increase in access of small farmers to technology; an increase in investments aimed at expanding the rural road infrastructure and crop storage facilities; secure land tenure and improved rental agreements; expansion of rural credit and innovative mechanisms for weather-based crop insurance; and improved access to information and information and communications (ICT) technology.

To the extent that innovation is strongly associated with risk-taking, risk-reduction mechanisms need to be introduced to avert devastating losses of income of small farm holders. Grants, tax incentives, innovative insurance policies and new forms of venture capital may be able to provide this kind of protection (Leeuwis and Hall, 2010).

The institutional failures that perpetuate poverty also need to be removed

The policy challenge resides in how to mobilize the resources needed to expand the range of supportive services that are critical to improving the capacity of small farm holders to innovate and to compete in dynamic markets. Increasing investments for rural development and shifting the focus of attention towards support of small-scale farm holders will require, in many contexts, overcoming the obstacles put in the path of change by prevailing power relations (Spielman, 2005). Rural poverty and food insecurity are frequently the result of "institutional failures" (including coordination failures, land insecurity, gender discrimination and marginalization of indigenous populations), which prevent the development of more dynamic food production systems.

One of the most contentious issues in most counties is land distribution. To a large extent, low income and food insecurity among small-scale farm holders can be traced back to the lack of adequate access to land. Traditional land reform designed to improve access to land and provide support to different forms of association among farmers would help to effect economies of scale in production and, most importantly, in the marketing of food crops. However, changing land distribution practices, securing property rights and creating incentives that benefit small farm holders often require the formation of political coalitions that might challenge the status quo.

In countries like Brazil, China and India, whose Governments had chosen to prioritize poverty reduction and food security, dynamic innovation systems emerged in support of agricultural development. In other instances, the scaling up of innovative practices—inter alia, for rice intensification, for farmers' training and in the case of India, for the watershed initiative mentioned above—was possible through the endorsement by international organizations, national non-governmental organizations and local governments of new practices in support of dissemination of knowledge, greater participation by and capacity development of farmers, building of missing infrastructure and improving access to credit, information and other supportive services.

National strategies for food security and sustainable agriculture need to explicitly recognize the politico-economic obstacles to inducing a radical transformation in agriculture that is focused on improving the productive capacity of small-scale food producers.

Gender-sensitive agricultural innovation

Innovation for sustainable food security must incorporate a special focus on women

Unless policies to promote innovation in agriculture have an explicit gender focus, women will continue to be disadvantaged with respect to accessing new technologies and supportive services. Women in rural areas face major labour constraints as a result of their multiple responsibilities: besides providing traditional family care, rural women are typically responsible for fetching water and firewood, tending animals and farming the house garden and often engage in wage employment. Simple labour-saving tools (including green cooking stoves and appropriate tools for planting and weeding) and better access to water for house consumption would help ease their time constraints.

It is important in fostering the creation of a dynamic innovation system that addresses women's needs, to grasp the impact of the institutions and local values that define their role. Very often, the creation of gender-sensitive systems of innovation in agriculture will also require a radical transformation of the institutional constraints that prevent better access by women to secure land tenure, credit and technical assistance.

Innovative partnerships

Successful innovation experiences in the last 30 years demonstrate the importance of building partnerships among multiple stakeholders so as to strengthen the capacity of small-scale farm holders to access technology, inputs and larger markets. While the corporate private sector has played an increasingly important role in accelerating innovation in agriculture through a variety of mechanisms, the risk of excluding small-scale farmers is also large. Through appropriate regulation to prevent monopolistic practices in food markets, and better access to information, credits and risk insurance, small-scale farm holders would be in a better position to engage in mutually beneficial partnerships with the corporate private sector.

Appropriate regulations, technical assistance and better access to supportive services are needed to prevent inequitable partnerships

Perhaps one of the most important drivers of change in recent years lies in the transformation in food retailing. The emergence of large supermarket chains, which control between 40 and 50 per cent of the food market in Latin America, about 10 per cent in China, 30 per cent in South Africa and 50 per cent in Indonesia, has concentrated the purchase of large quantities of food subject to strict quality standards, a phenomenon that has led to the displacement of traditional wholesalers and small retail shops. For small farm holders, participating in these markets depends on their capacity to meet strict quality standards and to achieve concerted commercialization of their products through cooperatives and other forms of association. The risk of exclusion, however, is large, especially for farms in remote and difficult to access areas (Berdegué, 2005). Technical assistance to farmers in meeting with quality standards would help to expand their opportunities for participation in larger markets.

Voluntary standards and certification programmes, payments for ecological services and production value chains ...

The proliferation of ethical and environmental certification processes in recent years is opening new opportunities for creating value chains that link small farm holders to larger exporting markets. For instance, voluntary standards and certification programmes in the banana industry address a wide range of issues including environmental protection, labour rights, safety and health at work, social equity and the welfare of local communities.[7] These can have substantial benefits for participating producers and traders by providing price premiums; improving market access and stability; helping to rationalize production, reduce costs, improve labour management and enhance the morale and participation of workers; improving the company image; and even aiding in the conservation of productive natural resources. Nevertheless, other types of standards aimed at food safety, quality, traceability and good agricultural practices, which are mainly developed by large firms in major markets, tend not to ensure price premiums, and may thus harm small-scale banana growers by significantly raising the costs they incur (Food and Agriculture Organization of the United Nations, 2008).

... can increase the productivity of small-scale farmers practising sustainable agriculture

Payments for ecological services with resources from businesses interested in protecting hydrologic services and Governments can play an important role in increasing the incomes of poor rural communities and maintaining ecological diversity (box III.3). However, new mechanisms for expanding payments for environmental services (PES) to small farm holders for the protection of natural resources, to conserve biodiversity and to increase carbon sequestration in agriculture and forestry need to be in place.

Box III.3

Payment for ecosystem services in Costa Rica

One approach to encouraging the conservation and restoration of forest ecosystems is to pay private landowners directly for conservation (Ferraro and Simpson, 2000). Payments for reforestation, forest management and conservation lead to improvement of the livelihoods of individuals and communities engaged in forestry.

In Costa Rica, alarming rates of deforestation in the 1970s led to the pioneering of a national-level payments for environmental services (PES) programme, facilitated by the recognition of ecosystem services in forest protection legislation in 1996. In this market-based system, landowners receive direct payments for environmental services provided by forestry ecosystems, including (a) mitigation of greenhouse gas emissions; (b) hydrologic services; (c) biodiversity conservation; and (d) provision of scenic beauty for purposes of promoting recreation and ecotourism (Malavasi and Kellenberg, 2002).

The national PES scheme is credited with having stopped the destruction of the Costa Rican rainforest and recapturing over one quarter of the country's land mass-to-forest cover in the period from 1987 to 2000. The scheme has also enhanced social development by rewarding more than 7,000 small- to medium-scale private landowners for the environmental services their property provides (Pax Natura, 2011).

In 2008, the programme's budget was close to \$13 million for an area of 652,000 hectares. The programme receives funds from businesses interested in protecting hydrologic services, which are matched by government funding from a fossil fuel tax, and multilateral loans and grants (Ecosystem Marketplace, 2010).

Source: UN/DESA.

7 Among the most common standards in the banana industry are those associated with organic agriculture, the Rainforest Alliance and the fair trade movement, along with SA 8000 and ISO 14001.

Civil society organizations play an important role as intermediaries between small-scale farm holders and other groups

Civil society organizations and private philanthropies are becoming important players in the area of agricultural innovation. Most of the recent stories of innovation characterized by pro-poor and positive environmental impacts have entailed the active participation of international and national civil society organizations, which engage in different activities depending on the context: advocacy and lobbying for pro-poor institutional change in rural areas; serving as intermediaries between research and agricultural practices; capacity-building among farmers and the dissemination of information and good practices; facilitating collective action and creation of farmers' organizations for the purchase of inputs and marketing of food; aiding in the creation of value chains so as to help reduce transaction costs; protecting against risk through creation of informal safety nets for farmers; strengthening the capacity of women to participate in marketing production and innovation; and, in the case of private philanthropies, directly funding research, capacity-building and access to technology.

Each type of activity has its own dynamic which does not necessarily interlock with others. Each actor will also have its own special interests whose pursuit may not always translate into improved welfare and enhanced innovative capacity of small farm holders.

Government regulations are important for strengthening fair and dynamic partnerships

Government policies have an important role to play in enhancing the contribution of the multiple stakeholders that are part of the Sustainable Agricultural Innovation System and creating a regulatory framework to "promote trust and cooperation, delimitation of contributions and rewards, timely information on compliance of obligations, enforcement of agreements, recognition and protection of the rights of each party" (Berdegué, 2005, p. 21). While any Government's policy will have to respond to the specific context of its own country, building stronger partnerships within an SAIS will require participants to collaborate in developing a clear-cut strategy directed towards achieving the objectives of agricultural reform while ensuring that there are resources adequate for expanding rural infrastructure and supporting provision of services to small-scale farmers.

National strategies for support of education, science and technology in addressing food security

Reviving agricultural R&D

Resources for agricultural research and development are limited and highly concentrated

At the heart of the food security problem is insufficient investment support for, and public attention focused on, small-scale farmers whose food production is mostly for local consumption. Since the 1980s, international support for agricultural research has decreased and national agricultural research centres have scaled back their programmes for the production and distribution of seeds (Dubin and Brennan, 2009). Expenditures for agricultural R&D in Africa, East and South-East Asia (excluding China) and the Middle East remain low (figure III.9).

Moreover, agricultural R&D investment is largely concentrated in a few countries. In 2000, developed countries accounted for 57 per cent of total public agricultural R&D. Among developing countries in Asia and the Pacific, China and India were responsible for 67 per cent of such investments; and in Latin America, Brazil alone accounted for 45 per cent of the total. In sub-Saharan Africa, annual agricultural R&D investment had grown by 0.6 per cent in 1981-2000, contracting slightly during the 1990s (Beintema and Elliott, 2009).

Figure III.9
Public agricultural R&D investment trends in developing countries, 1981-2008

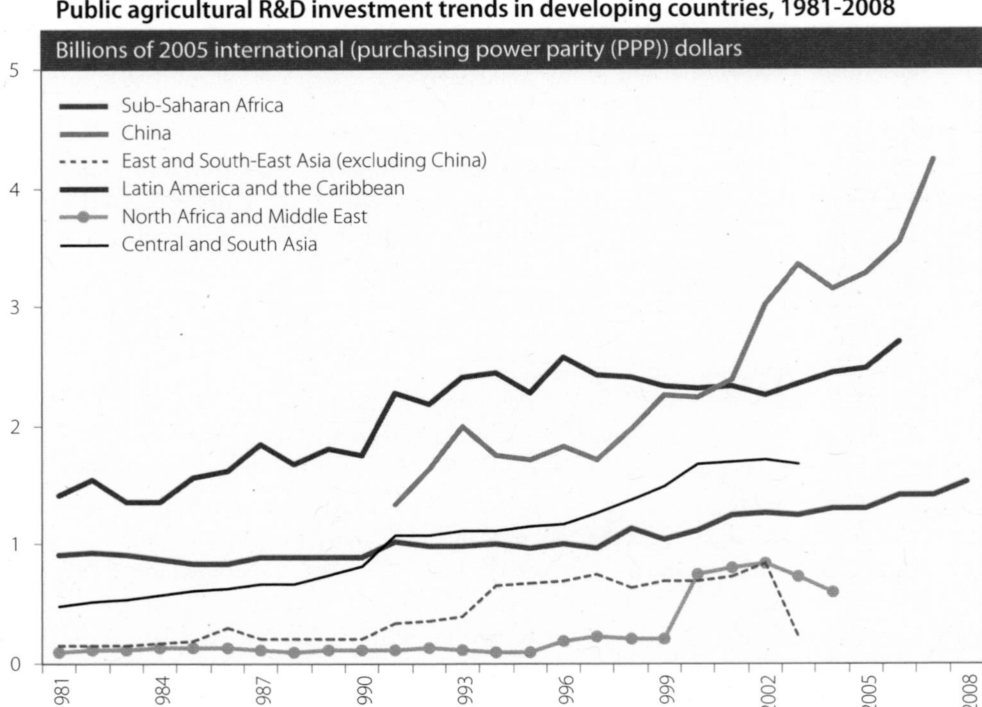

Source: UN/DESA estimates, based on Agricultural Science and Technology Indicators (ASTI), facilitated by the International Food Policy Research Institute (IFPRI) (http://www.asti.cgiar.org/data/).

While the corporate private sector has become a substantial player in agricultural R&D, especially in the production of agricultural chemical inputs, machinery and biotechnology, its focus has been centred largely on profitable research targeted towards meeting the demands of wealthy consumers and on intermediate inputs for large farmers (Ervin, Glenna and Jussaume, 2010).

National strategies for education, science and technology in agriculture need a larger supply of stable resources

While current agricultural knowledge and technology provide a range of alternatives for achieving sustainable agriculture, the adoption of new practices and technology requires additional investment in research and development to ensure adaptation to the diversity of agroecological conditions in which small-scale farm holders operate. In addition, rapidly changing climate patterns and food markets require continuous research and the development of new technology and crop management. Explicit national education, science and technology strategies are essential to accelerating productivity growth and environmental sustainability and there are three areas of development that need to be addressed by any national science and technology strategy for food security: agricultural research and development, including through the private sector; improved technical assistance to small-scale farm holders, mainly through extension services; and improved education of farmers, including innovative mechanisms for peer learning.

Agricultural research and development for food security

In drafting a national strategy for education, science and technology, it is important to have a clear picture of the agricultural research architecture so as to be able to identify the institutions currently involved, their interests, and the type of research that those institutions undertake. Such a perspective will facilitate the design of appropriate incentives to facilitate effective collaboration among scientists, farmers, the corporate private sector and non-governmental organizations. A clear mapping of the relationships among objectives, actors and resources will help to leverage existing capacities so as to facilitate the process of building dynamic Sustainable Agricultural Innovation Systems.

Public agricultural R&D for food security

Research whose goal is sustainable food security has the characteristics of a public good …

Agricultural research should consider climatic, soil and water conditions of the relevant agroecological region; technology and know-how are not easily transferable across regions without additional investment in adaptation (Pardey and Beintema, 2001). Hence, adaptation of technology to particular farming conditions should be central to the agenda of public research institutions in developing countries.

Agricultural R&D is the classic example of a public good: in the absence of public sector involvement, underinvestment in agricultural R&D will continue, especially in those areas where markets are small and consumers poor (the case of staples in developing countries is particularly relevant in this regard). The importance of farmers' capacity to innovate and adapt technology to their particular needs is widely recognized, but this has to be complemented—and is often guided—by formal agricultural R&D.

… and, as such, it requires adequate and stable financial support from Governments

Public institutions will continue to be the major source of formal agricultural R&D in developing countries; the significant economies of size, scale and scope that are achievable in agricultural research cause even private research to rely on the basic research and innovation originating in public institutions (ibid.). With few exceptions, national research institutions in developing countries lack adequate resources to operate efficiently through appropriate infrastructure, competitive salaries and research funds. Instability in operational budgets compromises their independence and capacity to operate efficiently. Agricultural research is cumulative and has long maturity cycles; discontinuity in funding and poor documentation of processes exacerbate permanent loss of knowledge. The development of a new variety of wheat, rice or corn, for example, requires 7-10 years of breeding (ibid.).

Regular allocations of public resources are important for maintaining research infrastructure and adequate salaries for scientific personnel. Funds generated internally from the sale of products and services (such as seeds and laboratory services) are becoming important in countries like Chile, China and Indonesia and may complement regular budgets. Yet the competition aimed at securing resources from different sources, which are often driven by commercial interests or by donor preferences, rather than by social and environmental concerns, leads to fragmentation of research objectives. Careful evaluation of funding sources helps to prevent diversion of research away from its focus on public goods (Echeverria and Beintema, 2009).

In addition to stable financial resources, public research institutions also require a radical change in their current linear hierarchic model of operation so as to improve their responsiveness to the needs of farmers, including through joint experimentation and learning.

In this regard, multidisciplinary teams comprising agronomists, water engineers and nutritionists are essential

Public research institutions also need to expand their traditional disciplinary approach to encompass an interdisciplinary focus in response to wide-ranging farmer demands. Transformation of diverse agroecological rural economies requires the expertise of biologists, agronomists, water engineers, nutritionists, economists and social and political scientists (Lipton, 2010). Participation of women, especially in sub-Saharan Africa where women constitute a large proportion of the agricultural labour force, will also be critical to enhancing their low levels of representation and decision-making in agricultural research and extension services and to addressing their specific needs.

Building the capacity of national public research centres is a long-term process requiring substantial and sustainable investments and radical changes in their organizational culture. Much of agricultural R&D resources in developing countries are concentrated in a few countries—Brazil, China and India—which have developed dynamic systems of innovation with capacity to engage in frontier research. In the case of small and poor countries, pooling resources to strengthen regional research agendas is perhaps the most effective option for improving their collective capacity. Promising experiences of regional and South-South agricultural cooperation include, for instance, agreements between research institutions of Brazil and China and African institutions.

Private sector research in climate-resistant crops

Through biotechnology, it may be possible to develop crops of great utility to the poor ...

... but the research agenda needs to be expanded to include consumption crops in poor countries

Rapid technological innovation for achieving food security and tackling climate change will require closer collaboration with the private sector towards expanding research in frontier areas. While the corporate private sector has increased its role in the development of technology in agriculture, we have chosen to focus attention below on private research in biotechnology, which remains controversial.

Biotechnology has the potential to improve crop varieties grown by the poor, by making them herbicide-resistant, less dependent on chemical pesticides and more resilient to water stress and by conferring on them a greater nutritional value. Biotechnology may therefore be able to respond to the variety of agroecological conditions in poor and food-insecure regions, provided the current research agenda can be expanded to reflect the challenges faced by small-scale farm holders. So far, private research in biotechnology has concentrated on the development of products that can be easily protected by patents and focused mainly on building resistance to weeds and insects in profitable plants (mainly soybeans, corn, cotton and canola), which are of interest to large-scale farmers.

While it is technically feasible to expand the research agenda to better contribute to food security, independent assessments of the larger impacts of this technology are urgently needed. Biotechnology has not fully responded to concerns about long-term environmental impacts and possible spillover effects to wild plant varieties. Bt cotton[8] and corn, for example, use less herbicides and pesticides, but if these crop varieties develop resistance to the less toxic chemical herbicides and pesticides, future more toxic inputs may be required.

In addition, recent research has found that the problem of gene flow, the spread of genes from genetically engineered (GE) crops into non-GE ones, is a more serious phenomenon than was originally thought. In this case, adoption of transgenic crops could have large negative ecological implications if "GE crops are adopted more widely in developing countries where domesticated crops have wild relatives" (Ervin, Glenna and Jussaume, 2010, p. 7).

Going forward, better understanding of the consequences of transgenics based on full disclosure of information, including rigorous assessments on a case-by-case basis, will be critical to informing decisions about the deployment of this technology on a larger scale in developing countries.

One legitimate concern in exploring the potential of biotechnology to contribute to food security and sustainable agriculture is the concentration of research and products in two large firms: DuPont Pioneer and Monsanto, which account for the largest

8 Bt cotton is a genetically modified variety that is resistant to insects.

proportion of the genetically modified crop acreage in the world (Ervin, Glenna and Jussaume, 2010). The cost of seeds and inputs may discourage use of this technology by small farm holders, especially if the market continues to be dominated by a few large companies which exert influence over prices.[9]

Research in biotechnology demands closer and more direct collaboration among public research institutions, the private sector and small-scale farmers …

Yet, biotechnology can still be an effective instrument for facilitating the transformation of agriculture in poor agroecological regions with low productive capacity under current technology (namely, in parts of Africa, Central America and Asia with degraded natural resources). However, the structure of incentives and governance of innovation in this area require radical changes, which ensure, inter alia, that (a) the objectives of food production and environmental sustainability become central to the research agenda in biotechnology; (b) all stakeholders, but especially small farm holders, can actively participate in shaping the research agenda; (c) scientific researchers consider the needs of small farm holders, consumer tastes and the characteristics of local markets and contexts; (d) there is full disclosure and an open flow of information; (e) peer reviewing to assess the possible unintended environmental consequences of biotechnology is practised; and (f) effective antitrust regulation is put in place (Wright and Shih, 2010).

… through innovative partnerships, including patent buyouts, prizes, joint ventures, co-financing and advance-purchase agreements

While there are no simple answers in this regard, publicly funded research should maintain an explicit focus on strategic priorities for food security, including improving yields and resistance of staples, improving the nutritional value of crops, facilitating sustainable use of natural resources and/or reducing the use of external chemical inputs. Innovative mechanisms designed to engage the private sector need to be explored: results-based performance contracts—for the development, for example, of improved seed or crop varieties with higher water-stress tolerance and greater responsiveness to fertilizers—granted on a competitive basis may be one means of stimulating private research. Patent buyouts, prizes and proportional prizes may be other means of doing so (Elliot, 2010; Bhagwati, 2005). Use of more traditional subsidies, co-financing arrangements and joint ventures should also be explored, within a framework of appropriate protocols for maintaining the public-good nature of research products (Pardey and Beintema, 2001).[10]

While it still needs to be tested in agriculture, the 2010 Advanced Market Commitment mechanism for the production of vaccines, whereby donors made a large advance purchase at a predetermined price in order to induce participation by large pharmaceutical companies, may offer significant lessons relevant to the effort to stimulate private research and technological innovation for food security.[11]

More generally, building partnerships with the corporate private sector is important, but in the specific case of food security, Governments and public research institutions in developing countries need to be fully involved in setting the research agenda, including comprehensive risk assessments and suitable regulations on the use of new technologies (Lipton, 2010).

---

9 Seed prices have increased by 30 per cent since 1996 when GE seeds were introduced, a price increase higher than that for any other input (Ervin, Glenna and Jussaume, 2010).

10 One of the problems connected with current associations between private companies and public universities is that the research products are often protected by the copyrights held by the private companies that have co-financed the research.

11 The Governments of Canada, Italy, Norway, the Russian Federation and the United Kingdom of Great Britain and Northern Ireland and the Bill and Melinda Gates Foundation signed an agreement with GlaxoSmithKline and Pfizer, Inc., by which the firms committed to supplying 30 million doses of vaccines each year for 10 years at a reduced price for developing countries, provided donors made additional payments for 20 per cent of the doses. See http://www.gavialliance.org/media_centre/press_releases/2010_03_23_amc_commitment.php (accessed 6 February 2011).

Technical support and extension services

The second pillar of an effective strategy for promoting education, science and technology in agriculture is the dissemination of information and technology, which during the green revolution, was mainly carried out by agricultural extension workers. In the current context, a larger number of actors (civil society organizations, the private sector, farmers and multilateral organizations) contribute towards this end.

Large-scale extension services in agriculture are important for effective technological adaptation

A survey conducted by the Global Conference on Agricultural Research for Development (GCARD) estimates that about one half billion agricultural extension workers exist globally, most of them being public workers. Although the number appears large, the general perception is that it is inadequate, especially when measured against the needs of small-scale farm holders who, for the most part, have been deprived of the services of such workers (Lele and others, 2010). Agricultural extension workers who have no particular interest in promoting the use of commercial products are still an important vehicle for the transmission of knowledge, information and training for small farm holders, provided that they have adequate training themselves, a clear mandate and appropriate incentives to perform their job.

... with special attention to female farmers

Exclusion of women from technical support needs to be explicitly addressed. In Africa, women receive 7 per cent of agricultural extension services and less than 10 per cent of credit offered to small-scale farm holders.[12] Moreover, inasmuch as educational curricula tend to exclude topics with particular relevance to women (such as nutrition, sanitation, hygiene, gender-specific tools and management), gender analysis and targeted initiatives must be incorporated in agricultural education, research and extension services (Davis and others, 2007).

In Ethiopia and Mozambique, for example, inadequate resources for expanding research and training facilities and retaining faculty members have compromised the quality of education received by students. Graduate education is more conceptual in nature than managerial and practically oriented and has thus failed to nurture innovative capacity among farmers in the range of services required to improve production and marketing, including their capacity for collective action (ibid.).

In India, a country with a long tradition of promoting agricultural R&D, Hall and others (1998) found little interaction occurring between scientists and extension service providers, or between production and post-harvest scientists. Institutional segregation by discipline and highly centralized management obscure the relevance of technical support to farmers and the building of partnerships among public agricultural R&D institutions, the private sector, farmer associations and civil society organizations. Scientists and extension service workers often have fairly fragmented perspectives on production and marketing and have been unable to make practical use of research findings and knowledge.

A longer-term commitment to providing adequate funding for public research and training needs to be accompanied by a new approach to technical education—one that is more practical in nature and oriented towards problem-solving and decision-making, and with greater capacity to involve farmers and civil society organizations in finding interdisciplinary and creative solutions to new problems.

---

12 New Agriculturist, "Gender revolution: a prerequisite for change" (July 2008). Available from http://www.new-ag.info/focus/focusItem.php?a=493.

Basic education and peer learning

The third pillar of an effective sustainable agricultural innovation system is basic education and adult literacy and training. The ability of farmers to innovate, learn from one another and adapt to change largely depends on their capacity to access and process information including through information and communications technology. Rapid expansion of quality education in rural areas, including adult literacy and training, should receive the highest priority in any strategy aimed at strengthening farmers' responsive capacity to rapidly changing agroecological and market conditions. Flexible land management and the capacity to innovate in production, storage and marketing practices and techniques require appropriate use of information and technology as part of a continuous learning process (Davis and others, 2007).

Formal and informal education and peer learning are essential for strengthening the innovative capacity of farmers

More innovative mechanisms for the transmission of knowledge and training also need strengthening. The experience of the Farm Field Schools—operating in 87 countries—shows that innovation and flexible natural resource management can be advanced through farmer-to-farmer learning, with participation from formal and informal research institutions (see also box III.1). In-service and on-the-job training and distance education have also proved effective and are increasingly complementing extension services.

Beyond rural education

Education is also central to bringing about the requisite societal transformation needed to ensure food security and protect the environment. Formal and informal education, extension services, advertising and information campaigns, and political and civil society mobilization are important means of creating more sustainable food production and consumption patterns.

Education aimed at changing behaviour is also important in respect of reducing waste and promoting the adoption of sustainable diets and consumption practices

On the production side, farmers need to be informed and trained and stimulated to adopt more sustainable practices. However, the challenge of feeding a rising and increasingly affluent population also requires behavioural changes in terms of consumption, including dietary patterns. In particular, the livestock sector, which has grown rapidly to meet the increasing demand for meat, is a prime cause of water scarcity, pollution, land degradation and greenhouse gas emissions. This has prompted calls for support for vegetarian diets.[13] However, the nutritional importance of animal protein, particularly in developing countries, and the differences, in the context of production efficiency and environmental impact, between different types of livestock,[14] may warrant, instead, warnings against consumption of red meat and dairy products (Godfray and others, 2010b). Publicity, advocacy, education and even legislation can also be used to bring about ideological, cultural and behavioural changes so as to reduce high levels of retail and domestic food waste in the developed world.

Building new institutions that pave the way towards sustainable agriculture and food security by strengthening the multiple nodes of the SAIS and changing behaviours is

13 See David Batty and David Adam, "Vegetarian diet is better for the planet, says Lord Stern", 26 October 2009. Available from http://www.guardian.co.uk/environment/2009/oct/26/palm-oil-initiative-carbon-emissions (accessed 14 March 2011).

14 According to certain estimates, cattle (under intensive production) consume 114-125 litres of water per animal per day compared with 1.3-1.8 litres in the case of chicken; cattle require 8 kilograms (kg) of cereal per animal to produce 1 kg of meat compared with a 1 kg feed requirement for chicken (Food and Agriculture Organization of the United Nations, 2006; Intergovernmental Panel on Climate Change, 2007b). The dairy and beef sector of the United Kingdom accounted for over 24 metric tons of carbon dioxide equivalent ($MtCO_2e$) of CH_4 and N_2O emissions in 2005, compared with 2 $MtCO_2e$ from the poultry sector (Radov and others, 2007).

a long-term process requiring commitment of resources, a clear vision of the overall direction of change, and capacities to adapt to a changing environment. National strategies to achieve food security and sustainable agriculture will help Governments ensure consistency in typically decentralized agricultural innovation systems, and help guide the direction of donor resources and private sector investments. Without this minimum framework, rural structural change may not occur in time to prevent irreversible human and environmental damage to the current food production and consumption systems.

Regional and global partnerships for food security and environmental sustainability

Payments for environmental services and better regulation of commodity markets could facilitate international cooperation towards food security and environmental protection

The international community has much to contribute to a global agenda for food security and environmental sustainability. Chapter VI examines the challenges associated with international cooperation in various areas. In the case of agriculture and sustainable land management, delivering on the financial pledges made in the aftermath of the food crisis of 2007-2008 would constitute a good down payment on realizing the commitment to the goal of eradicating hunger. Other areas where international action can be expected include:

- Reform of agricultural subsidies in OECD countries, including subsidies to biofuels, and support to new-generation biofuels to reduce the diversion of agricultural land use from food production.
- Increased international investment in agricultural R&D for food security with private sector participation in development. Adequate funding for the effective functioning of CGIAR during the green revolution was critical to facilitating rapid innovation through proactive adaptation and dissemination, often with supportive and facilitative (subsidized) public provisioning of infrastructure and other needed inputs. Reconstituting the global, regional and national capacities for agricultural R&D with international financial support can result in the generation of a rapid increase in agricultural productivity.
- New financing mechanisms to expand payments to small farm holders in developing countries for environmental services (PES) that help protect natural resources, to preserve biodiversity and to increase carbon sequestration in agriculture and forestry.
- Elimination of non-tariff barriers to food trade which prevent the expansion of markets to include small-scale producers in developing countries.
- Adoption of green/ecological footprint standards.
- Effective regulation of commodity futures markets to avert speculation with food prices.

In the very short term, preventing export bans on food crops and panic buying in response to weather-related catastrophes would help to reduce large price spikes. In addition, mechanisms to protect vulnerable populations utilizing safety nets and food assistance are necessary in order to reduce the impact of increasing food prices. Building global grain reserves may be an option in responding to food emergencies but the management and deployment of assistance require closer scrutiny so as to ensure an effective emergency response and to avert longer-term negative impacts on local food production systems.

Chapter IV
Reducing human harm from natural hazards

Summary

- The frequency of natural disasters, especially in the form of floods and storms, has quintupled over the past 40 years, the elevated disaster risk being partly due to the effects of climate change. Developing countries bear a higher share of the adverse consequences of that increased risk.
- Heightened disaster risk associated with poor management of the natural environment and human-induced climate change requires a long-term approach to reducing risk from natural events. An integrated and preventive framework embedded in national development strategies would be most effective.
- Existing technologies and knowledge systems—including those embodied in traditional and indigenous knowledge—are up to the tasks of reducing disaster risk and adapting to climate change. The bottleneck in their application to the local context lies in the cost of adaptation and investment, given other competing public priorities. To ensure that disaster risk management is accorded the appropriate attention, disaster reduction and adaptation programmes must be an integral part of national development strategies.

Introduction

In the 1970s, about 69 natural disasters were recorded worldwide every year. By the 2000s, this average had increased to 350 per year. Changes in the natural environment, owing in part to global warming, have elevated disaster risk and in consequence adaptation to those changes is testing human ingenuity. Developing countries tend to bear a disproportionate share of the adverse consequences of increased disaster risk since multiple vulnerabilities associated with lower levels of development and inadequate resources hinder them from more rapidly building up resilient infrastructure and knowledge capacities for risk reduction.

Vulnerability to disaster is highly correlated with the level of development and the incidence of poverty

Susceptibility to harm is highly correlated with inequities in respect of the level of development and the incidence of poverty. Overcoming those challenges within an environmentally constrained world means that technological transformation for green growth must be swift and inclusive. The uncertain availability of key inputs for economic growth and life survival such as renewable energy and water makes the utilization of technologies for disaster risk reduction and sustainable development more urgent. Putting an end to these inequities will require the inclusion of the appropriate technological content in the adaptation strategies and livelihood sphere of those who are poor and most vulnerable.

The present chapter assesses strategic options for facilitating and realizing the technological transformation needed to adapt to and reduce disaster risk, and to create the domestic capacity to respond swiftly and effectively to the increased adverse impacts of natural hazards on livelihoods and the likelihood of catastrophic events.

Multidimensional impacts of natural disasters

The number of natural disasters has quintupled over the past 40 years

As noted above, the number of natural disasters has quintupled over the past 40 years. Figure IV.1 depicts this trend for floods, storms, droughts, extreme temperatures, earthquakes, volcanoes, slides and wildfires. By far most of the increase can be accounted for by the greater incidence of hydro-meteorological disasters (floods, storms, droughts and extreme temperatures), which are associated with climate change. Further, the number of prolonged droughts has tripled.

The *World Economic and Social Survey 2008* (United Nations, 2008b, p. 81) stressed that, although geologic disasters can inflict severe damage, hydro-meteorological disasters "pose a greater threat of becoming large-scale (catastrophic) disasters and also account for much of the rising trend of reported disasters in recent decades".

In many countries and regions, the weather has become more erratic and often there have been spells of extreme temperatures. Some areas have been hit by much more intense rainfall in recent decades, while others have seen their dry seasons turn into prolonged droughts. Many countries regularly encounter both manifestations of these forces of nature: heavy storms and rainfall, and severe droughts.

The increased frequency of weather-related events is exacerbated by their increased intensity

The increased frequency of hydro-meteorological hazards is exacerbated by the increased intensity of these events. While the number of category 1 hurricanes and storms

Figure IV.1
Frequency of disasters, 1970-2009

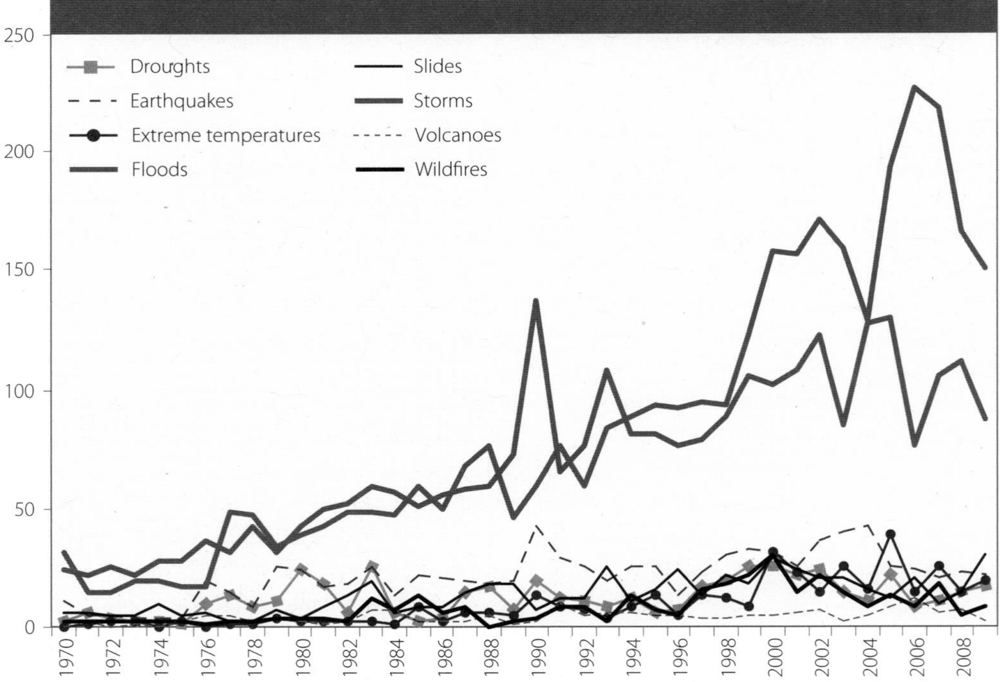

Source: UN/DESA, based on data from the Centre for Research on the Epidemiology of Disasters (CRED) International Disaster Database (EM-DAT), Université catholique de Louvain, Brussels, 2009. Available from www.emdat.net.

remained approximately constant throughout the 35-year period 1970-2004, hurricanes and storms in the strongest categories (4 and 5) have almost doubled in number in all ocean basins (Webster and others, 2005). The number of droughts that lasted from one to two years or longer tripled between 1970-1979 and 2000-2009.

Mapping disaster risks

Disasters are becoming more damaging to livelihoods

There has been a long-term declining trend in the average number of persons killed per disaster, leaving the average number of deaths per year from disasters more or less constant. At the same time, however, the increased frequency of natural disasters has contributed to a large increase in the number of persons affected by disasters and in the estimated costs of the damages incurred (figure IV.2). Damages have averaged \$88 billion per year since 2000, compared with an average of \$12 billion in the 1970s. While disasters have become less life-threatening, they have become more damaging to the livelihoods and well-being of the communities hit.

The human impact of disasters is significantly higher in developing countries

The human cost measured in terms of both the number of persons affected and the loss of human lives is significantly higher in developing countries, albeit with regional differences. According to figure IV.3, which shows the greater vulnerability of the populations of developing countries, the number of affected people (injured and homeless) is highest in developing Asia, although large parts of Africa and Latin America also show high degrees of impact. The forces of nature have also affected large numbers of persons per event in developed countries (most notably Australia and Spain), despite their generally greater resilience.

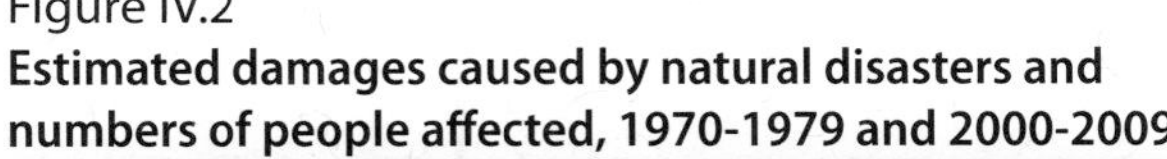

Figure IV.2
Estimated damages caused by natural disasters and numbers of people affected, 1970-1979 and 2000-2009

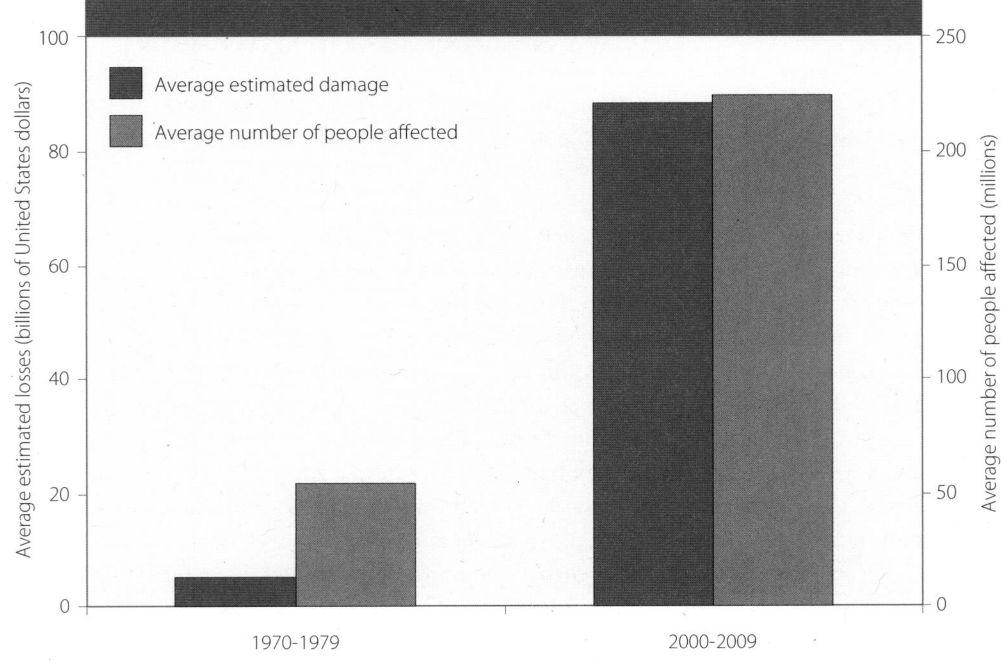

Source: UN/DESA, based on data from the Centre for Research on the Epidemiology of Disasters (CRED) International Disaster Database (EM-DAT), Université catholique de Louvain, Brussels, 2009. Available from www.emdat.net.

Figure IV.3
Number of persons affected per disaster,[a] by country, 1990-2009

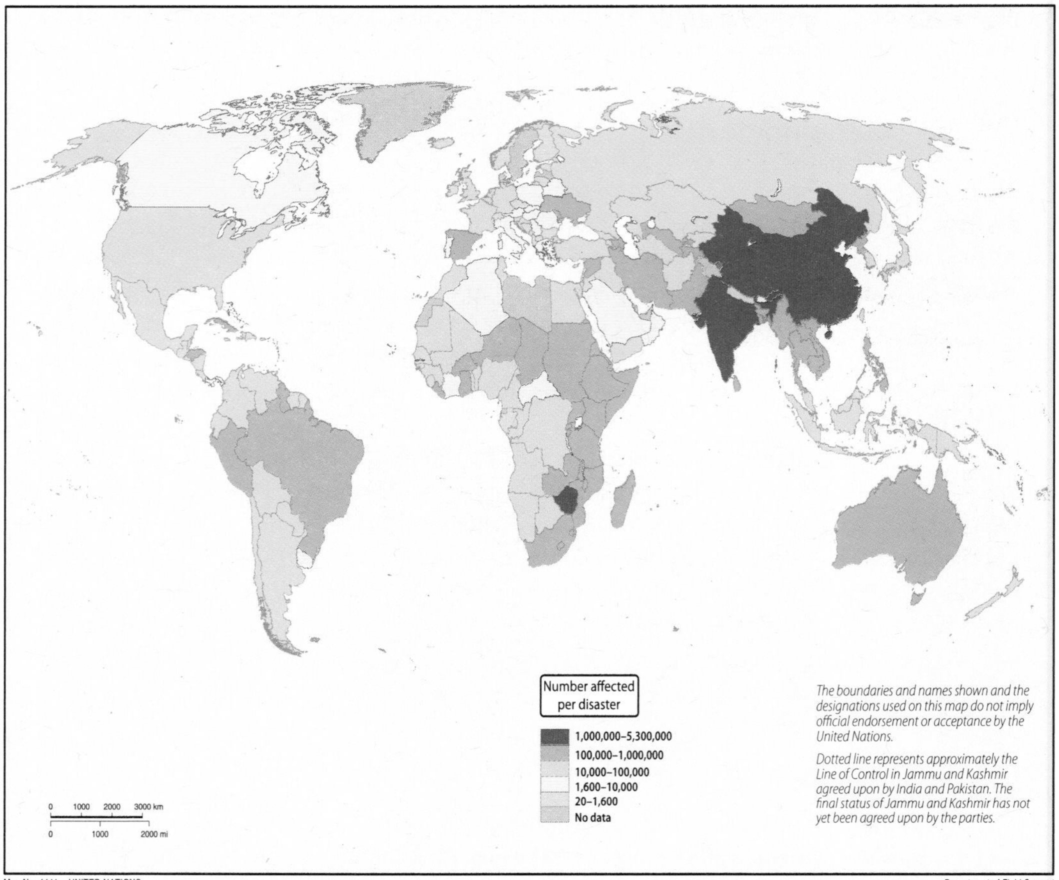

Number affected per disaster

1,000,000–5,300,000
100,000–1,000,000
10,000–100,000
1,600–10,000
20–1,600
No data

The boundaries and names shown and the designations used on this map do not imply official endorsement or acceptance by the United Nations.

Dotted line represents approximately the Line of Control in Jammu and Kashmir agreed upon by India and Pakistan. The final status of Jammu and Kashmir has not yet been agreed upon by the parties.

0 1000 2000 3000 km
0 1000 2000 mi

Map No. 4441 UNITED NATIONS
May 2011

Department of Field Support
Cartographic Section

Source: UN/DESA, based on data from the Centre for Research on the Epidemiology of Disasters (CRED) International Disaster Database (EM-DAT), Université catholique de Louvain, Brussels, 2009. Available from www.emdat.net.

Note: Grey areas represent countries where there was no disaster incidence, where data were not available or where there were no persons affected by disaster(s).

a Including floods, storms, droughts, extreme temperatures, earthquakes, volcanoes, slides and wildfires.

Most disasters have occurred in developing regions

While all regions are exposed to natural hazards, it is in developing regions that most disasters (comprising droughts, earthquakes, extreme temperatures, floods, slides, storms, volcanoes and wildfires) tend to occur (table IV.1). Also, by far most deaths, injuries and cases of homelessness (over 95 per cent) result from natural disasters in developing regions. The average number of persons killed per 100,000 inhabitants is five times higher in developing than in developed regions. Although the divergence between developing and developed regions continues when considering least developed countries and the group of small island developing States, the proportions vary. The number killed per 100,000 in least developed countries is 12 times higher than in developed regions and in small island developing States, more than 2½ times higher. Further, the number affected per 100,000 in least developed countries is 16 times higher than in developed regions and in small island developing States, about 10 times higher. The fact that the incidence of affected persons is somewhat below the developing-country average can be explained by the fact that many least developed countries and small island developing States tend to be less densely populated. Australia and New Zealand are exceptions owing to the higher incidence of climatic events in those countries, which have been affected by extreme temperatures, storms and floods, droughts and wildfires, as well as earthquakes, over the last 20 years.

Table IV.1
Frequency of natural disasters and impact by regions, 1970-2009

	Number of disasters	*Killed (thousands)*	*Affected (millions)*	*Killed (per 100,000)*	*Affected (per 100,000)*
Developing regions	**6 482**	**2 788**	**5 966**	**68**	**145 182**
Africa	1 200	705	370	109	56 982
Asia (excluding Japan)	3 478	1 828	5 401	61	179 051
Latin America and the Caribbean	1 575	250	191	57	43 717
Oceania	229	4	4	68	59 101
Developed regions	**2 451**	**153**	**84**	**14**	**7 364**
Australia and New Zealand	238	1	16	6	78 216
Europe	1 281	127	37	18	5 251
Japan	180	10	4	8	3 100
Northern America	752	15	27	5	9 356
Total	**8 933**	**2 941**	**6 049**	**56**	**115 361**
Memorandum items:					
Least developed countries	1 363	981	631	189	121 471
Small island developing States	636	18	35	37	72 760

Source: UN/DESA, based on data from the Centre for Research on the Epidemiology of Disasters (CRED) International Disaster Database (EM-DAT), Université catholique de Louvain, Brussels, 2009. Available from www.emdat.net.

Is climate change to blame?

The number of disasters that are climate-related has grown at an accelerating rate.

The number of climate-related disasters has grown at an accelerating rate since the 1950s, while geophysical disasters have followed a relatively stable upward trend, as was shown in figure IV.1. As this suggests the existence of a driver of increasing climate-related disaster events, researchers have tried through complex models to quantify to what extent weather shocks are related to climate change. The Intergovernmental Panel on Climate Change (IPCC) (2007a) warns, however, that results are often not conclusive, since climate models are constantly being updated and improved. The model-based analyses available to date suggest that climate change will result in warmer or fewer cold nights, warmer days and more occurrences of hot days over most land areas. The number of spells of warm weather and heatwaves, as well as the frequency and duration of droughts, will likely increase. This will result in decreased agricultural yields in most warm areas, where the majority of developing countries are located, and will have adverse effects on the availability and quality of groundwater. Climate change will also increase the frequency of heavy precipitation in most areas as well as the number of intense tropical cyclones in areas where they are at present occurring. Using model simulations, it has been estimated that each rise in tropical sea surface temperature by 1° C will increase the speed of hurricane surface winds by between 1 and 8 per cent and the degree of core rainfall by between 6 and 18 per cent (United States Climate Change Science Program, 2008).

Disaster-proofing can offer an opportunity to build infrastructure that utilizes more advanced technology

For many developing countries, environmental constraints and shocks are already part of a vicious cycle, which keep them trapped at a low level of income, undermines their resource base and restricts their ability to protect themselves from future shocks (United Nations, 2008b; 2009). While developing countries will need to take these adverse effects into account, they can also respond to them as offering an opportunity to make changes in living arrangements, build infrastructure that can absorb labour, and use more advanced technology for adaptation to and reduction of disaster risk.

Unequal impacts on livelihoods

Settlements of low-income people are often the most vulnerable

Developing regions bear the brunt of the adverse impacts of natural hazards (United Nations, 2008b; 2009). Droughts in sub-Saharan Africa and flooding in parts of Asia have already ravaged thousands of livelihoods, while heat spells have increased the risk of water scarcity in some countries. Also, urban development tends to increase environmental pressures that lead to disasters such as flooding, and settlements of low-income people are often the most vulnerable in this regard. Affluent groups—whether in developing countries or not—are often in a better position to withstand flooding, as the experience of the 2005 hurricane Katrina in New Orleans demonstrates (McGranahan, Balk and Anderson, 2007).

Unchecked climate change threatens to reduce agricultural yields and increase the number of malnourished children by 2050

Climate change has been associated with shifted growing seasons, threatened water sources and exacerbated food shortages. Unchecked climate change would reduce agricultural yields which, according to one estimate, could in turn cause a 20 per cent increase in the number of malnourished children by 2050 (Food and Agriculture Organization of the United Nations, 2009b). The adverse impacts on food production and nutrition would have ripple effects directly affecting the employment, income and livelihoods of both poor small farmers and urban-dwellers. In Bangladesh, for instance, the overflow of seawater has affected the livelihoods of fishermen, since rivers are now contaminated and fish banks have been decimated. By 2050, 70 million people in Bangladesh could be affected annually by climate change.

A greater frequency of extreme temperatures will have devastating consequences

The impacts of the symptoms of climate change have different dimensions. A greater frequency of extreme temperatures, for example, can have devastating consequences. In the summer of 2010, the Russian Federation faced the worst heatwave in its history, which caused 56,000 fatalities and left 100,000 homeless and over 500,000 hectares of forests destroyed by fires. In general, longer and drier seasons in Argentina, Canada, the Russian Federation, Ukraine and the United States of America have severely damaged harvests.

Similarly, the range of health risks from climate change and natural disasters is likely to be considerable, with all parts of the globe affected, as the unprecedented number of deaths in Europe from recent heatwaves has demonstrated. However, health vulnerability is very closely linked to other vulnerabilities, with the burden of climate-sensitive diseases imposed overwhelmingly on the poorest populations which also experienced the lowest coverage by health services. In fact, the people most vulnerable to climate change are those who have not been well protected by health sector interventions in the past. Meanwhile, it is not variation in the extent of climate change but in the magnitude of pre-existing health problems that has had the greatest influence on impacts in different regions. A recent assessment by the World Health Organization (WHO) (2009) estimates that the burden of disease imposed through the modest warming that has occurred since the 1970s is causing about 150,000 additional deaths annually in low-income countries from four climate-sensitive health outcomes—malnutrition, diarrhoeal disease and malaria. These additional deaths are concentrated in already vulnerable population groups; for instance, 90 per cent of the burden of malaria and diarrhoea, and almost all of the burden of diseases associated with undernutrition, are borne by children aged 5 years or under (Campbell-Lendrum, 2009; United Nations, 2009). Over the long term, higher temperatures will induce excessive levels of ozone and other air pollutants that provoke cardiovascular and respiratory diseases, and of pollen and other aero-allergens that trigger asthma, with the poor and the elderly being hardest hit (Beggs, 2004).

As many of the most important infectious diseases are highly sensitive to both temperature and precipitation conditions, higher temperatures will increase the rates of survival and replication of bacterial contaminants of food and water sources, which are responsible for imposing a large proportion of the burden of diarrhoeal disease, particularly in poor countries. Already, per capita mortality rates from vector-borne diseases are almost 300 times greater in developing regions than in developed ones (World Health Organization, 2009). The situation creates a double burden for women, who can be discriminated against based on their diseases-related afflictions (United Nations Children's Fund, 2008; UN Women Watch, 2011).

Per capita mortality rates from vector-borne diseases are almost 300 times greater in developing regions than in developed ones

Flooding may pose additional risks to human health. In Bangladesh, where arsenic contamination of groundwater is heavy, flooding increases the rate of exposure among rural populations. Long-term exposure to arsenic has deleterious health effects, including the increased incidence of certain cancers.

The most immediate effect of hydro-meteorological hazards on health and well-being is likely to be a function of the availability of water. It is estimated that one quarter of the population in Africa (about 200 million people) experience water stress (Ludi, 2009). Increasing temperatures and more variable precipitation are expected to reduce the availability of freshwater, making it more difficult to fulfil basic needs for drinking, cooking and washing. Meanwhile, a greater incidence of flooding, stemming, inter alia, from more intense precipitation and from sea-level rise in lower coastal zones, will further contaminate freshwater supplies, thereby further increasing water scarcity.

The most immediate effect of weather-induced hazards on health and well-being would be a function of the availability of water

The presence of large human populations in those zones has further increased the vulnerability of the coastal ecosystems. Two thirds of all cities worldwide with a population of more than 5 million are located within coastal areas with an elevation of less than 10 metres. Because of growing urban development and increased extraction of groundwater, among other factors, land has sunk in some places. The territory around Tianjin in China, for example, has been sinking at the rate of about five centimetres per year. In cities located in large river deltas, land areas have been disappearing because of sediment deposition. In the absence of added protection, lower land levels enhance the vulnerability to more frequent flooding, coastal erosion and the immersion of salt in groundwater.

Lower land levels increase vulnerability to more frequent flooding and coastal erosion

Natural hazards will thus have varying impacts on communities depending on the nature of the hazard and the location, resilience of infrastructure and preparedness of the population in affected areas. Table IV.2 summarizes some of the possible effects of increased climate-related natural disaster risks.

Enhanced risk of "extreme" disruptions?

Recent research confirms that major disruptions in the ecosystem, often referred to as "extreme events", have become more likely. Such events could already be occurring in the area of biodiversity (as evidenced by rapid extinction of species) and may be close to affecting fisheries and some water systems (Rockström and others, 2009).

The increased likelihood of extreme events led major stakeholders to reassess current climate change adaptation strategies through the preparation of a special report on the theme (Intergovernmental Panel on Climate Change, 2009). It is argued therein that "gradual and non-linear change to ecosystems and natural resources and increasing vulnerability further increases the consequences of extreme weather events" (p. 2). At the current global average temperature, the likelihood of extreme events has increased,

The likelihood of extreme events has increased

Table IV.2
Multiple potential impacts of changing climate conditions

Enhanced natural hazard risk	*Potential impacts*
Higher variability in local climate	• Major increase of hours lost due to extreme events
Sea-level rise	• Loss of coastal land • Problems in water supply and drainage systems • Increased risk of flood damages
More intensive droughts	• Increased water demand during hot, dry summers • Higher risk of fires, particularly in informal settlements • Increased risk of new vector-borne and water-borne diseases or changes in their spatial distribution
Increase in frequency and magnitude of flooding	• Disruption of the transport system • Increased risk of new vector-borne and water-borne diseases or changes in their spatial distribution • Major increase of hours and trips lost due to extreme events
Heatwaves	• Increased mortality and health risk due to the combination of heat and air pollution • Problems of energy supply • Increased water demand
Increased occurrence of storms and storm surges	• Increased risk of flooding • Possible contribution of storms and floods owing to the combination of extreme events to blockages of drainage systems

Source: Adapted from Birkmann and others (2010a).

and the threat of large-scale discontinuities such as "changes in the ocean conveyor-belt heat-distribution system or catastrophic thawing of the Arctic leading to massive releases of methane" grows if global warming leads to an average temperature rise of more than 2° C above pre-industrial levels. In particular, the risks of large sea-level rise and extreme weather events are currently larger than previously thought (World Bank, 2010a).

Extreme events are more likely to be cross-border

Extreme events are more likely to be cross-border, with serious damage being inflicted on different sectors of the economies affected. The 2004 tsunami in Asia and 2011 earthquake in Japan are recent reminders that the damages and losses resulting from disasters can be staggering, if the location and the existing level of resilience of the social and economic infrastructures renders the areas affected particularly vulnerable. Total damages and losses incurred by Indonesia were more pronounced in the social sector (health, education and housing), while in Sri Lanka it was the productive sectors (fisheries, industry and commerce, tourism and agriculture) that suffered more (Birkmann and others, 2010b).

There are uncertainties associated with predictions of possible disaster scenarios, which are often coloured by their own assumptions about future weather, degrees of global warming and tipping points (Gillett and others, 2011). In cases where the causes of the increasing risk of large disasters and catastrophes are sufficiently understood, shifts in individual and social behaviour and application of known technologies to reduce their impact are urgent.

Approaches to disaster risk reduction and climate change adaptation

Existing incremental approaches

Despite imminent threats, disaster risk management and adaptation to climate change in developed and developing countries alike have not been mainstreamed into broader decision-making processes (Adger and others, 2003; Huq and Reid, 2004). The challenge tends to be addressed by adding an "extra layer" to existing policy design and implementation mechanisms rather than by adjusting the original design so as to confront climate change in a more integrated way (O'Brien and others, 2008). Equating adaptation measures with emergency relief and placing the challenge within a framework of reliance on requests for donor support (a frequent approach) has not helped, having in fact given rise to an often bifurcated outlook, based on which efforts either focus on responses to the impacts of climate change (through coping measures) or seek to reduce exposure through climate-proofing existing projects and activities, particularly in the context of disaster risk management. While these two approaches share a common goal, there is a real danger that the perspectives underlying coping and proofing pull in different policy directions and that fragmented actions will end up, at best, creating a partial solution to problems and, at worst, causing new problems or aggravating existing ones (Sanchez-Rodriguez, Fragkias and Solecki, 2008).

Fragmented actions could, at worst, cause new problems or aggravate existing ones…

As discussed in *World Economic and Social Surveys 2008* and *2009* (United Nations, 2008b; 2009), there is indeed a real danger, already apparent in the response to natural disasters, that underlying structural causes of vulnerability and maladaptation will be ignored, including a number of closely interlinked and compounding threats to social and economic security.

…including a number of closely interlinked and compounding threats to social and economic security

Recent efforts to forge a more consistent approach to the adaptation challenge and weather shocks stress the central role of market incentives (Organization for Economic Cooperation and Development, 2008). These efforts usefully highlight the methodological challenge inherent in evaluating the costs and benefits of disaster risk reduction and adaptation to climate change, point to a role for positive incentives, and help expand the scope for more efficient coping and risk-reduction strategies.

However, such an approach tends to perceive the challenge in terms of a series of discrete and unconnected threats which can be addressed through incremental improvements made to existing arrangements, thereby ignoring the large-scale investments and integrated policy efforts that are likely to be called for in response to climate-related threats.

The need for an integrated approach

The alternative approach perceives adaptation in terms of building resilience with respect to climatic shocks and hazards by realizing higher levels of socio-economic development so as to provide threatened communities and countries with the requisite social and economic buffers. As elaborated in *World Economic and Social Surveys 2008* and *2009* (United Nations, 2008b; 2009), such an approach would contribute to meeting the larger development challenge of overcoming a series of interrelated socio-economic vulnerabilities.

The Hyogo Framework for Action supports the integration of climate change adaptation and disaster risk reduction into national development strategies

Disaster risk reduction strategies are now moving increasingly in this direction. Until 2005, those strategies had dealt with the adverse effects of natural hazards without explicitly recognizing the impact of climate change. Nevertheless, this experience allowed the accumulation of invaluable knowledge on how to cope with and reduce the adverse impact of disasters. As noted above, for most countries and at different income levels, a significant reduction of fatalities per disaster has been observed during the last two decades. However, the increased incidence of climatic disasters, that is, those linked to hydro-meteorological hazards, has required a reconsideration of disaster risk reduction strategies. Within the Hyogo Framework for Action 2005-2015: Building the Resilience of Nations and Communities to Disasters,[1] 168 Governments agreed to integrate climate change adaptation and disaster risk reduction by: (a) identifying climate-related disaster risks; (b) designing specific risk reduction measures; and (c) improving the use of climate risk information (para. 19 (c)). This approach focuses on responding effectively to more frequent and intense hydro-meteorological hazards and on the need to mainstream risk reduction into national development strategies.

A significant strain in the thinking on disaster risk reduction was focused on policy responses to volcanic eruptions, tsunamis and earthquakes. Climate change adaptation strategies, on the other hand, focus on increased resilience to hydro-meteorological hazards, with emphasis on finding a sustainable and preventive approach to disaster risk reduction. With greater consideration given to climatic hazards caused by human activity, disaster risk reduction strategies are becoming more long-term in perspective and more oriented towards prevention of disasters through investing in sustainable development.

Risk, uncertainty and catastrophes

In economics a key distinction is made between the concept of risk and that of uncertainty. In the present context, risk would apply to a situation where the probability and impact of an adverse event "can be inferred from past behaviour of the economy and the ecosystem" (Ocampo, 2011b, p. 19). Risk would then apply to a situation involving the likelihood of damages caused by hurricanes and tropical storms in certain parts of the world. Because the expected costs of such risks are quantifiable to a certain degree, resources can be set aside to insure against the potential damage.

Even where risks can be quantified, the impact of interactions among these risks could be uncertain

Uncertainty is a condition in which the probability and scale of adverse events cannot be inferred from past information. The uncertainty can arise with respect to the category of "known unknowns"; in this instance, awareness can exist concerning the possibility of a catastrophic event, such as a natural disaster, but with few clues regarding whether such a disaster could set in motion irreversible processes beyond certain thresholds. This form of uncertainty is incorporated, for instance, in some future climate change scenarios. Yet, even where risks can be quantified, the impact of interactions among these risks could be uncertain. In this regard, Rockström and others (2010) suggest that one type of uncertainty stems from "what human-induced surprises could be triggered, even though several of the risks have been identified [such as the] abrupt change in the African and Indian monsoons, accelerated melting of glaciers, abrupt savannization of rainforests [and the observed] abrupt collapse of the Arctic summer ice in 2007" (p. 34).

When the issue is one of risk, in particular in matters of diseases and other health challenges, it is incumbent on societies to invest in and set aside resources substantial enough to deal with the calculated impact of disasters and other threats to human

1 A/CONF.206/6 and Corr.1, chap. I, resolution 2.

life. When the risk and its distribution across the population can be calculated actuarially, private insurance could be utilized to raise the needed resources. Even when risks are well quantified, an adequate level of public investment is required to induce private investor participation, in, for example, general public health and seasonal flood control. When the existing domestic technology is not adequate for dealing with those risks, public authorities can either import it or invest in its development. Cost-benefit calculations can provide guidance on the level of public funding required, suitable financing modalities, and the manner in which risks are to be incorporated in national development strategies.

Detailed studies on the likelihood and potential costs of selected hazards would be advisable

However, when the threat belongs to the category of uncertain events, guidance will be limited on probability of impact and scale of the threat. The potential cost of extreme events raises the question how much a country can accomplish through preventive strategies and building resilience. Nevertheless, incorporating those threats in national planning is appropriate. Undertaking detailed studies on the likelihood of extreme events and the potential costs for selected hazards might also be considered by national authorities. The ferocity of onslaught of some recent natural hazards suggests that uncertainty in connection with natural events is quite pervasive and that building climate-proof infrastructure would not eliminate all risk.

Given the likelihood of extreme events, three sets of critical questions need to be posed when addressing the investment and technological challenges of providing protection:

- What kind of infrastructure would be resilient and how much should be invested in such infrastructure? Should precautions be taken to eliminate even the smallest possibility of a ruinous catastrophe? How should the costs and benefits of the necessary investments for present and future generations be weighed? In some cases, a more pointed question could be asked, namely, whether providing greater resilience is feasible at all in the case, for example, of some small island developing States and hence whether other "adaptation strategies" might be needed, such as massive evacuation of threatened populations;
- What kinds of research and development need to be promoted to achieve better protection against natural disasters, through the devising of better technological solutions in the area of climate-proofing of infrastructure and better management of the natural environment?
- How could these considerations be aligned with broader national sustainable development strategies and global disaster reduction strategies?

The road to technological transformation

Societies seeking to achieve the overall objective of reducing the impact of disaster risk are confronted with difficult choices as regards investment and technology policy. Because resources are finite, the coverage of disaster reduction is necessarily finite. The fact that the geographical context, the historical record in respect of disasters and projected climate change impacts vary from country to country implies that the nature and the scale of extreme events will vary from country to country as well. Strategy choices will be more limited in countries like the small island developing States that are more vulnerable to extreme events. Countries, operating within their limits, will eventually call on other countries for assistance when the scale of an actual disaster overwhelms domestic resources that can be devoted to disaster response and prevention.

While there are no general strategies for confronting these issues, national development strategies can identify explicitly the natural hazards that impose risks on projected development results and, on that basis, establish a prioritization of risks that must be addressed by investment and technology development programmes. National Governments can also identify the natural hazards that are regional in nature and then undertake to facilitate regional investment strategies.

Harnessing local technologies

For many poor countries, the strategic challenge is to combine the best local knowledge on adaptation with advanced expertise

For many poor countries, the strategic challenge is to combine the best local knowledge on adaptation with the expertise of qualified professionals and practitioners. The United Nations Framework Convention on Climate Change (2006) underlines that "(m)ost methods of adaptation involve some form of technology—which in the broadest sense includes not just materials or equipment but also diverse forms of knowledge" (preface). The Cancun Adaptation Framework (United Nations Framework Convention on Climate Change, 2011, decision 1/CP.16, sect. II) stresses that adaptation "should be based on and guided by the best available science and, as appropriate, traditional and indigenous knowledge, with a view to integrating adaptation into relevant social, economic and environmental policies and actions" (para. 12).

Through use of local knowledge, some communities have been able to cope with floods by building houses on stilts and cultivating floating vegetable plots, while remote satellite sensing has been able to provide more accurate weather forecasts for flood prevention. Such local action is vital. The visionary project of green integrated urban planning in Curitiba (Brazil) created a balance between promoting green economic growth and building resilience to more intense and frequent natural hazards, including floods, extreme temperatures and population density, and developing green areas (box IV.1). In Ho Chi Minh City (Viet Nam), where communities have been involved in mangrove rehabilitation, local action has been essential for effective adaptation (see below and annex IV.1).

Box IV.1

Smart and integrated urban planning in Curitiba, Brazil

While the population of Curitiba grew from 361,000 in 1960 to 1,828,000 in 2008, it did not experience the typical concomitants of expansion, namely, congestion, pollution and reduction of public space. For instance, the city's green area expanded from 1 square kilometre to over 50 square kilometres per person between 1970 and 2008, despite the fact that its population density increased threefold in the same period.

One of the key choices of urban planning had been growth in a "radial linear-branching pattern", which served to enhance green areas and encouraged, through a combination of land-use zoning and provision of public transport infrastructure, the diversion of traffic away from the city centre, the development of climate-resilient housing, and the location of services and industries along the radial axes.

By turning areas vulnerable to flooding into parks and creating artificial lakes to hold floodwaters, Curitiba has managed to address its potentially costly flooding problem. The cost of this strategy, including the relocation costs of slum-dwellers, is estimated to be five times less than that of building concrete canals. Among other results the property values of neighbouring areas appreciated and tax revenues increased.

Curitiba has also promoted waste management infrastructure and public awareness on waste separation and recycling. With 70 per cent of the city's residents actively recycling, 13 per cent of solid waste is recycled in Curitiba, compared with only 1 per cent in São Paulo.

Source: United Nations Environment Programme (2010a); and Rabinovitch (1992).

Institutional gaps

The Cancun Adaptation Framework reaffirmed the institutional focus by stressing that "adaptation … requires appropriate institutional arrangements to enhance adaptation action and support" (para. 2 (b)). One dimension of such arrangements would be the mainstreaming by Governments of investments in disaster risk reduction research and education into science, technology and production sector policies, thereby making them part of green national innovation systems, as discussed further in chapter V.

Societies also have to overcome political resistance to deployment of technologies on location. Harnessing the energies of different stakeholders with diverse interests during the process of creating a sustainable path of development is not an easy task for any Government. In 2005, the integration of different interests, ideas and activities into a three-year project to restore the Cheonggyecheon Stream in Seoul required often lengthy dialogues and negotiations. Under the leadership of the mayor, the city's political, business and residential communities found a way to coordinate their views on balanced urban growth and sustainable development. The rehabilitation of the local streams and improvements in water systems have enhanced resilience to floods.

The scope of technological transformation

Investments in climate change adaptation technologies can be part of building economic diversification strategies

The increased incidence of disasters and the higher likelihood of extreme events make investment in adaptation urgent. For the poorest countries, international cooperation will require emphasis on adaptation rather than on mitigation. For many developing countries, the demands of coping with the additional burdens of climate change will exceed domestic resources and require external support. In those countries, investment and technological choices will need to focus on addressing the most immediate hazards.

Reducing disaster risk in a sustainable manner will entail changes in the design of settlements and infrastructure, including roads, rail systems and power plants. Investments in technologies for adaptation must result in the installation of resilient infrastructures along with the creation of a diversified economy within the context of sustainable national development strategies (United Nations, 2008b; 2009).[2] Countries need to prepare a detailed assessment of their vulnerabilities, and of possible impacts of disasters, to establish priorities in respect of their responses. For example, the Federal Service for Hydrometeorology and Environmental Monitoring of the Russian Federation prepared impact indices for infrastructure depending on the frequency, intensity and duration of extreme weather events and climate volatility. In Siberia, as the level of risk to infrastructure built on permafrost has become increasingly unacceptable (owing to the reduction in the bearing capacity of permafrost soils in response to warmer weather), new building techniques are necessary to upgrade the infrastructure (United Nations Framework Convention on Climate Change, Subsidiary Body for Scientific and Technological Advice, 2010).

Existing technologies and knowledge systems for adaptation and disaster prevention

Technologies and knowledge systems for adaptation and disaster risk reduction are diverse and complex. Table IV.3 presents a typology of technology and knowledge systems for adaptation to and reduction of the adverse impacts of natural hazards.

2 See chap. II for an analysis of green technology strategies for climate change mitigation.

Table IV.3
Technology and knowledge-based systems for climate change adaptation

Adaptation strategy	*Floods*	*Droughts*	*Rise in sea level*	*Heatwaves*	*Storms*	*General adaptation technologies*
Infrastructure	Build dykes, gates and setback defences to protect coasts, industry and households; create upland buffers, reservoirs, floating communities/houses, and flood-resilient buildings/infrastructure	Create redundancy for aqueducts and water supply; build rainwater harvesting systems	Raise low-lying areas; elevate houses in high-risk zones; build floating communities and water plazas, sea walls and coastal defence structures; flood-proof new buildings	Modification of building design and construction	Implementation of sustainable urban drainage systems (storm water retention ponds, constructed wetlands)	Improve sanitation facilities in informal settlements; improve water treatment; genetic/molecular screening of pathogens
	Improve construction of low-income houses; housing construction in high-lying areas	Improve water supply infrastructure	Retrofitting; desalinization techniques	Plant trees	Improve construction of informal housing	Improve public transport; develop urban rail systems
	High-level storm sewers; fortify and adapt critical infrastructure, for example, larger diameters of pipes	Advanced recycling and efficient technologies in industrial cooling	Redevelop city parts	Urban shade-tree planting	Technology for monitoring and warning systems	Catalytic converters; tall chimneys
	Situate industrial systems away from vulnerable areas	New varieties of crops, irrigation systems, efficient windbreaks, erosion control techniques	Situate industrial systems away from vulnerable areas; use physical barriers to protect industrial installations	Installation of high albedo roofs; advanced recycling and efficient technologies in industrial cooling	Development of resilient infrastructure (storm water drainage, new sewage treatment installation); high-level storm sewers; flood proofing	Construction of sound housing for low-income groups
Regulation	Amend and enforce building standard codes; provide adequate flood insurance	Improve water efficiency standards	Amend and enforce building standard codes	Amend building codes	Improve regulation for informal housing	New buildings guidelines; emission controls
	Ban new buildings and increase land-use restrictions in high-risk zones/areas	Establish and enforce rules and regulations for water-use restrictions	Ban new buildings and increase land-use restrictions in high-risk zones/areas		Building standards (including in respect of increased risk of storms); amend building codes	New planning laws; traffic restrictions
	Improve regulation for informal settlements	Amend and enforce building standard codes				Watershed protection laws; water quality regulation

Table IV.3 (cont'd)

Adaptation strategy	*Floods*	*Droughts*	*Rise in sea level*	*Heatwaves*	*Storms*	*General adaptation technologies*
Management	Resettlement	Reduce pollution of freshwater; recycle water (grey water)	Resettlement	Urban greening programme; green roof programme; support green belts in the city	Monitoring, early warning and evacuation systems	In households, educate on removing items associated with transmission of water-borne diseases
	Update flood plain maps; implement/ update maps of flood evacuation zones	Develop comprehensive water strategy; integrate water resource planning	Monitor and assess climate impact indicators	Increase awareness of heat-related stress and management; heat-health alert system	Ban on new buildings in high-risk zones	City-wide strategic and integrated planning; urban planning to reduce heat island effects
	Training of task force to protect critical infrastructure	Change consumer behaviour	Local and regional climate models; systems for monitoring and early warning and evacuation systems	Public education on climate-related health threats; hygiene behaviour	Protection of mangrove forests	National health insurance schemes; vaccination; impregnated bednets; build-up of pit latrines
	Work with vulnerable neighbourhoods	Reduce leaking water pipes		Minimize paved surfaces	Task force to protect vital/critical infrastructure; use of storm shelters	Pollution warnings; boil-water alerts
	Establish emergency preparedness plans; establish public contingency plans	Establishment and training of task force to protect critical infrastructure; increase training in ecological fire management		Air quality management system; reduce energy required for air conditioning	Protect green belts that can help manage storm-water run-off	Lay out cities to improve efficiency of combined heat and power systems; optimize use of solar energy
	Improve flood warning and evacuation systems	Monitoring, early warning and evacuation systems; build awareness campaigns		Task force to protect vital/critical infrastructure	Protection of water catchment areas	Link urban transport to land-use patterns; promote mass public transportation; carpooling
		Temporary resettlement		Emergency preparedness plans	Emergency preparedness plans	Cluster homes, jobs and stores

Source: UN/DESA.

Technology policies in support of adaptation and disaster risk reduction can, based on their dimensions, be classified according to three categories: (a) infrastructure, (b) regulation and (c) management. High-level storm sewers and flood-proofing of new buildings, for example, come under infrastructure investment. New standards for water-use efficiency and improvement of building codes are examples of regulatory measures: Saint Lucia, for example, has revised its building codes so as to effect reduction in the adverse impacts of hurricanes, floods and extreme temperatures. The protection of mangrove forests, resettlement and green urban planning are examples of measures related to improving management expertise.

Most disaster reduction efforts can rely on known technologies and indigenous knowledge

As indicated in table IV.3, the building of floating communities, water plazas and coastal defence structures can be useful for tackling seawater-level rise as well as floods. Banning new buildings in high-risk zones can be useful for preventing the adverse impacts of storms and floods. Similarly, training to increase awareness of heat-related stress can be applied to reducing the impacts of droughts as well as heatwaves. The United Nations Framework Convention on Climate Change, Subsidiary Body for Scientific and Technological Advice (2010) notes that a rainwater harvesting system for the Caribbean Insular Area of Colombia, which has been effective in reducing pressure on the island aquifers, is also being used in the Plurinational State of Bolivia to reduce the adverse impact of droughts on the livelihoods of Aymara farmers.

From a consideration of the entries in the table, one concludes that the actions required for adaptation can rely heavily on known technologies and indigenous knowledge. The bigger challenge is to put into place the required technical capabilities and managerial skills to build dykes, improve construction of low-income housing, establish and enforce rules and regulations for water use, establish monitoring and early warning systems, and improve preparedness for emergencies and evacuation, all of which constitute key interventions for reducing disaster risk. Enhancing human resources in these areas is critical. Investments in disaster responses—including those that entail the expansion of infrastructure and basic services, which can have strong development impacts in the poorest countries—must be included in public sector planning. However, the set of disaster risk reduction projects does not constitute a development strategy. There are "hard choices" regarding how much of a country's limited investment resources can be devoted to these projects that have still to be made.

Technology gaps to be bridged

The scale of the required technological transformation will vary from context to context

As the scale of the required technological transformation will vary from context to context as a function of the degree of disaster risk, the adaptation technologies available, and the kinds of adaptation and disaster risk reduction strategies that countries have already put in place, the following questions will have to be asked: What is the degree of disaster risk for different countries? What are the actual adaptation technologies and knowledge systems in use? Which technological gaps should still be overcome? The choices to be made based on the answers must reflect the constraints on financial resources faced by many developing countries.

Although discussed in the relevant literature, not all of the existing adaptation technologies presented in the table have been widely used or integrated into ongoing projects. In fact, many of them have been implemented only in particular contexts and on differing scales. Annex IV.1 describes 25 ongoing adaptation projects selected from a databank of 135 (some of them including technological elements) operated in 70 countries.[3] Over 75 per cent of all projects tend to focus on the rural sector, attesting to what Birkmann and von Teichman (2010) have underscored, namely, that, in general, fewer adaptation strategies have been formulated for urban areas. The annex specifies the main types of disasters to which countries are subject, the kind of adaptation technologies being used, and the scale at which these are implemented.

About one third of all projects in the databank use technological strategies, often in combination with other components such as infrastructure, disaster risk reduction, awareness, planning and institution-building. The Grameen project, for example, combines technology and empowerment strategies by providing poor people with access to loans for home designs that are especially adapted to heavy rains and floods and, in addition, can be conveniently dismantled then reassembled in the face of severe flooding. Another advantage of this project is its national character, with the disaster-risk management sector integrated into the national development strategy of Bangladesh. Similarly, the Bogotá project, which reduces the risk of floods and landslides by improving risk-detection technology, emergency response, recovery finance, and awareness, uses a "cocktail" of tangible and intangible adaptation strategies, such as insurance, monitoring early warning systems, institution-building, improved infrastructure, and awareness, to achieve its objectives.

A national-scale project run by the Netherlands Climate Change Studies Assistance Programme operates along similar lines, focusing on institution-building, policy and efficient use of resource strategies in order to improve water management in Yemen. These projects demonstrate that technological improvement and capacity-building activities are central to increasing the resilience of vulnerable people, including women, children and older persons. In contexts where these groups have received equal access to preventive hazard management activities, the number of fatalities has been zero (World Bank, 2010a).

The United Nations Development Programme (UNDP) has also been active in facilitating technologies for climate change adaptation.[4] Tessa and Kurukulasuriya (2010) classify 29 UNDP country projects within four different cateogies: (a) projects implemented in the areas of agriculture/food security and water resources management (mainly in Africa), (b) projects on infrastructure for disaster risk management (in Asia, Africa and the Pacific), (c) projects designed to improve ecosystem management (forest, wetland and coastal ecosystems) and build capacity of stakeholders and institutions and (d) projects for sustainable land management whose aim is to improve the technical capacity of farmers and pastoralists and implement sustainable land management techniques.

Multinational projects to enhance adaptation technologies and risk reduction strategies are critical

Multinational projects set up to enhance adaptation technologies and risk reduction strategies are also important. For example, with the financial support of the World Bank, the Caribbean Community Secretariat is engaged in safeguarding the Community's coastal resources by enhancing risk communication strategies and running pilot projects designed to enhance the use of technology, planning methods and awareness campaigns. Similarly, the multinational rural project on disaster-risk management run by the non-governmental organization ActionAid engages communities in Bangladesh, Ghana, Haiti, Kenya, Malawi and Nepal in activities geared to making schools in high-risk areas safer, thereby enabling those schools to act as models during disaster risk reduction awareness campaigns. Strategies centred on raising awareness, institution-building and infrastructure investment support the implementation of this project.

3 The data bank was originally compiled by McGray, Hammill and Bradley (2007).

4 The Global Environment Facility (GEF) is the largest funder, with $66 million in grant contributions.

Facilitating multilateral adaptation projects is critical given the multidimensionality of the adverse impacts of many natural hazards. Box IV.2 offers an example of such a project, namely, the partnership between China and multilateral organizations established to strengthen technology-centred adaptation strategies.

Box IV.2

China's climate change adaptation programme and partnership framework

In the context of China's 2007 National Climate Change Strategy, the Government of China and a number of United Nations organizations[a] have signed off on a $19 million three-year joint programme to coordinate strategies and policies designed to enable communities to withstand the adverse impacts of climate change. The aim is to incorporate the Strategy into policies and legal measures, improve local capacities and partnerships for financing technology transfer and models, and ensure the adaptation of vulnerable communities to climate change.

Vulnerability assessment and adaptation constitute one of the major components of the programme, the other two being mitigation and climate change policy. The adaptation component addresses the areas of: (a) poverty reduction; (b) agriculture development in the Yellow River Basin, including vulnerability assessment and adaptation measures; (c) water management in the Yellow River Basin, including improved groundwater monitoring in high-risk areas; (d) a strategy for adapting China's health planning and practice to climate change; and (e) assessment of employment vulnerabilities and development of adaptation strategies.

While all of China is expected to feel the impact of climate change, poor areas are more vulnerable. In western China, glacial melting in the Himalayas and shifting patterns of land and water use for large upstream and downstream populations increase risks to livelihoods. On the south-east coast, rising sea levels threaten the lives of local people. Thus, vulnerability assessments and adaptation measures are needed, which tie in policies devised to eradicate poverty, combat diseases and ensure environmental sustainability.

Changes in temperature and precipitation have significant impacts on water resources. Analysis of the relation between climate change and hydrologic systems has proved useful in preventing water-related disasters. Owing to the increased reliance on groundwater in semi-arid and arid areas and the expected increased groundwater depletion and quality deterioration, assessment of actual changes in groundwater levels and quality and the impacts on livelihood is needed. This will allow for appropriate adjustment policies, including the imposing of restrictions and, where possible, the implementation of measures to recharge groundwater.

As climate change may lead to changes in the distribution of disease vectors and increases in vector-borne diseases, China's National Environment and Health Action Plan is focused on mainstreaming climate change into control policies for major health sensitive climate outcomes such as water stress/desertification, flooding, dust storms and smog, and on enhancing adaptive capacities.

The adverse impact of climate change on employment is still an unexplored area but the consequences are likely to be substantial. Major changes in crop distribution and yield would greatly affect people in rural areas and thus force migration into urban and industrial areas. There is a need for the Government and the commercial sector to assess the potential impacts on employment in order to formulate effective policies and responses. The focus on employment issues will complement and support other programme activities.

The programme intends to build on United Nations experience derived from past and ongoing projects and from grappling with high-level policy issues, to build on potential synergies among organizations in the United Nations family, to utilize the complementary support of other bilateral and multilateral organizations, and to focus on rural areas so as to maximize environmental and social co-benefits. The process of consultation among United Nations institutions and the Government of China, identification of priorities, creation of partnerships and pursuit of implementation and monitoring activities will all contribute to the creation of a model for replication in other countries.

Source: China climate change partnership framework document. Available from http://www.mdgfund.org/sites/default/files/China%20Environment_JP%20Signed.pdf.

a United Nations Environment Programme (UNEP), World Health Organization (WHO), Food and Agriculture Organization of the United Nations (FAO), International Labour Organization (ILO), United Nations Development Programme (UNDP), United Nations Educational Scientific and Cultural Organization (UNESCO), Economic and Social Commission for Asia and the Pacific/United Nations Asian and Pacific Centre for Agricultural Engineering and Machinery (ESCAP/UNAPCAEM), United Nations Children's Fund (UNICEF) and United Nations Industrial Development Organization (UNIDO).

Enabling sector-level disaster-resilient technological change

The energy challenge

The technological transformation needed in the energy sector (see chap. II) requires the installation of new types of energy plants and infrastructure, most pervasively in developing countries. As climate-proofing these facilities and related infrastructure will be necessary, developing countries must build a domestic capability in building and maintaining such structures. Risk reduction specialists recommend that storage facilities, factories, buildings, roads and water and sanitation infrastructures be relocated or reinforced against the likely impacts of longer droughts, intense precipitation, floods and sea-level rise. More intense and frequent floods in Albania, for example, prompted the Government to build smaller hydropower plants and larger water channels. By delivering energy more efficiently, these plants have the potential to open up avenues for sustainable development.

The need to climate-proof clean energy plants and infrastructure should not be neglected

Water and sanitation

The United Nations Framework Convention on Climate Change (2006) has discussed the inclusive framework for water management referred to as integrated water resource management (IWRM). This approach recognizes that water is a finite resource and that "(e)ssential water supplies should be accessible to all, and their distribution should be managed in a participatory fashion with a particular concern for the interests of the poor" (p. 16). This framework identifies forms of water-supply management that give consideration to ecosystems, including crop, livestock, fishing and forest activities.

Table IV.4 provides examples of adaptation technologies for water resources, which underline the multisectoral nature of water use and the dual (supply and demand) facets of adaptation technologies. Some technologies are traditional or locally based, for example, harvesting rainwater and building reservoirs and levees. Implementation of others requires specialized equipment or knowledge related, for example, to increased turbine efficiency and desalinization. Implementation of technologies for water management also requires regulatory mechanisms, such as the enforcement of water standards and the curbing of flood plain development.

In order to respond to the increased risk of epidemic outbreaks from climate change, countries in warm areas will have to enhance their systems for safely storing and treating water, for example, through waste-water recycling and desalinization. Investing in reliable water-conserving technologies for delivering clean water will be required in the households and settlements of many developing countries. Sustainable urban drainage systems utilizing rainwater harvesting, for example, can enhance resilience to excessive rainfall and eliminate the threat of the production of contaminated water, which provides a habitat for disease vectors such as mosquitoes.

Because of climate change, countries in warm areas will have to enhance their systems for safely storing and treating water

Water and sanitation systems must be made resilient with respect to the effects of heavy rainfalls and longer droughts. Ecological sanitation and toilet systems whose safe processing of human waste does not require water might become a key technology under water-scarce conditions.

Table IV.4
Adaptation technologies for water resources

Use category		*Supply side*	*Demand side*
Municipal or domestic		• Increase reservoir capacity • Desalinization • Make inter-basin transfers	• Recycle "grey" water • Reduce leakage • Use non-water-based sanitation systems • Enforce water standards
Industrial cooling		• Use lower-grade water	• Increase efficiency and recycling
Hydropower		• Increase reservoir capacity	• Increase turbine efficiency
Navigation		• Build weirs and locks	• Alter ship size and frequency of sailings
Pollution control		• Enhance treatment works • Reuse and reclaim materials	• Reduce effluent volumes • Promote alternatives to chemicals
Flood management		• Build reservoirs and levees • Protect and restore wetlands	• Improve flood warnings • Curb flood plain development
Agriculture	Rain-fed	• Improve soil conservation	• Use drought-tolerant crops
	Irrigated	• Change tilling practices • Harvest rainwater	• Increase irrigation efficiency • Change irrigation water pricing

Source: United Nations Framework Convention on Climate Change (2006), figure 5.

Health

Technologies for adaptation need to reduce the exposure of poor communities to the impacts of climate change by strengthening public-health systems and urban planning (including housing in risk-safe areas).

To deal with increased exposure to health risks, improved construction for housing and schools will be required

To deal with increased exposure to health risks, such as water- and vector-borne diseases, in areas where climate change will raise average temperatures, improved construction for housing and schools will be required. Adverse impacts of rising temperatures will require—just to protect health gains already achieved—increased investment in public-health infrastructure. Measures to reduce the health risks should be gender- and environment-sensitive, particularly in the context of development of technologies and public-health strategies.

Low-cost and low-technology solutions such as mosquito nets and water filters can be only a part of a larger integrated approach to building up effective public-health systems. Satellite mapping and geographical information systems, which are useful for local, regional and national surveillance of possible areas affected by malaria and other communicable diseases sensitive to climate shocks, allow health-care professionals to assess priorities, reallocate resources and prevent future outbreaks. The use of these technologies can be more effective if poor countries are able to access finance, knowledge and expertise.

Coastal zones

Sea-level rises endanger populations residing in low-elevation coastal zones

Sea-level rise increases the risk for populations residing in low-elevation coastal zones.[5] About 88 per cent of the people in low-elevation coastal zones (over half of whom live in urban areas) reside in developing countries. Low-elevation coastal cities such as Lagos, Cape Town, Maputo and Mombasa often have large concentrations of low-income urban-dwellers. Sites of economic production and strategic infrastructure concentrated in these cities are also vulnerable to climate change. Table IV.5 demonstrates that some of the most populous developing countries, such as China, India, Bangladesh, Viet Nam and Indonesia, have the largest number of people living in these zones. The table also indicates that among the top 10 countries with the highest shares of population in the low-elevation coastal zones, 8 are low-income or lower-middle-income countries.

Table IV.5
Countries with the largest total population and with the largest share of their population in a low-elevation coastal zone (LECZ), 2000

Top 10	*Country*	*Rank by total population in the LECZ (millions)*	*Country*	*Rank by share of population in the LECZ (percentage)*
1	China	143,880	Bahamas	88
2	India	63,188	Suriname	76
3	Bangladesh	62,524	Netherlands	74
4	Viet Nam	43,051	Viet Nam	55
5	Indonesia	41,610	Guyana	55
6	Japan	30,477	Bangladesh	46
7	Egypt	25,655	Djibouti	41
8	United States of America	22,859	Belize	40
9	Thailand	16,478	Egypt	38
10	Philippines	13,329	Gambia	38

Source: McGranahan, Balk and Anderson (2007), table 3.

Note: Countries or areas with a total population of under 100,000 people or smaller than 1,000 square kilometres were excluded from this list. If all countries had been included, 7 of the top 10 in the table would be countries or areas with fewer than 100,000 persons, the top 5 having more than 90 per cent of country or area in the Low Elevation Coastal Zone (Maldives, Marshall Islands, Tuvalu, Cayman Islands and Turks and Caicos Islands).

Three basic adaptation strategies are available to coastal communities and countries: protection, retreat and accommodation. For protection, "hard" options such as sea walls and "soft" options, such as restoring dunes, creating and restoring coastal wetlands, and reforestation, could be relevant. For retreat, the following might be appropriate: the requirement that setback zones for development be at a specific distance from the water's edge; legal restrictions on size and density of structures within risky areas; and specification of permitted forms of shoreline stabilization. In respect of accommodation, warning systems for extreme weather events, new building codes, and draining systems with increased pump capacity and wider pipes would be paramount (United Nations Framework Convention on Climate Change, Subsidiary Body for Scientific and Technological Advice, 2010).

More broadly, policy action on technological adaptations for new settlements encompasses three dimensions: (a) energy-efficient technology for new building structures;

5 Low-elevation coastal zones are defined as land areas contiguous with the coastline up to a 10-metre rise in elevation and whose width is often less than 100 kilometres.

(b) planning of settlements, including construction of appropriate infrastructure to protect against flooding (Netherlands), creation of green areas as flood buffers (Brazil) and design of multi land use cities to ease transportation and improve biodiversity (Seoul); and (c) making city services climate-friendly, for example, by offering affordable and efficient public transportation and adequate housing (see box IV.3).

Box IV.3

Green restoration projects in the Republic of Korea

Levels of flooding and drought are likely to worsen in the Republic of Korea and the threat of water scarcity and water overabundance becomes most acute when one considers demand and supply in the context of possible future socio-economic and natural changes. In order to respond effectively to expected climate irregularities, water control policies are becoming increasingly necessary.

Securing water resources is a critical dimension of climate change adaptation. In this regard it is planned, as part of the Four Major Rivers Restoration Project, that about 1.3 billion cubic metres of water will have been secured by 2012. The Project, launched in 2009, entails restoration of the Han, Nakdong, Geum and Yeongsan rivers and includes a number of related projects on their tributaries. A significant portion of the funds for adaptation ($28 billion) will be utilized for the Project (the total investment for "greening" the economy of the Republic of Korea is about $84 billion).

The project has five objectives: (a) to counter water scarcity by securing abundant water resources; (b) to implement well-coordinated measures for flood control; (c) to improve water quality and restore ecosystems; (d) to create multi-purpose spaces for local residents; and (e) to promote climate-resilient regional development centred on rivers. Overall, it is expected that the project will create 340,000 jobs and generate an estimated 40 trillion won ($31.1 billion) in positive economic effects.

The development of ecological defence systems will be continued through the setting up of forest protection and forest ecosystem management programmes. The Republic of Korea aims to increase the capacity of national forest resources from 862 million to 953 million cubic metres by enhancing forest protection and forest ecosystem management programmes. Forests and wetlands prevalent in a large part of the Korean Peninsula are being properly conserved and made more resilient so as to provide natural defences against storms, cyclones, flooding and sea-level rise.

The implementation of ecological restoration through reforestation can significantly enhance resilience. The review, under the UNEP-led study on the Economics of Ecosystems and Biodiversity, of a large number of restoration projects suggests that through ecological restoration, resilience improvements can be achieved in three significant areas of adaptation: (a) freshwater security; (b) food security (involving both artisanal fisheries and small-farm productivity); and (c) management of natural hazard risks (cyclones, storms, floods and droughts).

Source: United Nations Environment Programme (2010b).

Institutional change and capacity building

For disaster risk reduction technologies to be put in place effectively in poor countries, those countries need to strengthen their institutions. The United Nations Framework Convention on Climate Change[6]—acting under the Technology Transfer Framework—assessed the institutional gaps in developing countries in the course of undertaking technology needs assessments. Technology needs assessments track the need for new equipment and techniques ("hard technology") and for the practical knowledge and skills ("soft technology") required to adapt and reduce vulnerability to the adverse impacts of climate change (Hecl, 2010). In their technology needs assessments 68 countries highlighted capacity development as a technology priority.

6 United Nations, *Treaty Series*, vol. 1771, No, 30822.

It is crucial for Governments and the international community to support investment in capacity development, including in higher education focused on technologically oriented careers and in programmes that promote practices of sustainable consumption. The Government of Nigeria provides such support through a programme, in which specially trained instructors educate primary and post-primary school children in Lagos on climate change effects and environmental management. The young people then act as agents of change by reaching out to the larger society. "Climate change clubs" have been established in many primary and post-primary institutions having trained instructors.

The training of the next generation of technicians and professionals must be actively supported

Building local innovation capacity in developing countries is essential for the adaptation of renewable energy technologies. The training of the next generation of technicians and professionals must be actively supported, and national innovation plans should include support for local education and research and for their linkages with international innovation centres (United Nations, Department of Economic and Social Affairs, 2009).

Extension programmes can be important for building capacity among low-income urban communities

The challenge is to create institutional mechanisms that facilitate access of vulnerable communities not only to knowledge and finance but also to adaptation technologies. Fiscal systems whose purpose will be to transfer resources to technologically disadvantaged economic sectors and less educated populations need to be widely explored and carefully designed so as to reduce the impact of negative responses. Likewise, the active participation of all stakeholders, both women and men, in the implementation of adaptation technologies can promote greater support for the benefits of adaptation.

Extension programmes can be an important means of sharing information on technology transfer, building capacity among low-income urban communities and encouraging residents to form their own networks. Community organizations, for example, can be an effective information-sharing mechanism with the potential to provide cost-effective links between government efforts and community activities, while investment incentives and tax relief can entice the local private sector into engaging in technology transfer. Non-governmental organizations can play the role of intermediaries by facilitating investment, identifying adaptation technologies, and providing management and technical assistance.

Engaging the private sector requires the strengthening of countries' institutional base, including the provision of incentives to support, for example, architectural changes, hazard insurance and development of new consumer products. Policies to induce the participation of private insurance companies in the enforcement of standards can also be appropriate.

Financing and external transfers

Ballpark figures suggest that the cost of the resources needed for adaptation are significant but not prohibitive.

Adaptation technologies can be classified by sector and by stage of technological maturity (see table IV.6). The agriculture, livestock and fisheries sector lays claim to the bulk of these technologies, followed by the coastal zones and infrastructure sectors. The early warning and forecasting sector utilizes the largest number of technologies classified as "high". Global estimates for the additional annual investment and financial flows needed for technological adaptation to the adverse effects of climate change range from $32.6 billion to $163.1 billion in 2030 (United Nations Framework Convention on Climate Change, Subsidiary Body for Scientific and Technological Advice, 2009, table 8). These estimates, which include the costs of infrastructure, health, water supply and coastal

Table IV.6
Climate change adaptation technologies, by sector and stage of technological maturity[a]

Sector	Adaptation technologies		Percentage of technologies that are:		
	Number	*Percentage*	*High*	*Modern*	*Traditional*
Coastal zones	27	16.4	18.5	25.9	55.6
Energy	6	3.6		33.3	66.7
Health	18	10.9	38.9	38.9	22.2
Early warning and forecasting	13	7.9	84.6	15.4	
Infrastructure	23	13.9	8.7	47.8	43.5
Terrestrial ecosystems	8	4.8		25.0	75.0
Water resources	28	17.0	25.0	46.4	28.6
Agriculture, livestock and fisheries	42	25.5	21.4	31.0	47.6
Total	**165**	**100.0**	**41.0**	**57.0**	**67.0**

Source: United Nations Framework Convention on Climate Change, Subsidiary Body for Scientific and Technological Advice (2009), table 11. For the list of adaptation technologies, see annex II, table 20.

a Traditional/indigenous technologies are those that have been first developed in traditional societies to respond to specific local problems. Modern technologies comprise approaches that have been created since the first industrial revolution, including the use of synthetic materials, modern medicines, hybrid crops, modern forms of transportation and new chemicals. High technologies comprise technologies created based on recent scientific advances, including information and communications technology, computer monitoring and modelling, and engineering of genetically modified organisms.

projects, are based on assumptions on the likely course of climate change, although more detailed and localized studies are required to improve their accuracy. Further, assisting developing countries in obtaining realistic estimates on climate change impacts and extreme events will also improve the quality of the global database. While these numbers reflect a great deal of uncertainty, as the ballpark figures they suggest that the cost of the resources needed for adaptation is significant but not prohibitive.

In comparison with existing estimates, the Cancun commitment can be seen as only a first step in funding transfers to developing countries for climate change purposes

Under the Cancun Adaptation Framework, it was recognized "that developed country Parties (would) commit to … a goal of mobilizing jointly USD 100 billion per year by 2020 to address the needs of developing countries" (see FCCC/CP/2010/7/Add.1, decision 1/CP.16, para. 98). In comparison with existing estimates, the Cancun commitment can be seen as a modest first step in funding transfers to developing countries for climate change purposes. These funds would come "from a wide variety of sources, public and private, bilateral and multilateral, including alternative sources" (ibid., para. 99) with a "significant share of new multilateral funding for adaptation (flowing) through the Green Climate Fund" (ibid., para. 100).

The institutional mechanism that will implement and monitor the use of the "significant share" to be allocated for adaptation purposes has yet to be determined. It is clear, however, that the implementation of sustainable development plans in poor countries depends on stable sources of local finance and effective mobilization of resources at the international level. Concrete steps need to be taken to respond to the needs of developing countries.

The way forward

Drawing on indigenous knowledge, adapting existing technologies for the purpose of building infrastructure and housing and installing monitoring and response systems provide the key to successful disaster risk reduction efforts. However, investments in disaster risk reduction are constrained by competing investment claims on a finite public sector budget. Faced with the knowledge that one extreme disaster can wipe out the gains of decades of development investment, every society will still have to decide how much of its resources can be devoted to disaster risk reduction efforts. While projects designed to deal with seasonal and well-known risks would normally be given investment priority, domestic social priorities will shape how much technology and investment spending can be directed towards reducing longer-term hazards and truly catastrophic events. It is therefore critical that disaster risk reduction and climate change adaptation efforts be incorporated in national development strategies in order to ensure that priorities for disaster risk management are defined within that context.

Domestic social priorities will shape how much technology and investment spending can be directed towards reducing longer-term hazards and truly catastrophic events

Transborder natural hazards will require strengthening regional cooperation in the area of monitoring, forecasting and warning systems. Countries could also cooperate in disaster risk assessments and undertake multinational projects in risk reduction.

The longer-term hazards being imposed by climate change are global in source, but local in impact. Global cooperation will require facilitating technology transfer to developing countries. So that the advantages of foreign technology in adaptation and risk reduction projects can be realized, technology transfer should ensure that recipients have the capacity to install, operate, maintain and repair imported technologies. It might also be important for local adapters to be able to produce lower-cost versions of imported technologies and adapt imported technologies to domestic markets and circumstances. The international community has made a commitment to providing external assistance to local adaptation programmes and while most estimates suggest that the overall call on adaptation resources is not prohibitive, the operational modalities for predictable and adequate resource flows to developing countries still need to be agreed upon (see chap. VI).

The longer-term hazards being imposed by climate change are global in source, but local in impact

By protecting livelihoods against disaster, disaster risk reduction and climate change adaptation projects contribute to development (United Nations, 2008b). As noted, such projects have synergies with other development imperatives, including in the areas of construction, housing, transportation systems, basic services provisioning, manufacturing and employment absorption. The effort to manage the needed adaptation of both foreign and indigenous technology so as ensure the reduction of the impact of natural disasters and climate change should be embedded in the larger project of achieving national industrial development and innovation. This subject will be taken up in chapter V.

By protecting livelihoods against disaster, disaster risk reduction and climate change adaptation projects contribute to development

Annex table IV.1

Projects encompassing technological strategies for adaptation and disaster risk reduction

Country	*Highest disaster incidence, 1990-2009*	*Adverse impacts of changing environment*	*Strategies employed*	*Scale*	*Case description*
Argentina	Floods (29)	Damage to human settlements; decline in productivity of fisheries; decrease of crop yields; flooding; drought and aridity	Empowerment	Community (rural)	Argentina's rural electrification project grants scattered communities access to the technological and educational benefits of electricity, thereby helping them become resilient to floods, droughts and crop loss.
Bangladesh	Storms (84)	Water shortages; landslides; decrease of crop yields; decline in productivity of livestock and/or poultry; drought and aridity; flooding	Agriculture; resources; technology; empowerment	Community (rural)	**South***South*North and the Society for Wetland Eco-Research are implementing several measures (for example, crop diversification, disaster preparedness) targeting the threat of sea-level rise and storms.
Bangladesh	Storms (84)	Damage to human settlements; flooding	Technology; empowerment	National (urban and rural)	The Grameen Bank provides loans for two house designs that are specially adapted to heavy rains and floods, and can even be dismantled and reassembled, in severe flood events.
Colombia	Floods (42)	Flooding; landslides	Insurance; monitoring and early warning systems; institutions; infrastructure; awareness	Subnational (urban)	Concerned about floods and landslides, Bogota is improving risk-detection technology, emergency response, recovery finance and awareness.
Cuba	Storms (21)	Coastal inundation or erosion	Resources; infrastructure	National (urban and rural)	Cuba has developed beach restoration technology to restore ecological and functional value of its coasts.
India	Floods (141)	Water shortages; flood, drought	Technology	Subnational (rural)	Tarun Bharat Sangh (a non-governmental organization) has facilitated the construction of earthen check dams to retain monsoon water for times of drought.
Indonesia	Floods (85)	Damage to human settlements; flooding	Awareness; institutions; monitoring and early warning systems; planning	Community (urban)	The Red Cross is establishing institutional structures and in East Jakarta plans to take a proactive approach to climate change, including through awareness-raising and an early warning system.

Annex table IV.1 (cont'd)

Country	*Highest disaster incidence, 1990-2009*	*Adverse impacts of changing environment*	*Strategies employed*	*Scale*	*Case description*
Madagascar	Storms (29)	Drought and aridity; flooding	Monitoring and early warning systems; awareness; resources	National (rural)	WWF and Conservation International are analysing and raising awareness of the vulnerability of marine and terrestrial environments to climate change.
Mali	Floods (14)	Decrease of crop yields	Monitoring and early warning systems; awareness; technology	National (rural)	The Government of Mali and the Swiss Agency for Development and Cooperation use data collected by farmers to help them make planting decisions.
Mozambique	Floods (17)	Water shortages; drought and aridity	Technology; resources	Community (rural)	**South***South*North and local partners are supplying farmers with renewable energy to combat water shortage.
Multinational (Cameroon, Fiji, Tanzania (United Republic of))	Floods (37)	Flooding	Resources; planning; technology; institutions	Multinational (rural)	WWF is testing methods to restore degraded mangrove forests so as to make them resilient with respect to climate change.
Multinational (Bangladesh, Ghana, Haiti, India, Kenya, Malawi, Nepal)	Floods (297)	-	Institutions; awareness; policy; infrastructure	Community (urban and rural)	ActionAid is making schools in high-risk disaster areas safer, enabling them to act as models in disaster risk reduction.
Multinational (Southern African countries: Angola, Botswana, Comoros, Democratic Republic of the Congo, Madagascar, Malawi, Mozambique, Namibia, South Africa, Swaziland, Tanzania (United Republic of), Zambia, Zimbabwe)	Floods (157)	Spread of vector-borne diseases	Monitoring and early warning systems;	Multinational (urban and rural)	The Roll Back Malaria Initiative developed a monitoring and early warning system which uses climatic data to predict malaria outbreaks.
Multinational (West African countries: Cape Verde, Gambia, Guinea-Bissau, Mauritania, Senegal)	Floods (32)	Coastal inundation or erosion; decline in productivity of fisheries; biodiversity loss	Planning	Community (urban and rural)	UNDP is incorporating climate change concerns, such as coastal erosion and declining fish stocks, into integrated coastal management.
Nepal	Floods (20)	Damage to human settlements; flooding	Technology	Community (rural)	An intermediate technology development group project reduces the impact of floods by strengthening the capacity of local communities to set up early warning systems.

Annex table IV.1 (cont'd)

Country	*Highest disaster incidence, 1990-2009*	*Adverse impacts of changing environment*	*Strategies employed*	*Scale*	*Case description*
Nicaragua	Storms (15)	Landslides; flooding	Technology; monitoring and early warning systems	Community (rural)	The autonomous government of the North Atlantic Region has improved its early warning systems and disaster planning in order to cope with storms and floods.
Peru	Floods (23)	Decrease of crop yields; drought and aridity; flooding	Technology	Community (rural)	The waru waru restoration project has revived an ancient canalization technique designed to provide moisture to farms during drought, and drainage during heavy rains.
Philippines	Storms (136)	Flooding; drought and aridity	Resources; technology	Subnational (rural)	Oxfam set up a relief and rehabilitation programme in response to increased storms, droughts, floods and warfare. The programme includes food and medicine provision and credit and training for entrepreneurship.
Samoa	Storms (4)	Storm	Resources	Community (rural)	Matafa village is conserving nearby mangroves to safeguard biodiversity, provide income and protect the village from storm surges.
Samoa	Storms (4)	Flooding	Resources	Community (rural)	Lepa-Komiti Tumama is helping the village of Lepa store clean drinking water for use during floods.
South Asia (Bhutan, India, Nepal, Pakistan) Note: Data for China/Tibet not reported separately.	Floods (211)	Glacial lake outburst floodings; flooding	Monitoring and early warning systems	Multinational (urban and rural)	International Centre for Integrated Mountain Development is developing a database and early warning system for glacial lake outburst floods.
Tajikistan	Floods (19)	Water shortages; flooding; drought and aridity; landslides	Technology; institutions; policy	National (rural)	Oxfam is addressing the water provision problems associated with droughts and flooding by introducing new technologies, promoting new crops, and launching a disaster preparedness programme.

Annex table IV.1 (cont'd)

Country	*Highest disaster incidence, 1990-2009*	*Adverse impacts of changing environment*	*Strategies employed*	*Scale*	*Case description*
Tanzania (United Republic of)	Floods (22)	Decrease of crop yields	Technology; planning	Subnational (urban and rural)	United Republic of Tanzania is preparing for climate change impacts on the Pangani River by improving technical knowledge and watershed management.
Thailand	Floods (49)	Damage to human settlements; flooding	Technology; agriculture; resources	Community (rural)	As an example of autonomous adaptation, communities in the lower Songkhram River basin have modified their fishing gear and rice-growing strategies to adapt to climate changes such as flooding and drought.
Yemen	Floods (21), Storms (2)	Water shortages; drought and aridity	Resources; institution-building; policy	National (urban and rural)	Netherlands Climate Change Studies Assistance Programme in Yemen focuses on social-based adaptation to climate change, especially the water use planning.

Source: UN/DESA, based on McGray, Hammill and Bradley (2007).

Note:

Strategies employed comprise: agriculture: changing agricultural practices; awareness: raising awareness; empowerment: empowering people; infrastructure: improving infrastructure; institutions: building institutions; monitoring and early warning systems: establishing monitoring/early warning systems; planning: launching planning processes; policy: promoting policy change; resources: changing natural resource management practices; technology: promoting technology change.

Blue shading denotes UNDP projects.

Yellow shading denotes technological strategies.

Chapter V
National policies for green development

Summary

- Technological innovation is at the heart of sustainable development. "Catching up" with industrialized countries requires strong technology policies. A green sustainability-oriented national innovation system (G-NIS) should be an integral part of developing countries' national development strategies.
- Widespread adaptation and diffusion of green technologies require effective government industrial policies to "crowd in" private investment. Green technologies should be treated as infant industries, with appropriate support, including public sector investments in infrastructure, subsidies and access to credit.
- Building an innovative economy is not about overcoming price distortions or enforcing property rights. An innovative economy is based on interactive learning, information exchange, timely availability of finance and other resources, and coordination among firms, universities, research centres, policymakers and other actors.

Introduction

Technological innovation is at the heart of economic and social development. Building technological capacities can help developing countries "catch up" with more advanced countries, and innovation policy must play an important role in facilitating sustainable development. The present chapter argues that green sustainable development-oriented innovation policies should be an integral part of countries' national development strategies.

Green technologies have the potential to create new industries and jobs

The use of green technologies can have many benefits for developing countries. It can improve domestic infrastructure, help reach underserved communities that lack access to electricity, clean water and sanitation, and create jobs. Since many green products are initially developed in industrialized countries, technology transfer from developed to developing countries is a necessary part of this process. However, the conventional view that technology is developed in the North and simply transferred to the South is misleading. Technology transfer involves more than the importation of hardware: it involves the complex process of sharing knowledge and adapting technologies to meet local conditions. More broadly, innovation is not limited to new breakthroughs: most innovation involves incremental improvements and adaptations of existing technologies.

Technology transfer involves more than the importation of hardware

Innovation, in this sense, is widespread in many emerging market and developing countries. China and India, in particular, have become global leaders in some green technologies, such as solar photovoltaic (PV) panels, wind turbines, and electric and hybrid-electric vehicles, in part because they were able to improve and adapt existing technologies and production processes. Some low-income countries have also begun to develop domestic technological capacities, successfully adapt green technologies, and build new industries, such as the solar PV industry in Bangladesh.

Private investors are unlikely to invest in many new technologies without government support

In all cases, government policies have played important roles in the innovation process. Private investors are often unlikely to invest in many new technologies without government support, especially when these technologies are not cost-competitive with the technologies that are already in place. This is the case for many green technologies, in part because market prices do not fully incorporate the societal costs of using brown technologies, such as greenhouse gas emissions and other environmental risks, with which green technologies compete. Typical market-based solutions to this have been carbon taxes or "cap and trade" schemes aimed at incorporating the societal costs into market prices, along with strong intellectual property rights to encourage investment in green technologies. However, higher energy prices due to carbon taxes can have the perverse effect of disrupting economic development in poor countries, and strong property rights can impede knowledge transfer and inhibit innovation. Furthermore, this approach comes up against an affordability wall in most developing countries, which must nevertheless participate in this technological makeover as they attempt structural change over the next few decades.

Building an innovative economy is not about overcoming price distortions and enforcing property rights

More broadly, building an innovative economy is not about overcoming price distortions and enforcing property rights. An innovative economy is based on interactive learning, information exchange, and coordination among firms, universities, research centres, policymakers and other actors. The national innovation system (NIS) approach, which emphasizes the importance of these relationships, thus provides a more useful framework than a market-based approach for analysing innovation policy. A green sustainability-oriented NIS (G-NIS), which integrates the public-goods nature of many green technologies into the NIS framework, is particularly useful for innovation policymaking in the context of long-term sustainable development.

Green technologies should be treated as infant industries

This framework suggests that active industrial policies are necessary for the adaptation and diffusion of green technologies. Green technologies should be treated as infant industries, with appropriate support, including public sector investments in infrastructure, subsidies and access to credit (Ocampo, 2011b). Policies should also be designed to encourage interaction and knowledge-sharing among domestic and international firms, research institutes, universities, policymakers and other actors. Other policy suggestions based on a green systemic approach could encompass innovative sources of equity-linked financing and long-horizon green country funds.

Catching up with industrialized countries requires strong technology policies. The G-NIS approach emphasizes that policymakers do indeed need to make choices on how to best support innovation, and suggests a framework for government decision-making and investment.

Market and systemic failures

Many economists argue that the role of government is to correct market failures. In contrast, in an NIS or systems approach, the role of government is to correct systemic failures, which might include market failures, but can also include weak relationships between agents or institutions which are difficult to capture in traditional economic models. A systemic analysis also focuses on how changing incentives in one area negatively affect incentives in others.

Uncertainty, externalities and public goods-related problems

All investment is uncertain, but investment in innovation is particularly uncertain as the future outcomes of today's investment projects are unknown.[1] Innovation is also confronted with a public goods-related problem. Knowledge in its pure form is a public good, insofar as it is available to everyone and its use by one person does not limit its use by others. Hence, it is difficult for private firms to appropriate the full returns from research activity. In the market failure approach, patents are meant to confer a degree of ownership of the fruits of new knowledge by granting the innovators fixed-term monopoly rights.

The systemic approach, in contrast, emphasizes that strong intellectual property rights can also undercut knowledge-sharing, thereby impeding innovation. Further, even when such institutional mechanisms exist, investors still underinvest in research and development (R&D) (Mani, 2002). A typical policy response is to fund basic research through grants or public research institutes. The systems approach, however, might also suggest joint research grants to encourage collaboration among universities, research institutes and firms.

Innovation of green technologies is subject to heightened uncertainty, externalities, path dependencies, and additional public goods-related problems

Innovation with regard to green technologies is subject to heightened uncertainty, externalities, path dependencies, and additional public goods-related problems. Investment risk is heightened, since there is greater uncertainty about what the entire market, not just the specific technology, will look like in the future. Green technologies compete with brown technologies currently in use, most of which have large environmental externalities and other social costs that are not factored into market prices. As discussed above, carbon taxes and cap-and-trade schemes were supposed to be so designed as to address these issues. It appears, however, that the increase in price needed to cover all the externalities would likely be so large as to prove politically unfeasible (Mowery, Nelson and Martin, 2010). For developing countries, these schemes can be problematic, as they would raise the price of existing energy sources and other inputs, which could disrupt economic development, at least until new energy sources became available. And they can be particularly problematic, given the potential impact of higher energy prices on the poor. Industrial policies to encourage diffusion of green technologies provide an alternative policy prescription. Furthermore, there are opportunities in some poor countries for leapfrogging, which industrial policies could encourage.

Green technologies compete with brown technologies currently in use

There are also path dependencies associated with existing carbon technologies that are difficult for new technologies to overcome, even when the new technologies are potentially superior. For example, existing technologies have large sunk costs in infrastructure, which constrain their replacement. New technologies often have high operating expenses and are often less reliable in the early stages of development. This is true of most green technologies, even those like wind and solar PV that have longer histories (Mowery, Nelson and Martin, 2010.) It can also be difficult for any one new technology to overcome the dominant technology "regime" and change what is often an entire system, such as the energy system (Smith, 2009). Furthermore, existing technologies tend to serve entrenched interests, making it difficult for policymakers to support new technologies at the expense of existing ones.

Green technologies also have additional public goods-related problems. As discussed above, green technologies support infrastructure, reach underserved communities and promote equity, increase energy, food and water security, and have the potential to

1 Current market prices cannot convey accurate information about firms' investment (in other words, there are no futures markets for knowledge).

create new industries and jobs (Cosbey, 2011a). However, private investors tend to underinvest in green technologies because they are unable to capture these public benefits in their investment returns.

Finally, financial markets tend to be myopic and to be characterized by boom-and-bust cycles, which can be particularly severe in new illiquid investment sectors, such as green technology (Stiglitz and others, 2006). For example, although "green investment funds" had raised a large amount of capital prior to 2007, most experienced significant withdrawals during and after the financial crisis, as discussed below. Cyclically oriented financing cannot be counted on to support long-term sustainable development, and policymakers should focus on alternative forms of investment.

Systems of innovation

National innovation systems

Every country has a national innovation system, whether or not policymakers are conscious of it

The concept of a national innovation system (NIS) was first introduced in the 1980s (Nelson and Winter, 1982; Freeman, 1997). Although the general concept of a national innovation system is widely accepted (Nelson, 1993; Lundvall, ed., 2010; Metcalfe, 1994), there is no single definition. According to a broad definition, such as the one given by Edquist (2004), the NIS is "all important economic, social, political, organization, institutional, and other factors that influence the development, diffusion, and use of innovations". Hence, every country has an NIS, whether or not policymakers are conscious of it. It is a dynamic system that develops and changes over time. While it is not created by Governments, government policies can strengthen (or weaken) its efficiency.

Sector-specific green innovation systems

Sectoral innovation systems address differences in the innovation process across economic sectors

Innovation of green technologies covers a wide range of economic sectors, including energy, transportation, agriculture, industrial production, materials, buildings, water, and waste management (Johnstone, Hascic and Popp, 2010). These sectors differ with regard to characteristics such as firm size, the role of foreign direct investment (FDI), skill requirements, capital intensity, and the degree of integration into the global market. For example, while the energy sector tends to be dominated by a few large firms, agriculture in developing countries involves many small rural land holders, which can make knowledge-sharing and diffusion of innovation particularly challenging. An agricultural innovation system thus needs to focus on informal actors, such as community networks (Gallagher and others, 2011; Juma, 2011). Sectoral innovation systems (Malerba, 2002; Malerba and Nelson, 2008) address differences in the innovation process across economic sectors.

Because sector-specific innovation systems are specialized, they can be particularly useful as frameworks for sector-specific policy analysis. Chapters II and III examined energy and agricultural innovation systems; the discussion of both types of systems is fairly well developed in the literature (United Nations Conference on Trade and Development, 2010; Grübler and others, forthcoming bis; Juma, 2011). There is a significant literature on other sector-specific systems as well, such as chemicals, pharmaceuticals and electronics, but more research is needed on other sector-specific green sustainability-oriented innovation systems.

However, sole reliance on sector-specific systems could overlook economy-wide linkages especially relevant to green innovation since the impact of environmental externalities in one sector can affect other sectors. For example, hydroelectric plants are a clean energy source, but often have negative externalities, such as displacing people, harming agriculture, reducing fish populations, and deforestation.[2] On the other hand, they can also have positive externalities, such as lowering the risk of floods and providing irrigation for agriculture. A national system, especially one that is sustainability-oriented, provides a framework for promoting better understanding of all the relations and trade-offs involved in hydroelectric plants compared with other forms of energy. Though policymakers might consider many of these implications in any case, a green, sustainability-oriented national innovation system (a G-NIS) would provide a systematic framework for doing so.

Sole reliance on sector-specific systems could overlook economy-wide linkages

"Greening" national innovation systems

Greening an NIS involves incorporating unique features of sustainability into the systems framework.[3] There is a greater role for government and non-governmental organizations in a G-NIS framework because of the public-goods nature of green technologies. Although government policies are important in an NIS, particularly in the early stages of the development process, they are particularly important in a G-NIS, given the lack of domestic markets for green technologies. A G-NIS approach emphasizes incentives and industrial policies geared towards creating market demand throughout the innovation cycle (such as feed-in tariffs, low-interest loans and public procurement), which are not generally necessary for an NIS (Stamm and others, 2009). Because of the enhanced uncertainty associated with green technologies, policymakers might need to emphasize greater risk-sharing between the private and public sectors so as to stimulate private sector investment. In addition, the G-NIS takes account of environmental and other externalities, and incorporates technological, industrial and environmental policies within one framework.

A green innovation system emphasizes incentives and industrial policies geared towards creating market demand

Although G-NISs differ by country, based on existing institutions, human capital, business environment, infrastructure, geography and general level of development, they possess elements in common, as depicted in figure V.1. The innovation process is at the centre of the G-NIS. The actors in the system include firms, government agencies, universities, research institutes, training institutes, consumers, financial and non-financial institutions, private foundations and civil society.

Relationships and interactions among actors are crucial to the innovation process. These relationships include networks of innovators, research clusters, and coordination among universities and firms, upstream and downstream suppliers and their customers, and buyers and sellers. Institutions and infrastructure are the backdrop that shapes the innovation process; they are depicted as such as the light red circle in figure V.2. Industrial policies, such as public procurement, tax schemes and subsidies, define incentives for the actors and also shape the system.

Knowledge, increased capabilities and new technologies are important outputs of the system. These can be viewed as positive externalities of the system and are depicted in figure V.2 as arrows emanating from the G-NIS to the rest of the economy. The

Knowledge, increased capabilities and new technologies are important outputs of the system

2 The building of hydroelectric plants also leaves a significant carbon footprint.

3 The concept of a sustainability-oriented innovation system was first introduced by Stamm (Stamm and others, 2009; Rennkamp and Stamm, 2009) and the system was referred to as an SoIS.

Figure V.1
The innovation system

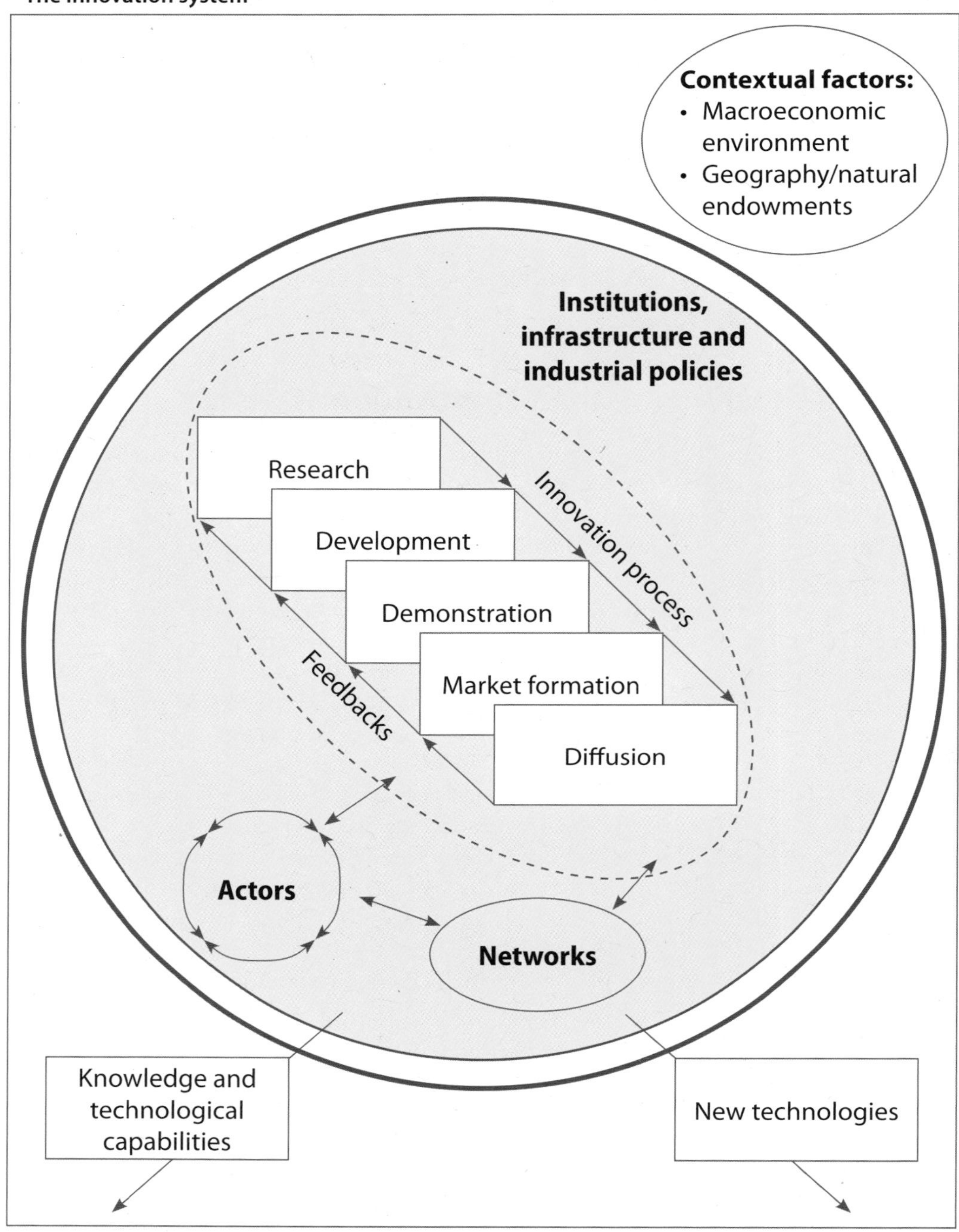

Source: UN/DESA.

remaining element of the G-NIS comprises contextual factors, such as the macroeconomic environment, geography and natural endowments. These are positioned exogenously to the system, and determine the context within which policies will or will not be effective.

Figure V.2
G-NIS financing

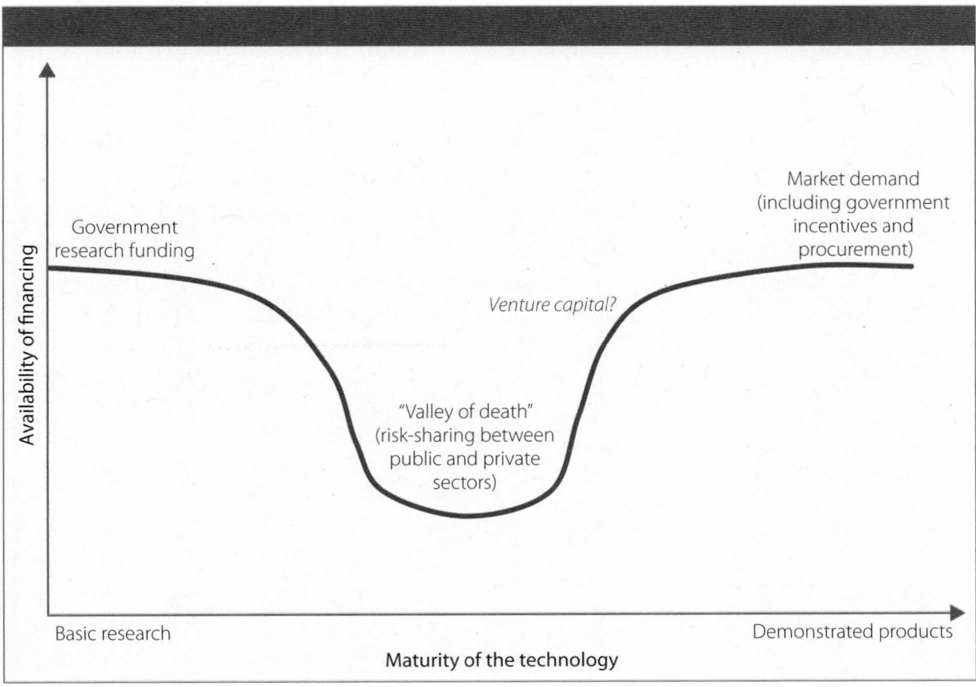

Sources: UN/DESA; and World Bank (2010a).

The innovation process

There are five phases in the innovation process. Market formation is added to the usual four phases

The innovation process is composed of interdependent phases (Mowery and Rosenberg, 1979), which feed back into one another, as depicted in figure V.1. The literature typically refers to four phases in the process: research, development, demonstration and diffusion (RDD&D). Following Grübler and others (forthcoming bis), "market formation" is added to the usual four, since markets for new green products do not automatically develop after the diffusion stage.

The five phases do not necessarily follow in order: some are sometimes skipped or inapplicable to a given technology or process (Gallagher and others, 2011; Grübler and Messner, 1998). In addition, there are feedbacks between stages, so that phases often occur simultaneously. For example, during the diffusion process, end-users provide producers with feedback, which should lead to product improvements and further adaptations.

Basic research, development and demonstration (RD&D)

Figure V.2 depicts the development phases (RD&D) of the innovation process, along with the type of financing typically available for the different phases. The government is often the main actor in basic research, through funding for universities or public research laboratories. In the United States of America, Europe and, more recently, China, many technological breakthroughs of the past decades, including innovations in aeronautics and electronics, were facilitated or funded by Governments (United Nations, Department of Economic and Social Affairs, 2008).

The government is often the main actor in basic research, while development and demonstration are based on entrepreneurial experimentation within firms

Development and demonstration, which are based on entrepreneurial experimentation, generally take place within firms. Entrepreneurs potentially continue to acquire commercially useful product-related information during these phases, which then feeds back into research. For example, several types of wind turbines were experimented with before the three-blade vertical-axis turbine was developed. Similarly, the development of hybrid vehicles entailed entrepreneurial experimentation among Japan's car manufacturers (Grübler and others, forthcoming bis).

However, financing for these advanced stages of product development is generally limited, particularly in the so-called valley of death, for which the investment risk is still high, but government financing often limited (Gallagher and others, 2011). Funding for this stage often comes from the entrepreneur's own savings or from family members. Venture capitalists tend to fund projects that have already been demonstrated in the marketplace, although they have been hesitant to take risks associated with some investments in green technologies, especially in developing countries, as discussed below. Thus, the development phase of many technologies—and particularly green technologies—needs to be supplemented by government policies.

Market formation and diffusion

In the case of green technologies, market demand is primarily determined by government policies

Diffusion and widespread use of technologies are a critical part of the innovation process, and are usually financed by the private sector. However, many clean energy technologies fail to transition from product development to diffusion not necessarily because of technological problems, but because they are too expensive relative to existing brown technologies or too difficult to integrate into existing systems (owing to path dependencies) or scale up, or because of lack of market demand for other reasons.

As discussed in chapter II, historically, market formation of new energy products focused on creating protected "niche" markets. These markets shield products from full commercial competition in the initial stages of product development, based on the expectation that some end-users would be willing to pay a higher price for high-quality technologies, and that as a result these technologies will not need to be subsidized. However, as there are few niches today in which cost-insensitive end-users are willing to pay for environmental public goods, this strategy is less appropriate for green technologies.

Policies aimed at market formation include environmental regulations

The role of government in the market formation stage can be critical to overcoming barriers to market formation and diffusion. As discussed below, policies aimed at market formation include environmental regulations, minimum production quotas, public procurement policies, subsidies and feed-in tariffs, as well as risk-sharing policies designed to encourage greater private sector investment.

Coordination and networks

Because innovation is based on interactive learning, information exchange, coordination and feedback are important throughout the innovation process. Indeed, innovation, adaptation and diffusion are dependent on such interactions. Coordination between researchers and firms is critical, as are interactions between firms and networks and clusters. Further, interactions between domestic and international firms facilitate the ability of domestic firms to tap into global knowledge and build domestic capacities. Interactions among government agencies, firms, research institutes, universities and civil society can help inform policymaking.

Cooperation among universities, research institutions and firms

There is evidence that cooperation among universities, public research organizations and firms is likely to stimulate private sector R&D (Jaumotte and Pain, 2005), and that when such interactions do not exist, there is likely to be less innovation (Soete, Verspagen and ter Weel, 2009). In countries with high levels of innovation, such as the United States, Sweden and Singapore, these linkages tend to be strong. However, knowledge is not automatically transferred from university and research centres to commercial applications. In the newly industrialized countries in Asia, Governments made efforts to help stimulate these relationships (Kim and Nelson, eds., 2000), through, for example, grants for collaborative R&D, as well as science and technology parks.

Knowledge is not automatically transferred from university and research centres for commercial application

In many developing countries, however, the linkages between universities and firms are weak. In Mexico, R&D is concentrated in universities, but the universities do not necessarily interact with private firms (Casas, 2005). In Africa, universities tend to be centralized, and are often unknown to producers not located nearby (Metcalfe and Ramlogan, 2005). Incorporating private sector inputs in education policy, as in several newly industrialized countries and some Latin American countries, can stimulate greater cooperation between firms and universities, as discussed below. In addition, collaborative R&D projects, joint conferences and seminars, and policies that encourage mobility of researchers between the public and private sector can help address this problem. For example, in Sweden, university professors are mandated to interact with firms and stakeholders outside the university, in addition to engaging in teaching and research (Edquist, 2006).

Networks, clusters and science parks

Learning and knowledge spillovers tend to be stronger with geographical proximity (Walz, 2010; Archibugi and Pietrobelli, 2003), and knowledge transfer between firms is often informal (Grübler and others, forthcoming bis). Clusters and networks of firms that encourage interactions among firms' personnel can facilitate knowledge spillovers.

Research networks are also important for information-sharing, and several emerging market and developing countries are taking steps to build such networks. Colombia has created a network of national research institutes whose goal is to develop sustainable energy technologies, and universities in Singapore have been developing green construction and water technologies (Cannady, 2009). Least developed countries, however, often do not have the resources or critical mass needed to build such networks. These countries should therefore form regional R&D networks and engage in South-South collaboration to leverage the resources of all members. For example, several Central African nations recently formed a university network of researchers engaged in work in the medical field (Cannady, 2009).[4] Regional networks could also offer valuable opportunities to leverage resources of wealthier countries.

Least developed countries form regional R&D networks and engage in South-South collaboration

To the extent that geographical proximity encourages increased knowledge spillovers, local science parks, which co-locate domestic and foreign firms, universities, research centres, laboratories and related businesses, can be used to facilitate green innovation. Science parks have been established successfully in both developed and emerging market economies and are being planned in several African developing countries, such as Senegal (Tavares, 2009) and Ghana. There has been some discussion of also building regional science parks in Africa as an alternative to national parks. For example, a project

4 See http://www.edctp.org/Networks-of-Excellence.641.0.html.

being run by the United Nations Educational, Scientific and Cultural Organization (UNESCO) is examining the possibility of setting up a science park in Nairobi, which will then serve as a model for other such "technopolises" across Africa (United Nations Educational, Scientific and Cultural Organization, 2011a).

Science parks can also offer support services, financial services and infrastructure (including buildings, meeting rooms, telephone, Internet, power and transportation), although business incubators can also assume this role, as discussed below. In addition, in some countries, such as India, firms in science parks are exempted from import duties and quotas, as well as from capital controls on repatriating currency.

The most important function of a science park is to foster interactions among actors

Experience suggests that the most important function of a science park is to foster interactions among actors. However, policymakers have sometimes focused on the physical presence of the park at the expense of fostering interactions and knowledge spillovers. Without a deliberate effort to encourage interactions, there is a risk that science parks will end up as real estate operations, instead of contributing to innovation and development. On the other hand, if linkages or industry clusters already exist, it might not be necessary to build an expensive science park as a means of bringing actors together. Other means of encouraging interactions and sharing may be more useful and affordable. Lower-cost options could include setting up resource centres, and technology transfer centres for firms in or near universities, and organizing frequent conferences and seminars in order to bring together domestic and foreign scientists, engineers, entrepreneurs, practitioners and policymakers. Furthermore, it is possible that, over time, virtual science parks will replace physical parks. However, to the extent that (as noted above) the goal of the park is to encourage interactions among actors, the importance of physical proximity cannot be underestimated. It is therefore unlikely that physical parks will be completely replaced by virtual counterparts, at least for the near future. While it is possible to organize "online conferences and dialogues", sustaining interactions and virtual networking appears to be more difficult.

International networks and technology transfer

Technology transfer is effective only if supplemented by indigenous research and domestic capabilities

Because much green technology is developed globally, international interactions play an important role in transferring technological knowledge. This can be facilitated through traditional forms of technology transfer, although it could also include other forms of knowledge sharing, transfer and collaboration. Traditional mechanisms for technology transfer are FDI, imports and licensing. Experience demonstrates, however, that these measures are effective only if supplemented by indigenous research and domestic capabilities (Li, 2008; Fu, 2008; Mani, 2002). Indeed, one primary motive for engagement by developing-country firms in domestic R&D is the desire to acquire knowledge developed elsewhere (Cohen and Levinthal, 1990; Grübler and others, forthcoming bis). Such indigenous research is not necessarily limited to basic research in a university or institute and may very well include "learning by doing" and experimentation.

Traditional mechanisms for technology transfer are foreign direct investment (FDI), imports and licensing

Today, countries also make use of alternative methods for technology transfer, such as joint R&D with international companies, outward FDI (including the acquisition of foreign firms by domestic entities), R&D overseas in existing knowledge centres, global joint ventures, movement of people through migration and foreign education, and participation in global value chains to gain access to knowledge transferred within the supply chain (Lema and Lema, 2010; Fu, Pietrobelli and Soete, 2010). Scientific journals and conferences provide access to international research, and much technical information is available on the Internet. In addition, traditional measures, such as FDI and joint ventures, have at times been accompanied by investment requirements and other policies to promote more efficient technology transfer, as discussed below. Some of these mechanisms may be quite different from those utilized by Organization for Economic Cooperation and Development (OECD) countries. Although certain mechanisms (such as outward FDI) require more resources, this is not the case for all, and less developed countries should therefore not exclude these forms of knowledge transfer.

FDI and investment performance measures

Technology spillovers through FDI can occur through several modes, such as movement of trained labour from foreign to domestic firms, vertical spillovers between foreign or domestic suppliers and their customers, joint ventures between foreign and local firms, and transfers between foreign firms and their local affiliates. However, from the foreign firm's perspective, the purpose of FDI is to generate a profit, not to transfer technology, and often firms will try to limit, rather than promote, knowledge transfer (Fu, Pietrobelli and Soete, 2010).

Knowledge spillovers from FDI are likely the result of explicit policies pursued by the Government

The empirical evidence for the effectiveness of knowledge spillovers from FDI is mixed (Fu, Pietrobelli and Soete, 2010). In countries like Singapore and China, where there is evidence of positive spillovers, they are likely the result of explicit policies pursued by the Government (Mani, 2002; Lema and Lema, 2010). China, for example, implemented local content requirements that required foreign firms to purchase inputs from domestic sellers, and, in some cases, also imposed training requirements and mandated joint R&D programmes. Mexico, on the other hand, which did not have such policies in place, was less successful in capturing spillovers from FDI. One estimate is that domestic firms in Mexico provided only about 5 per cent of the inputs for foreign firms, while firms in China provided over 20 per cent (Gallagher and Shafaeddin, 2010).

In addition, there is a risk that FDI can reduce or crowd out indigenous R&D (Organization for Economic Cooperation and Development, 2002). In China, this phenomena has been attributed to competition for talent between foreign and domestic firms (Fu and Gong, 2011), which is likely to be even more pronounced in countries with more limited technological capacities. The movement of workers between foreign and domestic firms could help counteract this tendency somewhat, at least over a longer time-horizon. In China, clusterings of innovative foreign firms were more likely to lead to knowledge spillovers (Chen, Li and Shapiro, 2009), which is a further argument for the establishment of science parks or lower-cost alternatives.

Technology transfer through imports: Kenya and Bangladesh

Importing machinery and equipment is generally regarded as another mechanism for technology transfer. However, it is not clear how effective this mechanism is insofar as importing machinery does not necessarily mean that countries have mastered how the machinery is designed. Countries first need to service, maintain and "reverse-engineer" the machinery to understand the technology embedded within it, which requires local capacities and indigenous R&D.

Bangladesh first imported solar home systems, and then used the opportunity to build a local servicing and manufacturing industry

The cases of solar PV in Bangladesh and Kenya provide contrasting studies on technology transfer through imports. Both countries have rural populations that suffer from poor access to electricity; both have ample sunshine, which enables solar home systems (SHS) to be somewhat competitive with alternative sources of energy in rural areas; in both cases, private firms imported SHS; and both have had relative success in SHS distribution. However, only Bangladesh used the opportunity to build a local manufacturing industry.

In Kenya (see box V.1), the dealerships that initially imported the solar equipment in the early 1990s had very little technical expertise; imports were plagued with quality problems, which domestic firms lacked the expertise to service. As of 2009, most technicians still lacked sufficient technical training (Hankins, Anjali and Kirai, 2009). The lack of domestic competencies also meant that Kenya lacked the institutional capacity to implement and enforce standards. In addition, lack of domestic financing meant that the systems reached mainly the wealthiest rural population. Further, local firms did not engage in indigenous research or significant adaptation.

Box V.1

Solar PV in rural Kenya

Kenya's off-grid solar PV household system (SHS) market is a commercial market, with very little government involvement. It represents vibrant solar markets, with 150,000 units having been sold in 2004 and close to 300,000 in 2009 (REN21, 2010). Yet, despite this relative commercial success, the industry has been plagued by quality problems (Jacobson and Kammen, 2007), owing to a lack of domestic expertise and capabilities as well as a weak regulatory framework.

Kenya had begun to import solar PV household systems in relatively significant numbers in the 1990s. However, the development of the industry was hampered by the above-mentioned lack of domestic expertise. For example, only 17 per cent of solar technicians were able to correctly size the battery for an SHS (Duke, Jacobson and Kammen, 2002). A significant portion of the imported panels were of extremely poor quality and many households that purchased the poor-quality systems lost most or all of their investment (ibid.). As of 2009, the training of technicians remained weak, with the estimated 2,000 installation technicians who service SHS generally lacking in sufficient formal training (Hankins, Angali and Kirai, 2009).

Despite the quality problems, demand for the systems has continued to grow owing to the lack of viable alternatives in rural areas. However, financing is limited and, when available, tends to be prohibitive, adding up to 80 per cent to the overall cost of the systems (Ondraczek, 2011). Purchasers of SHS are thus among the wealthiest rural households, with almost half of the SHS owned by the top 10 per cent of the rural population (Jacobson, 2005). Because of the lack of financing, demand for SHS has also tended to be "component-based", meaning that suppliers sell pieces at a time, rather than entire systems, which has compounded quality problems (Hankins, Anjali and Kirai, 2009).

In response to pressure from local users, the Kenya Bureau of Standards drafted performance standards for solar products. However, the Bureau did not have the necessary expertise to design and enforce these standards. As there are still no domestic accredited laboratories in Kenya, the accreditation for quality standards takes place abroad (Jacobson and Kammen, 2007), which inevitably increases domestic costs and limits potential feedback between consumers and suppliers. As of 2009, enforcement of standards is still weak, which has led to a market perception among consumers of solar PV of its being "second rate" (Hankins, Anjali and Kirai, 2009). As regards building domestic industries and ancillary services, most of the parts for SHS are still imported, although there are three domestic manufacturers of local batteries and nine manufacturers of lamps (International Energy Agency, Photovoltaic Power Systems Programme, 2003).

Source: UN/DESA.

Bangladesh has begun to export solar panels to Africa

The case of Bangladesh (see box V.2) contrasts starkly with that of Kenya. Owing to its vocational education system, Bangladesh had a stronger human resource base at the outset than Kenya. Grameen Shakti (SK), a subsidiary of Grameen Bank, invested in building local capacities: trained engineers taught less skilled workers how to service the units. It also engaged in in-house research, which reduced costs and helped SK develop ancillary business. Bangladesh used its microfinance network to finance SHS and reach

Box V.2

Importing solar PV in Bangladesh

The solar household systems (SHS) industry in Bangladesh partnered with microfinance institutions, international organizations and the Government. Grameen Shakti (GS), a subsidiary of Grameen Bank, began importing solar home units in 1996. By 2010, it had sold 650,000 to off-grid rural customers in Bangladesh (Gallagher and others, 2011).

The establishment of a standardized technical and vocational infrastructure over 50 years ago created a base of expertise, which enabled the development of the industry. The vast majority of field engineers who sell, install and maintain SHS in Bangladesh have received a diploma in engineering from the Bangladesh Technical Education Board. These engineers, many of whom are women, also train less educated women on how to construct and repair component parts of solar PV systems, which creates a positive effect cascading down to less educated workers.

Financing for SHS sales is generally conducted through microfinance. To aid in this effort, the Government set up the financial institution IDCOL (Infrastructure Development Company Limited) in 1997, with financing from the World Bank. IDCOL works with partner organizations (such as GS), which sell the units and provide financing to customers. To ensure quality standards, these organizations are required to sell components approved by a technical standards committee, including experts from Government, the rural electrical agency and the technical university.

In addition to being involved in sales, GS is engaged in indigenous research, which has helped GS reduce the cost of the panels, adapt the technology and develop accessories, such as a mobile phone battery charger (Chhabara, 2008). Initially, most of the panel components were imported, but today, all the parts are produced domestically. In this regard, Rahimafrooz, a local firm that initially manufactured lead-acid batteries for the systems, has expanded its operation to include exports to Nepal and Bhutan. More recently, Rahimafrooz set up the first solar panel assembly plant in Bangladesh (Parvez, 2009) and has begun to export panels to Africa (Ahmed, 2011); in addition, it has signed a memorandum of understanding with TATA BP Solar on building a 5 megawatt (mw) solar power plant in Bangladesh (Daily Star, 2010), thereby further building international linkages.

In addition to creating employment through these new manufacturing industries, the off-grid solar sector has created thousands of jobs in rural Bangladesh. GS itself employs more than 7,500 individuals and operates 45 technology centres run by women engineers. These centres have trained over 3,000 rural women who generally lack access to other income-generating opportunities.

Source: Gallagher and others (2011).

broader populations. The Government set up a State-owned infrastructure development company and set standards to support financing and ensure quality. At the same time, companies in Bangladesh took advantage of the growth of the sector to provide ancillary services. Today, all the components of the systems are produced domestically. Further, Bangladesh has set up its first solar assembly plant and begun to export panels to Africa.

The cases of Bangladesh and Kenya offer several lessons on the use of imports to effect technology transfer. First, in Bangladesh, domestic capabilities were crucial for the servicing and operation of units, as well as for building ancillary businesses and spurring employment and growth. The experience of Bangladesh demonstrates the importance of vocational education, on-the-job training, and the role that women can play in fostering green innovation. Second, in Bangladesh, indigenous research helped cut costs and led to successful adaptation, as well as the development of new businesses. Third, regulators need institutional capacity to be able to enforce quality standards. Fourth, coordination among university, regulators and foreign and domestic firms was an important element in Bangladesh's success, whereas these linkages were weak in Kenya. Finally, in Bangladesh, the Government enforced quality standards and developed a rural energy development fund to overcome financing shortfalls.

Licensing and alternative modes of technology transfer: China and India

The third traditional mechanism, licensing agreements, has been used fairly extensively for green technologies. The effectiveness of licensing for knowledge spillovers is dependent on local capabilities and R&D.

Licensing agreements have been used for green technologies

Both China and India used licensing agreements as part of their initial investments in clean-energy wind and solar technologies, and supplemented licensing with indigenous research, often conducted in collaboration with domestic universities and research institutes supported by subsidies and public investment. Over time, licensing shifted to co-development with foreign partners, as firms attempted to build learning networks (Lema and Lema, 2010).

Companies can develop strategic partnerships with international firms and universities through collaborative R&D

Although there were differences in strategies (firms in China focused on building domestic learning networks, while companies in India focused on international learning networks), companies in both countries developed strategic partnerships with international firms and universities through collaborative R&D. For example, India's wind company Suzlon built R&D centres and manufacturing units in Germany, the Netherlands and the United States in order to tap into foreign expertise (Lewis, 2007a). While China's wind turbine industry was initially focused on the domestic market, the solar industry concentrated on exports to take advantage of government subsidies for solar energy in developed countries, emphasizing the importance of international markets to domestic innovation systems (Fu, 2011).

Both countries also benefited from human resources trained abroad. Many of the leaders in China's most important solar firms had spent time studying abroad, and either returned to China to start their own firms or were recruited to join existing ones (Gallagher and others, 2011).

From brain drain to brain gain

The cases of China and India point to a potential role for the diaspora in transferring international knowledge. However, many developing countries experience the reverse effect: outmigration of skilled labour to developed countries, which has increased rapidly over the past two decades (Docquier, Lohest and Marfouk, 2007). From the perspective of building domestic capabilities, the challenges for policymakers are first, how to keep educated people from leaving by developing opportunities at home; and second, how to draw those participating in the diaspora back to the country, or find other ways to encourage them to share their expertise and skills and form business linkages (United Nations Conference on Trade and Development, 2007).

Some advanced emerging markets and newly industrialized economies, such as China, the Republic of Korea and Taiwan Province of China, have set up programmes to encourage emigrants to return. China has set up more than 100 special high-technology parks to draw back nationals from overseas (Dahlman, 2008). In Taiwan Province of China, there is a State information clearing house for potential employers and returning researchers, with airfare and other subsidies for those who return (Davone, 2007).

The ability to draw back diaspora members can be an important element in knowledge transfer

However, the effectiveness of many of these strategies is conditional on a country's level of development (United Nations Conference on Trade and Development, 2007). While newly industrialized countries such as China can take advantage of the temporary migration of students and workers to develop scientific capacities, very few African countries are in this position. Nonetheless, as difficult as it is to draw back diaspora members, the ability to do so can be an important element in knowledge transfer, and could be especially important for countries with weak education systems. In fact, a number of countries have programmes that encourage citizens to obtain their student education abroad by financing it, on condition that those students bring home their skills by working in the home country, generally in the public sector, for a number of years after graduation, or after acquiring work experience.

To attract new generations of scientists, policymakers need to build a scientific infrastructure accompanied by changes in culture by promoting innovation and collaboration (Tole and Vale, 2010). In essence, steps that countries should already be taking to spur sustainability-oriented innovation could help attract the diaspora, thereby creating a virtuous cycle.

Education

Education can play multiple roles in a G-NIS. It can influence consumption choices and teach consumers about the environment; build skills necessary for innovation, technological adaptation and the institutional capacity; raise awareness among policymakers; and generate positive externalities, such as the positive benefits conferred by educated parents (particularly women) on their children (Schultz, 2002).

Partnerships with the private sector can help policymakers determine an appropriate education strategy

Building the technological capacities necessary for green innovation requires both learning-by-doing and formal education. Countries need to orient their education systems towards developing a skills base for innovation across sectors, such as agriculture, energy and transportation, and should (as this chapter argues) develop vocational training, although the nature of educational reforms will, of course, depend on a country's economic structure, fiscal means and level of development. In addition, non-traditional forms of education can increase coordination between educators and firms, as well as enhance access to and lower costs of education.

Partnerships with the private sector can help determine the most appropriate education and training strategy for a country. For example, in the Republic of Korea, the partnership of the private and public sectors played a role in the development of Government-led investment in the vocational training system (Hawley, 2007). Similarly, Governments in several Latin American countries have forged successful partnerships with private companies aimed at improving technical education (Alvarez and others, 1999). These partnerships can also help strengthen interactions between agents in the economy.

Education, consumption and environmental behaviour

Information campaigns and civil society mobilization can raise public environmental sensitivity and responsibility, and foster sustainable behaviour in areas such as energy conservation and recycling. Studies have shown that educating consumers regarding their energy consumption patterns can reduce consumption (by about 11 per cent in the United States, according to one study), by switching from high- to low-energy items (Gardner and Stern, 2008).

Education for conservation can impact consumer and firm behaviour

Education for conservation can have an even greater impact on firms. A United Nations Industrial Development Organization (UNIDO)-United Nations Environment Programme (UNEP) programme focused on training, awareness creation and policy advice has led to significant savings by firms through conservation. For example, in Kenya, the paper manufacturer Chandaria Industries experienced savings of 40 per cent in energy, 48 per cent in materials and 181 per cent in water through involvement in the programme.

Carbon dioxide (CO_2) emission intensity was reduced by 28 per cent, waste water by 64 per cent and waste intensity by 62 per cent (United Nations Industrial Development Organization, 2010).

Formal education

Vocational schooling can be particularly useful in building technological skills

There is some debate regarding whether developing countries should focus their efforts on improving primary, secondary or tertiary education. Primary education is critical for developing a semi-skilled labour force. In low-income countries with large rural sectors, it can be vital for equipping farmers with the basic skills necessary to their being informed on and implementing sustainable agricultural and forestry practices. However, while the significance of achieving universal primary education is highlighted by its inclusion as a Millennium Development Goal, secondary, vocational and tertiary education are just as important in the field of green technology. Secondary education can provide core skills and knowledge needed for countries' economic growth. Vocational schooling can be particularly useful in building technological competencies; successful vocational education also provides important links between education and industry. For example, in both Bangladesh (see box V.2) and China, the presence of a pool of workers trained in vocational schools was instrumental for the development of domestic solar PV industries (Gallagher and others, 2011). In Brazil, the National Employers' Federation is a major provider of high-quality training in areas with labour-market shortages.

Governments may benefit from targeted interventions in scientific fields

However, the provision of vocational education can be relatively costly; in sub-Saharan Africa, for example, it is up to 14 times more expensive than general secondary education (Johanson and Adams, 2004). Thus, Governments may benefit from targeted interventions in scientific fields. Tertiary education, especially in science and engineering, can help countries become globally competitive and build technological capacities (World Bank, 2010b).

Recent progress in education in developing countries

Many technical and vocational programmes suffer from weak linkages to employment markets

An assessment of educational outcomes reveals huge variations among and within countries at all levels of education. Overall progress towards universal primary education in the past decade has been encouraging, with the net enrolment ratio having reached 87 per cent at the end of the school year, 2008, in the developing world (table V.1). Nevertheless, UNESCO (2011b) estimates that over 50 million children will still be out of school in 2015 and that in many countries the quality of education remains weak. Despite some improvements, secondary school enrolment remains a problem in many developing regions (table V.2). Countries vary enormously in respect of coverage of technical and vocational education. However, many technical and vocational education programmes suffer from underinvestment, poor quality and weak linkage to employment markets. Tertiary enrolment in developing countries has increased, but remains relatively low in many regions, with enrolment being only 6 per cent in Africa.

Lower female access to education remains a problem in many parts of the world. Although gender disparities have been narrowing in developing countries, they are still pronounced in technical and vocational education and in scientific and technical fields in tertiary education (Hyde, 1993). On the other hand, in some countries, such as Bangladesh, training of women has been critical in building the green technology sector (see box V.2).

Table V.1
Primary enrolment, 1999 and 2008

Percentage

	Net enrolment ratio		Gross enrolment ratio	
	School year ending		School year ending	
	1999	2008	1999	2008
World	**82**	**88**	**98**	**107**
Developed countries and areas	96	95	103	101
Europe	97	96	105	103
North America	94	93	101	99
Australia and New Zealand	95	97	100	105
Japan	100	100	101	102
Developing countries and areas	80	87	98	108
Africa	61	77	81	100
Asia (excluding Japan)	85	90	100	110
Latin America and the Caribbean	92	94	121	116
Oceania	..	..	81	..

Source: United Nations Educational, Scientific and Cultural Organization Institute for Statistics (Montreal, Canada).
The gross enrolment ratio (GER) is defined as total enrolment at a specific level of education: regardless of age, expressed as the proportion of the population in the official age group corresponding to this level of education. The gross enrolment ratio may exceed 100 per cent because of early or late entry and/or grade repetition.

Innovative approaches to education

There are a host of new mechanisms designed to lower costs and improve access to education, many of which can focus on vocational training. These innovative approaches supplement the formal education system and focus on the skills necessary for green jobs.

Use of e-learning programmes and satellite schools in higher education can lower the risk of brain drain

At the primary level, partnerships connect schools in Africa with the United Kingdom of Great Britain and Northern Ireland (United Kingdom of Great Britain and Northern Ireland, British Council, 2011). Access to secondary education can be expanded through distance learning via television or other media, utilized by many Latin American countries (World Bank, 2007b). Costa Rica has focused on vocational training for small enterprises through government collaboration with non-governmental organizations and businesses in creating a one-year technical vocational degree (Alvarez and others, 1999). At the tertiary level, distance learning can drastically lower the cost of high-quality education, as demonstrated by Mexico's virtual Millennium University (Alvarez and others, 1999). The use of e-learning programmes and satellite schools in higher education has the added benefit of not necessitating the physical relocation of students to developed countries and can thereby lower the risk of brain drain. Community learning centres can be used to enhance basic education, train teachers, develop local businesses and strengthen civil society, offer access to information and communications technology (ICT) tools, and provide populations in small villages with valuable information (United Nations Educational, Scientific and Cultural Organization, 2011a).

In many countries, there is a shortage of skilled labour, such as engineers, maintenance staff and site managers in green economy sectors, although the needs vary by sector. For example, sustainable agriculture is knowledge-intensive and requires farmer training through extension services, farmer field schools and/or adult literacy campaigns, as discussed in chapter III.

Table V.2
Secondary, vocational and tertiary enrolment, 1999 and 2008

Percentage

	Secondary		*Tertiary*		*Vocational*	
	Gross enrolment ratio		*Gross enrolment ratio*		*Share of technical/ vocational in total secondary education*	
	School year ending		*School year ending*		*School year ending*	
	1999	*2008*	*1999*	*2008*	*1999*	*2008*
World	**59**	**68**	**18**	**27**	**11**	**11**
Developed countries	98	99	54	70	17	16
Developing countries and areas	52	63	11	20	9	10
Africa	32	41	8	10	12	10
Asia (excluding Japan)	53	66	11	20	..	..
Latin America and the Caribbean	80	89	21	38	11	11
Oceania	34	..	4	..	..	..

Source: United Nations Educational, Scientific and Cultural Organization Institute for Statistics (Montreal, Canada).

Labour market policies

Education and training need to be accompanied by labour-market policies that encourage an appropriate match between job-seekers and employers. Governments can help facilitate labour mobility and job searches through various interventions, including vocational training, as discussed above, and employment services, competency assessment programmes and skills certification (World Bank, 2010b). These policies can have the ancillary benefit of leading to increased knowledge spillover and faster technology transfer. Costs associated with a transition to a green economy, including unemployment arising from the shift from high-carbon industries, will need to be minimized through targeted measures such as worker retraining, potentially backed by international-level support through development assistance, including Aid for Trade.

Green development requires effective labour-market institutions, including various forms of protection for workers

Building the appropriate skills base for a green economy needs to be accompanied by effective labour-market institutions, including various forms of protection for workers. Green jobs need to entail decent work, with adequate wages, safe working conditions, job security and worker rights (United Nations Environment Programme, 2008). Jobs in some sectors considered green, such as the electronics recycling industry in Asia and the biofuel feedstock plantations sector in Latin America, actually expose workers to environmental and other risks. Recycling, for example, is an important sustainable industry in many developing countries: In China, 1.3 million people are employed in the formal waste collection system, an additional 2.5 million are informal workers or scrap collectors, and as many as 10 million people are involved in other areas of recycling; and in Brazil, half a million people are involved in materials collection activities (United Nations Environment Programme, 2008). Yet, recycling jobs are often hazardous, with safety and environmental rules non-existent. Labour-market institutions and regulations need to address these issues.

Institutions, industrial policies and infrastructure

There are a wide range of institutions and fiscal incentives that can promote or impede innovation. Institutions comprise laws, rules and established social and cultural practices that affect incentives and behaviour (Edquist, 1997),[5] such as patent laws, cap-and-trade systems and regulations. As elsewhere in the G-NIS, there should be two-way relationships between these elements and the rest of the system. Domestic institutions and existing infrastructure set incentives and affect how the actors behave. Infrastructural or institutional rigidities that arise can hamper innovation.

Public sector investments in infrastructure could be required to support industrial policy efforts

Because of the lack of market demand for sustainable technologies, government industrial policies designed to stimulate private sector investment need to be at the heart of the G-NIS. Such policies treat green economy activities as "infant industries", requiring appropriate support, including regulatory requirements, government procurement, subsidies (preferably performance-related and time-bound), access to credit and, possibly, some level of trade protection, as discussed in chapter VI. In many countries, public sector investments in infrastructure would be required to support these industrial policy efforts. In addition, the policy framework should include a government agency structure that can facilitate the establishment of stable but flexible institutions.

Regulation

Regulations should be designed to be innovation-friendly

Regulatory mechanisms, such as targets and standards, are often designed as tools to limit or prohibit certain forms of behaviour (United Nations Environment Programme, 2011). However, regulations should also be designed to be innovation-friendly. Environmental regulations, such as limits placed on emissions, pesticides in food, pollution and water contamination, have the first-order effect of improving the environment, but can also be drivers of domestic demand for green technologies.

Targets are already being utilized in many developing countries. For example, renewable energy targets, which set goals for green energy, usually at 5-20 per cent of total energy consumption, are used by 45 developing countries (REN21, 2010). However, the effectiveness of these targets varies by country, and many countries are likely to miss their 2010 targets. An alternative measure used in many countries, particularly those with public energy companies, is to mandate energy companies to source a certain percentage of energy from renewable sources (Kempener, Diaz Anadon and Condor Tarco, 2010). These more direct targets are somewhat easier to manage and enforce.

Standards can create demand for green technologies

Standards, including energy-efficiency codes for buildings and air, water, and fuel efficiency standards, can create demand for green technologies, while improving the environment and health. For example, fuel efficiency standards in China led to the adoption of and improvements in fuel efficiency technologies (Gallagher, 2006). Similarly, water safety standards can stimulate the development of systems for safely storing and treating water, for example, through waste-water recycling and desalinization, or improve on traditional or local-based technologies, such as harvesting rainwater. Such standards can be implemented progressively over time if necessary, through regulation that has been announced in advance, to give agents time to adjust.

5 Note that this list does not include organizations (such as government agencies), which are categorized as actors.

One effective programme for setting standards has been Japan's Top Runner Programme for appliances, discussed in chapter II. This programme is based on collaboration among various actors. The most energy efficient product on the market sets the "Top Runner Standard", which all corresponding manufacturers and products will aim to achieve in the next stage. Energy efficiency standards are then set by the Ministry of Economy, Trade and Industry and its advisory committees, comprising representatives from academia, industry, consumer groups, local governments and mass media.

Other regulations include outright mandates. For example, the Republic of Korea has a policy of "extended producer responsibility" which requires companies to recycle packaging. This programme has increased recycling by 14 per cent and estimated savings by $1.6 billion (United Nations Environment Programme, 2011). Other mandates include direct requirements for green technologies. For example, Bangladesh mandates the utilization of solar PV in new construction; Israel mandates utilization of solar hot water; and other countries, such as Brazil, have mandates for biofuels.

Quantity-based restrictions can often reduce risk more effectively than price-related interventions

Economists are traditionally partial to price-based mechanisms, such as taxes, over quantity-based regulations, such as those mentioned above. However, the case to be made for price-based interventions is far from clear-cut, and theoretical work in economics has shown that quantity-based restrictions can reduce risk more effectively than price-related interventions (Stiglitz and others, 2006). Further, quantity-based interventions are typically easier to administer than more complex price-based incentives, making them particularly useful tools for countries with weak administrative capacity.

Government procurement, subsidies and other incentives

Government procurement, such as purchases of clean bus fleets, is designed to create market demand, subsidies and tax credits are designed to lower an investor's initial investment, while feed-in tariffs (FITs) are designed to guarantee a higher return. Many of these instruments are already utilized by developing countries. Green investment tax credits are used in 18 developing countries, public investment is used in 17, while feed-in tariffs, which guarantee prices to clean energy producers above the existing market price, are used in 17, including Algeria, Mongolia, Sri Lanka and Uganda (REN21, 2010). Many of these mechanisms have been criticized for locking in subsidies that then become politically difficult to remove, although putting time limits on them can help reduce this risk somewhat.

Industrial policies can also be used to accelerate changes in behaviour

Industrial policies can also be used to accelerate changes in behaviour and practices. If well designed, some of these tools can have multiple benefits. For example, paying farmers for carbon sequestration would remove CO_2 from the atmosphere (mitigation), enhance soil resilience (adaptation) and improve production by improving crop yields (Ocampo, 2011a).

Carbon instruments

Another set of instruments are designed to incorporate environmental externalities into carbon technologies to "get prices right", thereby making sustainable technologies more competitive with existing technologies. These include cap-and-trade policies and carbon taxes. As discussed above, both sets of policies are particularly problematic for poor developing countries, as the likely increase in energy costs could disrupt economic development, at least until new energy sources are available.

Cap-and-trade is a quantity control, since it limits the amount of carbon that firms can produce; but it has been designed to be more in line with market mechanisms than the regulatory controls discussed above. The advantage of a cap-and-trade system versus priced-based mechanisms, such as a carbon tax, lies in the fact that a cap puts a legal limit on pollution, while the tax sets a price under the assumption that quantity will adjust, based on the higher price. A carbon tax has the advantage of raising revenue for the government. In addition, some studies have indicated that under certain conditions a carbon tax is more likely to spur innovation (Scotchmer, 2010).[6]

Strong administrative capacity is needed to implement cap-and-trade schemes

Perhaps most importantly, for developing countries without strong administrative capacity, domestic cap-and-trade schemes could be extremely difficult to implement. The 2007-2008 financial crisis revealed the ease with which financial markets could be manipulated, even in the most advanced markets; hence, the risk of manipulation, market failures and distorted incentives would be extremely high in most developing countries. Moreover, with respect to getting prices right, it is likely that both carbon taxes and cap-and-trade programmes would have to be so large as to be politically infeasible (Mowery, Nelson and Martin, 2010).

Investment requirements and trade protection

Many newly industrialized economies used investment requirements to build domestic industries

In addition to price incentives and quantity restrictions, many newly industrialized economies used investment requirements and protectionist measures to build and protect domestic industries. For example, both India and China adjusted customs duty requirements to protect the development of domestic solar and wind industries (Lema and Lema, 2010). China also imposed investment requirements on FDI, including local content, joint venture, local hiring and mandatory seminar requirements, with the goal of encouraging technology transfer from foreign to domestic companies (Lewis, 2007a; 2007b).

International intellectual property rights can limit technology transfer and the ability to engage in domestic innovation

However, as discussed in chapter VI, these measures, as well as many of the quantity and price incentives discussed above, might be considered illegal under World Trade Organization rules, which could potentially limit policy scope and thus make it difficult for developing countries to "catch up". In fact, according to Gallagher and Shafaeddin (2010, p. 37): "OECD governments have begun to dub China's policies as 'forced transfers' and have undertaken investigations and task forces in order to eliminate or reduce them". Further, international intellectual property rights can limit technology transfer and the ability to engage in domestic innovation, although the extent will depend on the economic sectors involved, the economic activities and the level of development, as discussed in chapter VI.

Infrastructure and business environment

To spur innovation, industrial policy measures need to be supplemented by public sector investment in domestic infrastructure. Such investment can have multiple benefits. For example, public sector investment in clean transportation or in energy, water and sanitation services can reduce poverty, improve health and create a better investment climate.

6 According to Scotchmer, when the demand for energy is inelastic, cap-and-trade regulation may lead to incomplete diffusion of a new technology, whereas tax regulation offers an incentive to fully diffuse the innovation.

Countries can support business incubators and technology transfer centres

Innovation and entrepreneurial activity also require facilities, legal and businesses services, and access to telecommunications services. An alternative for countries that do not have a supportive infrastructure is to build business incubators and technology transfer centres capable of providing these services. These can be either independent or structured as elements in a science park, as is the case in Tunisia (World Bank, 2010b).

A second important element is the nature of the business environment, which is influenced by the extent to which bureaucracy impacts the ease of doing business. Although every context differs, in general, the government should focus on reducing the red tape that unnecessarily impedes entrepreneurship, while distinguishing between those regulations that serve a purpose and those that simply foster inefficiency. For example, investors might view regulations that require documentation of environmental risks as being simply red tape, even though these regulations are a necessary element of a country's regulatory framework.

Government agencies

Institutions in many countries, such as those in Africa, are subject to rigidities, which make it difficult for them to respond to the changing needs of a developing economy's innovation system (Oyelaran-Oyeyinka, 2005). While overcoming institutional rigidities can be difficult, a government agency structure that is designed to promote innovation can better manage a G-NIS and thus help overcome some of these obstacles.

The goal is to leave in place the flexibility of a diffused governmental organization, while maintaining coordination

The Economic Commission for Africa (ECA) (United Nations, Economic Commission for Africa, 2007) identified three types of structures for government agencies: pluralist, coordinated and centralist. Pluralist structures have independent government agencies and ministries with no coordinating mechanism, an arrangement that could lead to a high cost in terms of overlap and gaps. In the coordinated system, government departments initiate their own programmes, but a coordinating body nevertheless exists. This type of structure has tended to lead to rivalries among ministries and its effectiveness is being called into question by many of the OECD countries that have utilized it. In a centralist system, the full range of green technological projects and issues are coordinated by a single ministry. An inter-ministerial committee formulates policy, approves the technology budget and oversees all decisions related to technology policy. The goal is to leave in place the flexibility of a diffused governmental organization, while maintaining a central coordinating body.

The Economic Commission for Africa (United Nations, Economic Commission for Africa, 2007) concluded that the centralist system is the most appropriate structure for developing countries, such as those in Africa. Given that a G-NIS is a complex system, a coordinating body is likely to play an important role in designing policy. However, in a G-NIS framework, it is important to include all key stakeholders in the design process, including the private sector and civil society. There is no one-size-fits-all solution, and which structure is most relevant will depend on the specifics of the country.

Whatever structure is chosen needs to be coupled with mechanisms for monitoring and evaluation so as to limit the capture of politicians by the private sector. It is also important to ensure the connection between the coordinating body and the highest political authorities, since without a strong visible political commitment, short-term urgent priorities in other areas can displace attention and resources.

Financing

One of the most important functions of the G-NIS is to mobilize the capital needed to finance innovation. In theory, the government would finance public goods, such as infrastructure and possibly education, and leave the rest to the private sector. However, as discussed earlier, the lines blur with regard to investments in innovation of green technologies because of their status as public goods.

Which source of financing makes the most sense for a country will depend on its financial market structure and the level of risk in the project. There are also international public funds available to help countries finance investments in green technologies, including through the United Nations Framework Convention on Climate Change,[7] the World Bank Group, and other sources of aid as discussed in chapter VI.

Private sector green funds

So-called green funds have tended to be myopic and extremely pro-cyclical

So-called green funds are mutual funds and hedge funds that invest in sustainable technologies. However, these funds tend to be myopic and extremely pro-cyclical, increasing during boom periods and falling during economic downturns. This is partly because the fund managers themselves are short-sighted, and partly because their own funding sources tend to grow during boom periods and collapse during economic recessions (Stiglitz and others, 2006). For example, investors redeemed $1.2 billion from renewable energy funds in the first 10 months of 2010 as changes in regulation and the credit crunch dimmed the outlook for solar and wind projects, after those funds had grown by $1.2 billion in 2009 (Sills, 2010). In essence, these funds are green hot money and Governments should be wary of the type of financing they offer.

Venture capital

Generally, venture capital has not been available for investments in green technologies in developing countries owing to the high risks involved

Venture capital (VC) is the form of financing typically used in the diffusion stage of the innovation process, not least because many venture capitalists can assist in business development. Unlike green funds, VC tends to have relatively long lock-ups, meaning that investors cannot withdraw their investments for a period of 7-10 years.[8] Generally, VC has not been available for investments in green technologies in developing countries owing to the high risks involved, as discussed above. Although a significant amount of VC had been raised for investments in green technology prior to the financial market crisis, most of the funds were invested in developed countries. Approximately one quarter of the funds were never deployed at all, because green investments had been viewed as too risky—even in developed countries (World Bank, 2010b).

Microfinance institutions and microfinance

Microfinance can play a role in reaching rural populations which currently lack access to electricity, clean water and cooking stoves. Microfinance and micro-consignment[9] are

7 United Nations, *Treaty Series*, vol. 1771, No. 30822.

8 Nonetheless there is evidence that investments of venture capital in R&D are somewhat pro-cyclical (Barlevy and Tsiddon, 2006; Ouyang, 2009).

9 In micro-consignment, the consumer pays off the price of the product over time, with the distributor owning the product until it is fully paid off.

currently being used for solar lamps, water purifiers and stoves (Rosenberg, 2011). Further opportunities exist in the areas of cleaner cooking products, biofuels and low-emissions agriculture (Rippey, 2009).

Some microfinance institutions have set up subsidiary companies to provide financing for clean energy products

Several microfinance institutions, such as Grameen Bank in Bangladesh, have also successfully set up subsidiary companies which use their microcredit networks to extend loans for clean energy products, such as off-grid solar systems, as discussed in box V.2. Much of the financing for these loans comes from banks set up by government or multilateral institutions. Similarly, Sri Lanka's renewable energy project is based on a network of microfinance institutions that work with solar companies (REN21, 2010).

Foreign direct investment

FDI can be a source of long-term investment. Although there is evidence that FDI is also somewhat pro-cyclical (Stiglitz and others, 2006), it is significantly less so than portfolio investment. However, as discussed above, to be effective in technology transfer, FDI needs be supplemented by domestic policies designed to encourage knowledge spillovers.

Long-term institutional investors

Long-term investors include domestic and international pension funds, as well as sovereign wealth funds (SWFs).[10] Although funds differ, all of these investors tend to have relatively long investment-horizons, and can, to some extent, avoid succumbing to the myopia discussed above. In addition, because SWFs and public pension funds represent citizens, many of them are conscious of the need to behave in a socially responsible way: green investments can enhance their legitimacy and reputation in this regard (Bolton, Guesnerie and Samama, 2010).

Several large public pension funds and sovereign wealth funds have begun to invest in clean energy projects

Pension funds tend to be relatively conservative investors, since their liability structure is based on future payments to pensioners, which are meant to be relatively stable. Therefore, it could be difficult for pension funds to invest in the earlier stages of green technological innovation in developing countries, owing to the high uncertainty associated with many of the projects. Nonetheless, several large public pension funds, such as the public sector funds of Canada and the Netherlands, have begun to invest in clean energy projects. Government policies that emphasize risk-sharing policies could be particularly important for these investors.

Moreover, several SWFs have also already made significant green investments. Most SWFs have a mandate to preserve and transfer wealth to future generations. Therefore, green investments make sense to them from an asset-liability perspective, since the risks associated with climate change can be seen as a potential liability to nation States (Bolton, Guesnerie and Samama, 2010).

Private and public sector risk-sharing

There is enormous uncertainty associated with the innovation process and the lack of markets for many green products

As the above analysis makes clear, the main impediments to private sector investment in green innovation are the enormous uncertainty associated with the innovation process and the lack of markets for many green products. Mechanisms designed to facilitate

10 However, many seemingly long-term investors, such as pension funds (both domestic and international), manage their investment with a short-term bias.

sharing of risk between the government and the private sector can be used to overcome these impediments to some degree. These include traditional forms of risk-sharing, such as public-private partnerships, as well as more innovative mechanisms, such as equity-linked financing, rural funds and national green long-horizon funds.

Public-private partnerships (PPP) and development banks

Both the government and the private sector invest jointly in public-private partnerships, and share the costs of the projects. In the United States, public-private partnerships are an important component of government innovation policy (Audretsch, Link and Scott, 2002) and have been particularly helpful in overcoming the risks associated with the introduction of new technologies into the market. A prominent example is the 1986 United States Clean Coal Technology Program, which was created to address the acid rain problem. The industry covered almost two thirds of the project costs, and a Department of Energy (DOE) study found that "cost sharing between (the) DOE and industrial collaborators frequently improved the performance of RD&D programs and enhanced the level of economic and other benefits associated with such programs" (National Research Council, 2001).

Public sector development banks provide an alternative funding channel for long-term investment in many developing countries. Development banks have been important in Brazil, China and India, particularly in infrastructure. Local public banks, often dedicated to financing rural projects, are one such source of financing. These banks usually lend through private companies, non-governmental organizations and microfinance groups and, more recently, have lent through rural energy funds. In the case of both public-private partnerships and development banks, it is important that mechanisms be set up to judge their effectiveness and minimize potential abuse.

It is important to set up mechanisms to judge the effectiveness of and minimize potential abuse in public-private partnerships

Rural renewable energy funds

Rural energy funds have been set up in countries such as Bangladesh, Mali, Senegal and Sri Lanka (REN21, 2010). These funds have the triple advantage of reducing poverty, improving infrastructure (including access to electricity) and stimulating investment in green technological adaptation and diffusion. Rural funds tend to combine financing with advice on engineering, project management and feasibility studies.

Equity-linked financing

Many government policies discussed in this chapter and elsewhere, such as government subsidies, tax breaks and low-interest loans, are transfers from the government to private sector firms, meant to "crowd in" private investment. In essence, taxpayers subsidize private sector activity, but if the firm succeeds, the entrepreneurs earn all the profits.

Risk-linked financing provides an alternative to outright grants or low-interest loans. Similar to a gross domestic product (GDP)-linked bond (Griffiths-Jones and Sharma, 2006), equity-linked loans or bonds allow the lender (in this case, the government) to share in the potential upside of successful projects.[11] If the firm fails, the

Risk-linked financing provides an alternative to outright grants and low-interest loans

11 The financing could be structured as a loan (with non-voting equity warrants attached), whose repayment would be based on the success of the venture. In the event of success, the firms' owners could buy out the government's stake at a price on the basis of pre-agreed rules.

country's taxpayers lose their investment—but that loss is similar to what they would have paid out in traditional subsidies; however, if the firm succeeds, the government will have a financial stake in the firm and the taxpayers will be compensated for the risks they have taken. These are relatively simple structures that can provide low-risk financing for firms, while still ensuring that taxpayers are compensated for their investments.

National green long-horizon funds

National green long-horizon funds can be set up to enable the sharing of risk between the public and private sectors and the "crowding in" of private investment

Much attention has been focused on global funds for clean technology, which constitute an important part of the global effort to combat climate change, as discussed in chapter VI. From a domestic perspective, long-horizon domestic clean energy funds could be part of the G-NIS framework. Such funds would raise capital from long-term investors. One unique aspect of the structure is that the investors with shorter time-horizons would not be allowed to participate in the fund.[12] The government would either invest alongside private investors, or give a guarantee and put up a fraction of the capital. Either way, the government would maintain some equity in the fund to compensate for its share of the risk-taking, so that taxpayers could earn returns on the investments.

Investors would likely be drawn to the fund for several reasons.[13] First, they would have a stake in a field with enormous potential, but with reduced risk. Second, with the government taking the same risks as the investor, the government and investors' interests would be more or less aligned, thereby making it much less likely that the government would put in place policies that harm the fund's investments. Thus, one type of political risk usually faced by investors would be removed. Third, because Governments establish the regulatory and policy framework, they tend to have inside knowledge of what type of projects makes the most sense for their country. This is particularly relevant in the case of green technologies where market demand is primarily determined by government policies, thereby making the government a valuable co-investor.

The government can also derive several advantages from this type of structure. First, the government can leverage its own investments and attract investors who normally might not invest in the early phases of the innovation process. Second, the fund would likely be off balance sheet, since, for accounting purposes, it would be treated as an investment rather than as an expenditure. The implication is that it would not affect the budget, and the government could possibly issue "green bonds" to finance additional projects. Third, the fund—unlike the usual fiscal incentives, many of which are giveaways to investors—would enable the government to keep an equity stake in the projects it finances.

The investment strategy of the fund would focus on innovation. Nevertheless, the question still remains, how will the fund go about choosing which investments to finance? The answer to this question is particularly significant in the present context, because it offers insights relevant to the broader question of how a government should go about choosing its investments.

12 As measured by their liquidity provisions.

13 As the fund will invest in direct equity, the existence of a well-developed bond or equity market would not be a prerequisite for its workability.

Policy implications

A framework for government decision-making

There is a continuing debate on how a government should intervene in markets. Some argue, pointing to the success of East Asia, that government should select or target particular activities or firms. Others point to government failures, and argue that government interventions are meant to improve markets without favouring specific activities (Lall and Teubal, 1998), such as by setting standards and letting the private sector make the decision on how best to meet those standards. Yet, while standards are an important tool, they are unlikely, as discussed above, to be sufficient to spur innovation of green technologies to the extent necessary. Without other forms of government support, it is unlikely that clean technology markets will develop; thus, Governments still need to subsidize green technologies. Hence the question remains, how does the government choose which technologies or sectors are to be subsidized?

The objectives of the G-NIS suggest several general guidelines. First, the government should commit to sustainably oriented investments. Second, it should give priority to investments in infrastructure that might be critical to "crowding in" private investment. Third, it should look to investments that have positive externalities elsewhere in the system, with higher potential for learning spillovers. While a more detailed answer to the question will inevitably depend on the specific characteristics of a country, this chapter sets out a framework for responding to it through use of an analogy to financial asset management (which is one reason that the fund construct above is so useful).

When it has unique insight into the appropriateness of certain investments, a Government should take advantage of that knowledge to direct investment choices

Grübler and others (forthcoming bis) have suggested that Governments should create a diversified portfolio comprising a blend of technologies, based on a granular approach, which spreads risk across a broad range of smaller-scale innovations without the Government's being required to make premature selections of a few capital-intensive projects. However, larger projects are sometimes the most appropriate, especially for small economies and developing countries, and the small, diversified approach would preclude this option. Further, a diversified portfolio is the best approach for investing only if the following conditions are satisfied: (a) the returns of the investments are uncorrelated, and (b) the investor does not have any unique knowledge or comparative advantage over other investors. If an investor has unique knowledge, it is likely more profitable to invest on that information than to diversify. Venture capitalists invest all the time in more concentrated portfolios while still maintaining a degree of diversification across multiple investments. Many of these investments are in fact based on educated guesses regarding what government policy will look like.

Similarly, when a government or a non-governmental organization has unique insight, like the Government of Brazil in respect of sugar and biofuels or Grameen on the potential for solar in rural Bangladesh, it can—and should—take advantage of that knowledge. More broadly, a diversified index fund approach makes sense when a Government does not have unique insight; a more concentrated venture capital-type approach (which nonetheless still maintains some degree of diversification) makes sense when the government does have that insight.

Building insight at the government level is, of course, not always straightforward. Government learning is an interactive process based on experimentation. Feedback from private sector innovators, research labs, suppliers and demanders are a crucial part of the decision-making process. The G-NIS emphasizes the importance of interaction between policymakers and the private sector, universities, and research institutes, which can further enhance government decision-making. Furthermore, most Governments know more than any other actors about future regulatory structure, legal framework and players in the system, and often have more information on various existing projects in relevant sectors.

As in the private sector, not all government investments will be profitable and some will fail

As in the private sector, not all government investments will be profitable and some will fail. After all, more than 50 per cent of new businesses in the United States fail in the first four years of their existence (Shane, 2008). Successful venture capitalists are right only part of the time,[14] while the gains of the winners compensate for the failures of the losers. However, particular investment failures do not mean that the strategy itself is a failure. It is important to change perceptions of the meaning of government failure. A country fund structure, as discussed above, could be helpful in doing so, since it incorporates individual decisions into a larger framework. In addition, as the fund would likely be managed by an independent manager, it could also help address some of the issues associated with government mismanagement.

Governments should be judged on the success of overall strategies and not on the success of specific projects

Nonetheless, government failures do exist, owing to mismanagement, incompetence and/or fraud. History has shown that without a strong governance structure, government programmes can become riddled with favouritism and cronyism. Well-structured rules for assessment and monitoring investments are a crucial element in the innovation process. In the newly industrialized countries in Asia, for example, effective policies were linked to mechanisms set up to judge their effectiveness, with a flexible policy regime capable of adapting to failed policies (Kim and Nelson, eds., 2000). Implementing such a strategy is no doubt difficult, but improvements in the structure of government agencies can be a step in the desired direction.

Policy reforms under the G-NIS

The G-NIS provides a coherent systemic framework for understanding innovation policies

Strong technology and innovation policies are needed to meet the challenges associated with achieving sustainable green growth. The G-NIS provides a coherent systemic framework for understanding innovation policy. Policies within the G-NIS should correct inefficiencies in the *system,* rather than specific market failures. For example, if systemic inefficiency is due to a lack of coordination between universities and firms, the Government might offer grants for joint R&D, deploy the funds needed to start a science park and/or encourage mobility between research institutions and firms.

Policy choices will depend on the specificities of a country, including the level of development and administrative capacity

Nonetheless, one size does not fit all, and policy choices will depend on the specificities of a country, including the level of development and administrative capacity. Table V.3 sums up many of the policy measures discussed throughout this chapter and provides some general examples of how policies might apply to countries with weak, medium and strong administrative and innovative capacity. Overall, policies in the G-NIS should promote technological capacity-building, technological transfer, interactive learning and entrepreneurship based on education, knowledge spillovers and learning-by-doing.

Industrial policies are at the heart of the G-NIS. There will, of course, be some failures associated with these policies, but it is time to reassess the meaning of government failure so as to judge government performance from a broader perspective—one that is focused on the importance of building long-term sustainable green growth.

---

14 Some estimates put the proportion of the time that successful venture capitalists are correct at as low as 10 per cent (Grübler and others, forthcoming bis). Based on back-of-the-envelope estimates, the figure, while possibly higher than 10 per cent, is likely less than 50 per cent.

Table V.3
A sample of green technology policy options for countries at different levels of development and administrative capacity

	Administrative and innovative capacity		
	Weak	*Medium*	*Strong*
Formal education	Primary and secondary education, emphasis on vocational training; begin to strengthen tertiary education, including educating some people abroad	Primary, secondary, and tertiary education; emphasis on vocational training; strengthening of tertiary education	Higher demand for capabilities; greater emphasis on tertiary education, including at the postgraduate and doctorate level
Technology transfer	FDI and global value chains in conjunction with domestic research and policies; encourage joint ventures with foreign firms and mobility between firms	Reverse engineering of imports, FDI and global value chains in conjunction with domestic research and policies; encourage joint ventures with foreign firms, mobility between firms and return of diaspora members	Outward FDI; joint research with international firms; sharing of scientific research
Other industrial policies	Emphasize regulations and quantity-based incentives; possible investment regulations; investments in infrastructure	Wide range of quantity- and price-based incentives; possible investment regulations; investments in infrastructure	Wide range of quantity- and price-based incentives; focus on domestic and export markets
Additional market formation policies	Public procurement	Public procurement, feed-in tariffs	Public procurement, feed-in tariffs
Other risk-sharing mechanisms	Public-private partnerships; development banks; country funds; equity-linked financing; rural infrastructure funds	Public-private partnerships; development banks; country funds; equity-linked financing; rural infrastructure funds	Public-private partnerships; development banks; equity-linked financing; country funds; rural infrastructure funds
Focus on building linkages between…	Universities and firms; regional knowledge networks; science parks; movement of people	Universities and firms; regional knowledge networks; science parks; movement of people	Build international knowledge networks; joint R&D with international firms; outward FDI
Intellectual property rights	Weak intellectual property rights regimes	Advantages to both weak and strong systems	Likely a stronger system; though still encourage knowledge-sharing in key sectors

Source: UN/DESA.

Chapter VI
Building a global technology development and sharing regime

Summary

- A sustained scaling up and reform in international cooperation and finance are required to achieve the global technological revolution. Within the next three to four decades, individual-country efforts and efforts undertaken across the various areas of technology will need to "add up" to the global requirements for reducing environmental degradation while increasing human economic activity in pursuit of eliminating poverty.
- Green industries can be considered infant industries. Restoring State capacities for technological development, particularly in developing countries, is critical. Multilateral trade disciplines, which now heavily restrict industrial development, need to be reformed to enable the promotion of economic activities based on green technologies in a fair manner among all countries.
- Creating a publicly led global technology sharing regime and building networks of international technology research and application centres will be indispensable. To achieve the global objective of rapid technological diffusion, a greater variety of multilateral intellectual property modalities will have to be deployed.
- To facilitate the introduction of the new green technologies, investment rates in developing countries will have to be raised by at least 2-4 per cent and sustained at the higher level over the next four decades. Affording developing countries macroeconomic policy space is necessary for achieving higher investment rates needed for sustainable development. This will require improved financial regulation coordination, effective controls over volatile private capital flows, and strengthened international financing mechanisms for long-term investments and for external shocks.

Two key global challenges

As discussed in previous chapters, effective national education and innovation systems must match and build upon existing local conditions. It is expected that a great variety of national strategies and institutional approaches will emerge. The present chapter evaluates the global regime that will be required to advance and sustain these diverse national approaches.

The expected variety of country strategies must "add up" to meet global objectives

Significant and sustained upgrading of developing-country technological capabilities is a necessary ingredient in achieving sustainable development. At the international level, there are two interrelated challenges associated with achieving this end. The first challenge is to ensure that technological development and diffusion induced by individual-country Government and private sector efforts "add up"; that is, they need to induce sufficient progress towards sustainable development goals by making energy systems low on carbon emissions, producing more energy-efficient and less waste-generating appliances, and ensuring food security through sustainable agricultural production methods. International mechanisms must be able to aggregate the expected variety of country strategies. Much-strengthened international mechanisms for technological and industrial evaluation, planning, stimulation and cooperation will be needed. Multiple stakeholders, including Governments, private sector agents, the scientific community and other parts of civil society, will need to be held accountable for their actions and commitments through adequate monitoring systems.

Significant reforms in existing mechanisms for international trade, aid, finance and technology-sharing are needed

The second challenge is to unleash from individual countries the actions and creativity needed to meet the global goals of poverty reduction and environmental sustainability. At present, the multilateral trading system and bilateral and regional free trade agreements and investment treaties erect barriers that constrain national innovation and industrial development. Significant reforms in existing mechanisms related to international trade, aid, finance and technology-sharing are needed. It will also require expanded investment and financial flows and technological cooperation. International rules should facilitate developing countries' ability to incorporate green technological development into their own national development strategies.

The body of the chapter begins with a brief description of the bases of international cooperation in sustainable development and technological development and diffusion, followed by a discussion of the challenges related to ensuring that the efforts of individual stakeholders indeed add up to the achievement of sustainable development goals. The chapter then examines existing deficiencies in multilateral arrangements and concludes with a consideration of the reforms needed to overcome these deficiencies.

Global sustainable development commitments

Expanding action towards nurturing and upgrading green production and consumption technologies in developing countries must be a priority of international cooperation. In the context of the climate challenge, the Expert Group on Technology Transfer under the United Nations Framework Convention on Climate Change[1] (United Nations Framework Convention on Climate Change, Subsidiary Body for Scientific and Technological Advice, 2009, para. 216) summarized the problem as follows: "The implementation challenge is to stimulate the development of a continuously changing set of technologies (currently consisting of approximately 147 mitigation technologies and 165 technologies for adaptation) that are at different stages of technological maturity and have different requirements for further development. Those technologies need to be adapted for, and transferred to, about 150 developing countries, each with its own needs for specific technologies and enabling environments to support them."

Proposals to reorient the global regime towards publicly led technological diffusion have been justified on the grounds of poverty eradication

It is noteworthy that since 1992, pursuant to the adoption of Agenda 21 (United Nations, 1993), one of the outcomes of the United Nations Conference on Environment and Development (the "Earth Summit"), held in Rio de Janeiro in June 1992, proposals to reorient the global technological regime towards diffusion shaped by public goals have been justified on the grounds of poverty eradication and environmental sustainability. Agenda 21 embodied a political commitment based on principles—not action. This political commitment has been reaffirmed in subsequent political agreements.

1 United Nations, *Treaty Series*, vol. 1771. No. 30822.

The United Nations Framework Convention on Climate Change, an agreement focused on the shared State responsibilities in response to the challenge of climate change (unlike Agenda 21 which focused on development-related responsibilities), reiterates the commitment in its article 4, which states that "(T)he developed country Parties and other developed Parties included in Annex II shall take all practicable steps to promote, facilitate and finance, as appropriate, the transfer of, or access to, environmentally sound technologies" (para. 5).

Chapter 34 of Agenda 21, entitled "Transfer of environmentally sound technology, cooperation and capacity-building", contains the earliest reference to the issue and sets out the key parameters involved. It identifies the "need for favourable access to and transfer of environmentally sound technologies, in particular to developing countries, through supportive measures that promote technology cooperation and that should enable transfer of necessary technological know-how as well as building up of economic, technical, and managerial capabilities for the efficient use and further development of transferred technology"; and calls on Governments, the private sector and research institutes to play their role in technology transfer, while recognizing the role of long-term partnerships in systematic training and capacity-building at all levels (para. 34.4).

An important precedent for action in the realm of international technological diffusion has been provided under the auspices of the Consultative Group on International Agricultural Research (CGIAR) (as discussed in chap. III), which supported research in and application of innovative food production technologies as a response to the perceived danger of the outstripping of food production by population growth. The CGIAR created technology intended for the public domain (even though it had been financed originally by private foundations) and in this regard established many important models of cooperative global technology regimes, placing a special emphasis on the needs of developing countries.

Do stakeholders' actions towards sustainable development add up?

Public interventions must be directed at accelerating and scaling up research and diffusion of green technology more broadly

Since the Earth Summit, there has been a growing body of multilateral technology transfer commitments driven by the goal of sustainable development and reflecting an important emerging international understanding that, at the international level, greater public sector involvement in technology development and diffusion is indispensable. The challenge lies in how to mobilize all stakeholders to deliver on these commitments and how to ensure their actions and initiatives add up so as to ensure that sustainable development objectives will be achieved. At the international level, public interventions have to be directed at accelerating and scaling up research and diffusion of green technology more broadly in order to (a) reverse the situation in respect of the status of change in energy technology, which has remained at the level of the global fuel mix of the 1970s; (b) restore land productivity while increasing food production; and (c) reduce human harm from increasingly extreme natural events, as discussed in chapters II, III and IV, respectively.

For mitigation technology in particular, an interim report of the Chair of the above-mentioned Expert Group on Technology Transfer (United Nations Framework Convention on Climate Change, Subsidiary Body for Scientific and Technological Advice, and Subsidiary Body for Implementation, 2008) provides an estimate of the relative impact of various sectors (table VI.1). Reducing greenhouse gas emissions caused by energy use (see chap. II) and forestry (discussed under land management in chap. III) makes

Table VI.1
Estimated sectoral distribution of emissions reduction potential and mitigation technologies

Sector	*Estimated contribution to total reduction potential in 2020 (percentage)*	*Number of technologies (and as percentage share of total)*	*Stage of technological maturity*				
			Research and development (percentage)	*Demonstration (percentage)*	*Deployment (percentage)*	*Diffusion (percentage)*	*Commercially mature (percentage)*
Agriculture	8–17	8 (5%)	0	0	100	0	0
Buildings	2–40	35 (24%)	3	3	51	23	20
Energy supply	14–30	32 (22%)	9	38	28	13	13
Forestry	9–39	9 (6%)	0	67	0	11	22
Industry	8–17	17 (12%)	0	6	24	71	0
Transport	7–13	37 (25%)	19	11	27	19	24
Waste	2–8	9 (6%)	11	0	22	33	33
Total		**147 (100%)**	**12 (8%)**	**24 (16%)**	**51 (35%)**	**35 (24%)**	**25 (17%)**

Source: United Nations Framework Convention on Climate Change, Subsidiary Body for Scientific and Technological Advice, and Subsidiary Body for Implementation (2008), table 10.

the greatest possible contribution to climate change mitigation. Moving towards more sustainable agriculture (chap. III) and energy-efficient buildings can also have significant and almost comparable, mitigation effects, depending on the technology involved. Out of the total of 147 technologies included in table VI.1, 51 (or 35 per cent) and, in particular, all of the agricultural technologies, are in the deployment stage of technological maturity. As discussed in chapter III, the technological deployment effort will require public sector support and is best directed at smallholder farmers. While the transport sector, which is a key energy end-user (chap. II), has the greatest number of technologies at the very basic research maturity stage compared with other sectors, some of those technologies are already commercially viable, implying that the rapid adoption of mature transportation technologies can yield quick results.

Upgrading agricultural technology will be critical in reducing GHG emissions from that sector (chap. III) while increasing food production by 70-100 per cent by 2050. New technologies in energy-efficient buildings more resilient to extreme weather events can contribute between 2 and 40 per cent to emissions reductions (table VI.1).

Private-public sector roles in technology development and diffusion

Because the challenge is to widely test, diffuse and scale up green technologies, private sector participation is critical. Maintaining stable incentives through long-term public policy is indispensable for private investment and risk-taking in green technology. The recent volatility in the prices of crude oil and carbon permits are not conducive to beneficial private risk-taking.

Increased technological deployment stimulates further private sector technical innovation

The role of advanced economies through a combination of their own tax and regulatory policies will be crucial in sustaining stable international prices for green technology development and deployment; increased technological deployment will stimulate further private sector technical innovation. Chapter V discussed how national development strategies and innovation systems can accelerate the shift towards the adoption of green technologies in order to meet sustainable development objectives. One of the roles of the proposed national innovation system (G-NIS), presented in chapter V, is "market formation" through policies such as public procurement and investment risk-sharing to stimulate private investment in the scaling up of applications of new technologies until they become cost-competitive with old technologies.

Technology development and diffusion of industrialized and developing countries must add up

For green technologies that are already commercially competitive or almost competitive, the public sector role at the international level must be to ensure that developing countries are able to deploy these technologies at a speed and scale consistent with their development needs and the global community's sustainable development objectives. A key public intervention is adequate and stable development financing for deployment of such technologies. The growing international cooperation in establishing innovative sources of development financing can be a stable, long-term and less politically contingent basis of such financing (see United Nations, General Assembly, 2009). Proposed charges on international transportation, for example, might be able to ensure both carbon efficiency and revenue benefits (United Nations, 2010a).

While some large emerging market economies, such as India, China and Brazil, appear able to undertake the required technological effort on their own and are already competing with industrialized countries, the overwhelming majority of developing countries are not in the same situation. If the international technological development and diffusion regime is to promote sustainable development, its rules and mechanisms will have to ensure affordable access to new green technologies as a developmental imperative.

Public financing will help increase the size of the market and thereby spur private companies to increase scale and continue to drive costs lower. Public action is also needed to ensure that critical new technology is available at reasonable cost. Technologies should be purchased at prices comparable with those of risky projects over extended time periods. The implications for the multilateral intellectual property regime are discussed further below.

Cooperative international scientific efforts need to be scaled up

Strengthening and configuring the role of the international public sector in promoting development of as yet non-commercial technologies constitute an urgent priority. Indeed, there exist a variety of separate technologies that offer large possibilities for crossovers and joint development. There are a variety of key players from among Governments, academia and research institutions, and private companies that compete and coordinate based on individual self-interest.

The precedents set by the work of the Intergovernmental Panel on Climate Change (IPCC), the United Nations Framework Convention on Climate Change and players within the international arena of civil society groups provide the international community with a body of knowledge and methods of reaching consensus on technical issues. While these achievements are directly related to climate change and reflect only a subset of all green economy-building goals, they do encompass all the key technological sectors whose efforts are required for sustainable development. The issue is how to translate the outcomes of this form of "knowledge consolidation and validation" into guides for concrete action.

The work of the Intergovernmental Panel on Climate Change provides the international community with precedents for methods of reaching consensus on technical issues

Governments should facilitate the creation of multi-country working bodies whose membership would be drawn from officials, academia and the private sector and whose aim would be to identify policies for, and approaches to, accelerated international technological diffusion and sharing in specific areas of technology. Each of these bodies could sustain an international network of experts with the capacity to undertake technology assessments, including the identification of areas where additional funding would be required and where changes in public policy—entailing, for example, placement of certain technologies in the public domain—would be appropriate. Applying the model of the CGIAR, these networks would raise funds and accept funding from public and private donors to finance research, experimentation and deployment. The Framework Convention Expert Group on Technology Transfer provides a template for this kind of effort (box VI.1).

Box VI.1

Expert Group on Technology Transfer

The Expert Group on Technology Transfer was established in 2001 by the Conference of the Parties to the United Nations Framework Convention on Climate Change as an institutional arrangement whose purpose would be to facilitate the implementation of the technology transfer framework provided by the Marrakesh Accords.[a] The Expert Group keeps the Conference of the Parties informed on the status and progress of its work in annual reports; and over the years, it has produced targeted and instructive products which the Conference of the Parties can use in formulating specific climate change mitigation and adaptation technology strategies.

According to its terms of reference, the Expert Group organizes workshops and prepares technical papers, reports and handbooks that analyse and identify ways of facilitating and advancing technology transfer activities. Based on these activities, the Expert Group makes recommendations to the Subsidiary Body for Scientific and Technological Advice (SBSTA).

One of the Expert Group's emerging work areas related to mechanisms for technology transfer encompasses innovative options for financing the development and transfer of technologies. A major output of the work in this area has been a practitioners' guidebook designed to assist project developers in developing countries in preparing project proposals that will meet the standards of international finance providers.

The focus of another important work area is the development of tools that can support countries in meeting their special needs for adaptation to climate change. A major output has been a background paper that sets out the lessons learned in specific sectors (coastal zones, water resources, agriculture, public health and infrastructure), including 15 case studies. The report highlights potential policy recommendations for strengthening the transfer of technologies for adaptation.

Pursuant to its reconstitution at the thirteenth session of the Conference of the Parties to the Framework Convention within the context of implementing the Bali Action Plan,[b] the strengthened Expert Group elaborated a programme of work for 2008-2009 that included the identification of mechanisms for technology transfer, including innovative financing, cooperation with relevant conventions and intergovernmental processes, endogenous development of technology and collaborative R&D of technologies.

In Bali, the Conference of the Parties at its thirteenth session was requested to develop, as part of its future programme of work, a set of performance indicators that could be used by the Subsidiary Body for Implementation to regularly monitor and evaluate the effectiveness of implementation of the technology transfer framework for meaningful and effective actions to enhance the implementation of article 4.5 of the Framework Convention. The work comprises three tasks: developing a set of candidate performance indicators, testing the set of performance indicators, and preparing recommendations for their use (United Nations Framework Convention on Climate Change, Subsidiary Body for Scientific and Technological Advice, 2008). The performance indicator system will serve as a methodological mechanism for evaluating and monitoring the development and transfer of environmentally sound technologies.

a FCCC/CP/2001/13/Add.1 and Corr.1, sect. II.

b FCCC/CP/2007/6/Add.1, decision 1/CP.13.

Source: UN/DESA (2008), pp. 40-41.

Deficiencies of existing mechanisms

Sustainable development is unattainable within the existing international frameworks. To achieve this goal, all efforts need to yield (or "add up" to) the necessary technological changes in energy and transport, in agriculture and land management, and in disaster risk reduction management, as elaborated in previous chapters. Five key constraints on the effort required have to be overcome.

Private investment-dependent technological diffusion would be too slow

Newer green technologies are characterized by a higher cost of operation relative to existing technologies

Currently, an overwhelming proportion of environmental technology is in private hands (including in universities, which have become dependent on intellectual property income in recent decades). Technology transfer relies heavily on foreign direct investment (FDI) flows, technical cooperation provisions in external assistance grants and loans and export credit agency financing. The newer green technologies are characterized by a higher cost of operation relative to existing technologies and will tend to incur additional costs specific to their deployment in developing countries because of domestic deficiencies in human skills and infrastructure ascribable to dependence on older technology. Chapter V highlighted the fact that, because technological development is path-dependent, the public sector has consistently played an indispensable role in inducing and facilitating large technological shifts. Because protection of the natural environment is a public good, there is an obvious justification for strong technology and industrial policies and one cannot expect freely operating markets to provide the right incentives conducive to large-scale investment in green technologies.

Under the United Nations Framework Convention on Climate Change, the five key elements underpinning the framework "for meaningful and effective actions" in implementing technology transfer entail a strong role for the public sector. The elements identified are: (a) technology needs assessments; (b) technology information; (c) enabling environments; (d) capacity-building; and (e) mechanisms to facilitate institutional and financial support for technology cooperation, development and transfer. In actual practice:

> (T)he focus of implementation has generally been on creating conditions in developing countries conducive to foreign investment and building capabilities to absorb and utilize imported technologies. Less emphasis has been placed on measures which governments of technology supplier countries can and should take to facilitate and accelerate technology transfer. Nor, until now, have there been effective methods of measuring and verifying the extent of environmentally sound technology transfer.[2]

Operationally, the TRIPS Agreement involves the recognition and enforcement of nationally created private intellectual property

The dependence on private transfers makes the international intellectual property regime a potentially decisive determinant of technological upgrading in developing countries. A multilateral intellectual property regime emerged in the 1990s within the framework of the Agreement on Trade-related Aspects of Intellectual Property Rights (TRIPS) regime of the World Trade Organization (World Trade Organization, 1994) and numerous bilateral and regional trade and investment treaties. Operationally, the TRIPS Agreement encompasses the recognition and enforcement of nationally created private intellectual property rights by World Trade Organization member States. Least developed countries that are World Trade Organization members obtained a grace period

2 United Nations, Department of Economic and Social Affairs, 2008, p. vi.

until 2013—and until 2016 specifically for pharmaceuticals—to recognize these property rights in their national policies. At the national level, the regime has two functions: (a) categorizing of intellectual knowledge as private property and (b) utilizing a State-enforced monopoly-of-use award as the main approach to recognizing private property and motivating private innovation. Non-owners of property must pay for the privilege to use, adapt and undertake further innovations of the technology. Because most intellectual property is owned in the developed countries, intellectual property becomes a cost of development for post-TRIPS developing countries, to be budgeted among all the other spending required to overcome underdevelopment.

World Trade Organization member States retained important flexibilities and safeguards under the TRIPS Agreement

World Trade Organization member States have retained important flexibilities and safeguards under the TRIPS Agreement. (United Nations, 2010b, p. 65). Countries can interpret the three criteria of patentability (novelty, inventive step and industrial applicability) in line with strategic domestic objectives. Governments can also issue compulsory licences and undertake "parallel imports" for stated social objectives, provided adequate compensation is made. Developing countries "with the capacity to do so" can take advantage of these flexibilities consistent with their development ambitions.

In practice, these flexibilities have been difficult to exploit (United Nations, 2010c, pp. 82-83). For one thing, trade-oriented countries seek to maintain a "welcoming reputation" towards foreign companies. Moreover, many countries are signatories to bilateral treaties which require stronger-than-TRIPs intellectual property protection.

It is difficult to find evidence that stronger property rights are a significant motivator of innovation in countries below the technological frontier

The existence of an enforceable global intellectual property regime is part of the climate in which developing countries must attempt to pursue sustainable development. Country case-studies reported in Odagiri and others (2010) suggest that, while the TRIPS has stymied national innovation, notably in the pharmaceutical industry, it has not been as constraining in other industries, particularly those requiring product assembly. Quite significantly, these case studies also suggest that it is difficult to find evidence that stronger property rights are a significant motivator of innovation in countries below the technological frontier. Overall, except for pharmaceuticals, the TRIPS does not appear to have a strong impact in its first 10 years because of specific characteristics of industries. Most of the cited case studies dealt with countries with successful industrial development policies, whose promotion of creative activities and determination enabled them to get around intellectual property-related obstacles when their attempts to purchase a given technology at a reasonable price failed.

Patenting is very aggressive in various areas of green technology

Patenting is very aggressive in various areas of green technology. For example, a small group of private companies is actively patenting plant genes with a view to securing ownership of the rights to the genes' possible future "climate readiness" (Shashikant, 2009, p. 23). There has been a rapid increase in international patenting activity specifically in climate change mitigation technologies, compared with other technologies (figure VI.1). The intense interest in green technologies and the growing competition among major economies (which include some developing countries such as India and China) suggests that it would be foolhardy to presume that the relatively benign impact of the TRIPS on countries with strong industrial policies would be benign in the case of green technology.

As a contrast, the example of rapid international diffusion during the green revolution in agriculture of the 1960s and 1970s (see chap. III) has been an important precedent for publicly led, rather than private sector-dependent international technology transfer. Under the auspices of the CGIAR, "miracle seeds" were placed in the public domain to assist in the pursuit of the global objective of raising food production so as to keep up with population growth.

Figure VI.1
Increase in climate change mitigation technologies, 1975-2006

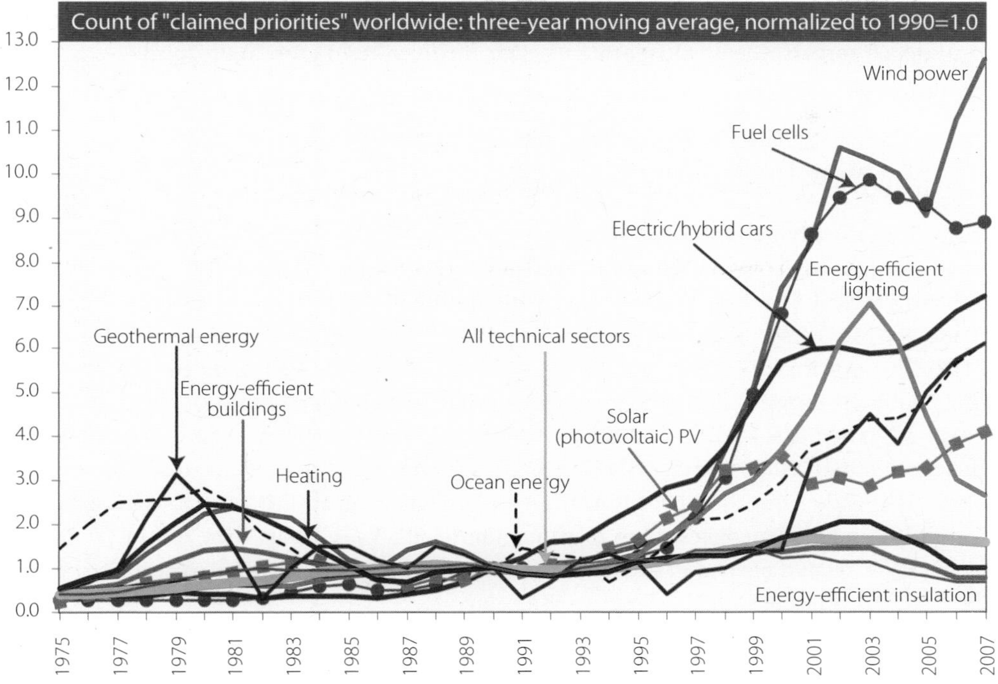

Source: OECD, Working Party on Global and Structural Policies (2010), figure 3. Available at http://www.oecd.org/environment/innovation.

Note: "Claimed priorities" are patent filings in which an applicant reserves the right to file the application in other jurisdictions and thus signify the potential for international application.

Inadequate investment rates due to volatile global markets and fiscal constraints

In developing countries, enhanced domestic resource mobilization (private savings and public revenues) is key for the required additional investment effort for sustainable development over the medium term. However, many developing countries have poorly developed markets for long-term financing and a weak fiscal basis, which limits the scope for substantial increases in domestic funding for long-term investment in the near term. An additional, and inadvertent, constraint on domestic investment in developing countries arises from deficiencies in the global financial and payments system. A number of developing countries hold a significant portion of domestic savings as international reserves, which have been largely invested in financial assets in developed countries to the tune of more than $500 billion per year[3] (United Nations, 2011), which compares unfavourably with a required developing-country green investment of about $1.1 trillion per year, as indicated below. Volatile global capital and commodity markets are an important reason behind this costly form of self-protection and the substantial net transfer of financial resources to advanced market economies.

The combination of volatile global financial flows and open capital accounts unduly restricts domestic fiscal policy

For many developing countries, the combination of volatile global financial flows and open capital accounts unduly restrict domestic fiscal policy to a profile characterized by a deflationary bias, small deficits and volatile public investment spending in response to external shocks. Particularly for countries with still weak export capacities, such as commodity exporters, and limited access to international borrowing, fiscal policy

3 Between 2000 and 2010, the aggregate investment in developed countries' assets was $5.5 trillion by developing countries and $0.8 trillion by economies in transition (United Nations, 2011).

has a limited ability to smooth consumption and sustain public investment rates so as to crowd in private risk-taking. Public authorities have been forced to postpone or terminate infrastructure and other long-term investment projects during downturns because of strict fiscal deficit targets, thereby jeopardizing their medium-term growth prospects.

Inadequate financing for technological development and transfer

Financial obstacles hinder technological development at every stage

Inadequate financing has been consistently identified by developing countries as the greatest obstacle to their rapid adoption of clean technologies (figure VI.2). At every stage of technological development, there are public sector and private sector obstacles put in the way of their finding the needed financing (this is succinctly summarized in table VI.2). These obstacles can be economic—financing for green technologies competes with other public priorities and inadequate internal rates of return restrain private risk-taking (chap. V). They can also be political, such as hesitation on the part of Governments to intervene in markets in the face of resistance from vested interests or consumer preferences (chap. II). There may also be constraints on domestic capabilities, such as those stemming from insufficient investment in education (chap. V). Finally, there are international cooperation-related obstacles, such as those associated with conflicts between export credit agency conditions and local financial requirements.

Figure VI.2
Economic and market barriers to technology transfers, as reported in technology needs assessments

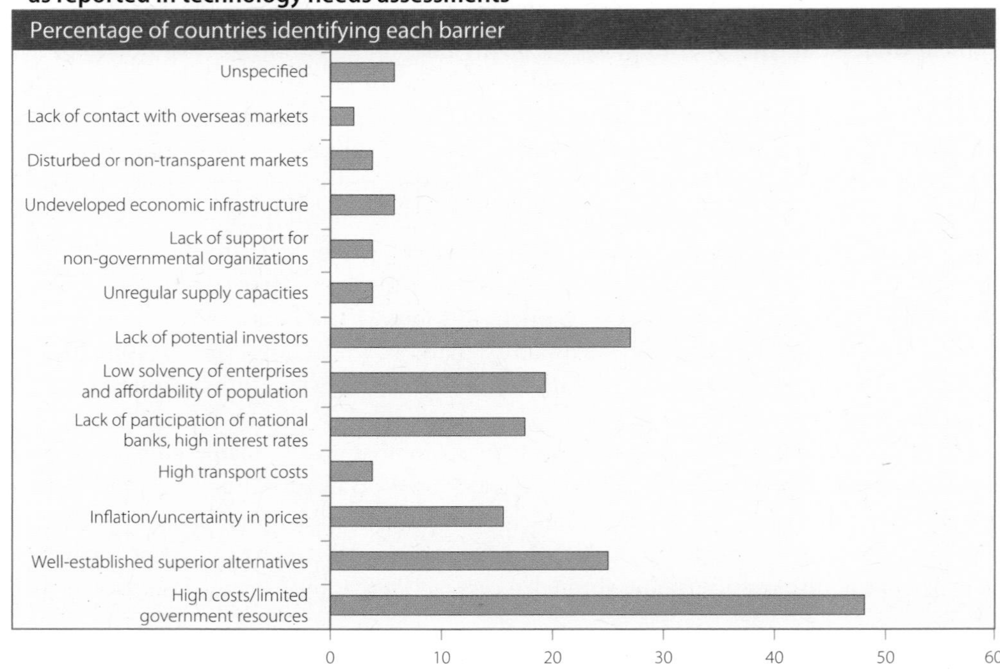

Source: United Nations Framework Convention on Climate Change, Subsidiary Body for Scientific and Technological Advice, (2009), figure 6.

Table VI.2
Specific financing barriers related to different stages of technological maturity

Stage of technological maturity	*Categories of gaps and barriers*	*Financing barriers*	
		Public finance	*Private finance*
Research and development	Proof of concept	• Other political priorities for public finance • Uncertain outcomes of fundamental research • Uncertain results of education and training	• Insufficient rate of return • Spillover effects preventing financiers from capturing benefits of investment
Research and development	Technical	• Other political priorities for public finance	• Lack of good technical information, resulting in high-risk profiles • Spillover effects preventing financiers from capturing benefits of investment
Research and development, demonstration	Scale	• Relatively high costs of scaling up from prototype scale	• Lack of technological record, resulting in high-risk profiles
Research and development, demonstration, deployment	Costs	• High costs involved in reaching significant deployment	• Lack of policy for overcoming costs, leading to low internal rate of return
Research and development, demonstration, deployment, diffusion	Economic	• Unwillingness to interfere in the market, especially when drastic changes harm vested interests • Inflexibility of tax policy	• Energy pricing and subsidies; lack of or insufficient carbon price • High upfront capital costs • Lack of valuation of co-benefits, leading to low internal rate of return • Requirement of large parallel infrastructure, leading to high upfront costs
Research and development, demonstration, deployment, diffusion	Social	• Vested interests in social/ consumer preferences • Underinvestment in education and training	• Lack of consumer or user market • Split incentives (principal-agent problem) • Lack of labour skills
Research and development, demonstration, deployment, diffusion	Institutional	• Vested interests in institutional settings • Public finance policy failures	• Lack of regulatory framework • Absence of international standards • Technology lock-in • Lack of match between export credit agency conditions and local finance conditions for environmentally sound technologies

Source: United Nations Framework Convention on Climate Change, Subsidiary Body for Scientific and Technological Advice, and Subsidiary Body for Implementation (2008), table 11.

Investment requirements for sustainable development

There is a proliferation of estimates of required investment levels needed to achieve sustainable development. In chapter II, investment needs for the energy transformation were estimated at $1.6 trillion per year during 2010-2050. Chapter III presented the objective of achieving food security for an increasing world population. In this regard, Nelson and others (2009) suggest that investment requirements for achieving the objective of maintaining calorie intake to counteract the potential decline in yields due to climate change is about $7 billion per year from the year 2000. Published estimates of developing-country financing requirements for adaptation vary from $50 billion to $100 billion per year (O'Connor, 2009). For developed countries, published estimates range from between $15 billion and $150 billion per year (Stern, 2007).

The variety of assumptions and methodologies explains the wide range in required sustainable development investment estimates

The variety of assumptions and methodologies used in different studies explains the wide range of published estimates of sustainable development investment requirements. Some differences stem from different target objectives (for example, 550 versus 450 ppmv CO_2 atmospheric concentration). There are also divergences in coverage of investment included (for example, whether or not to include the construction of additional transportation infrastructure in the estimates of costs of installing wind farms in remote areas or costs for the diffusion of improved, sustainable agricultural technology). More often than not, there is a tendency to underestimate investment requirements in infrastructure and shelter in developing countries and the costs from climate change of increased mortality and disease burden (O'Connor, 2009). The estimate of Nelson and others (2009) of the investment costs of ensuring food security, cited in the previous paragraph, does include additional infrastructure cost (roads and irrigation systems), based on region-specific cost estimates.

It is important to distinguish between baseline investment and incremental investment needs

There is also the important distinction between total investment, which includes both a baseline projection of investment costs for (traditional and green) energy production under business-as-usual assumptions and the incremental costs of an acceleration of the energy transition, and an investment estimate solely reflecting additional ("incremental") investment under what would have been a baseline scenario. The $1.6 billion per year investment requirement for energy transformation, set out in chapter II and, based on a specific scenario in the Global Energy Assessment (GEA) of 2009, includes both the investment needs under a business-as-usual scenario investment and the additional investment requirements for scaling up renewable energy technology and enhancing energy efficiency. The International Energy Agency (IEA) (2009) reports only a required incremental investment in 2020 of $427 billion globally (on top of investments required to match projected population and income growth), with almost $200 billion in non-Organization for Economic Cooperation and Development (OECD) countries, to achieve stabilization at 450 ppmv CO_2-equivalent by 2050 (the global investment cost is projected to rise to $1.2 trillion in 2030, or 1.1 per cent of world gross product (WGP). This estimate would be in line with the total investment (incremental plus base) requirement of the specific GEA scenario of $1.6 billion per year, the latter figure being about 2.5 per cent of WGP.

Finally, the fact that assumptions of the base scenario regarding other variables, such as population and economic growth (which also have interactions with each other and with investment itself), will affect the estimates, explains why every reported estimate is specific to a chosen scenario.

The United Nations Environment Programme (2011) makes another set of scenario choices and proposes an investment requirement estimate of about 2 per cent of WGP from 2010 to 2050 (in level terms, this would amount to $1.3 trillion in 2010). This represents an estimate of incremental investment requirements relative to the baseline scenario as defined by UNEP.

Timely progress in achieving mitigation will significantly reduce adaptation costs

All estimates are subject to a host of caveats and uncertainties. They rest on debatable assumptions about cost and technology learning curves, about the degree of interaction between technological change across sectors and about the extent to which the continuum between climate change mitigation, adaptation and disaster risk prevention are taken into account. For example, accelerated progress in achieving mitigation will likely significantly reduce adaptation costs.

Table VI.3 presents an estimate of required investment levels across the various sectors covered by this *Survey,* with an attempt to offer some consistency in scenarios across sectors. It makes the strong assumption that mitigation efforts will be undertaken in a timely manner. It incorporates estimates for meeting universal access to modern energy and adequate access to food by 2030. The values in table VI.3 are broadly in line with the UNEP 2011 estimates, but suggest the investment needs to induce the green energy transformation would be higher. It is important to note, however, that the figures are not strictly comparable, as the underlying model-based scenarios tend to differ across the studies.

Given these caveats, by the estimates reported in table VI.3, it would seem reasonable to put the overall incremental investment requirements for achieving sustainable development objectives at about 3 per cent of WGP.

The overall incremental investment requirements for achieving sustainable development objectives would be about 3 per cent of world gross product

Among the items in table VI.3, the estimate for agricultural investment is solely for developing countries alone and it is assumed (based on available studies) that roughly 80 per cent of the adaptation investments would need to be undertaken in developing countries. Incremental investment requirements for climate change adaptation and sustainable agriculture are only 6-7 per cent of the green investment total, based on the "central" estimates reported in table VI.3. In other words, most of the additional resources would be needed for investing in the green energy transformation. About two thirds of energy and energy end-use investments would need to take place in developing countries, and most of these would be in development of new energy systems, in contrast with developed countries, where they would be for replacing and transforming existing capital invested in energy systems.

Financial transfers for developing countries

About $1.1 trillion will be needed per year for incremental investments in green technology in developing countries

Hence, much of the incremental investment in green technology will need to take place in developing countries. Even as the majority of the basic research and development is expected to occur in developed countries, developing countries will have a potentially bigger role in demonstration, deployment and diffusion, including the cost of building related infrastructure. In developing countries, the new technologies can be installed not just to replace existing "brown" activity but also to increase the scale of economic activity.

For climate change mitigation, the largest potential for increasing the supply of clean primary energy supply is in developing countries (chap. II; United Nations, 2009). Hence, the bulk of the incremental investment for the energy transformation would need to take place in developing countries, even though on a per-project basis costs are higher in developed countries. At least one half of the related estimated incremental investments for climate change mitigation and, as per the assumptions underlying the estimates in table VI.3, all incremental investments in sustainable agriculture for food security would need to take place in developing countries. Applying a rough proportion of 60 per cent[4] of incremental investment for developing countries suggests at least $1.1 trillion incremental investment per year in developing countries.

4 A proportion of 60 per cent in favour of developing countries is in line with current proportions in the energy sector. Table VI.3 suggests that adaptation (based on the assumption that mitigation will be undertaken in a timely manner) and agriculture's incremental investment requirements represent no more than 6-7 per cent of the total, even though 100 per cent of these sectors' reported estimates are required for developing countries. Sixty per cent can be seen as a lower bound for the proportion of global investment needed for developing countries.

Table VI.3
Estimates of required investment levels for sustainable development

Sectors/themes	*Time frame*	*Range of estimates*	*Energy supply*	*Energy end-use (appliances, etc.)*	*Adaptation*	*Agriculture and food*	*Row total*
Assumed goals			Stabilize greenhouse gas concentrations to limit warming to <2° C (with at least 50 per cent probability)	Significant end-use efficiency increase and greenhouse gas stabilization to < 2° C	Minimum investments in securing livelihoods, assuming successful mitigation	Increasing agricultural yields to ensure global food security without further expanding agricultural land	
Incremental investment requirements	**Annual, 2000-2050, in billions of 2010 US dollars**	**Range**	400-1600	–	50-160	15-30	
		Central estimate	**1,000**	**800**	**105**	**22**	**1,927**
		Estimates from other sources	340-1360 (IPCC, 2007b) 465 (Riahi and others, forthcoming)	125-1,400 (UN/DESA estimates based on Wilson and Grübler, 2010)		67 (FAO, Global Perspectives Studies Unit, 2006) 14 (Fan and Rosegrant, 2008)	
Comments			Energy supply only. Investment needs in end-use appliances are several times this amount	Energy end-use appliances (not just energy components)	These numbers assume stabilization of greenhouse gas concentrations below 450 ppmv. Without mitigation, adaptation needs might be 10-100 times as large	Data refer to **developing countries only**. Includes investment in primary agriculture and related downstream services, but excludes public investment in rural roads and education	
Investment needs for a business-as-usual (BAU) scenario	**Annual, 2000-2050, in billions of US dollars**	**Central estimate**	**1,400**	**1,000**	**–**	**200**	**2,600**
		Estimates from other sources	1,200 (Rao, 2009; van Vuuren and others, unpublished) 870 (International Energy Agency, 2008b)	380-4200 (UN/DESA estimates based on Wilson and Grübler, 2010)		142 (FAO, Global Perspectives Studies Unit, 2006)	
Total investment needs to achieve objectives	**Annual, 2000-2050, in billions of US dollars**	**Range**	1600-2600	–	50-160	200-240	
		Central estimate	**2,400**	**1,800**	**90**	**220**	**4,510**
		Estimates from other sources	820-2260 (Riahi and others, forthcoming)	500-5600 (UN/DESA estimates based on Wilson and Grübler, 2010)	49-171 of which 27-66 for developing countries (United Nations Framework Convention on Climate Change, 2007); 86-109 (United Nations Development Programme, 2007) 9-41 (World Bank, 2007a).	209 (FAO, Global Perspectives Studies Unit, 2006)	

Table VI.3 (cont'd)

Sectors/themes	*Time frame*	*Range of estimates*	*Energy supply*	*Energy end-use (appliances, etc.)*	*Adaptation*	*Agriculture and food*	*Row total*
Additional investment needs (additional to BAU)	**Cumulative 2000-2050, in trillions of US dollars**	**Range**	20-70	6-70	2-7	0.6-1.2	
		Central estimate	**46**	**40**	**4.5**	**1.2**	**92**
		Estimates from other sources	17-68 (IPCC, 2007b) 25-80 (van Vuuren and others, 2007)	**6-70** (UN/DESA estimates based on Wilson and Grübler, 2010)		3.4 (FAO, Global Perspectives Studies Unit, 2006)	
			-10 to 48 (Stern, 2007) (less reduction) 45-90 (IEA, 2008b) 15 (Rao, 2009)				
Investment needs for BAU	**Cumulative, 2000-2050, in trillions of US dollars**	**Central estimate**	**60**	**95**	**–**	**~10** [1.3 (for food only) 9.0 (all agriculture in developing countries)]	**165**
		Estimates from other sources	26 (International Energy Agency, 2008b) (only until 2030) 60 (Rao, 2009; van Vuuren and others, unpublished)	19-210 (UN/DESA estimates based on Wilson and Grübler, 2010)		7.1 (FAO, Global Perspectives Studies Unit, 2006)	
Total investment needs to achieve objectives	**Cumulative, 2000-2050, in trillions of US dollars**	**Range**	80-130	–	2-7	10-12	
		Central estimate	**106**	**135**	**4.5**	**11.2**	**257**
		Estimates from other sources	36-93 (Riahi and others, forthcoming)	**25-280** (UN/DESA estimates based on Wilson and Grübler, 2010)	2.5-8.6 (United Nations Framework Convention on Climate Change, 2007)	10.5 (FAO, Global Perspectives Studies Unit, 2006)	

Source: UN/DESA.

Note: The yellow-shaded areas denote annual estimates in 2010 United States dollars; the blue-shaded areas denote cumulative estimates for 2000-2050.

Since the Rio conference in 1992, there have been many efforts to enhance resource availability for investments in sustainable development

Since the Earth Summit, there have been many efforts to secure the finance needed for sustainable development. Recently, at the United Nations Climate Change Conference held in Copenhagen in December 2009, developed countries pledged to provide $30 billion during 2010-2012 and $100 billion per year by 2020 towards the cost of fighting climate change in poorer countries. There is also a proposal, set out in a recent International Monetary Fund (IMF) Staff Position Note, exploring the use of special drawing rights (SDRs) to start a "Green Fund" with new financing flows of about $17 billion a year during the "start-up phase" (2011-2013), increasing quickly to $100 billion by 2020 (Bredenkamp and Pattillo, 2010). In November 2010, the Secretary-General's Advisory Group on Energy and Climate Change (United Nations, 2010c) reported that the $100 billion transfer target is achievable through a combination of public and private financing mechanisms.

Aid to the environment has not kept pace with the average increase in aid programmes

Official development assistance (ODA) from Organization for Economic Cooperation and Development/Development Assistance Committee countries, as aid for the environment, increased steadily, by 5 per cent per annum, from 1998 to 2007 to reach almost $18 billion in 2009 (figure VI.3). Nevertheless, aid to the environment has not kept pace with the 8 per cent average increase in aid programmes, losing share to aid for health and population and government services. Nonetheless, the absolute level ($18 billion) could be considered as being in the range of the Copenhagen pledges of $30 billion for climate financing to developing countries during 2010-2012. If the flows committed to in Copenhagen are indeed realized as "additional" to, and not a recategorization of, existing commitments, these would seem like a doubling of transfers, but, because sustainable investment requires investments in many other sectors such as energy, fall considerably short based on total estimated needs. Moreover, the Secretary-General's high level advisory panel did not interpret the corresponding $100 billion pledge for 2020 as financed only from ODA but from a mix of many sources, including private investment.

Figure VI.3
Aid commitments from OECD/DAC countries for core environment and water supply and sanitation, 1998-2009

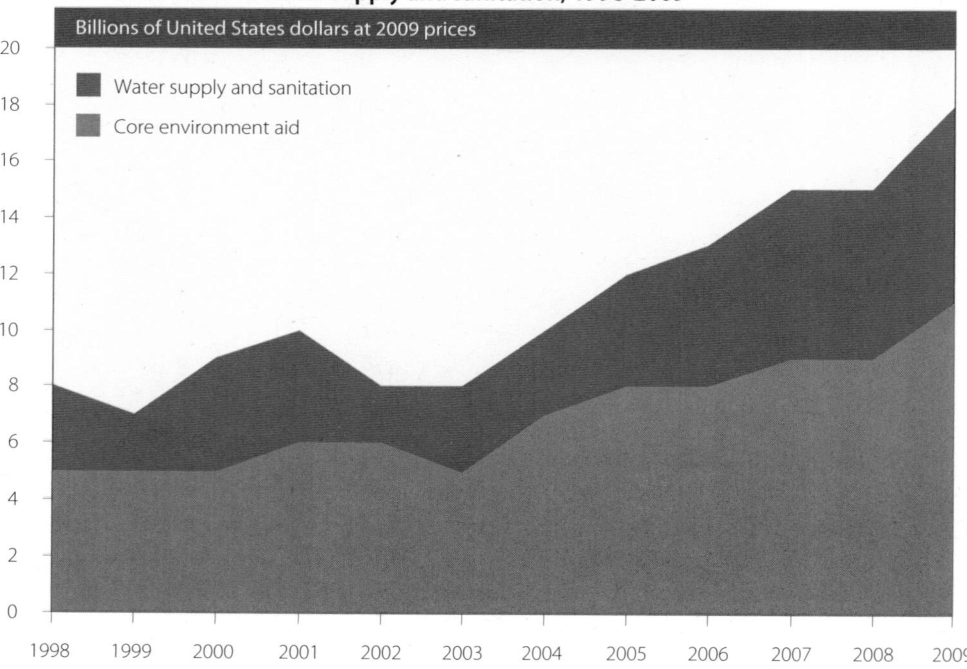

Source: OECD-DAC Creditor Reporting System.
Note: For the definition of "water supply and sanitation" and "core environment aid", see Castro and Hammond (2009).

At the multilateral level, there exists a diversity of specific funding streams. They are presented in table VI.4, showing a wide range of pledged funding for developing countries channelled through a plethora of financing mechanisms. A total of $18 billion has been pledged, $2 billion deposited and $734 million disbursed (O'Connor, 2009).

Table VI.4
Bilateral and multilateral funds for mitigation (M) of and adaptation (A) to climate change

Fund	*Total amount (millions of dollars)*	*Period*
Funding under the United Nations Framework Convention on Climate Change		
Strategic Priority on Adaptation	50 (A)	GEF3-GEF4
Least Developed Country Fund	172 (A)	As of October 2008
Special Climate Change Fund	91 (A)	As of October 2008
Adaptation Fund	300-600 (A)	2008-2012
Bilateral initiatives		
Cool Earth Partnership (Japan)	10,000 (A+M)	2008-2012
ETF-IW (United Kingdom)	1,182 (A+M)	2008-2012
Climate and Forest Initiative (Norway)	2,250	
UNDP-Spain MDG Achievement Fund	22 (A) / 92 (M)	2007-2010
GCCA (European Commission)	84 (A) / 76 (M)	2008-2010
International Climate Initiative (Germany)	200 (A) / 564 (M)	2008-2012
IFCI (Australia)	160 (M)	2007-2012
Multilateral initiatives		
GFDRR	15 (A) (of $83 million in pledges)	2007-2008
UN-REDD	35 (M)	
Carbon Partnership Facility (World Bank)	500 (M) (140 committed)	
Forest Carbon Partnership Facility (World Bank)	385 (M) (160 committed)	2008-2020
Climate Investment Funds, including:	6,200 (A+M)	2009-2012
Clean Technology Fund	4,800 (M)	
Strategic Climate Fund, including	1,400 (A+M)	
Forest Investment Programme	350 (M)	
Scaling up renewable energy	200 (M)	
Pilot Program for Climate Resilience	600 (A)	

Source: World Bank (2010a), table 6.4.

Abbreviations: ETF-IW, Environmental Transformation Fund-International Window; GCCA, Global Climate Change Alliance; IFCI, International Forest Carbon Initiative; UN-REDD, United Nations Collaborative Programme on Reduced Emissions from Deforestation and Forest Degradation; GFDRR, Global Facility for Disaster Reduction and Recovery; GEF, Global Environment Facility.

Restricted domestic policy space from international trade and investment regimes

A restricted domestic policy space in developing countries could be a barrier to rapid introduction of green technology

Over the medium term, the restricted domestic policy space of developing countries in the area of industrial development, stemming from multilateral and bilateral trade commitments and bilateral investment agreements, could be a barrier to rapid introduction of green technology in those countries. Technologies in general and green technologies in particular are mostly imported from abroad. During the period when new domestic capabilities in new industries and products are being built, local producers would need to enjoy a period of protection from foreign competition. It is also critical that the relationship with foreign companies provide benefits to the local economy in terms of technology transfer. To build green sectors, which bear many of the characteristics of infant industries (chap. V), domestic authorities require policy space for industrial policies.

The multilateral trading system provides restricted space for industrial policies

The multilateral trading system, as currently constituted, provides restricted space for such policies. Bilateral trade treaties normally contain even more restrictive provisions. Because industrial policies tend to promote capabilities of residents and domestic corporations and thus discriminate against foreign nationals, only a limited number of activities, such as basic research and regional development, are permitted under World Trade Organization rules. Two recent complaints from the United States, regarding Canada's feed-in-tariff scheme and China's subsidies for clean energy technologies, could eventually be brought to the World Trade Organization's dispute resolution mechanism. A potential result of these actions is a haphazard set of specific industrial policies that would be allowed and of specific ones that would be prohibited. Trends in the Doha trade negotiations suggest that the industrial policy space now afforded to developing countries through higher bound tariffs for manufactured goods could be headed for further reduction.

Incoherence and weaknesses in international governance

The global governance system does not maintain effective mechanisms for coordination among specialized areas of governance

Many developing-country Governments face challenges in restoring their capacity to develop strong technology policies, as discussed in chapter V. Creating public capacities in managing and promoting technological development is doubly challenging in the international arena, where there are no systems of coordination and governance comparable with those existing in national contexts. In the context of both practice and policy, establishing the requisite public sector role in the area of economic and development cooperation at the international level presents a distinct challenge. The recent global financial crises in food, energy and finance exposed serious shortcomings in institutions and rules which were created, for the most part, more than 60 years ago (United Nations, 2010c). The global governance system does not maintain effective mechanisms for coordination among specialized areas of governance and does not prevent the adoption of conflicting decisions. Moreover, a set of important public international institutions—with authority over, for example, the coordination of financial regulation, debt resolution and the movement of natural persons—are missing.

The objective of sustainable development is cross-cutting with respect to international efforts in development, environmental policy and technical cooperation

The objective of sustainable development is a cross-cutting issue with respect to international efforts in development, environmental policy and technical cooperation. There are some evolving international mechanisms designed to address the challenges that arise in areas of intersection, notably within the United Nations Framework Convention on Climate Change. For example, Convention outcomes have consistently emphasized the critical importance of technology diffusion under public sector leadership. This will require amending the global trade and financial regime which relies almost exclusively on private channels for the international diffusion of technology. Efforts in this regard will be tested as individual States and private companies seek to survive or gain dominance in green technology through actions in the arenas of aid, trade and finance.

Reforming multilateral trading rules and international finance to accelerate green technology development and diffusion

Achieving the global technological revolution and overcoming the deficiencies of existing mechanisms require sustained scaling up and reform in international cooperation and finance. First, an international regime for technology sharing will have to be established to facilitate sustainable development in developing countries and will have to include utilization of a broader set of tools in the domain of intellectual property and multilateral trade policies. Second, securing adequate development finance and policy space for energizing developing-country efforts to upgrade production technologies towards environmental sustainability is indispensable. Third, international governance and cooperation have to be upgraded.

Establishing an effective global technology development and diffusion regime

Expanding action in nurturing and upgrading green production and consumption technologies in developing countries must be a key goal of international cooperation. As discussed, publicly guided *international* mechanisms of technological diffusion have limited precedents. Historically the bulk of technological knowledge has been embodied and transferred as private property through the operations of private companies.

The Montreal Protocol created a financing pool governed jointly by both contributing and beneficiary countries to pay for the costs of transition to new technology

Elements from the successful experience of the CGIAR in promoting the rapid worldwide diffusion of new agricultural technologies through a publicly supported global and regional network of research institutions can be part of the design of the global regime. The 1987 Montreal Protocol on Substances that Deplete the Ozone Layer[5] is an example of a successful global framework within which sovereign States can move towards implementing a swift and radical shift away from polluting technologies worldwide, with special support to developing countries in adopting new technologies. The support included the creation of a financing pool funded by developed countries but governed jointly by both contributing and beneficiary countries to pay for the costs of transition to new technology.

In the climate change area, building international public policymaking capability can draw upon already existing international scientific networks and the multi-stakeholder example provided by the work of the Intergovernmental Panel on Climate Change. The international community took the first step in regard to this challenge in reaching agreement at the sixteenth session of the Conference of the Parties to the United Nations Framework Convention on Climate Change held in Cancun, Mexico, in November/December 2010, on setting up a Technology Executive Committee (TEC) as a policymaking body to implement a framework for meaningful and effective actions designed to enhance the implementation of commitments on technology transfer. At the same session, agreement was reached on establishing an operational body to facilitate networking among national, regional, sectoral and international technology bodies, to be called the Climate Technology Centre and Network (CTCN).

5 United Nations, *Treaty Series*, vol. 1522, No. 26369.

Orienting the intellectual property rights regime towards stimulating innovation of green technologies

Granting intellectual property rights should always remain a public policy action with the intention to stimulate—not restrict—private initiative

Managing global intellectual property rights is also crucial and a logical overriding principle. Granting intellectual property rights should be a public policy action and should always remain so, consistent with the policy's intention to stimulate—not restrict—private initiative in technological development. The starting point of public policy would be treating "compliance with climate change policies as a public good" (Maskus and Okediji, 2010, p. viii). At the present time, the granting of a patent is the most widespread and lucrative technological development incentive. What is required at the national level is a public policy that ensures a higher standard and more transparent and rigorous processes for recognizing international intellectual property. Developing countries particularly should raise the standard for patent registration in their jurisdictions. Studies indicate that, particularly at lower levels of development, there is no evidence that greater protection of intellectual property rights has promoted domestic technological development or diffusion (Odagiri and others, 2010; Dosi, Marengo and Pasquali, 2007).

The intellectual property regime should not prevent non-owners of the technology from undertaking experiments and test applications that could improve such technology

Obtaining agreement among countries on public policies needed to accelerate invention and diffusion is critical. Currently, protecting private intellectual property rights by enforcing exclusive use and deployment by its owner is the main approach. Internationally, a wider mix of public sector strategies will be required to spur green technological development. There is a need to guarantee a sufficient commercial incentive to private parties to undertake research using subsidies and public purchases of technology at reasonable cost, while constraining monopolistic practices which restrict both diffusion and further development. This means that the intellectual property regime should not prevent non-owners of the technology from undertaking experiments and test applications that could improve the technology or that could help build new domestic capabilities. One discordance under the otherwise successful Montreal Protocol to reduce harmful substances was the fact that chemical manufacturers in India were unsuccessful in buying the technology for producing approved coolant chemicals at reasonable cost from the small group of manufacturers in developed countries that owned it.

Limitations on compulsory licensing do not fit well with the public purpose of climate change compliance

Maskus and Okediji (2010) make the case for reforming the international intellectual property system on behalf of "environmentally sound technologies" (ESTs). Drawing on experiences in industrialized countries, they state that compulsory licences "are a valid tool to facilitate access to technology under well-defined conditions" (p. viii). Some of these conditions are set out in the limitations and exceptions provisions of the TRIPS Agreement, which need to be incorporated in domestic regulations of technology recipients. Limitations on compulsory licensing do not fit well with the public purpose of achieving climate change compliance. For example, under article 31 (f) of the Agreement, World Trade Organization members cannot use compulsory licences to produce for export markets. If these licences are mainly applied to enable countries to comply with emissions targets, production for export purposes is not of commercial interest to technology recipients. On the other hand, Maskus and Okediji (2010, p. 34) point out that "ironically, given that climate change is a global public good, it would actually be beneficial to have production for export purposes, as ultimately this would increase the number of ESTs in circulation".

A range of policy tools could be considered by the international community:

1. *Placing basic technology or technology with multiple uses in the public domain*

The international community or self-selected groups of countries (including groupings among developing countries) could convene expert committees to determine which technologies meet the criteria of basic technology. To place them in the public domain, countries could either exercise the power of eminent domain in respect of those technologies (through a concerted application of individual-country compulsory licensing rights[6] under the TRIPS, for example) or purchase them at a reasonable rate of compensation. Jurisprudence in the many industrialized countries, including the United States of America, is an abundant source of precedents and grounds for the application of compulsory licensing, not to mention federal powers reserved for converting private property to public use on grounds of eminent domain or under anti-trust laws (ibid., p. 31). Box VI.2 summarizes some existing precedents in the United States legal system.

2. *Awarding cash prizes for technical solutions to defined problems*

The international community or self-selected groups of countries could form expert committees that would define problems requiring technological solutions and award prizes for solutions. Countries in the consortia would contribute to the pool for the awards.

Box VI.2

Compulsory patent licensing in the United States of America

In the United States of America, compulsory patent licensing provisions have been addressed in specific legislation. Some relevant examples include:

- ***The Atomic Energy Act,***[a] which allows for such licensing when the patented innovation is "(u)seful in the production or utilization of special nuclear material or atomic energy". The Atomic Energy Commission can determine whether a compulsory patent licence should be granted and the reasonable royalty owed by the licensee.
- ***The Bayh-Dole Act,***[b] which permits compulsory patent licensing when a recipient of federal grants and contracts "has not taken, or is not expected to take within a reasonable time, effective steps to achieve practical application of the subject invention". The federal Government can also exercise its "march-in rights" by showing that a compulsory patent licence is necessary "to alleviate health or safety needs" or "to meet requirements for public use specified by Federal regulations".
- ***The Clean Air Act***[c] also provides for compulsory patent licences when the patented innovation is necessary to comply with the emission requirements, where no reasonable alternative is available, and where non-use of the patented innovation would lead to a "lessening of competition or a tendency to create a monopoly". A district court can, with the assistance of the Attorney General, determine whether a compulsory patent licence should be granted and can set the reasonable terms.

There are many cases where developed-country Governments have granted or threatened to grant compulsory licences to overcome the patent barrier for various purposes. Courts in many of these countries have also utilized compulsory licencing through opting for payment of royalties by the infringing party to the patent-holder in lieu of granting an injunction to the patent-holder. Developing countries are also increasingly making use of the provision of compulsory licences, although largely for purposes of either importing or producing affordable generic medicines.

a 42 United States Code Section 2183; see also http://www4.law.cornell.edu/uscode/42/2183.html and http://www.cptech.org/ip/health/cl/us-misc.html.

b 42 United States Code Section 7608; see also http://www4.law.cornell.edu/uscode/42/7608.html.

c 35 United States Code Section 203; see also http://www4.law.cornell.edu/uscode/35/203.html.

Source: Shashikant (2009), p. 43.

6 Compulsory licences are allowed only for the purpose of serving the domestic markets. Patent-holders are still protected in export markets.

3. *Listing technologies in pools and permitting qualified parties (such as developing countries or firms in developing countries) to use the technology without compensation until its use has borne commercial fruit*

Private and public property owners would be invited to contribute their technology to the pool. Users of the technology would begin paying reasonable royalties (at previously agreed rates) when they had achieved commercial returns from its use.

The international community could come to a decision on which brown technologies would be banned from a certain date

Establishing funding pools to facilitate technology transfer is a critical element in ensuring that individual technology development initiatives add up to global objectives. These kinds of pools do not exist at present. These can be applied to purchase technology or to fund research and award prizes. The international community could come to a decision on which brown technologies would be banned from a certain date; countries requiring the alternative technology could draw on these funds to fulfil their obligations. With these funds, it should be possible to establish international innovation networks in different areas of technology. The private sector must continue to play a vital role in technological development, particularly in adapting and developing basic inventions for actual application.

The new international regime should allow special and differential access to new technology by level of development. For example, developing-country Governments and firms could be allowed to adapt technology but would pay royalties only when its use begins to yield commercial returns. Where exclusive private sector rights of use to vital technology are a hindrance to developing other needed technology or to widespread use, the technology regime must have a mechanism for imposing a "compulsory licence" which places the technology in the public domain, as is done in areas of public health.

Multilateral trading rules should grant developing countries greater flexibility in conducting industrial policies

It is important to guarantee sufficient policy space in developing countries for their own industrial development

Present project-oriented loan conditionality and the proliferation of international financing mechanisms thwart developing countries' efforts to design and implement coherent strategies for sustainable development. From the multilateral trade regime and bilateral treaties which include restrictions on "investment measures"—such as prohibitions on imposing technology transfer or domestic content requirements—shackle attempts at implementing industrial policy at a time when developed-country industrial interventions for building green technologies are proliferating. Thus, it is important that developing countries be guaranteed sufficient policy space for their own industrial development.

Historically, rich countries' agricultural subsidies under the multilateral trade regime have been a source of vexation. The requirements of accelerated technological diffusion to promote sustainable agriculture (chap. III) and national adaptation to climate change (chap. IV) suggest that faster progress in eliminating the harmful effects of these subsidies on developing countries has to be part of a global environmental regime.

Consistent with the aim of promoting green technological development and transformation, the multilateral trade regime must begin to recognize the role of industrial policy in creating "green space".

The multilateral trade regime would not be a hindrance to industrial policies affecting non-tradable sectors (such as infrastructure construction), including industrial policy for green objectives, as long as those policies were not affected by a country's bilateral trade or investment agreements. Environmental regulations and interventions affecting public education, strengthening integrated planning, improved transparency, accountability and law enforcement, reform of environmental laws, building codes and transportation standards, and upgraded measurement and indicators for monitoring (Cosbey, 2011a) would not run afoul of World Trade Organization disciplines.

For tradable sectors, a greater range and higher levels of bound tariffs are often key tools: fiscally constrained developing countries can utilize them to develop specific industries. Further, as regards the tradable sectors, the possible implications of recognizing the need for green policy space will require a revisiting of the restrictions contained in the World Trade Organization Agreement on Trade-related Investment Measures (TRIMs) (World Trade Organization, 1994) and the Agreement on Subsidies and Countervailing Measures (ibid.).

Recognizing green policy space might require revisiting restrictions contained in the TRIMS Agreement

Establishing a multilateral regime that recognizes the role of national industrial policy and coordinates transfers of financial and technical resources towards developing countries is a challenge that can be addressed explicitly by international agreement or resolved de facto through trade disputes and rulings of the World Trade Organization dispute settlement mechanism (ibid., p. 56). The disadvantage of the latter approach is that it will create a possibly extended period of uncertainty with regard to public policy and private investment (Cosbey, 2011b). It would be preferable for the revisiting of these agreements to be undertaken under the auspices of the World Trade Organization, even as the non-completion of the Doha negotiations represents an impediment to opening negotiations on new issues.

Policies that promote domestic green industries at the expense of foreign competitors and can be subject to dispute could take the following forms (ibid., p. 54):

- Research, development and deployment support to domestic green sectors
- Conditional support for green sectors, designed to foster green infant industries
- Regulations, standards and prohibitions based on production and processing methods (PPM)

Policies that promote domestic green industries at the expense of foreign competitors can be subject to trade disputes

The first policy type, which encompasses the early stages of innovation, while relatively uncontroversial, does put developing countries with more limited fiscal resources at a disadvantage. In the case of policy type two, World Trade Organization agreements restrict subsidies to domestic industries conditional on export performance or domestic content.

The principle providing the logical basis for PPM policies (type three) affirms that the way in which a product is made determines its environmental impact. The question is whether countries can protect their domestic industries by imposing border adjustment tariffs based on the way in which potential imports are produced. PPM-based policies are constrained by General Agreement on Tariffs and Trade (GATT)-related rules and the World Trade Organization Agreement on Technical Barriers to Trade (World Trade Organization, 1994). GATT-World Trade Organization rules provide exceptions to these constraints in two environmentally related areas. Clause (b) of GATT article XX provides exceptions for measures "necessary to protect human, animal or plant life or health" and clause (g) excepts measures "relating to the conservation of exhaustible natural resources if such measures are made effective in conjunction with restrictions on domestic production or consumption". Khor (2010, p. 8) argues that these exceptions apply only within the context of the preamble of the article which prohibits measures "applied in a manner which would constitute a means of arbitrary or unjustifiable discrimination between countries where the same conditions prevail, or a disguised restriction on international trade".

Environmental standards have been effective industrial policy instruments for accelerating technological transformations. At present, technical standards are often determined by Governments (unilaterally or through agreements among a reduced number of countries) or set by private companies. Wider participation of all parties in the setting

Wider participation of all parties in the setting of international standards, especially developing countries, can help eliminate unfair trade practices

of these standards, especially developing countries, should guarantee that environmental standards (including through green labels and ecological footprint certificates) do not become a means of promoting unfair trade protectionism. The Montreal Protocol process, which identified the substances that would be banned and the pace of their elimination, may again serve as an example: the Montreal Protocol provided financial support for adjustment to the agreed standards. A similar, but much more ambitious mechanism to compensate countries economically disadvantaged by the standard-setting of other countries could be devised as part of global financing mechanisms for sustainable development. In addition, a global technology policy mechanism, such as the Technology Executive Committee established in Cancun in November/December 2010, could serve as an appellate body where parties adversely affected by such standard-setting could seek a ruling from an expert panel on whether the standards were supported by scientific and practical consideration, as opposed to being protectionist actions.

World Trade Organization disciplines constrain green industry development in *both* developing and developed countries. If the objective is the acceleration of green technological development, rethinking and renegotiating World Trade Organization disciplines will require attention to two facets: (a) what type of indicators of green development—novelty, level of riskiness, high initial cost—should be agreed upon as providing a reasonable basis for discriminating temporarily in favour of domestic industries and (b) how to embody the "common but differentiated responsibilities" principle in the application of trade disciplines promoting sustainable development.

Financing of green technology transfers necessitates domestic and international financial reforms

To achieve the timely diffusion of the new green technologies, investment rates in most developing countries will have to be raised by about $1 trillion per year for the period from 2010 to 2050. For developing countries, particularly, there is a need to eliminate internationally imposed restraints on long-term financing of domestic investment in pursuit of sustainable development.

The availability of public resources is important in financing start-ups in green sectors

Ensuring that domestic resources mobilized for investment are channelled to green investment and industries is the first and most important step. The availability of public resources is important in financing start-ups in green sectors. Overcoming domestic resource constraints through broadening the revenue base and creating the capacity to raise long-term finance by building domestic bond markets will be needed to raise public resources. Effective capital-account management and prudential regulations would go hand in hand with strengthened international tax cooperation with other countries. National Governments should also facilitate the rise of robust domestic financial sectors through effective supervision and regulation. All of these steps will permit Governments to acquire tools for counter-cyclical policy critical to sustaining private savings and investment activities.

Higher investment rates and the need to import technology and equipment will induce higher external deficits. Low-income countries would require increased external assistance to finance these deficits. More advanced developing countries that are able to access international private markets and FDI can finance the bulk of their external deficits in this way. Reforms in sovereign debt mechanisms and rules to establish orderly markets will increase the flow of long-term development financing available to developing countries.

A reversal of the current situation of net financial transfers from developing countries to developed countries is required. Inadequate regulation of volatile international private asset flows and deficiencies in reserve payments and exchange-rate mechanisms have motivated developing countries to accumulate developed countries' liquid financial assets, leading to perverse transfers (United Nations, 2010c). Reforming the international financial system is a precondition for financing sustainable development because, once achieved, this will allow developing countries as a group to redirect their savings towards their own development financing needs. Enhanced global and regional reserve pooling arrangements will reduce the need for self-protection through individual-country reserves accumulation (United Nations, 2010c) and could free substantial resources (including from sovereign wealth funds) for long-term financing in green investments. Moreover, it would facilitate effective net resource transfers to developing countries.

A reversal of the current situation of net financial transfers from developing countries to developed countries is required

Ensuring that developing countries have sufficient policy space within which to generate long-term financing from domestic sources (Ocampo, 2011b, p. 30), through cooperative efforts at capital regulation, for example, will reduce the volume of external financing needed and the vulnerability to external debt crises. This will need to be matched by a "development-oriented" macroeconomic policy approach, which requires effective capital-account controls and counter-cyclical fiscal and monetary policies (United Nations, 2010c), as part of the toolkit for sustainable development.

Developing countries must have sufficient policy space with which to generate long-term finance from domestic sources

Foreign investment and private flows

Based on recent experience, FDI flows can play an important role in diffusing green technology in developing countries, as long as recipient countries adopt a strategic stance with regard to foreign investors by actively including technology acquisition in investor programmes. The precedents come from the rise of internationally competitive firms in China, such as Goldwind, through joint ventures and technology-sharing (United Nations, Department of Economic and Social Affairs, 2008; and chap. V). Within the framework of national innovation systems, developing countries can incorporate technology transfer provisions in foreign investment approvals. At the international level, this will require relaxing the provisions of the Agreement on Trade-related Investment Measures that restrict technology transfer requirements.

Upgrading levels and capabilities of global governance

The proposed reshaping of national development efforts and strengthened international cooperation in technological development and cooperation, external assistance, investment finance and trade rules will require stronger mechanisms of global governance and coordination. Within the next three to four decades, all of these efforts must "add up" to the achievement of what appear today to be almost unattainable targets, such as an almost three-fourths reduction in per capita carbon emissions and the eradication of poverty, which will involve an almost 10-fold increase in the availability of modern energy to those now counted as poor.

The bulk of the efforts directed towards technological transformation must occur at the country level and be built upon local conditions and resources (chap. V). The need for an effective global technology policymaking body has already been mentioned. There are several conditions for success. First, more effective monitoring and verification of performance on international commitments are needed. When establishing mechanisms

The bulk of efforts for technological transformation must occur at the country level and build upon local conditions and resources

of mutual accountability, lessons can be drawn from existing models in other areas, such as the trade policy review process of the World Trade Organization.

Second, much greater coherence among the elements of the now rather disjointed multilateral architectures for the environment, technology transfer, trade, aid and finance will be required in coordinating the likely diverse set of country strategies for green growth and ensuring that they add up to global targets for environmental sustainability. For example, the expansion of international financial services facilitated under the World Trade Organization General Agreement on Trade in Services (World Trade Organization, 1994) unduly restricts the capacity of individual countries to regulate domestic financial markets. Establishing a better definition of the scope of the responsibilities of the disparate mechanisms involved and ensuring the coordination of their activities by existing bodies (such as the Economic and Social Council, which has an official coordination mandate) will require agreement among dominant economic countries (United Nations, 2010c).

There is a need to build mutual confidence in international public technology policymaking

Third, there is a need to build capacity and (given the limited precedents) mutual confidence in international public policymaking on technology. A particularly important technical issue involves deciding which technologies are most appropriately placed in the public domain, either through purchase at reasonable cost from private owners or through compulsory licencing. As emphasized in chapter II, particularly in the case of energy technologies, there is a need to build mechanisms providing effective technical input to international technology policymaking bodies with sufficient independence from political and commercial interests. As already noted, the tradition of the Intergovernmental Panel on Climate Change, which facilitated technical input conditioned by political accountability, can provide a foundation on which to build at the international level.

International mechanisms should be able to monitor the performance of donors and recipients on their commitments

Fourth, the governance of international financing mechanisms will have to be upgraded to strengthen coordination and reinforce accountability. At present, there seem to be too many funds and programmes which have mobilized insufficient resources (United Nations, 2009) and are overly project-oriented and subjected to donor policy conditionality (rather than aligned with national sustainable development strategies). Funding mechanisms can incorporate governance principles like those of the Paris Declaration regarding donor alignment to national priorities. It is also important that international mechanisms be established that can decide on guiding principles and standards for financial transfers and monitor performance of donors and recipients on their commitments at the aggregate level. Building on the successful Montreal Protocol approach has been proposed in the climate change framework negotiations conducted by the Group of 77 and China. This will involve the creation of a board that would report to the Conference of the Parties to the United Nations Framework Convention on Climate Change. The board would ensure equitable representation with geographical balance. Donor flows that were not subject to the policies of the board would not count towards fulfilment of those donors' commitments under the Convention.

Having agreed in 1992 that sustainable development is a goal to be shared among developed and developing countries, the global community will need to make rapid progress in strengthening global, and particularly economic, governance. It would be advantageous for international bodies and mechanisms to identify universally agreed targets and specific global ones which could be utilized to help monitor progress and ensure accountability for the actions undertaken. Indeed, improved governance could make diverse actions undertaken in a variety of sectors and countries add up to what is required at the global level.

Bibliography

Adger, W. N., and others (2003). Adaptation to climate change in the developing world. *Progress in Development Studies*, vol. 3, No. 3, pp. 179-195.

Africare, Oxfam America and WWF-ICRISAT Project (2010). More rice for people, more water for the planet. Hyderabad, India.

Agrawala, Shardul, and Samuel Fankhauser, eds. (2008). *Economic Aspects of Adaptation to Climate Change: Costs, Benefits and Policy Instruments*. Paris: Organization for Economic Cooperation and Development.

Ahmed, Mushir (2011). Solar energy use sees major growth. *Financial Express* (Dhaka), vol. 18, No. 77 (30 January). REGD NO DA 1589. Available from http://www.thefinancialexpress-bd.com/more.php?news_id=124464&date=2011-01-30.

Alire, Rod (2011). The reality behind biodegradable plastic packaging material: the science of biodegradable plastics. Redwood City, California: FP International. Available from http://www.fpintl.com/resources/wp_biodegradable_plastics.htm.

Altieri, Miguel A. (2008). Small farms as a planetary ecological asset: five key reasons why we should support the revitalization of small farms in the global South. Oakland, California: Food First/Institute for Food and Development Policy. 15 April. Available from http://www.foodfirst.org/en/node/2115.

Alvarez, Benjamín, and others (1999). Education in Central America. Development Discussion Paper, No. 711 (June). Cambridge, Massachusetts: Harvard University, Harvard Institute for International Development.

Archibugi, D., and C. Pietrobelli (2003). The globalisation of technology and its implications for developing countries: windows of opportunity or further burden? *Technological Forecasting and Social Change*, vol. 70, No. 9, pp. 861-883.

Audretsch, David B., Albert N. Link and John T. Scott (2002). Public/private technology partnerships: evaluating SBIR-supported research. *Research Policy*, vol. 31, No. 1 (January), pp. 145-158.

Ausubel, Jesse H. (2007). Renewable and nuclear heresies. *International Journal of Nuclear Governance, Economy and Ecology*, vol. 1, No. 3, pp. 229-243.

Bai, Z. G., and others (2008). Global assessment of land degradation and improvement: 1. identification by remote sensing. Report 2008/01. Wageningen, Netherlands: ISRIC—World Soil Information, Food and Agriculture Organization of the United Nations.

Baker, Elaine, and others (2004). Vital waste graphics. Nairobi: Basel Convention Secretariat, UNEP Division of Environmental Conventions, Grid-Arendal and UNEP Division of Early Warning Assessment—Europe.

Barlevy, G., and D. Tsiddon (2006). Earnings inequality and the business cycle. *European Economic Review*, vol. 50, No. 1, pp. 55-89.

Baumert, Kevin A., Timothy Herzog and Jonathan Pershing (2005). *Navigating the Numbers: Greenhouse Gas Data and International Climate Policy*. Washington, D.C.:World Resources Institute.

Beggs, P. J. (2004). Impacts of climate change on aeroallergens: past and future. *Clinical and Experimental Allergy*, vol. 34, No. 10, pp. 1507-1513.

Beintema, Nienke, and Howard Elliott (2009). Setting meaningful investment targets in agricultural research and development: challenges, opportunities and fiscal realities. Paper prepared for the Expert meeting on "How to Feed the World in 2050", organized by FAO, Rome, 24-26 June 2009.

Berdegué, Julio A. (2005). Pro-poor innovation systems. Background paper commissioned by the International Fund of Agricultural Development, December.

Berry, Len, Jennifer Olson and David Campbell (2003). Assessing the extent, cost and impact of land degradation at the national level: findings and lessons learned from seven pilot case studies. Report commissioned by Global Mechanism of the United Nations Convention to Combat Desertification, with support from the World Bank.

Besley, Timothy, and Louise J. Cord, eds. (2007). *Delivering on the Promise of Pro-Poor Growth: Insights and Lessons from Country Experiences*. Washington, D.C.: World Bank; Basingstoke, United Kingdom: Palgrave Macmillan.

Bhagwati, Jagdish (2005). Development aid: getting it right. *OECD Observer*, No. 249 (May).

Bhatia, Arti, H. Pathak and P. K. Aggarwal (2004). Inventory of methane and nitrous oxide emissions from agricultural soils of India and their global warming potential. *Current Science*, vol. 87, No. 3 (August), pp. 317-324.

Birkmann, Jörn, and Korinna von Teichman (2010). Integrating disaster risk reduction and climate change adaptation: key challenges - scales, knowledge, and norms. *Sustainability Science*, vol. 5, No. 2, pp. 171-184.

Birkmann, Jörn, and others (2010a). Adaptive urban governance: new challenges for the second generation of urban adaptation strategies to climate change. *Sustainability Science*, vol. 5, No. 2, pp. 185-206.

_________ (2010b). Extreme events and disasters: a window of opportunity for change? analysis of organizational, institutional and political changes, formal and informal responses after mega-disasters. *Natural Hazards*, vol. 55, No. 3 (December), pp. 637-655.

Bolton, Patrick, Roger Guesnerie and Frederic Samama (2010). Towards an international green fund. Mimeo. October.

Bosetti, V., and D.G. Victor (2011). Politics and economics of second-best regulation of greenhouse gases: the importance of regulatory credibility. *Energy Journal*, vol. 32, No. 1.

Braun, Arnoud, and Deborah Duveskog (2008). The Farmer Field School approach: history, global assessment and success stories. Background paper commissioned by the International Fund for Agricultural Development for the *IFAD Rural Poverty Report 2009* (October).

Brazil, Associação Nacional dos Fabricantes de Veículos Automotores (2008). Brazilian automotive industry yearbook 2008. São Paolo, Brazil.

Bredenkamp, Hugh, and Catherine Pattillo (2010). Financing the response to climate change. IMF Staff Position Note, No. SPN10/06. Washington, D.C.: International Monetary Fund. 25 March.

British Petroleum (2010). Statistical review of world energy 2010. London: British Petroleum. Available from http://www.bp.com/productlanding.do?categoryId=6929&contentId=7044622.

Brooks, S., and M. Loevinsohn (2011). Shaping agricultural innovation systems responsive to food insecurity and climate change. Background paper prepared for *World Economic and Social Survey 2011.*

Bundesnetzagentur (2009). Bundesnetzagentur official website (www.bundesnetzagentur.de) (accessed 21 April 2011).

Campbell-Lendrum, D. (2009). Saving lives while saving the planet: protecting health from climate change. Background paper prepared for *World Economic and Social Survey 2009.*

Cannady, Cynthia. (2009). Access to climate change technology by developing countries: a practical strategy. *ICTSD Intellectual Property and Sustainable Development Series Issue Paper*, No. 25. Geneva: International Centre for Trade and Sustainable Development. September.

Carin, Robert (1969). Power industry in Communist China. Hong Kong: Union Research Institute.

Casas, R. (2005). Exchange and knowledge flows between large firms and research institutions. *Innovation: Management, Policy and Practice*, vol. 7, No. 2-3, pp. 188-199.

Castro, Rocio, and Brian Hammond (2009). The architecture of aid for the environment: a ten year statistical perspective. CFP Working Paper Series, No. 3. Washington, D.C.: Concessional Finance and Global Partnerships Vice Presidency, World Bank. October. Table A.2.

Chakravarty, Shoibal, and others (2009). Sharing global CO_2 emission reductions among one billion high emitters. *Proceedings of the National Academy of Sciences*, vol. 106, No. 29, pp. 11884-11888.

Chant, Lindsay, Scott McDonald and Arjan Verschoor (2008). Some consequences of the 1994-1995 coffee boom for growth and poverty reduction in Uganda. *Journal of Agricultural Economics*, vol. 59, No. 1 (February), pp. 93-113.

Chen, Dong, Jing Li and Daniel Shapiro (2009). FDI knowledge spillovers and product innovations of Chinese firms. SLPTMD Working Paper Series, No. 028. Oxford: University of Oxford, Department of International Development.

Chhabara, Rajesh (2008). Grameen's World Bank deal brings solar power to Bangladesh. Climate Change Corp, 23 April. Available from http://www.climatechangecorp.com/content.asp?ContentID=5283.

Cohen, W. M., and D. A. Levinthal (1990). Absorptive capacity: a new perspective on learning and innovation. *Administrative Science Quarterly*, vol. 35, No. 1 (March), pp. 128-152.

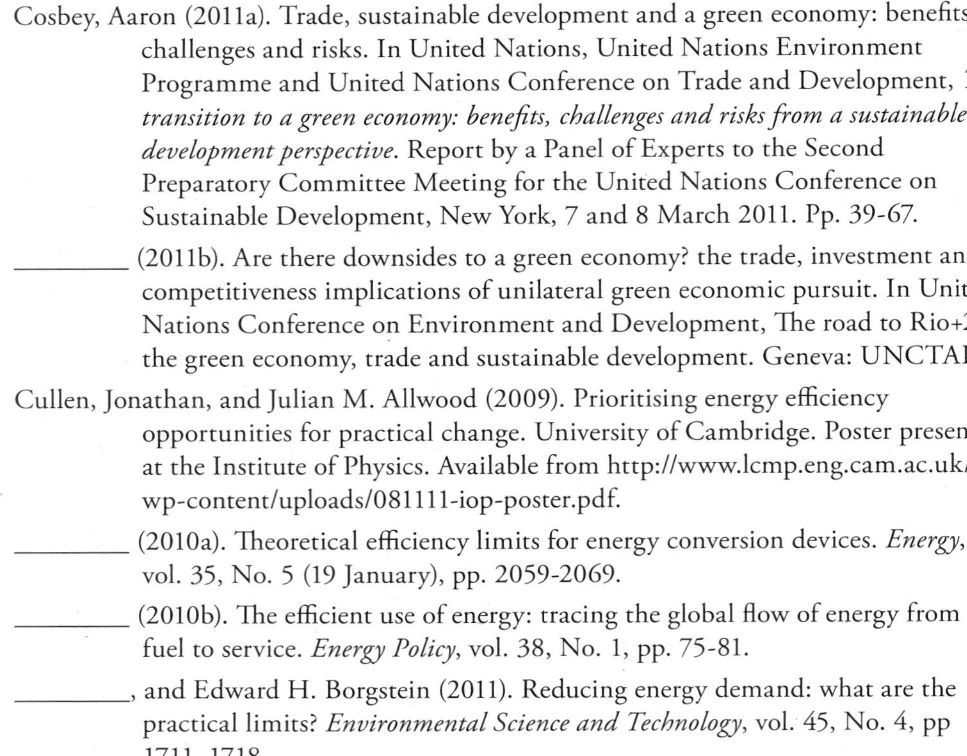

Cosbey, Aaron (2011a). Trade, sustainable development and a green economy: benefits, challenges and risks. In United Nations, United Nations Environment Programme and United Nations Conference on Trade and Development, *The transition to a green economy: benefits, challenges and risks from a sustainable development perspective*. Report by a Panel of Experts to the Second Preparatory Committee Meeting for the United Nations Conference on Sustainable Development, New York, 7 and 8 March 2011. Pp. 39-67.

________ (2011b). Are there downsides to a green economy? the trade, investment and competitiveness implications of unilateral green economic pursuit. In United Nations Conference on Environment and Development, The road to Rio+20: the green economy, trade and sustainable development. Geneva: UNCTAD.

Cullen, Jonathan, and Julian M. Allwood (2009). Prioritising energy efficiency opportunities for practical change. University of Cambridge. Poster presented at the Institute of Physics. Available from http://www.lcmp.eng.cam.ac.uk/wp-content/uploads/081111-iop-poster.pdf.

________ (2010a). Theoretical efficiency limits for energy conversion devices. *Energy*, vol. 35, No. 5 (19 January), pp. 2059-2069.

________ (2010b). The efficient use of energy: tracing the global flow of energy from fuel to service. *Energy Policy*, vol. 38, No. 1, pp. 75-81.

________, and Edward H. Borgstein (2011). Reducing energy demand: what are the practical limits? *Environmental Science and Technology*, vol. 45, No. 4, pp 1711–1718.

Dahlman, Carl (2008). Innovation strategies of three of the BRICS: Brazil, India and China - what can we learn from three different approaches? SLPTMD Working Paper Series, No. 023. Oxford: University of Oxford, Department of International Development.

Daily Star (2010). Rahimafrooz plans 5MW solar power plant. Business Desk, 31 October. Dhaka. Available from http://www.thedailystar.net/newDesign/news-details.php?nid=160646.

Davis, Kristin, and others (2007). Strengthening agricultural education and training in sub-Saharan Africa from an innovation systems perspective: case studies of Ethiopia and Mozambique. IFPRI Discussion Paper, No. 00736 (December). Washington, D.C.: International Food Policy Research Institute.

Davis, Steven J., Ken Caldeira and H. Damon Matthews (2010). Future CO_2 emissions and climate change from existing energy infrastructure. *Science*, vol. 329, No. 5997, pp. 1330-1333.

Davone, Richard (2007). Diasporas and development. Resource paper prepared for the Global Workshop on Migration of Talent and Diasporas of the Highly Skilled, Buenos Aires, 26 and 27 April 2005. Available from http://info.worldbank.org/etools/docs/library/152385/richarddavone.pdf.

Deininger, Klaus, and others (2010). *Rising Global Interest in Farmland: Can It Yield Sustainable and Equitable Benefits?* Washington, D.C.: World Bank.

DeLong, J. Bradford (1998). Estimating world GDP, one million B.C.-present. Berkeley, California: University of California, Berkeley. Available from http://www.j-bradford-delong.net/TCEH/1998_Draft/World_GDP/Estimating_World_GDP.html.

Deutsche Energie-Agentur (DENA) (2005). *Energiewirtschaftliche Planung für die Netzintegration von Windenergie in Deutschland bis zum Jahr 2020.* Köln, Germany. 24 February.

Deutsche Gesellschaft für Internationale Zusammenarbeit (2011). International fuel prices 2010/2011: data preview January 2011. Available from www.gtz.de/de/dokumente/giz2011-international-fuel-prices-2010-2011-data-preview.pdf (accessed 25 April 2011).

Deutsche Physikalische Gesellschaft (DPG) (2010). *Elektrizität: Schlüssel zu einem Nachhaltigen und klimaverträglichen Energiesystem—eine Studie der Deutsche Physikalische Gesellschaft.* Bad Honnef, Germany. June.

Diamond, Jared (2005). *Collapse: How Societies Choose to Fail or Succeed.* New York: Viking Press.

Dixon, John A., David P. Gibbon and Aidan Gulliver (2001). *Farming Systems and Poverty: Improving Farmers' Livelihoods in a Changing World.* Rome: Food and Agriculture Organization of the United Nations; Washington, D.C.: World Bank.

Dobrov, Gennady M. (1979). The strategy for organized technology in the light of hard-, soft-, and org-ware interaction. *Long Range Planning*, vol. 12, No. 4 (August), pp. 79-90.

Docquier, Frédéric, Olivier Lohest and Abdeslam Marfouk (2007). Brain drain in developing countries. *World Bank Economic Review*, vol. 21, No. 2, pp. 193-218.

Dosi, Giovanni, L. Marengo and C. Pasquali (2007). Knowledge, competition and innovation: is strong IPR protection really needed for more and better innovations? 13 Mich. Telecomm. Tech. L. Rev. 471 (2007).

Dregne, H. E. (1990). Erosion and soil productivity in Africa. *Journal of Soil and Water Conservation*, vol. 45, No. 4 (July/August), pp. 431-436.

Dubin, H. J., and John P. Brennan (2009). Fighting a "shifty enemy": the international collaboration to contain wheat rusts. In *Millions Fed: Proven Successes in Agricultural Development*, David J. Spielman and Rajul Pandya-Lorch, eds. Washington, D.C.: International Food Policy Research Institute. Pp. 19-24.

Duke, R. D., A. Jacobson and D. M. Kammen (2002). Photovoltaic module quality in the Kenyan solar home systems market. *Energy Policy*, vol. 30, No. 6 (6 May), pp. 477-499.

Duro, Juan Antonio, and Emilio Padilla (2011). Inequality across countries in energy intensities: an analysis of the role of energy transformation and final energy consumption. *Energy Economics*, vol. 33, No. 3 (May), pp. 474-479.

Echeverria, Ruben G., and Nienke M. Beintema (2009). Mobilizing financial resources for agricultural research in developing countries: trends and mechanisms. Rome: Global Forum on Agricultural Research (GFAR).

Ecosystem Marketplace (2010). Costa Rica water-based ecosystem services markets: forest trends. Available from http://www.ecosystemmarketplace.com/pages/dynamic/web.page.php?section=water_market&page_name=crwb_market (accessed 12 April 2011).

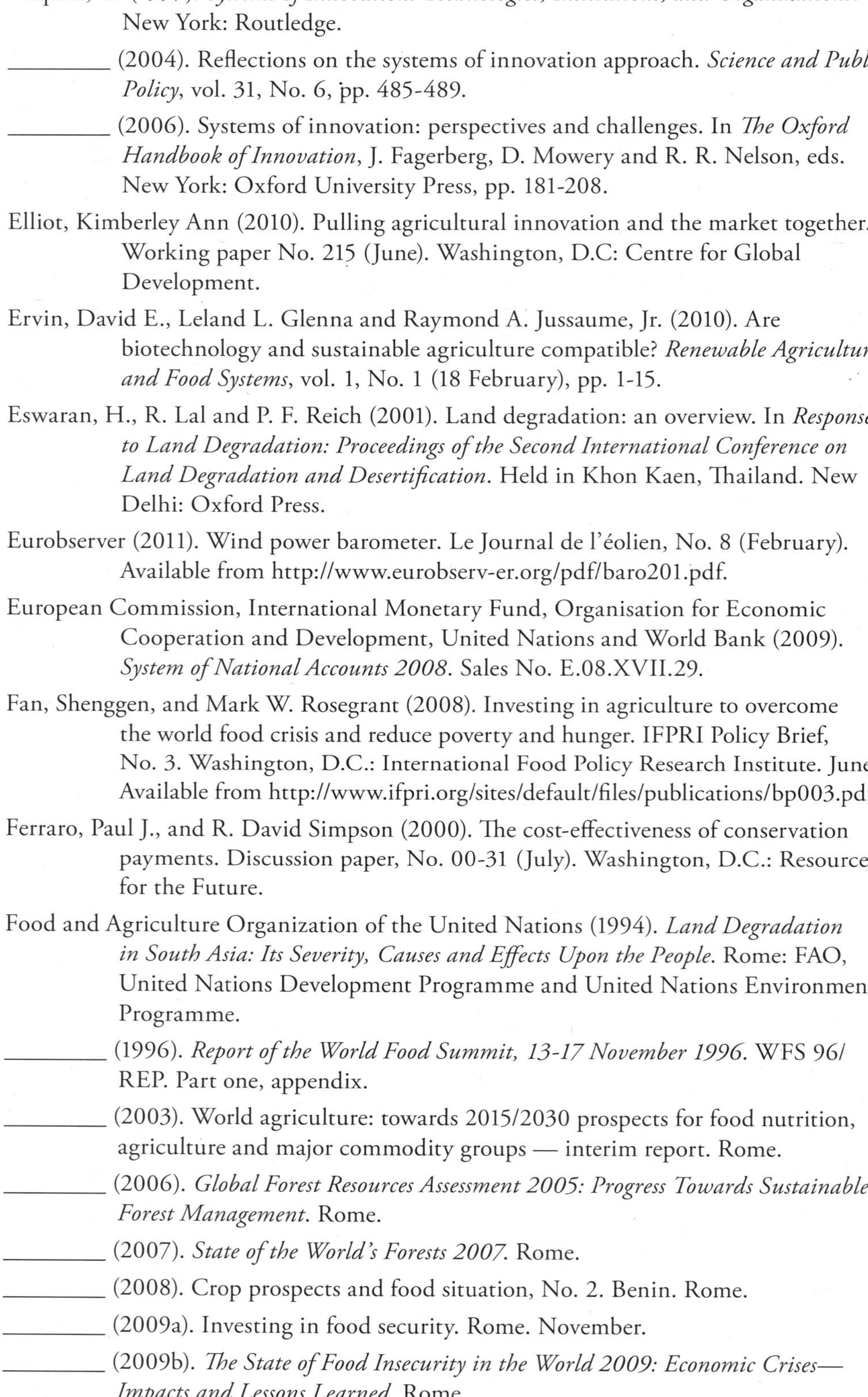

Edquist, C. (1997). *Systems of Innovation: Technologies, Institutions, and Organizations.* New York: Routledge.

________ (2004). Reflections on the systems of innovation approach. *Science and Public Policy*, vol. 31, No. 6, pp. 485-489.

________ (2006). Systems of innovation: perspectives and challenges. In *The Oxford Handbook of Innovation*, J. Fagerberg, D. Mowery and R. R. Nelson, eds. New York: Oxford University Press, pp. 181-208.

Elliot, Kimberley Ann (2010). Pulling agricultural innovation and the market together. Working paper No. 215 (June). Washington, D.C: Centre for Global Development.

Ervin, David E., Leland L. Glenna and Raymond A. Jussaume, Jr. (2010). Are biotechnology and sustainable agriculture compatible? *Renewable Agriculture and Food Systems*, vol. 1, No. 1 (18 February), pp. 1-15.

Eswaran, H., R. Lal and P. F. Reich (2001). Land degradation: an overview. In *Responses to Land Degradation: Proceedings of the Second International Conference on Land Degradation and Desertification.* Held in Khon Kaen, Thailand. New Delhi: Oxford Press.

Eurobserver (2011). Wind power barometer. Le Journal de l'éolien, No. 8 (February). Available from http://www.eurobserv-er.org/pdf/baro201.pdf.

European Commission, International Monetary Fund, Organisation for Economic Cooperation and Development, United Nations and World Bank (2009). *System of National Accounts 2008.* Sales No. E.08.XVII.29.

Fan, Shenggen, and Mark W. Rosegrant (2008). Investing in agriculture to overcome the world food crisis and reduce poverty and hunger. IFPRI Policy Brief, No. 3. Washington, D.C.: International Food Policy Research Institute. June. Available from http://www.ifpri.org/sites/default/files/publications/bp003.pdf.

Ferraro, Paul J., and R. David Simpson (2000). The cost-effectiveness of conservation payments. Discussion paper, No. 00-31 (July). Washington, D.C.: Resources for the Future.

Food and Agriculture Organization of the United Nations (1994). *Land Degradation in South Asia: Its Severity, Causes and Effects Upon the People.* Rome: FAO, United Nations Development Programme and United Nations Environment Programme.

________ (1996). *Report of the World Food Summit, 13-17 November 1996.* WFS 96/REP. Part one, appendix.

________ (2003). World agriculture: towards 2015/2030 prospects for food nutrition, agriculture and major commodity groups — interim report. Rome.

________ (2006). *Global Forest Resources Assessment 2005: Progress Towards Sustainable Forest Management.* Rome.

________ (2007). *State of the World's Forests 2007.* Rome.

________ (2008). Crop prospects and food situation, No. 2. Benin. Rome.

________ (2009a). Investing in food security. Rome. November.

________ (2009b). *The State of Food Insecurity in the World 2009: Economic Crises—Impacts and Lessons Learned.* Rome.

_________ (2010a). *The State of Food Insecurity in the World 2010: Addressing Food Insecurity in Protracted Crises*. Rome.

_________ (2010b). Global forest resource assessment 2010: key findings. Rome.

_________ (2011). *The State of Food and Agriculture 2010/2011: Women in Agriculture — Closing the Gender Gap for Development*. Rome.

_________, Global Perspectives Studies Unit (2006). World agriculture: towards 2030/2050 - prospects for food, nutrition, agriculture and major commodity groups. Interim report. Rome. June.

Food and Agriculture Organization of the United Nations, International Fund for Agricultural Development and International Labour Organization (2010). *Gender Dimensions of Agricultural and Rural Employment: Differentiated Pathways out of Poverty*. Rome: FAO, International Fund for Agricultural Development and International Labour Organization.

Foresight (2011). The future of food and farming: challenges and choices for global sustainability. London: Government Office for Science.

Freeman, Chris (1997). The "National System of Innovation" in historical perspective. In *Technology, Globalisation and Economic Performance*, D. Archibugi and J. Michie, eds. Cambridge, United Kingdom: Cambridge University Press. Pp. 24-49.

Fri, R.W. (2003). The role of knowledge: technological innovation in the energy system. *Energy Journal*, vol. 24, No. 4, pp. 51-74.

Fu, Xiaolan (2008). Foreign direct investment, absorptive capacity and regional innovation capabilities: evidence from China. *Oxford Development Studies*, vol. 36, No. 1, pp. 89-110.

_________ (2011). Key determinants of technological capabilities for a green economy in emerging economies. Background paper prepared for *World Economic and Social Survey 2011*.

_________, and Yundan Gong (2011). Indigenous and foreign innovation efforts and drivers of technological upgrading: evidence from China. SLPTMD Working Paper, No. 016. Oxford: University of Oxford, Department of International Development.

Fu, Xiolan, Carlo Pietrobelli and Luc Soete (2010). The role of foreign technology and indigenous innovation in emerging economies: technological change and catching up. Inter-American Development Bank Technical Notes, No. IDB-TN-166 (September). Washington, D.C.: Inter-American Development Bank, Institutional Capacity and Finance Sector.

Gallagher, Kelly Sims (2006). Limits to leapfrogging in energy technologies? Evidence from the Chinese automobile industry. *Energy Policy*, vol. 34, No. 4 (March), pp. 383-394.

_________, and others (2011). Harnessing energy: technology innovation in developing countries to achieve sustainable prosperity. Background paper prepared for *World Economic and Social Survey 2011*.

_________ (forthcoming). Trends in investments in global energy RD&D. Wiley Interdisciplinary Reviews: Climate Change.

Gallagher, K. P., and M. Shafaeddin (2010). Policies for industrial learning in China and Mexico. *Technology in Society*, vol. 32, No. 2, pp. 81-99.

Gardner, G. T., and P. C. Stern (2008). The short list: the most effective actions US households can take to curb climate change. *Environment: Science and Policy for Sustainable Development*, vol. 50, No. 5, pp. 12-25.

Gaskins, D., and B. Stram (1991). A meta plan: a policy response to global warming. Center for Science and International Affairs Discussion Paper, No. 91-3. Cambridge, Massachusetts: John F. Kennedy School of Government, Harvard University. June.

Gilbert, Christopher L. (2008). How to understand high food prices. Discussion paper, No. 23. Trento, Italy: Department of Economics, University of Trento. Available from http://www.unitn.it/files/23_08_gilbert.pdf.

Gillett, Nathan P., and others (2011). Ongoing climate change following a complete cessation of carbon dioxide emissions. *Nature Geoscience*, vol. 4, No. 2 (February), pp. 83-87.

Global Energy Assessment (forthcoming). *The Global Energy Assessment*. Cambridge, United Kingdom: Cambridge University Press.

Global Wind Energy Council, World Institute of Sustainable Development, and Indian Wind Turbine Manufacturing Association (2011). Indian wind energy outlook 2011. Brussels: Global Wind Energy Council; Pune, India: World Institute of Sustainable Development; Chennal, India: Indian Wind Turbine Manufacturing Association. Available from http://www.indianwindpower.com/pdf/iweo_2011_lowres.pdf.

Godfray, H. Charles J., and others (2010a). The future of the global food system. *Philosophical Transactions of the Royal Society B: Biological Sciences*, vol. 365, No. 1554, pp. 2769-2777.

_________ (2010b). Food security: the challenge of feeding 9 billion people. *Science*, vol. 327, No. 5967, pp. 812-818.

Griffith-Jones, Stephany, and Krishnan Sharma (2006). GDP-indexed bonds: making it happen. DESA Working Paper, No. 21 (April). New York: Department of Economic and Social Affairs of the United Nations Secretariat. ST/ESA/DWP/2006/21.

Group of 8 (2008). Leaders' statement on global food security, Hokkaido, Japan, 8 July. Available from http://www.mofa.go.jp/policy/economy/summit/2008/doc/doc080709_04_en.html.

_________ (2009). Chair's summary, L'Aquila, Italy, 10 July. Available from http://www.g8italia2009.it/static/G8_Allegato/Chair_Summary,1.pdf (accessed 4 April 2011).

Grübler, Arnulf (1998). *Technology and Global Change*. Cambridge, United Kingdom: Cambridge University Press.

_________ (2004). Transitions in energy use. In *Encyclopedia of Energy*, vol. 6. Amsterdam: Elsevier. Pp. 163-177.

_________ (2008). Energy transitions. In The Encyclopedia of EARTH. Washington, D.C.: Environmental Information Coalition and National Council for Science and the Environment. 13 February.

_________, and Sabine Messner (1998). Technological change and the timing of mitigation measures. *Energy Economics*, vol. 20, No. 5-6, pp. 495-512.

Grübler, Arnulf, and Keywan Riahi (2010). Do governments have the right mix in their energy R&D portfolios? *Carbon Management*, vol. 1, No. 1, pp. 79-87.

Grübler, Arnulf, and others (forthcoming). The energy technology innovation system. In *The Global Energy Assessment*. Cambridge, United Kingdom: Cambridge University Press.

_________ (forthcoming bis). Policies for innovation. In *The Global Energy Assessment*. Cambridge, United Kingdom: Cambridge University Press.

Hall, Andy (2010). Entrepreneurs: what sort do we really need? Link Look (June). United Nations University.

_________, Jeroen Dijkman and Rasheed Sulaiman V. (2010). Research into use: investigating the relationship between agricultural research and innovation. UNU- MERIT Working Paper Series, No. 2010-44 (July). Maastricht, Netherlands: United Nations University - Maastricht Economic and Social Research and Training Centre on Innovation and Technology.

Hall, Andy, and others (1998). Institutional developments in Indian agricultural R & D systems: emerging patterns of public and private sector activity. (October). Chatham, United Kingdom: Food Security Department, Natural Resources Institute; Hyderabad, India: National Centre for Agricultural Economics and Policy Research.

Hamrin, Jan, Holmes Hummel and Rachael Canapa (2007). Review of the role of renewable energy in global energy scenarios. Paper prepared for the International Energy Agency (IEA) Implementing Agreement on Renewable Energy Technology Deployment. San Francisco, California: Center for Resource Solutions. June.

Hankins, Mark, Saini Anjali and Paul Kirai (2009). Target market analysis: Kenya's solar energy market. Berlin: Deutsche Gesellschaft für technische Zusammenarbeit (GTZ). November. Available from http://www.gtz.de/de/dokumente/gtz2009-en-targetmarketanalysis-solar-kenya.pdf.

Hawley, Josh (2007). Public private partnerships in vocational education and training: international examples and models. Washington, D.C.: World Bank. Available from http://siteresources.worldbank.org/EXTECAREGTOPEDUCATION/Resources/444607-1192636551820/Public_Private_Partnerships_in_Vocational_Education_and_Training.pdf (accessed 29 March 2011).

Hazell, Peter B.R. (2009). Transforming agriculture, the green revolution in Asia. In *Millions Fed, Proven Successes in Agricultural Development*, David J. Spielman and Rajul Pandya-Lorch, eds. Washington, D.C.: International Food Policy Research Institute. Pp. 25-32.

_________, and others (2010). The future of small farms: trajectories and policy priorities. *World Development*, vol. 38, No. 10 (October), pp. 1453-1526.

Hecl, Vladimir (2010). Technology needs assessments under the UNFCCC process. Power Point presentation at the Latin American and Caribbean Regional Workshop on Preparing Technology Transfer Projects for Financing, Belize City, 5 May.

Heymann, Matthias (1998). Signs of hubris: the shaping of wind technology styles in Germany, Denmark, and the United States, 1940-1990. *Technology and Culture*, vol. 39, No. 4, pp. 641-670.

Hirschberg, Stephan, and others (2006). Strengths and weaknesses of current energy chains in a sustainable development perspective. *ATW-Internationale Zeitschrift fur Kernenergie*, vol. 51, No. 7 (July), pp. 447-457.

________ (2009). Final report on sustainability assessment of advanced electricity supply options. Deliverable D10.2 - RS2b. New Energy Externalities Developments for Sustainability (NEEDS), Project No. 502687. Project co-funded by the European Commission within the Sixth Framework Programme. April.

HM Government (2010). *The 2007/2008 Agricultural Price Spikes: Causes and Policy Implications*. London.

Holden, S. T. (1991). Peasants and sustainable development: the Chitemene region of Zambia — theory, evidence and models. Unpublished PhD dissertation. Ås, Norway: Department of Economics and Social Sciences, Agricultural University of Norway.

Holdren, John P. (2006). The energy innovation imperative: addressing oil dependence, climate change, and other 21st century energy challenges. *Innovations: Technology, Governance, Globalization*, vol. 1, No. 2, pp. 3-23.

Huq, Saleemul, and Hannah Reid (2004). Mainstreaming adaptation in development. *IDS Bulletin*, vol. 35, No. 3, pp. 15-21.

Hyde, Karin A.L. (1993). Sub-Saharan Africa. In *Women's Education in Developing Countries: Barriers, Benefits and Policies*, E. M. King and M. A. Hill, eds. Baltimore, Maryland: The Johns Hopkins University Press. Chap. 3.

Intergovernmental Panel on Climate Change (2001). *Climate Change 2007: Mitigation—Contribution of Working Group III to the Fourth Assessment Report of the Intergovernmental Panel on Climate Change*, B. Metz and others, eds. Cambridge, United Kingdom: Cambridge University Press. Available from http://www.grida.no/publications/other/ipcc_tar/?src=/climate/ipcc_tar/.

________ (2007a). *Climate Change 2007: Synthesis Report*. Geneva.

________ (2007b). *Climate Change 2007: Impacts, Adaptation and Vulnerability—Contribution of Working Group II to the Fourth Assessment Report of the Intergovernmental Panel on Climate Change*, M. L. Parry and others, eds. Cambridge, United Kingdom: Cambridge University Press.

________ (2009). Managing the risks of extreme events and disasters to advance climate change adaptation. Scoping Paper - IPCC Special Report, submitted to IPCC at its thirtieth session, Antalya, Turkey, 21-23 April. Available from http://www.ipcc.ch/meetings/session30/doc14.pdf.

International Assessment of Agricultural Knowledge, Science and Technology for Development (2009). *Agriculture at a Crossroads: Global Report*, Beverly D. McIntyre and others, eds. Washington, D.C.: Island Press.

International Energy Agency (2008a). Deploying renewables: principles for effective action. Paris: OECD. Available from http://www.iea.org/G8/2008/G8_Renewables.pdf.

________ (2008b). *Energy Technology Perspectives 2008 - Scenarios and Strategies to 2050*. Paris: OECD.

________ (2009). *World Energy Outlook 2009*. Paris: OECD.

________ (2010a). Energy balances of non-OECD countries, 2010 ed. Paris. Available from http://www.iea.org/Textbase/nptoc/greenbal2010TOC.pdf.

________ (2010b). *World Energy Outlook 2010*. Paris: OECD.

________, Photovoltaic Power Systems Programme (2003). 16 case studies on the deployment of photovoltaic technologies in developing countries. Paris. September. IEA-PVPS T9-07:23.

International Energy Agency, United Nations Development Programme and United Nations Industrial Development Organization (2010). Energy poverty: how to make modern energy access universal? Special early excerpt of the World Economic Outlook 2010 for the United Nations General Assembly on the Millennium Development Goals. September. Available from http://www.worldenergyoutlook.org/docs/weo2010/weo2010_poverty.pdf.

International Food Policy Research Institute (2002). Green revolution, curse or blessing? Washington, D.C.

________ (2005). The future of small farms. Proceedings of a research workshop, Wye, United Kingdom, 26-29 June 2005, jointly organized by International Food Policy Research Institute (IFPRI)/2020 Vision Initiative, Overseas Development Institute (ODI) and Imperial College, London. Washington, D.C.

International Fund for Agricultural Development (2011). *Rural Poverty Report 2011: New Realities, New Challenges — New Opportunities for Tomorrow's Generation*. Rome.

IUCN, Species Survival Commission (2004). *2004 Red List of Threatened Species: A Global Species Assessment*, J. E. M. Baillie and others. Gland, Switzerland.

Jackson, Tim (2009a). Prosperity without growth? the transition to a sustainable economy London: Sustainable Development Commission.

________ (2009b). *Prosperity Without Growth: Economics for a Finite Planet*. London: Earthscan.

________ (2010). Philosophical and social transformations necessary for the green economy. Background paper prepared for *World Economic and Social Survey 2011*.

Jacobson, Arne (2005). The market for micro-power: social uses of solar electricity in rural Kenya. Working Paper No. 9. Nairobi: Egerton University, Tegemeo Institute of Agricultural Policy and Development.

________, and D.M. Kammen (2007). Engineering, institutions, and the public interest: evaluating product quality in the Kenyan solar photovoltaics industry. *Energy Policy*, vol. 35, No. 5, pp. 2960-2968.

Japan, Energy Conservation Center (2008). Top-Runner Program: developing the world's best energy-efficient appliances, revised ed. Tokyo.

Jaumotte, Florence, and Nigel Pain (2005). An overview of public policies to support innovation. *OECD Economics Department Working Paper*, No. 456 (December). Paris.

Jayne, T. S., and others (2003). Smallholder income and land distribution in Africa: implications for poverty reduction strategies. *Food Policy*, vol. 28, No. 3, pp. 253-275.

Johanson, Richard K., and Arvil V. Adams (2004). *Skills Development in Sub-Saharan Africa*. World Bank Regional and Sectoral Studies. Washington, D.C.: World Bank.

Johnstone, Nick, Ivan Hascic and David Popp (2010). Renewable energy policies and technological innovation: evidence based on patent counts. *Environmental and Resource Economics*, vol. 45, No. 1 (January), pp. 133-155.

Jonas, M., and others (2010). Dealing with uncertainty in greenhouse gas inventories in an emissions constrained world. Paper prepared for the Third International Workshop on Uncertainty in Greenhouse Gas Inventories, Lviv, Ukraine, 22-24 September 2010.

Jones, Darryl, and Andrzej Kwiecinski (2010). Policy responses in emerging economies to international agricultural commodity price surges. *OECD Food, Agriculture and Fisheries Working Papers*, No. 34. Paris.

Juma, Calestous (2011). *The New Harvest: Agricultural Innovation in Africa*. New York: Oxford University Press.

Junginger, M., A. Faaij and W. C. Turkenburg (2005). Global experience curves for wind farms. *Energy Policy*, vol. 33, No. 2 (January), pp. 133-150.

Kaeb, Harald (2011). European bioplastics: introduction. Available from http://www.european-bioplastics.org/.

Kayombo, B., and R. Lal (1994). Response of tropical crops to soil compaction. In *Soil Compaction in Crop Production*, B. D. Sloane and C. Van Ouwerkkerk, eds. Amsterdam: Elsevier. Pp. 287-315.

Kempener, Ruud, Laura Diaz Anadon and Jose Condor Tarco (2010). Energy innovation policy in major emerging countries. Belfer Center for Science and International Affairs Policy Brief (December). Cambridge, Massachusetts: Harvard University, John F. Kennedy School of Government.

Khor, Martin (2010). The climate and trade relation: some issues. *South Centre Research Paper*, No. 29 (May). Geneva: South Centre.

________ (2011a). Global debate on green economy. *Star online* (Petaling Jaya, Malaysia). 24 January. Available from http://thestar.com.my/columnists/story.asp?col=globaltrends&file=/2011/1/24/columnists/globaltrends/7856802&sec=Global%20Trends.

________ (2011b). Challenges of the green economy concept and policies in the context of sustainable development, poverty and equity. In United Nations, United Nations Environment Programme and United Nations Conference on Trade and Development, *The transition to a green economy: benefits, challenges and risks from a sustainable development perspective*. Report by a Panel of Experts to the Second Preparatory Committee Meeting for the United Nations Conference on Sustainable Development, New York, 7 and 8 March 2011. Pp. 68-96.

Kim, Linsu, and Richard R. Nelson, eds. (2000). *Technology, Learning and Innovation: Experiences of Newly Industrializing Economies*. Cambridge, United Kingdom: Cambridge University Press.

Kossoy, Alexandre, and Philippe Ambrosi (2010). State and trends of the carbon market 2010. Washington, D.C.: World Bank.

Lal, Rattan (1998). Soil erosion impact on agronomic productivity and environment quality. *Critical Reviews in Plant Sciences*, vol. 17, No. 4 (4 July), pp. 319-464.

Lall, S., and M. Teubal (1998). "Market-stimulating" technology policies in developing countries: a framework with examples from East Asia. *World Development*, vol. 26, No. 8, pp. 1369-1385.

Landes, David S. (1969). *The Unbound Prometheus: Technological Change and Industrial Development in Western Europe from 1750 to Present*. Cambridge, United Kingdom: Cambridge University Press.

Lapidos, Juliet (2007). Will my plastic bag still be here in 2507? how scientists figure out how long it takes your trash to decompose. *Slate*. 27 June. Available from http://www.slate.com/id/2169287/.

Laxmi, Vijay, and others (2003). Household energy, women's hardship and health impacts in rural Rajasthan, India: need for sustainable energy solutions. *Energy for Sustainable Development*, vol. 7, No. 1 (March), pp. 50-68.

Leeuwis, Cees, and Andy Hall (2010). Facing the challenges of climate change and food security: the role of research, extension and communication institutions — final report. (October). Rome: Food and Agriculture Organization of the United Nations, Wageningen University and UNU-MERIT.

Lele, Uma, and others (2010). Transforming agricultural research for development. Paper commissioned by the Global Conference on Agricultural Research (GCARD) for the Global Conference on Agricultural Research in Development, Montpellier, France, 28-31 March 2010.

Lema, Rasmus, and Adrian Lema (2010). Whither technology transfer? the rise of China and India in green technology sectors. Paper prepared for the 8th GLOBELICS International Conference "Making Innovation Work for Society: Linking, Leveraging and Learning", Kuala Lumpur, 1-3 November.

Lewis, Joanna I. (2007a). Technology acquisition and innovation in the developing world: wind turbine development in China and India. *Studies in Comparative International Development*, vol. 42, No. 3, pp. 208-232.

________ (2007b). A review of the potential international trade implications of key wind power industry policies in China. Paper prepared for the Energy Foundation China Sustainable Energy Program. San Francisco, California: Center for Resource Solutions. October.

Li, Xuan (2008). Patent counts as indicators of the geography of innovation activities: problems and perspectives. South Centre Research Paper, No. 18 (December). Geneva: South Centre. December.

Lipton, Michael (2010). From policy aims and small-farm characteristics to farm science needs. *World Development*, vol. 38, No. 10 (October), pp. 1399-1412.

Ludi, Eva (2009). Climate change, water and food security. *ODI Background Note* (March). London: Overseas Development Institute.

Lund, H., and B. V. Mathiesen (2009). Energy system analysis of 100% renewable energy systems: the case of Denmark in years 2030 and 2050. *Energy*, vol. 34, No. 5, pp. 524-531.

Lundvall, Bengt-Åke, ed. (2010). *National Systems of Innovation: Toward a Theory of Innovation and Interactive Learning*. London: Anthem Press.

Lutz, Ernst, ed. (1998). *Agriculture and the Environment: Perspectives on Sustainable Rural Development*. Washington, D.C.: World Bank.

MacKay, David J.C. (2008). *Sustainable Energy–Without the Hot Air*. Cambridge, United Kingdom: UIT Cambridge Ltd.

Maddison, Angus (2007). *Contours of the World Economy, 1 - 2030 AD: Essays in Macro-Economic History*. New York: Oxford University Press.

Malavasi, Edgar Ortiz, and John Kellenberg (2002). Program of payments for ecological services in Costa Rica. Paper prepared for a conference of the IUCN Forest Conservation Programme.

Malerba, F. (2002). Sectoral systems of innovation and production. *Research Policy*, vol. 31, No. 2, pp. 247-264.

________, and Richard R. Nelson (2008). *Catching Up: In Different Sectoral Systems*. Globelics Working Paper Series, No. 08-01. Aalborg, Denmark: Global Network for the Economics of Learning, Innovation, and Competence Building Systems (Globelics), Department of Business Studies, Aalborg University.

Mani, S. (2002). *Government, Innovation and Technology Policy: An International Comparative Analysis*. Cheltenham, United Kingdom: Edward Elgar.

Marchetti, Cesare, and Nebojsa Nakicenovic (1979). The dynamics of energy systems and the logistic substitution model. RR-79-13 (December). Laxenburg, Austria: International Institute for Applied Systems Analysis. Available from http://cesaremarchetti.org/abstract.php?id=23.

Maskus, Keith, and Ruth Okediji (2010). Intellectual property rights and international technology transfer to address climate change: risks, opportunities and policy options. *ICTSD Issue Paper*, No. 32 (December). Geneva: International Centre for Trade and Sustainable Development.

McGranahan, Gordon, Deborah Balk and Bridget Anderson (2007). The rising tide: assessing the risks of climate change and human settlements in low elevation coastal zones. *Environment and Urbanization*, vol. 19, No. 1 (April), pp. 17-37.

McGray, Heather, Anne Hammill and Rob Bradley (2007). *Weathering the Storm: Options for Framing Adaptation and Development*. Washington, D.C.: World Resources Institute. Available from http://pdf.wri.org/weathering_the_storm.pdf.

Mehra, Rekha, and Mary Hill Rojas (2008). A significant shift: women, food security and agriculture in a global marketplace. Washington, D.C.: International Center for Research on Women (ICRW).

Metcalfe, J.S. (1994). Evolutionary economics and technology policy. *Economic Journal*, vol. 104, No. 425, pp. 931-944.

________, and R. Ramlogan (2005). Limits to the economy of knowledge and knowledge of the economy. *Futures*, vol. 37, No. 7, pp. 655-674.

Meyer, Niels I. (2007). Learning from wind energy policy in the EU: lessons from Denmark, Sweden and Spain. *European Environment*, vol. 17, No. 5, pp. 347-362.

Millennium Ecosystem Assessment (2005). *Ecosystems and Human Well-Being: Synthesis.* Washington, D.C.: Island Press.

Minx, Jan, and others (2009). Understanding changes in UK CO_2 emissions 1992-2004: a structural decomposition analysis. London: United Kingdom Department for Environment, Food and Rural Affairs. December.

Mitchell, Donald (2008). A note on rising food prices. World Bank Policy Research Working Paper, No. 4682. Washington, D.C.

Moe, E. (2010). Energy, industry and politics: energy, vested interests, and long-term economic growth and development. *Energy*, vol. 35, No. 4, pp. 1730-1740.

Molden, David, and Charlotte de Fraiture (2004). Investing in water for food, ecosystems and livelihoods. Blue Paper prepared for the Comprehensive Assessment of Water Management in Agriculture, organized by International Water Management Institute, Stockholm, August 2004.

Moutinho, Paulo, and Stephan Schwartzman, eds. (2005). *Tropical Deforestation and Climate Change.* Belém, Brazil: Instituto de Pesquisas Ambiental da Amazonia; Washington, D.C.: Environmental Defense.

Mowery, D., and N. Rosenberg (1979). The influence of market demand upon innovation: a critical review of some recent empirical studies. *Research Policy*, vol. 8, No. 2, pp. 102-153.

Mowery, David C., Richard R. Nelson and Ben Martin (2010). *Technology Policy and Global Warming: Why New Policy Models are Needed (Or Why Putting New Wine in Old Bottles Won't Work).* London: National Endowment for Science, Technology and the Arts (NESTA). October.

MS Swaminathan Research Foundation and World Food Programme (2008). Report on the state of food insecurity in rural India. Rome: WFP.

Nakicenovic, Nebojsa, Arnulf Grübler and Alan McDonald (1998). *Global Energy: Perspectives.* Cambridge, United Kingdom: Cambridge University Press.

National Research Council (2001). *Energy Research at DOE: Was It Worth It? Energy Efficiency and Fossil Energy Research 1978 to 2000.* Washington, D.C.: National Academy Press.

Nelson, Gerald C., and others (2009). *Climate Change: Impact on Agriculture and Costs of Adaptation.* IFPRI Food Policy Report. Washington, D.C.: International Food Policy Research Institute. October.

Nelson, Richard R. (1993). *National Innovation Systems: A Comparative Analysis.* New York: Oxford University Press.

_________, and S. G. Winter (1982). *An Evolutionary Theory of Economic Change.* Cambridge, Massachusetts: Belknap Press (of Harvard University Press).

Nemet, Gregory, and Daniel Kammen (2007). U.S. energy research and development: declining investment, increasing need, and the feasibility of expansion. *Energy Policy*, vol. 35, No. 1, pp. 746-755.

O'Brien, Karen, and others (2008). Disaster risk reduction, climate change adaptation and human security. *Global Environmental Change and Human Security (GECHS) Report*, No. 2008: 3. Report prepared for the Royal Norwegian Ministry of Foreign Affairs by the Global Environmental Change and Human Security (GECHS) Project. Oslo: University of Oslo. Available from http://www.gechs.org/downloads/GECHS_Report_3-08.pdf.

O'Connor, David (2009). Clarifying climate change financing estimates. Informal note. New York: Division for Sustainable Development, Department of Economic and Social Affairs of the United Nations Secretariat.

Ocampo, José Antonio (2011a). Summary of background papers. In United Nations, United Nations Environment Programme and United Nations Conference on Trade and Development, *The transition to a green economy: benefits, challenges and risks from a sustainable development perspective.* Report by a Panel of Experts to the Second Preparatory Committee Meeting for the United Nations Conference on Sustainable Development, New York, 7 and 8 March 2011. Pp. 1-14.

_________ (2011b). The Macroeconomics of the Green Economy. In United Nations, United Nations Environment Programme and United Nations Conference on Trade and Development, *The transition to a green economy: benefits, challenges and risks from a sustainable development perspective.* Report by a Panel of Experts to the Second Preparatory Committee Meeting for the United Nations Conference on Sustainable Development, New York, 7 and 8 March 2011. Pp. 14-38.

Odagiri, Hiryuki, and others (2010). Conclusion. In *Intellectual Property Rights, Development, and Catch-up: An International Comparative Study*, Hiryuki Odagiri, and others, eds. Oxford: Oxford University Press. Pp. 412-430.

Oldeman, L. R. (1998). Soil degradation: a threat to food security. Report 98/01. Wageningen, Netherlands: International Soil Reference and Information Centre.

Ondraczek, J. (2011). The sun rises in the East (of Africa): a comparison of the development and status of the solar energy markets in Kenya and Tanzania. Working Paper FNU-195 (4 March). Hamburg, Germany: University of Hamburg, Research Unit Sustainability and Global Change.

Organization for Economic Cooperation and Development (2002). *Science and Technology Industry Outlook, 2002.* Paris.

_________ (2008). *Economic Aspects of Adaptation to Climate Change: Costs, Benefits and Policy Instruments.* Paris.

_________, Working Party on Global and Structural Policies (2010). Climate policy and technological innovation and transfer: an overview of trends and recent empirical results. 7 July. ENV/EPOC/GSP(2010)10/FINAL. Paris.

Organization for Economic Cooperation and Development and Food and Agriculture Organization of the United Nations (2010). *OECD-FAO Agricultural Outlook 2010-2019.* Paris: OCED; Rome: FAO.

Ortiz, Isabel, Jingqing Chai and Matthew Cummins (2011). Escalating food prices: the threat to poor households and policies to safeguard a recovery for all. UNICEF Social and Economic Policy working paper (11 February). Available from http://ssrn.com/abstract=1760162.

Ouyang, Min (2009). On the cyclicality of R&D. Paper prepared for the University of California Riverside Conference on "Business Cycles: Theoretical and Empirical Advances", Riverside, California, 10 and 11 April.

Oyelaran-Oyeyinka, B. (2005). Systems of innovation and underdevelopment: an institutional perspective. *Science Technology Society*, vol. 11, No. 2 (September), pp. 239-269.

Pacala, Stephen (2007). Equitable solutions to greenhouse warming: on the distribution of wealth, emissions and responsibility within and between nations. Speech prepared for the IIASA Conference on Global Development: Science and Policies for the Future, 13-16 November 2007. Available from www.iiasa.ac.at/Admin/INF/conf35/docs/speakers/speech/ppts/pacala.pdf; www.iiasa.ac.at/iiasa35/docs/speakers/speech/pdf/Pacala_speech.pdf.

Pahle, Michael, Lin Fan and Wolf-Peter Schill (2011). How emission certificate allocations distort fossil investments: the German example. *DIW Discussion Paper*, No. 1097 (January). Berlin: Deutsches Institut für Wirtschaftsforschung.

Pardey, Philip G., and Nienke M. Beintema (2001). *Slow Magic: Agricultural R & D a Century after Mendel.* (26 October). Washington, D.C.: International Food Policy Research Institute.

Parvez, Hossain Sohel (2009). Rahimafrooz to set up solar panel assembling plant. *Daily Star* (Dhaka), 24 June. Available from http://www.thedailystar.net/newDesign/news-details.php?nid=93896.

Pax Natura (2011). Payment for environmental services (PES) program highlights. Available from http://www.paxnatura.org/CostaRicanPESProgram.htm.

Pearce, David, Anil Markandya and Edward Barbier (1989). *Blueprint for a Green Economy.* London: Earthscan.

Polyani, Karl (1944). *The Great Transformation: The Political and Economic Origins of Our Times.* Boston, Massachusetts: Beacon Press.

Pretty, J. N., and others (2006). Resource-conserving agriculture increases yields in developing countries. *Environmental Science and Technology*, vol. 40, No. 4, pp. 1114-1119.

Rabinovitch, Jonas (1992). Curitiba: towards sustainable urban development. *Environment and Urbanization*, vol. 4, No. 2 (October), pp. 62-73.

Radov, Daniel, and others (2007). Market mechanisms for reducing GHG emissions from agriculture, forestry and land management. London: Department for Environment, Food and Rural Affairs. 18 September. Available from http://archive.defra.gov.uk/evidence/economics/foodfarm/reports/ghgemissions/wholerep.pdf.

Rapsomanikis, George (2009). *The 2007-2008 Food Price Swing: Impact and Policies in Eastern and Southern Africa. FAO Commodities and Trade Technical Paper*, No. 12. Rome: Food and Agriculture Organization of the United Nations.

Rao, S. (2009). Investing in a climate friendly future. IIASA, Laxenburg, Austria: International Institute for Applied Systems Analysis (IIASA).

Rehfuess, Eva, Sumi Mehta and Annette Prüss-Üstün (2006). Assessing household solid fuel use: multiple implications for the Millennium Development Goals. *Environmental Health Perspectives*, vol. 114, No. 3 (March), pp. 373-378.

REN21 (2010). *Renewables 2010 Global Status Report.* Paris: REN21 Secretariat.

Rennkamp, B., and A. Stamm (2009). Towards innovation systems for sustainability: the role of international cooperation (from innovation for sustainability in a changing world). Paper prepared for the Second South African-German Dialogue on Science for Sustainability, Pretoria, 26 and 27 October.

Riahi, Keywan, Arnulf Grübler and Nebojsa Nakicenovic (2007). Scenarios of long-term socio-economic and environmental development under climate stabilization. *Technological Forecasting and Social Change*, vol. 74, No. 7, pp. 887-935.

Riahi, Keywan, and others (forthcoming). The GEA scenario: energy transition pathways for sustainable development. In *The Global Energy Assessment*. Cambridge, United Kingdom: Cambridge University Press.

Rippey, P. (2009). Microfinance and climate change: threats and opportunities. CGAP Focus Note, No. 53 (February). Washington, D.C.: Consultative Group to Assist the Poor.

Rockström, Johan, and others (2009). A safe operating space for humanity. *Nature*, vol. 461, No. 7263 (24 September), pp. 472-475.

________ (2010). Making progress within and beyond borders. In *Global Sustainability: A Nobel Cause*, Hans Joachim Schellnhuber and others, eds. Cambridge, United Kingdom: Cambridge University Press.

Roehrl, Richard Alexander, and Keywan Riahi (2000). Technology dynamics and greenhouse gas emissions mitigation: a cost assessment. *Technological Forecasting and Social Change*, vol. 63, No. 2-3, pp. 231-261.

Roehrl, Richard Alexander, and Ferenc Toth (2009). A critical comparison of geological storage of carbon dioxide and nuclear waste in Germany: status, issues, and policy implications. Paper prepared for the Eighth Conference on Applied Infrastructure Research, Berlin, 9 and 10 October 2009.

Rosenberg, Tina (2011). When microcredit won't do. *New York Times*. Opinionator, 31 January. Available from http://opinionator.blogs.nytimes.com/2011/01/31/when-microcredit-wont-do/.

Sanchez, Pedro A. (2002). Soil fertility and hunger in Africa. *Science*, vol. 295, No. 5562 (15 March), pp. 2019-2020.

Sanchez-Rodriguez, Roberto, Michail Fragkias and William Solecki (2008). Urban responses to climate change: a focus on the Americas. Report prepared for the International Workshop on Urban Responses to Climate Change, New York, 26 and 27 September 2007. June. Available from http://ccsl.iccip.net/ur2cc.pdf.

Sandén, Björn A., and Christian Azar (2005). Near-term technology policies for long-term climate targets: economy wide versus technology specific approaches. *Energy Policy*, vol. 33, No. 12, pp. 1557-1576.

Sarris, Alexander (2009). Evolving structure of world agricultural trade and requirements for new world trade rules. Paper presented at the FAO Expert Meeting on "How to Feed the World in 2050", Food and Agriculture Organization of the United Nations, Rome, 24-26 June 2009.

Schot, J., and F.W. Geels (2008). Strategic niche management and sustainable innovation journeys: theory, findings, research agenda, and policy. *Technology Analysis and Strategic Management*, vol. 20, No. 5, pp. 537-554.

Schultz, T. P. (2002). Why government should invest more to educate girls. *World Development*, vol. 30, No. 2, pp. 207-225.

Scotchmer, S. (2010). Cap-and-trade, emissions taxes, and innovation. In *Innovation Policy and the Economy*, vol. 11, Josh Lerner and Scott Stern, eds. Chicago, Illinois: University of Chicago Press.

Shane, S. A. (2008). *The Illusions of Entrepreneurship: The Costly Myths That Entrepreneurs, Investors, and Policy Makers Live By*. New Haven, Connecticut: Yale University Press.

Shashikant, Sangeeta (2009). IPRs and technology transfer issues in the context of climate change. Background paper prepared for *World Economic and Social Survey 2009*.

Sills, Ben (2010). BlackRock blames loan crisis for clean-energy outflow. *Bloomberg News*, 26 December. Available from http://www.businessweek.com/news/2010-12-26/blackrock-blames-loan-crisis-for-clean-energy-outflow.html (accessed 25 March 2011).

Smakhtin, Vladimir, Carmen Revenga and Petra Döll (2004). *Taking into Account Environmental Water Requirements in Global-Scale Water Resources Assessments. Comprehensive Assessment Research Report*. Colombo: Comprehensive Assessment Secretariat.

Smil, Vaclav (2004). World history and energy. In *Encyclopedia of Energy*, vol. 6. Amsterdam: Elsevier. Pp. 549-561.

_________ (2010a). *Energy: Myths and Realities: Bringing Science to the Energy Policy Debate*. Washington, D.C.: American Enterprise Institute for Public Policy Research. Press.

_________ (2010b). *Energy Transitions: History, Requirements, Prospects*. Santa Barbara, California: Praeger.

Smith, Keith (2009). Climate change and radical energy innovation: the policy issues. TIK Working Papers on Innovation Studies, No. 20090101. Oslo: University of Oslo, Centre for Technology, Innovation and Culture.

Soete, L., B. Verspagen and B. ter Weel (2009). Systems of innovation. UNU-MERIT Working Paper Series, No. 2009-062. Maastricht, Netherlands: United Nations University - Maastricht Economic and Social Research and Training Centre on Innovation and Technology. December.

Spielman, David J. (2005). Innovation systems perspectives on developing-country agriculture: a critical review. International Service for National Agricultural Research (ISNAR) Division Discussion Paper, No. 2 (27 September). Washington, D.C.: International Food Policy Research Institute. Available from http://www.ifpri.org/sites/default/files/publications/isnardp02.pdf.

_________, and Rajul Pandya-Lorch (2009). Fifty years of progress. In *Millions Fed: Proven Successes in Agricultural Development*, David J. Spielman and Rajul Pandya-Lorch, eds. Washington, D.C.: International Food Policy Research Institute. Pp. 1-18.

Stamm, Andreas, and others (2009). Sustainability-oriented innovation systems: towards decoupling economic growth from environmental pressures? *DIE Discussion Paper*, No. 20/2009 (November). Bonn: Deutches Institut für Entwicklungspolitik (German Development Institute).

Steinfeld, Henning, and others (2006). *Livestock's Long Shadow: Environmental Issues and Options*. Rome: Food and Agriculture Organization of the United Nations.

Stern, Nicholas (2007). *Stern Review: The Economics of Climate Change*. Cambridge, United Kingdom: Cambridge University Press.

Stiglitz, Joseph E. (2002). *Globalization and Its Discontents.* New York: W.W. Norton and Company.

________, and others (2006). *Stability with Growth: Macroeconomics, Liberalization and Development.* New York: Oxford University Press.

Szargut, J. (1988). Energy and exergy analysis of the preheating of combustion reactants. *International Journal of Energy Research*, vol. 12, No. 2 (March-April), pp. 45-58.

Tan, Xiaomei, and others. (2010). *Scaling Up Low-Carbon Technology Deployment - Lessons from China.* Washington, D.C.: World Resources Institute.

Tavares, Raymond (2009). Science and technology parks: an overview of the ongoing initiatives in Africa. *African Journal of Political Science and International Relations*, vol. 3, No. 5 (May), pp. 208-233.

Taylor, Margaret (2008). Beyond technology-push and demand-pull: lessons from California's solar policy. *Energy Economics*, vol. 30, No. 6, pp. 2829-2854.

________, and others (2007). Government actions and innovation in clean energy technologies: the cases of photovoltaic cells, solar thermal electric power, and solar water heating. Pier Project report. Sacramento, California: California Energy Commission. October.

Tessa, Bertrand, and Pradeep Kurukulasuriya (2010). Technologies for climate change adaptation: emerging lessons from countries pursuing adaptation to climate change. *Journal of International Affairs*, vol. 64, No. 1 (fall/winter), pp. 17-31.

Thapa, Dipti, and Marjory-Anne Broomhead (2010). Opportunities and challenges for a converging agenda: country examples. Conference edition background paper prepared for the The Hague Conference on Agriculture, Food Security and Climate Change, organized by the World Bank, The Hague, October 2010.

Timmer, C. Peter (2009). Rice price formation in the short run and the long run: the role of market structure in explaining volatility. CGD Working Paper, No. 72 (21 May). Washington, D.C.: Center for Global Development.

Tole, S., and R.D. Vale (2010). Young leaders for biology in India. *Science*, vol. 329, No. 5998, p. 1441.

United Kingdom of Great Britain and Northern Ireland, British Council (2011). Partnerships in education: innovative approaches to learning. Available from http://www.britishcouncil.org/morocco-support-education-partnership.htm.

United Nations (1993). *Report of the United Nations Conference on Environment and Development, Rio de Janeiro, 3-4 June 1992*, vol. I, *Resolutions Adopted by the Conference.* Sales No. E.93.I.8 and corrigendum. Resolution 1, annex I (Rio Declaration on Environment and Development). Resolution 1, annex II (Agenda 21).

________ (2008a). Comprehensive framework for action. Prepared by the High-level Task Force on the Global Food Crisis. 15 July.

________ (2008b). *World Economic and Social Survey 2008: Overcoming Economic Insecurity.* Sales No. E.08.II.C.1.

________ (2009). *World Economic and Social Survey 2009: Promoting Development, Saving the Planet.* Sales No. E.09.II.C.1.

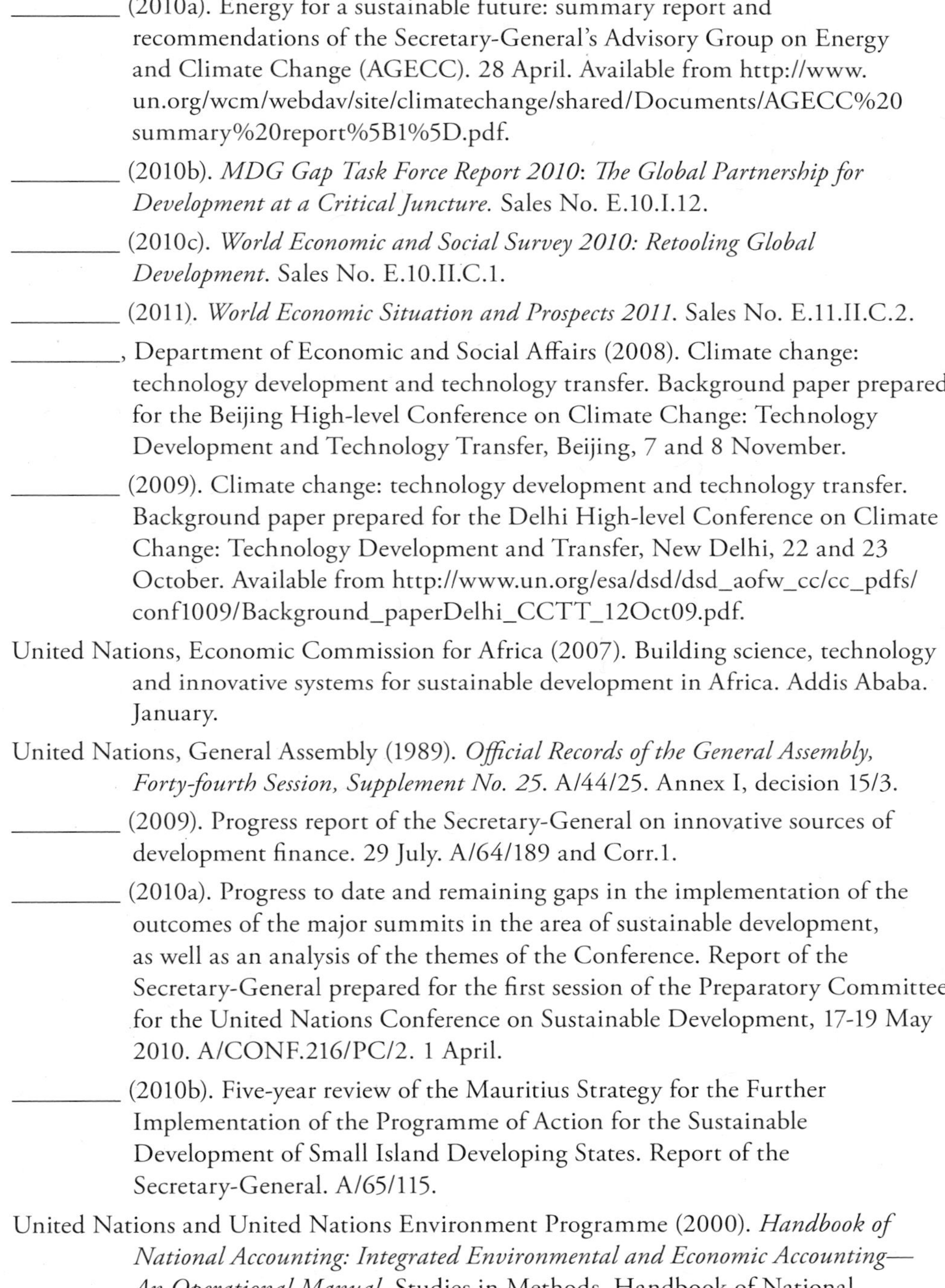

________ (2010a). Energy for a sustainable future: summary report and recommendations of the Secretary-General's Advisory Group on Energy and Climate Change (AGECC). 28 April. Available from http://www.un.org/wcm/webdav/site/climatechange/shared/Documents/AGECC%20summary%20report%5B1%5D.pdf.

________ (2010b). *MDG Gap Task Force Report 2010: The Global Partnership for Development at a Critical Juncture.* Sales No. E.10.I.12.

________ (2010c). *World Economic and Social Survey 2010: Retooling Global Development.* Sales No. E.10.II.C.1.

________ (2011). *World Economic Situation and Prospects 2011.* Sales No. E.11.II.C.2.

________, Department of Economic and Social Affairs (2008). Climate change: technology development and technology transfer. Background paper prepared for the Beijing High-level Conference on Climate Change: Technology Development and Technology Transfer, Beijing, 7 and 8 November.

________ (2009). Climate change: technology development and technology transfer. Background paper prepared for the Delhi High-level Conference on Climate Change: Technology Development and Transfer, New Delhi, 22 and 23 October. Available from http://www.un.org/esa/dsd/dsd_aofw_cc/cc_pdfs/conf1009/Background_paperDelhi_CCTT_12Oct09.pdf.

United Nations, Economic Commission for Africa (2007). Building science, technology and innovative systems for sustainable development in Africa. Addis Ababa. January.

United Nations, General Assembly (1989). *Official Records of the General Assembly, Forty-fourth Session, Supplement No. 25.* A/44/25. Annex I, decision 15/3.

________ (2009). Progress report of the Secretary-General on innovative sources of development finance. 29 July. A/64/189 and Corr.1.

________ (2010a). Progress to date and remaining gaps in the implementation of the outcomes of the major summits in the area of sustainable development, as well as an analysis of the themes of the Conference. Report of the Secretary-General prepared for the first session of the Preparatory Committee for the United Nations Conference on Sustainable Development, 17-19 May 2010. A/CONF.216/PC/2. 1 April.

________ (2010b). Five-year review of the Mauritius Strategy for the Further Implementation of the Programme of Action for the Sustainable Development of Small Island Developing States. Report of the Secretary-General. A/65/115.

United Nations and United Nations Environment Programme (2000). *Handbook of National Accounting: Integrated Environmental and Economic Accounting—An Operational Manual.* Studies in Methods, Handbook of National Accounting, Series F, No. 78. Sales No. E.00.XVII.17.

United Nations Children's Fund (2008). Arsenic mitigation in Bangladesh. Available from http://www.unicef.org/bangladesh/Arsenic.pdf.

United Nations Conference on Trade and Development (2007). *The Least Developed Countries Report 2007: Knowledge, Technological Learning and Innovation for Development.* Sales No. E.07.II.D.8.

________ (2010). *Technology and Innovation Report 2010: Enhancing Food Security in Africa through Science, Technology and Innovation*. Sales No. E.09.II.D.22.

United Nations Development Programme (2007). *Human Development Report 2007/2008: Fighting Climate Change—Human Solidarity in a Divided World*. Basingstoke, United Kingdom: Palgrave Macmillan.

United Nations Educational, Scientific and Cultural Organization (2011a). Creation of pilot science park in Africa. Available from http://www.unesco.org/new/en/natural-sciences/science-technology/sti-policy/african-sti-policy/creation-of-a-pilot-science-park-in-an-african-country/ (accessed 18 March 2011).

________ (2011b). *Education for All Global Monitoring Report 2011: the Hidden Crisis - Armed Conflict and Education*. Paris.

United Nations Environment Programme (2002). *Global Environment Outlook 3: Past, Present and Future Perspectives*. London: Earthscan.

________ (2008). UNEP background paper on green jobs. Nairobi. Available from http://www.unep.org/labour_environment/pdfs/green-jobs-background-paper-18-01-08.pdf.

________ (2010a).Green economy: developing country success stories. Geneva: Division of Technology, Industry and Economics. Available from http://www.unep.org/pdf/GreenEconomy_SuccessStories.pdf.

________ (2010b). Overview of the Republic of Korea's National Strategy for Green Growth. Prepared by the Programme as part of its Green Economy Initiative. Geneva: Division of Technology, Industry and Economics, Economics and Trade Branch. April.

________ (2011). Towards a green economy: pathways to sustainable development and poverty eradication - a synthesis for policy makers. Nairobi.

United Nations Forum on Forests (2007). Report of the United Nations Forum on Forests on its seventh session (24 February 2006 and 16 to 27 April 2007). *Official Records of the Economic and Social Council, 2007*, Supplement No. 22. E/2007/42.

United Nations Framework Convention on Climate Change (2006).*Technologies for Adaptation to Climate Change*. Bonn: Adaptation, Technology and Science Programme of the UNFCCC Secretariat. Available from http://unfccc.int/resource/docs/publications/tech_for_adaptation_06.pdf.

________ (2007). Investment and financial flows to address climate change. Bonn. Available from http://unfccc.int/resource/docs/publications/financial_flows.pdf.

________ (2011). Report of the Conference of the Parties on its sixteenth session, held in Cancun from 29 November to 10 December 2010: addendum. Part two: action taken by the Conference of the Parties at its sixteenth session. FCCC/CP/2010/7/Add.1. Available from http://unfccc.int/resource/docs/2010/cop16/eng/07a01.pdf#page=4.

________, Subsidiary Body for Scientific and Technological Advice (2008). Proposed terms of reference for a report on performance indicators and for a report

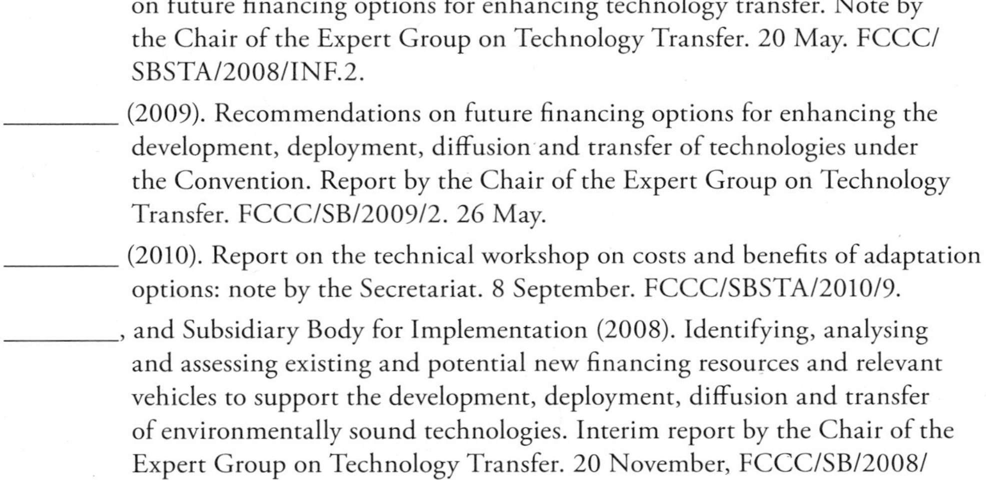

on future financing options for enhancing technology transfer. Note by the Chair of the Expert Group on Technology Transfer. 20 May. FCCC/SBSTA/2008/INF.2.

_________ (2009). Recommendations on future financing options for enhancing the development, deployment, diffusion and transfer of technologies under the Convention. Report by the Chair of the Expert Group on Technology Transfer. FCCC/SB/2009/2. 26 May.

_________ (2010). Report on the technical workshop on costs and benefits of adaptation options: note by the Secretariat. 8 September. FCCC/SBSTA/2010/9.

_________, and Subsidiary Body for Implementation (2008). Identifying, analysing and assessing existing and potential new financing resources and relevant vehicles to support the development, deployment, diffusion and transfer of environmentally sound technologies. Interim report by the Chair of the Expert Group on Technology Transfer. 20 November, FCCC/SB/2008/INF.7.

United Nations Industrial Development Organization (2010). Enterprise benefits from resource efficient and cleaner production. Vienna. Available from http://www.unido.org/fileadmin/user_media/Services/Environmental_Management/Cleaner_Production/RECP_Peru.pdf.

United States Climate Change Science Program (2008). Weather and Climate Extremes in a Changing Climate: Regions of Focus: North America, Hawaii, Caribbean, and the U. S. Pacific Islands. Report by the United States Climate Change Science Program and the Subcommittee on Global Change Research, Thomas R. Karl, and others, eds. Synthesis and Assessment Product 3.3. Washington, D.C.: United States Department of Commerce and National Oceanic and Atmospheric Administration (NOAA) National Climatic Data Center.

United States Department of Energy, Carbon Dioxide Information Analysis Center (2011). List of countries by carbon dioxide emissions per capita. Available from Wikipedia (http://en.wikipedia.org/wiki/List_of_countries_by_carbon_dioxide_emissions_per_capita) (accessed 1 March 2011).

University of East Anglia, Overseas Development Group (2006). Global impacts of land degradation (August). Norwich, United Kingdom.

UN Women Watch (2011). Women, gender equality and climate change. Fact sheet. Available from http://www.un.org/womenwatch/feature/climate_change/ (accessed 1 March 2011).

van den Bergh, Jeroen C.J.M, and others (2007). *Evolutionary Economics and Environmental Policy: Survival of the Greenest*. Cheltenham, United Kingdom: Edward Elgar Publishing.

van Vuuren, D. P., and Keywan Riahi (2008). Do recent emission trends imply higher emissions forever? *Climatic Change*, vol. 91, No. 3, pp. 237-248.

van Vuuren, D. P., and others (2007). Stabilizing greenhouse gas concentrations at low levels: an assessment of reduction strategies and costs. *Climatic Change*, vol. 81, No. 2, pp. 119-159.

_________ (unpublished). Exploring scenarios that keep greenhouse gas radiative forcing below 3 W/m2 in 2100. *Energy Economics.*

von Braun, Joachim (2009). Overcoming the world food and agriculture crisis through policy change and science. Prepared for the Trust for Advancement of Agricultural Sciences (TAAS), Fourth Foundation Day Lecture, organized by International Food Policy Research Institute, New Delhi, 6 March 2009. Available from http://www.ifpri.org/publication/oming-world-food-and-agriculture-crisis-through-policy-change-and-science.

von Weizsäcker, Ernst U., Amory B. Lovins and L. Hunter Lovins (1998). *Factor Four: Doubling Wealth-Halving Resource Use—The New Report to the Club of Rome.* London: Earthscan.

Vos, Robert (2009). Green or mean: is biofuel production undermining food security? In *Climate Change and Sustainable Development: New Challenges for Poverty Reduction*, M. A. Mohammed Salih, ed. Cheltenham, United Kingdom: Edward Elgar Publishing.

Waggoner, P.E., and J. H. Ausubel (2002). A framework for sustainability science: a renovated IPAT identity. *Proceedings of the National Academy of Sciences*, vol. 99, No. 12 (11 June), pp. 7860-7865.

Walz, Rainer (2010). Competences for green development and leapfrogging in newly industrializing countries. *International Economics and Economic Policy*, vol. 7, Nos. 2-3, pp. 245-265.

Webster, P. J., and others (2005). Changes in tropical cyclone number, duration and intensity in a warming environment. *Science*, vol. 39, No. 5742 (16 September), pp. 1844-1846.

Wernick, Iddo K., and others (1997). Materialization and dematerialization: measures and trends. In Technological Trajectories and the Human Environment, Jesse H. Ausubel and H. Dale Langford, eds. Washington, D.C.: National Academies Press. Pp. 135-156.

Wilson, Charlie, and Arnulf Grübler (2010). Lessons from the history of technology and global change for the emerging clean technology cluster. Background paper prepared for *World Economic and Social Survey 2011.*

Wilson, Charlie (forthcoming). Historical scaling dynamics of energy technologies: a comparative analysis.

Wood, Stanley, Kate Sebastian and Sara J. Scherr (2000). *Pilot Analysis of Global Ecosystems: Agroecosystems.* Washington, D.C.: International Food Policy Research Institute and World Resources Institute.

World Bank (2003). *World Development Report 2003: Sustainable Development in a Dynamic World — Transforming Institutions, Growth, and Quality of Life.* Washington, D.C.: World Bank; New York: Oxford University Press.

_________ (2004). *Sustaining Forests: A Development Strategy.* Washington, D.C.

_________ (2007a). *Enhancing Agricultural Innovation: How to Go Beyond the Strengthening of Research Systems.* Washington, D.C.: World Bank.

_________ (2007b). *Building Knowledge Economies: Advanced Strategies for Development.* Washington, D.C.

_________ (2008a). World Bank President to G8: "World entering a danger zone". News and Broadcast (2 July). Available from http://web.worldbank.org/WBSITE/EXTERNAL/NEWS/0,,contentMDK:21828803~pagePK:34370~piPK:34424~theSitePK:4607,00.html (accessed 12 January 2011).

_________ (2008b). Food price crisis imperils 100 million in poor countries. News and Broadcast. Available from http://web.worldbank.org/WBSITE/EXTERNAL/NEWS/0,,contentMDK:21729143~pagePK:64257043~piPK:437376~theSitePK:4607,00.html (accessed 12 January 2011).

_________ (2009). *Global Economic Prospects 2009: Commodities at the Crossroads.* Washington, D.C.

_________ (2010a). *World Development Report 2010: Development and Climate Change.* Washington, D.C.

_________ (2010b). *Innovation Policy: A Guide for Developing Countries.* Washington, D.C.

_________ (2011). Food price watch. Available from http://www.worldbank.org/foodcrisis/food_price_watch_report_feb2011.html (accessed 24 March 2011).

_________, Independent Evaluation Group (2008). *The Welfare Impact of Rural Electrification: A Reassessment of the Costs and Benefits—An IEG Impact Evaluation.* Washington, D.C.

World Business Council for Sustainable Development (2011). Innovating for green growth: drivers of private sector RD&D. Geneva.

World Commission on Environment and Development (1987). *Our Common Future.* Oxford: Oxford University Press.

World Energy Council and Food and Agriculture Organization of the United Nations (1999). The challenge of rural energy poverty in developing countries. London: World Energy Council.

World Health Organization (2009). Gender, climate change and health. Draft discussion paper. Geneva. Available from http://www.who.int/globalchange/publications/reports/final_who_gender.pdf.

World Trade Organization (1994). *Legal Instruments Embodying the Results of the Uruguay Round of Multilateral Trade Negotiations, done at Marrakesh on 15 April 1994.* Sales No. GATT/1994-7. Geneva: GATT secretariat.

World Water Assessment Programme (2003). *Water for People, Water for Life: The United Nations World Water Development Report.* Oxford: Berghahn Books.

Wright, Brian, and Tiffany Shih (2010). Agricultural innovation. *NBER Working Paper*, No. 15793 (March). Cambridge, Massachusetts: National Bureau of Economic Research.

Xiao, Y. L., and F. Y. Nie (2009). *A Report on the Status of China's Food Security.* Beijing: China Agricultural Science and Technology Press.

United Nations publication
Sales No. E.11.II.C.1
ISBN 978–92–1–109163–2
eISBN 978–92–1–054758–1

Printed at the United Nations, New York
11–27775